American Furniture

AMERICAN FURNITURE 2001

Edited by Luke Beckerdite

Published by the CHIPSTONE FOUNDATION

Distributed by University Press of New England

Hanover and London

Cover Illustration: Detail of the pediment of a high chest, Philadelphia, 1750–1755. (Chipstone Foundation; photo, Gavin Ashworth)

Design: Wynne Patterson, Pittsfield, VT
Typesetting: Aardvark Type, Hartford, CT
Prepress: GIST, New Haven, CT
Printing: Meridian Printing, East Greenwich, RI

Published by the Chipstone Foundation, 7820 North Club Circle, Milwaukee, WI 53217
Distributed by University Press of New England, Hanover, NH 03755
© 2001 by the Chipstone Foundation
All rights reserved
Printed in the United States of America   5 4 3 2 1
ISSN 1069–4188
ISBN 1–58465–056–7

Contents

Editorial Statement   VII
Luke Beckerdite

Preface   IX
Allen M. Taylor

Introduction   XI
Luke Beckerdite

First Flowers of the Wilderness: Mannerist Furniture from a Northern   I
Essex County, Massachusetts, Shop
Robert F. Trent, Peter Follansbee, and Alan Miller

When Good Cabinetmakers Made Bad Furniture: The Career and   65
Work of David Evans
Eleanore P. Gadsden

Early New York Turned Chairs: A *Stoelendraaier's* Conceit   88
Erik Gronning

The Lisle Desk-and-Bookcase: A Rhode Island Icon   120
Brock Jobe

A Salem Cabinetmakers' Price Book   152
Dean Thomas Lahikainen

Two Early Eighteenth-Century *Schränke*: Rare Survivals of the   220
German Joiner's Art in the Hudson River Valley
Peter M. Kenny

Book Reviews   243

The White House: Its Historic Furnishings and First Families, Betty C.
Monkman; review by Elisabeth D. Garrett

Early American Decorative Arts, 1620–1860: A Handbook for Interpreters,
Rosemary Troy Krill with Pauline K. Eversmann; review by Gilian Ford
Shallcross

Rural New England Furniture: People, Place, and Production, Peter Benes,
editor; review by Anne Woodhouse

American Furniture: Understanding Styles, Construction, and Quality,
John T. Kirk; review by Ted Landsmark

Recent Writing on American Furniture: A Bibliography   255
Gerald W. R. Ward

Index   266

Editorial Statement

American Furniture is an interdisciplinary journal dedicated to advancing knowledge of furniture made or used in the Americas from the seventeenth century to the present. Authors are encouraged to submit articles on any aspect of furniture history, essays on conservation and historic technology, reproductions or transcripts of documents, annotated photographs of new furniture discoveries, and book and exhibition reviews. References for compiling an annual bibliography also are welcome.

Manuscripts must be typed, double-spaced, illustrated with black-and-white prints or transparencies, and prepared in accordance with the *Chicago Manual of Style*. Computer disk copy is requested but not required. The Chipstone Foundation will offer significant honoraria for manuscripts accepted for publication and reimburse authors for all photography approved in writing by the editor.

Luke Beckerdite

Preface

The Chipstone Foundation was organized in 1965 by Stanley Stone and Polly Mariner Stone of Fox Point, Wisconsin. Representing the culmination of their shared experiences in collecting American furniture, American historical prints, and early English pottery, the foundation was created with the dual purpose of preserving and interpreting their collection and stimulating research and education in the decorative arts.

The Stones began collecting American decorative arts in 1946, and by 1964 it became apparent to them that provisions should be made to deal with their collection. With the counsel of their friend Charles Montgomery, the Stones decided that their collection should be published and exhibited.

Following Stanley Stone's death in 1987, the foundation was activated by an initial endowment provided by Mrs. Stone. This generous donation allowed the foundation to institute its research and grant programs, begin work on three collection catalogues, and launch an important new journal, *American Furniture*.

Allen M. Taylor

Introduction

Luke Beckerdite

This volume of *American Furniture* is dedicated to the memory of John Bivins, a dear friend and brilliant scholar who passed away in August of this year. John was one of the first decorative arts historians to recognize the need for a journal devoted solely to American furniture. He participated in seminars that inspired the Chipstone Foundation to begin publishing *American Furniture* and served on the editorial advisory board from 1993 to 2001.[1]

It would be virtually impossible to overstate John's impact on the American decorative arts field. A graduate of Guilford College, he joined the staff of the North Carolina Department of Archives and History in 1966 and subsequently became Curator of Furnishings for the Historic Sites Division. Shortly after publishing his first book, *The Longrifles of North Carolina* (1968), he took the position of Curator of Crafts at Old Salem, the restored Moravian Village in Winston-Salem, North Carolina. During his eight-year tenure with that organization, John also served as Curator of Collections and Director of Restoration and published *The Moravian Potters in North Carolina* (1975), which set a new standard for books on American ceramics.[2]

In 1975, John left Old Salem to pursue a career as a gunmaker—a trade he had practiced for more than a decade. Renowned for applying European fine arts standards to the production of historic American forms, he influenced the work of leading contemporary arms makers such as Monte Mandarino, Mark Silver, and Mike Ehinger, all of whom were journeymen in John's shop. Today the term "Bivinsesque" is often used to describe firearms of this genre. John's immense influence on the contemporary arms field is also the result of his lectures and workshops presented at the National Muzzleloading Rifle Association Gunsmithing Seminars and numerous publications on gunmaking and arms conservation in *Rifle Magazine*, *Muzzleblasts*, and the *Journal of Historic Arms Making Technology*.[3]

John's greatest contributions to the history of American furniture began in 1979, when he became Director of Publications at the Museum of Early Southern Decorative Arts. During his tenure, MESDA's *Journal of Early Southern Decorative Arts* attained national prominence and on three occasions articles in that publication received the Robert C. Smith Award. Believing that focused regional studies were more important than collection catalogues, John conceived and initiated MESDA's Frank L. Horton Series of Monographs. Not surprisingly, the first installment was John's *Furniture of Coastal North Carolina, 1700–1820* (1988), which received the Charles Montgomery Award and is considered by many to be the finest regional furniture study ever published.[4]

In 1990, John left MESDA to pursue a career as a professional carver and independent scholar. He conserved and replicated architectural carving for George Mason's house Gunston Hall, and for the Miles Brewton House and St. Michael's Church in Charleston; produced a series of videos on connoisseurship; and continued to publish books and articles on American furniture. Most recently, John completed the manuscript for *The Furniture of Charleston, 1680–1820,* which will be released in 2002 as part of the Horton Series.[5]

John's legacy encompasses much more than words can express. He was a generous and inspirational colleague, a gifted teacher, and a kind and loyal friend. Many of our lives and careers have been enriched, if not shaped, by the time we spent with John, and I know his sense of humor, his delight in discovery, and the memory of his kind face will never fade.

1. The first seminar to discuss the feasibility of establishing a journal on American furniture was sponsored by the Kaufman Americana Foundation and held at the National Gallery of Art in 1987. The second seminar, sponsored by the Chipstone Foundation, was held at the Yale University Art Gallery in 1988.

2. *The Moravian Potters in North Carolina* received the Mayflower Cup award presented by the North Carolina chapter of the American Association of State and Local History.

3. The National Muzzleloading Rifle Association Gunsmithing Seminars were co-sponsored by the University of Western Kentucky at Bowling Green.

4. *The Furniture of Coastal North Carolina* also received the Mary Ellen LoPresti Award for Excellence in Art Publishing.

5. The video series titled *Authenticating Antique Furniture* is distributed by Estate Antiques in Charleston, South Carolina. Jim Pratt was the executive producer.

Partial list of publications by John Bivins

Longrifles of North Carolina. York, Pa.: George Shumway, 1968.

The Moravian Potters in North Carolina. Winston-Salem, N.C.: Old Salem, Inc., 1975.

"Decorative Cast Iron on the Virginia Frontier," *Antiques* 101, no. 3 (March 1972): 535–39.

"A Piedmont North Carolina Cabinetmaker: The Development of a Regional Style," *Antiques* 102, no. 5 (May 1973): 968–73.

"Fraktur in the South: an Itinerant Artist," *Journal of Early Southern*

Decorative Arts 1, no. 2 (November 1975): 1–23.

"Baroque Elements in North Carolina Moravian Furniture," *Journal of Early Southern Decorative Arts* 2, no. 1 (May 1976): 38–63.

"Carolina Colloquial: Furniture with that Carolina Accent," *Antiques World* (December 1980): 42–47.

Moravian Decorative Arts in North Carolina: A Guide to the Old Salem Collection. With Paula Welshimer. Winston-Salem, N.C.: Old Salem, Inc., 1981.

"Isaac Zane and the Products of Marlboro Furnace," *Journal of Early Southern Decorative Arts* 11, no. 1 (May 1985): 15–65.

"Charleston Rococo Interiors, 1765–1775: The Sommers Carver," *Journal of Early Southern Decorative Arts* 12, no. 2 (November 1986): 1–129.

The Furniture of Coastal North Carolina, 1700–1820. Winston-Salem, N.C.: Museum of Early Southern Decorative Arts, 1988.

Wilmington Furniture, 1720–1860. Wilmington, N.C.: St. John's Museum of Art and Historic Wilmington Foundation, 1989.

"The Cupola House: An Anachronism of Style and Technology." With James Melchor, Marilyn Melchor, and Richard Parsons. *Journal of Early Southern Decorative Arts* 15, no. 1 (May 1989): 57–132.

"A Catalogue of Northern Furniture with Southern Provenances," *Journal of Early Southern Decorative Arts* 15, no. 2 (November 1989): 43–92.

"Furniture of the Lower Cape Fear," *Antiques* 137, no. 5 (May 1990): 1202–1213.

The Regional Arts of the Early South: A Sampling from the Collection of the Museum of Early Southern Decorative Arts. With Forsyth Alexander. Chapel Hill: University of North Carolina Press for the Museum of Early Southern Decorative Arts, 1991.

"Furniture of the North Carolina Roanoke River Basin in the Collection of Historic Hope Foundation," *Journal of Early Southern Decorative Arts* 22, no. 1 (Summer 1996): 42–90.

"The Convergence and Divergence of Three Stylistic Traditions in Charleston Neoclassical Case Furniture, 1785–1800," in *American Furniture*, ed. Luke Beckerdite, pp. 47–105. Hanover, N.H.: University Press of New England for the Chipstone Foundation, 1997.

"Rhode Island Influences in the Work of Two North Carolina Cabinetmakers," in *American Furniture*, ed. Luke Beckerdite, pp. 78–108. Hanover, N.H.: University Press of New England for the Chipstone Foundation, 1999.

Furniture of the North Carolina Roanoke River Basin in the Collection of Historic Hope Foundation. Windsor, N.C.: Historic Hope Foundation, 2000.

The Furniture of Charleston, 1680–1820. With Bradford L. Rauschenberg. Winston-Salem, N.C.: Museum of Early Southern Decorative Arts, forthcoming.

American Furniture

Robert F. Trent,
Peter Follansbee,
and Alan Miller

First Flowers of the Wilderness: Mannerist Furniture from a Northern Essex County, Massachusetts, Shop

▼ O F A L L T H E seventeenth-century furniture made in Essex County, the only objects that rival the work of Thomas Dennis of Ipswich are case pieces and tables with histories of ownership in the towns of Beverly, Topsfield, Ipswich, Newbury, Andover, and North Andover. Unlike most early joinery, the products of this anonymous shop are unusually diverse in design, construction, and decoration. Several examples show the influence of Boston furniture in the London style—most notably in the use of drawer dovetails, multiple channel moldings with mitered inserts, and classical turning sequences. At the same time, these Essex County pieces depart from Boston practice in having channel moldings with mitered inserts on drawer fronts rather than on case stiles. The architectural jetties on four cupboards from this shop have no direct precedent in British furniture. With their dramatic overhangs and turned pendants, these jetties differ from framed examples, which often capture large turned pillars. Several of the ornamental details and some of the architectural tropes used by the artisans in this shop appear to be indebted to sixteenth-century French joinery, specifically to the Second School of Fontainebleau.

Many of the pieces in the Essex County group have carved initials and dates. Most of the original owners, identified through genealogical research or by process of elimination, were members of the Puritan gentry, including the Appleton family of Ipswich and the Perkins families of Ipswich and Topsfield. The Appletons never acquired vast wealth, but they became socially prominent and prosperous through intermarriage with such grandees as John Winthrop, Thomas Dudley, Henry Dunster, Simon Bradstreet, Rev. John Woodbridge, Rev. Nathaniel Rogers, Major-General Daniel Denison, Rev. Samuel Phillips, and Richard Dummer. Their extended family included five presidents of Harvard College and ministers from the coveted pulpits of Watertown, Cambridge, Topsfield, Rowley, Ipswich, and Newbury.[1]

Although this Essex County shop did produce relatively standardized objects, such as joined chests, the compositional and ornamental variety of its major forms is difficult to explain using the tools of conventional furniture history. The artisans continually refined their designs, working toward some ideal aesthetic goal. Because the easiest way for seventeenth-century joiners to earn a living was to produce standardized forms using repetitive work methods, this departure from the norm seems counterproductive. It is difficult to imagine that any of the objects illustrated here were stock-in-trade, but the nature of the relationship between the makers and patrons remains unclear. Customer preference undoubtedly influenced the shop's designs, and the allure of the unique was probably a selling point. The furniture produced by these joiners presents direct evidence of that most elusive mystery with which the art historian must struggle—the nature of the creative process.

The Historiography of Essex County Furniture
The case pieces and tables attributed to this shop are hardly newcomers to decorative arts literature. A description of the cupboard base that descended in the Appleton family (fig. 21) appeared in an article by William H. Sumner in the *New England Historic and Genealogical Register* in October 1855. This furniture also attained a measure of prestige through its association with prominent Puritans and with the joined oak forms of the English Arts and Crafts movement, which became popular in the United States after the Civil War. Salem, Massachusetts, antiquarian Henry Fitz Gilbert Waters (1833–1913) commissioned replicas of several cupboards in the group and marketed them as period objects. A centennial exhibition of colonial artifacts held at Plummer Hall in Salem in December 1875 included fraudulent examples, as did Clarence Cook's superficial but popular book *The House Beautiful* (1877). Waters and his cabinetmaker undoubtedly studied and made drawings of period examples, several of which remained in the families of original owners in Boston, Beverly, and Ipswich. That is the only plausible explanation for the replicas having riven oak and the unusual secondary wood sycamore, which occurs in furniture from this shop.[2]

Waters also acquired and conserved several period examples. During the 1880s, he met furniture historian Irving W. Lyon, who subsequently employed him to conduct genealogical research in England. Lyon illustrated only two genuine Essex County pieces in his seminal work *The Colonial Furniture of New England* (1891), and his papers indicate that he was suspicious of Waters. Subsequent books by Esther Singleton and Frances Clary Morse followed Lyon's example in illustrating objects from the Waters collection, but these authors chose some of the spurious examples and made no significant new comments about the objects.[3]

Wallace Nutting illustrated newly discovered objects from this shop in *Pilgrim Century Furniture* (1921, 1924) and *Furniture Treasury* (1927). In the latter book, he speculated that the maker lived "somewhere from Salem to Newburyport" and that "a little research . . . should locate the town and perhaps the workmen." His remarks apparently motivated Lyon's equally capable son, Irving P. Lyon, to conduct research on Essex County joinery during the 1930s. The results of his work—two articles in *Old-Time New England* and six articles in *Antiques*—set a new standard for documentary investigation and formal analysis. While his father pioneered the use of probate inventories in American decorative arts scholarship, Irving P. Lyon developed a methodology that assessed traditional histories of ownership through genealogical research, identified workmen in a variety of public records, and combined this information with technical study to distinguish various shop traditions. He identified Ipswich joiner Thomas Dennis as the maker of a large group of carved furniture, and most of his attributions are accepted today. Lyon erred, however, in attributing examples from this Essex County shop to Dennis. He theorized that Dennis' work evolved over forty years to encompass an applied ornament style, and his argument remained unchallenged for twenty years.[4]

In 1960, Helen Park published two articles that questioned some of Lyon's attributions. Her work inspired Benno M. Forman's research on Essex County joinery, which he conducted while a student in the Winterthur Program between 1966 and 1968. Forman scrutinized public records to identify furniture craftsmen and analyzed the design and structural details of all the objects known to him. In his thesis and a subsequent article, he separated Essex County production from the London-style joinery of the Boston-Charlestown area. Forman followed this impressive achievement by attributing what Lyon had referred to as the "geometric-panels" phase of Dennis' production to the Symonds shops of Salem, Rowley, and Topsfield. However, by not challenging the attribution of the Staniford chest of drawers (fig. 1) to Dennis, Forman implicitly accepted Lyon's theory that Dennis moved from a carved style to an applied ornament style. In addition to the authority of Lyon's articles, Forman placed great emphasis on the many documents linking Dennis with Thomas (1648–1730) and Margaret (Harris) (1657–1750) Staniford, the original owners of the chest.[5]

Using probate inventories, Forman cited benches, molding planes, fine tenon saws, and holdfasts as evidence of the joiner's trade and suggested

Figure 1 Chest of drawers, northern Essex County, Massachusetts, 1678. Oak, sycamore, maple, and tulip poplar with oak and sycamore. H. 42", W. 44¾", D. 19⅞". (Courtesy, Winterthur Museum.)

that most carpenters did not own such tools. To some extent, he pushed the joiner/carpenter distinction almost to the point of joiner *versus* carpenter. By eliminating carpenters as candidates for furniture makers, he made it easier to attribute schools of joinery to specific artisans or shop traditions. Many seventeenth-century joiners did architectural work, and numerous artisans referred to as carpenters made joined furniture of good quality. As the furniture attributed to this Essex County shop reveals, its makers could produce elaborate stylistic effects with the simplest equipment.[6]

In *New England Begins: The Seventeenth Century* and in two subsequent articles, Robert F. Trent asserted that the entire Essex County group was not the work of Dennis but possibly associated with the Emery shop tradition of Newbury. A chest made for Thomas and Margaret Staniford in 1676 clarified this distinction when it appeared in 1982. Clearly a product of Dennis' shop, it differed from an Essex County chest of drawers made for the same couple two years later (fig. 1). This article does not defend Trent's Emery attribution, but it does argue that this Essex County shop was located in the vicinity of Ipswich or Newbury.[7]

The Shop Becomes Established

The chest of drawers illustrated in figure 1 has the most credible provenance of any piece attributed to this shop. It descended from Thomas and Margaret Staniford through several generations of the Heard family of Ipswich. Her grandmother, Margaret (Reade) Lake (1598–1672), was one of three sisters who married members of the Puritan elite about the time of the Great Migration from England to the Massachusetts Bay. Elizabeth Reade (1616–1672) was John Winthrop, Jr.'s second wife, and Martha Reade (b. 1602) married Deputy Governor Samuel Symonds of Ipswich. Abandoned by her husband John Lake, Margaret often lived in John Winthrop, Jr.'s household.[8]

The Staniford chest of drawers is the earliest dated example from New England. With its oak façade, unusual drawer arrangement, and distinctive carving, it differs significantly from seventeenth-century Boston work. In that city, the London-trained joiners of the intermarried Mason and Messinger families made Italo-Netherlandish case pieces with drawers of varied heights, Corinthian base and waist moldings, Ionic entablatures, and vertical channel moldings with mitered inserts. Although Boston case pieces often have oak side frames and panels, their façades are invariably walnut and/or cedrela. No surviving example has carved decoration; however, the table shown in figure 23 and firebacks cast at the Saugus Ironworks from patterns supplied by Boston joiners have simple relief carving similar to that on London case pieces.[9]

The concept of a chest of drawers as a specialized form spread from Boston to other areas of New England. Boston three- and four-drawer chests typically have drawer ornament divided differently. On the former, the upper drawer typically has three geometric panels, the second drawer has two, and the third drawer has three. On the latter, each drawer has two panels separated by a central plaque or reserve. The Staniford example is

unusual in having five drawers, all of equal height. Although precedents for this arrangement can be found in continental baroque furniture, most of the associated stylistic conventions did not arrive in New England until the 1690s. The maker of the Staniford chest also departed from Boston practice in the division of his drawer ornament. The upper drawer has three panels, the second has two, the middle has three, the fourth has two, and the bottom has three. Although the drawers are unmarked and interchangeable, this arrangement appears to be correct given the location of the small half-columns and the relationship of the initial and date plaques to those on other pieces in the group. The practice of alternating the ornamental divisions on successive drawer fronts became a staple of this shop's vocabulary and may have influenced the work of other Essex County joiners.

The moldings and large half-columns (fig. 2) of the Staniford chest divide the façade into a frieze/column/surbase composition. Mitered moldings, plaques of various sizes, and shallow strapwork carving give the drawers and façade a staccato quality that differs significantly from seventeenth-century Boston and London chests. Boston case pieces occasionally have inset and applied plaques, but they are usually framed by applied mitered moldings. On the Staniford chest, the plaques incised with letters or numerals were intended to contrast with other parts of the case. Their edges are exposed, and they are made of tulip poplar and maple, which would have been green and light yellow respectively.

The painted decoration may have been added after Margaret Staniford's death in 1750. When new, the chest's oak and ebonized maple components resembled those on other pieces in the group. The only other pigment found on furniture from this shop is red, which occurs on the strapwork carving and applied arches of two cupboards.[10]

The painted decoration covers several repairs that collectively alter the composition of the chest. One drawer in the middle row of three is replaced, as are the large and small blocks between the top and the large half-columns. These blocks cover portions of the channel moldings on the stiles, which were probably visible originally, as they are below the large half-columns. With the blocks removed and small half-columns placed on either side of the channel moldings, the uppermost drawer would lose much of its frieze-like emphasis.

The joiner used a scratch-stock (fig. 3) to cut almost all of the moldings (see fig. 4) on the framed elements and appliqués of the Staniford chest and other pieces in the group. Although molding planes are ancient tools and were certainly present in seventeenth-century America, most New England joiners, including those in the Essex County shop, produced small mold-

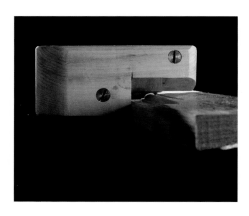

Figure 3   Modern scratch-stock made by Philip Ruhl, Quakertown, Pennsylvania, 2000. (Photo, Gavin Ashworth.)

Figure 4   Detail of the stopped moldings produced by a scratch-stock cutter on the right side frame of the chest of drawers illustrated in fig. 53. (Photo, Gavin Ashworth.)

ings with scratch-stocks. Unlike molding planes, which have shaped angled blades, conforming soles, and remove wood by cutting, scratch stocks have upright blades, L-shaped frames that act as depth stops, and remove wood by scraping. Because they do not have a conforming sole, scratch-stocks can produce curved moldings either when worked by hand against a piece of curved stock or when mounted on a rotating arm. They scrape on the forward and backward strokes, often producing slight irregularities or "chatter marks" exactly perpendicular to the molding unless the tool is skewed. These marks are clearly visible on the moldings produced in this shop. On the bottom drawer of the Staniford chest, the scratch-stock channels are subdivided into panels with mitered inserts that may have been chopped with a special die. A similar feature appears on the stiles of Boston case pieces, but its use on horizontal drawer fronts and rails appears unique to this Essex County group.[11]

The small half-columns on the chest may have been influenced by Boston work, whereas the large half-columns (fig. 2)—distinguished by stacks of barrel turnings—resemble those on case furniture made in Paris and its environs during the late sixteenth and early seventeenth centuries. This same magnificent furniture provided the immediate antecedents for French-Canadian buffets that are often described as Louis XIII but are more properly Henri IV, if not Henri II, in style.

Surveys of French furniture reveal that late medieval case pieces were organized with Gothic tracery in the panels and miniature applied buttresses on the stiles and on the muntins between the panels. This formula was reworked during the Mannerist period by substituting floral carving or rondels with profile busts in the panels and pilasters or turned appliqués on the stiles and muntins. Adaptations of these stacked reel and baluster turnings, known as "candelabra," were derived from Roman frescoes in the Golden House of Nero and were a staple of French court design. In time, the candelabra lost their bases and became floating abstractions, but their visual emphases in the composition of façades remained the same. As codified by the group of Italian and French architects and designers now known as the Second School of Fontainbleau, these exquisitely proportioned forms, with extreme thick and thin passages, were the object of much scrutiny by connoisseurs. Italian architect Sebastiano Serlio (1475–1554) had a profound influence on French court styles during this period. His *Architettura* (1537–1547) contains a lengthy discussion about drawing classical vases, translated in the English edition (1611) as "cups" or "vessels" (fig. 5). In the study of classical proportions, vases were almost as important as the five orders of columns:

> It is an excellent thing for a man to study or practise . . . with the Compasse, whereby in time men may find out that which they never imagined: as this night it happened unto me, for that seeking to find a neerer rule, to make ye forme of an Egge [than] . . . Albertus Durens hath set downe: I found this way to make an Anticke [Roman] vessell, placing the foote beneath at the foot of an Egge, and the necke with the handles above upon the thickest part of the Egge.[12]

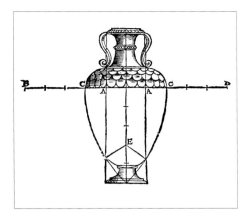

Figure 5 Detail of a "cup" illustrated in the 1611 London edition of Sebastian Serlio's *Five Books of Architecture*. "Cups" or "Vessels" were usually depicted with feet and covers with finials.

Figure 6 Detail of the water-sawn sycamore bottom boards of a drawer in the chest of drawers illustrated in fig. 1. Sycamore is difficult to rive and is water-sawn in all of the objects in the Essex County group.

The existence of Roman and French prototypes for certain details found on the Essex County group is the rationale for describing the applied turnings on the Staniford chest and related case pieces as "half-columns" rather than "split spindles"—a modern term used by many American authors. Although it is unlikely that the turner owned a copy of *Architettura* or was of direct French descent, he was an extremely accomplished artisan with an acute knowledge of classical proportion and form. The fact that all of the half-columns and pillars on furniture from the Essex County group are by the same hand suggests that the shop collaborated with the same turner for twenty-five years or that the shop master was also a turner.[13]

The drawer construction of the Staniford chest is typical of this shop. Each front is made from a wedge-shaped piece of riven oak that tapers in section from top to bottom. The joiner (or joiners) used the broadest dimension for the base to accommodate a rabbet for nailing on the bottom boards and planed similar rabbets in the ends to receive the drawer sides. In many instances, these workmen used two wrought nails with short shanks to secure the sides to the front. Often the nails protrude just above the surface, but occasionally they are countersunk. Some drawer fronts were too thin at the top to receive nails from the sides. On these examples, the joiners drove nails through the upper corners of the front into the end grain of the sides. The drawer bottoms on pieces from this shop are usually water-sawn sycamore or riven oak. All of the bottom boards are oriented front-to-back, and they have fine tongue-and-groove, V-shaped, or butt joints. Drawer backs are invariably nailed, and on some examples they are housed in rabbets on the back ends of the drawer sides. As on many pieces of seventeenth-century case furniture, drawers from this group are side-hung. Workmen in the shop occasionally departed from these construction practices, but the combination of details cited above are standard.[14]

Abundant forests and a shortage of skilled labor promoted distinctive timbering and woodworking practices in New England. Water-powered sawmills were located on just about every stream. The principal product of these mills was white pine boards. In contrast, oak logs were almost always riven—split radially to align the face with the medullary ray plane. On the Staniford chest, the oak components are riven, but the top and drawer bottoms are water-sawn sycamore (fig. 6). Some objects attributed to this shop have water-sawn oak, an extremely rare feature on New England furniture. The most common use of this wood was three-inch by five-inch joists and studs for house frames.[15]

The sides and back of the chest have superimposed vertical panels of approximately equal size (figs. 1, 7). Most joiners preferred to use repeatable designs and standardized components to expedite assembly. Although seventeenth-century woodworkers chose trees and harvested timber with specific parts in mind, they often had to produce smaller components when they encountered defects in the wood or made errors in the riving process. This sort of decision making probably became more critical later in the seventeenth century, when supplies of oak diminished in the vicinity of older towns. A variety of panel widths and configurations are evident on

Figure 7 Detail of the back of the chest of drawers illustrated in fig. 1. The tenons of two drawer supports are visible on the center rail. These supports are for the middle tier of three drawers, an odd feature possibly specified by the patron.

later pieces in the Essex County group. Like the water-sawn oak, sycamore, and pine used by this shop, these features may have resulted from timber shortages.

The maker of the Staniford chest often used marks similar to those found in architectural joinery to designate the orientation and alignment of individual components and assembled frames. These marks are often visible on the internal surfaces and outside backs of case pieces, but no consistent pattern is discernable. The marks on the Staniford chest are less comprehensive and more random than those on the cupboard illustrated in figure 36. On the latter piece, every component is marked, in some instances in a seemingly contradictory fashion. Many seventeenth-century joiners used marking systems, but few are as elaborate as those associated with this shop.[16]

The Staniford chest has two features that do not occur on other case pieces attributed to this shop. All of the framing members of the back have molded and chamfered decoration on their inside surfaces. It is unlikely that the joiners simply erred and flipped the back 180 degrees during assembly, since few pieces in the Essex County group have backs with molded and chamfered decoration on either surface. Also unusual are the two diagonal braces dovetailed to the bottom rails at the front and rear. Although their precise function is unknown, they resemble wind braces in house framing and may have been used to prevent the case from wracking. These features, which contrast with the mature construction and ornament of the chest, are the only indications that it may have been one of the first examples produced by this shop.

Dated two years later than the chest, the cupboard shown in figure 8 reputedly belonged to Peter Woodbury of Beverly, Massachusetts. Irving W. Lyon illustrated it in *Colonial Furniture of New England,* and his son sub-

Figure 8   Cupboard, northern Essex County,
Massachusetts, 1680. Red oak, maple, sycamore,
and tulip poplar, with oak and sycamore.
H. 57¾", W. 50", D. 21⅝". (Courtesy, Winterthur Museum.)

sequently published its family history. Just as misinterpretations of the
Staniford chest caused previous scholars to consider it a product of Thomas
Dennis' shop, the history of the Woodbury cupboard diverted attention
from its more likely origin in Ipswich or Newbury. The Woodbury cupboard and Staniford chest are undoubtedly from the same shop. Their
drawer construction is identical, including the use of water-sawn sycamore
bottom boards. The cupboard also has sycamore moldings surrounding the
drawer fronts and date panel of the lower case.[17]

The upper pillars of the cupboard (fig. 9) are taller and slightly more complex than the ones below (fig. 10). Similarly, the four large half-columns at
the front corners of the storage compartment (fig. 11) are more intricate
than the two at the rear (fig. 12). To some degree, this hierarchy of ornament conforms to the superimposition of orders in classical architecture. As
on the outer façade of the Colosseum of Emperor Vespasian in Rome, the

Figure 9   Detail of the upper right pillar of the cupboard illustrated in fig. 8.

Figure 10   Detail of the lower right pillar of the cupboard illustrated in fig. 8.

orders in multi-storied structures were arrayed according to a decorum in which the Doric order was always placed under the Ionic, the Ionic under the Corinthian, and the Corinthian under the Composite.

The joiner of the Woodbury cupboard introduced surface arcades as a decorative element for the side panels of the storage compartment (fig. 8). Arcades are the most architectonic feature of this shop's design vocabulary. They are literal translations of classical design, interspersed with Mannerist conceits. The joiner used a scratch-stock cutter to mold the jambs, which function as abutments of the arch. On the earliest cupboards from this shop, the jambs rest on tapered plinths. This feature is not architecturally correct, but the tradesmen in this shop used it as an expedient and economical solution because they were already making a series of tapered imposts onto which the upper ends of the jambs abut. The joiner of the Woodbury cupboard molded the curves of the arches with a "sweep," a scratch-stock cutter mounted on a trammel. He also used the same cutter to make the moldings on the jambs below.[18]

Figure 13 Chest, Boston, Massachusetts, 1660–1700. Oak, cedrela, and walnut with oak and white pine. H. 30½", W. 45", D. 20½". (Chipstone Foundation; photo, Gavin Ashworth.)

On the Woodbury cupboard, turned bosses decorate the arch spandrels, and pendants drop from the keystones rather than the center imposts in correct architectural fashion. Similar pendants and bosses appear on five firebacks cast at Saugus Ironworks between 1655 and 1662. Although Boston woodworkers produced the casting patterns, they used several details found on furniture from the Essex County group including drop-ground carving and scratch-stock and sweep-generated moldings.[19]

The Boston chest illustrated in figure 13 and a chest of drawers with doors (Yale University Art Gallery) have panels with composite applied arches comprised of scratch-stock and sweep-generated moldings. Although furniture from that town may have inspired the arcades produced by the Essex County joiners, the lack of dated metropolitan parallels makes any speculation tentative. Other New England shops decorated panels with surface arches, but it is unlikely their furniture influenced this Essex County group.[20]

The framing of the upper storage compartment resembles that of English cupboards but is considerably more complex. The stiles of the trapezoidal case are pentagonal in cross-section, to allow for ninety-degree shoulders on the connecting rails (fig. 14). This enabled the maker to use stronger joints than if angled shoulders united the parts. Boston joiners used a somewhat different approach. A cupboard that reputedly belonged to Isaac and Elizabeth Lawton of Portsmouth, Rhode Island, has a trapezoidal upper case with rectangular rear stiles and side rails cut at an angle and toe-nailed to the faces of the rear stiles.[21]

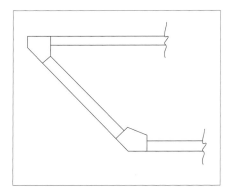

Figure 14 Drawing showing the framing of the trapezoidal storage compartment of the cupboard illustrated in fig. 8. (Drawing by Peter Follansbee; artwork by Wynne Patterson.)

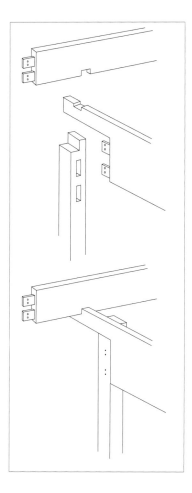

Figure 15 Drawing showing the framing of the jetty on the cupboard illustrated in fig. 8. (Drawing by Peter Follansbee; artwork by Wynne Patterson.)

The construction of cupboards in the Essex County group is superior to that of contemporary Boston examples. The trapezoidal section of the Woodbury cupboard is recessed, a design that appears to be unique to this shop. The tops of the rear stiles have tenons that engage mortises in the bottom edge of the long rear rail that passes over them. This rail joins the square corner stiles, and two turned rear pillars support the overhang. British and New England cupboards with trapezoidal frames usually have rear stiles positioned at the extreme corners and pillars that support the front stiles.

The Woodbury cupboard also deviates from standard design in having a jetty on the side and rear façades. The deep side rails between the lower front and back stiles are seated in notches in the rear stiles and protrude out toward the back of the cupboard. The top edge of this extension and the lower edge of the upper rear rail are joined with a half-lap or notch. Continuing beyond the cupboard's side, the upper rear rail joins the suspended back stiles to form the rear jetty (fig. 15). The side jetty extends from the narrow rail tenoned to the top of the front stiles. All of the overhanging sections of the jetties are sealed with soffit boards, which help reinforce the frame and protect the contents of the cupboard from dust and vermin. The soffit boards are nailed to the upper edge of the inner sections of each overhang, and their beveled edges are set in grooves in the inner face of the suspended rails.

Figure 16   Chest of drawers, northern Essex County, Massachusetts, 1675-1685. Oak and maple with oak and pine. H. 44¼", W. 46¼", D. 20⅝". (Courtesy, Peabody Essex Museum.) The piece has been dismantled, repinned, and glued, and the back of each drawer, the top of the case, and the crossetted central plaques on the drawers are replacements. Scribed layout lines for the original appliqués are still visible. About half of the bilaterally symmetrical sphere-and-column appliqués are restored. The original ones relate to those on the cupboard illustrated in fig. 17.

An early four-drawer chest (fig. 16) attributed to this shop is illustrated in the third edition of Luke Vincent Lockwood's *Colonial Furniture in America* (1926). It and the cupboard illustrated in figure 17 are the only case pieces with scalloped ornament integral to the lower rail, rather than applied under it. Three of the drawer dividers or rails on the chest have multiple astragal moldings with carved imbrication, a motif that appears on a related example dated 1685 (fig. 53). The large applied half-columns flanking the drawers are thirty-six inches high, the largest ones on any object from this shop. The lowest element of these appliqués repeats the straight-sided vase turning on a leaf table (fig. 22) and cupboard (fig. 17) from the same shop.[22]

Although the joiner who made the chest shown in figure 16 used tangentially-sawn oak for his drawer fronts, he hewed and planed the boards to produce a wedge-shaped cross section. This is the only known instance of a New England joiner reworking sawn material to accommodate joinery practices based on the use of riven timber. All other case pieces attributed to this shop have drawer fronts made of riven oak.[23]

A cupboard formerly owned by Henry Fitz Gilbert Waters (fig. 17) may be the earliest example from this shop. It departs from the design vocabulary of the other cupboards in having horizontally configured spandrel appliqués and structural channel-molded muntins, rather than applied ones, separating the side panels of the trapezoidal storage compartment. Each panel is a separate theater for its own arch, which is comprised of appliqués including a keystone with a long turned pendant and canted imposts and

Figure 17 Cupboard, northern Essex County, Massachusetts, 1675–1685. Oak and maple with oak and pine. H. 58½", W. 46½", D. 20". (Private collection; photo, Gavin Ashworth.) The door, top, middle and lower shelves, upper pillars, and some applied ornaments have been restored based on related examples from the same shop. The feet of the cupboard are original, and they have long cylindrical necks like the finials on the half-columns of the chest illustrated in fig. 16. The cupboard is shown prior to restoration in Wallace Nutting, *Furniture Treasury,* 2 vols. (Framingham, Mass.: Old America Co., 1928), no. 458.

jamb plinths. These multiple arch panels appear to be the genesis of the surface arcades found on later cupboards from the same shop. Moldings produced by the same scratch-stock cutters also link the Waters cupboard with other pieces in the group. The ogee with fillet on the arches, jambs, and lower rails of the frieze appears on the cupboards illustrated in figures 21 and 27.[24]

Cupboards made by the Harvard College joiners in Cambridge, Massachusetts, may have inspired certain details found on furniture in the Essex County group. The overall composition of the Waters cupboard (fig. 17) is strikingly similar to that of the Cambridge example shown in figure 18. Both cupboards have an open base with a lower shelf, integral turned front feet, channel-molded stiles that extend to the floor in the back, and a single drawer with a central plaque and applied half-columns flanked by rectangular panels trimmed with moldings. Like their Essex County contemporaries, the Harvard joiners also decorated case panels with composite arch appliqués.[25]

The base of a British cupboard (see fig. 100) is an even closer cognate to the Waters cupboard. Although the former example's history is unknown, it is probably from a coastal town or city where local artisans were exposed

Figure 18 Cupboard attributed to the Harvard College joiners, Cambridge, Massachusetts, 1670–1700. Oak and maple with pine. H. 53⅞", W. 46⅝", D. 20⅛". (Courtesy, Winterthur Museum.)

Figure 19 Detail of the shaped lower rail of the cupboard illustrated in fig. 17. (Photo, Gavin Ashworth.)

to Italian and French designs. Its molded and scrolled lower rail is very similar to that of the Waters cupboard, and its pillar has design sequences closely related to turnings in the Essex County group. If the pierced brackets on the British example are original, they could prefigure those on the cupboard illustrated in figure 75.[26]

The scalloped lower rail on the Waters cupboard (figs. 17, 19) resembles that on the chest illustrated in figure 16. Like the Staniford chest of drawers

(fig. 1), these objects have turned ornament that appears somewhat embryonic when compared with other work from the Essex County group. The lower pillars of the Waters cupboard (fig. 20) have much thicker necks than any of the later ones associated with this shop, and the cove and astragal

Figure 20 Detail of the lower right pillar of the cupboard illustrated in fig. 17. (Photo, Gavin Ashworth.)

elements interrupting the balusters are deep and unusually complex. The profile of these pillars echoes that of the large half-columns on the chest shown in figure 16. Similarly, the small half-columns flanking the cupboard's drawer are compressed versions of the horizontal appliqués on the drawers of the chest.

Like several objects in this group, the cupboard or chest base illustrated in figure 21 has a credible provenance. In an 1855 article titled "The Eliot Bureau," William H. Sumner proposed that the initials "IAE" on the base referred to Rev. John Eliot (1604–1690) of Roxbury, Massachusetts. Forty years later, Irving P. Lyon refuted Sumner's assertion and identified John and Elizabeth (Rogers) Appleton of Ipswich as the original owners. John (1652–1739) was born in Ipswich and married Elizabeth on November 23, 1681. She was the daughter of John Rogers, pastor of the church in Ipswich and later president of Harvard College. Among the many positions Appleton held were Judge of Probate, and Chief Justice of the Court of Common Pleas.[27]

Although Sumner must be credited for saving the cupboard base and recording its condition, the restoration done under his supervision altered the piece to the extent that its original appearance is difficult to discern. Unlike "standard" cupboards in this group, the base has no framed overhang on the front. It does, however, have side jetties related to those on three cupboards (figs. 8, 36, 75) and superimposed side panels similar to those on two chests (figs. 1, 16). Based on this configuration, the piece was probably a chest of drawers with a door rather than a cupboard with a recessed façade. Only two other American examples of this sophisticated form survive—one from Boston (Yale University Art Gallery) and the other from New Haven (Museum of Fine Arts, Boston). The Appleton base may have had an upper case, perhaps with a cupboard, or like the Boston chest, a compartment with a tier of drawers. Unfortunately, the top boards are replaced and no evidence of a superstructure survives.[28]

Notches in the rear stiles indicate that the Appleton base originally had supports for four drawers. This also suggests that the door had iron dovetail hinges and that the pintles described in Sumner's article were later additions. A door hung between the front stiles with pintle hinges would have prevented the drawers from sliding out of the case. The original hinges were probably nailed to the inside edge of the door frame and the inner face of the front stile. This attachment may account for the unusual orientation of the front stiles, which have the narrow face on the façade and the wide face on the side. The aforementioned Boston and New Haven chests differ in having doors that fit over the stiles and dovetail hinges that are nailed to the front of the stiles and the inside face of the door.[29]

A round joined leaf table (fig. 22) shares several features with many of the case forms in the Essex County group. Only two other New England examples of this form are known, and both are from Boston (see fig. 23). Because the frame of the table is trapezoidal, like the storage compartments of contemporary cupboards and presses, Wallace Nutting described it as a "card table in the court cupboard style." There is no reason to assume that such tables were intended specifically for gaming, however, nor is there any evi-

Figure 21   Base of a chest of drawers or cupboard, northern Essex County, Massachusetts, 1681. Oak and maple with oak and sycamore. H. 44⅛", W. 47", D. 22¼". (Courtesy, Harvard University.) The back and bottom boards, which constitute all of the surviving secondary wood, are water-sawn sycamore. The vertical back boards are set in grooves in the top rail and stiles and nailed to an inner lower rail. The pendants, small turned "bosses," and half-columns on the overhanging stiles are replacements, whereas the half-columns on the door and stiles are original. The planed edge moldings on the lower rails are also period, indicating that the case never had an applied base molding.

Figure 22   Leaf table, northern Essex County, Massachusetts, 1680–1685. White oak and maple. H. 28", W. 36⅜", D. 35⅝" (open). (Courtesy, Metropolitan Museum of Art, gift of Mrs. J. Insley Blair; photo, Gavin Ashworth.) The frame and bottom of the drawer is missing and the original front is fixed in place. The pendant under the left frieze is original. Similar drops were present on the addorsed brackets on five other objects attributed to this shop. Like the Staniford chest (fig. 1), the table has paint dating from the eighteenth century. The rails are mahoganized and the top is marbleized.

Figure 23   Leaf table, Boston, 1660–1680. Walnut, oak, cedrela, and maple with oak and white pine. H. 28¾", W. 28¾", D. 28¾" (open). (Chipstone Foundation; photo, Gavin Ashworth.)

Figure 24   Detail of the water-sawn board used for the shelf of the leaf table illustrated in fig. 22. (Photo, Gavin Ashworth.)

dence supporting Nutting's theory that the Essex County example "was presumably made to accompany one of the court cupboards." Leaf tables undoubtedly served a variety of functions including dining, gaming, and other domestic pursuits.[30]

The joiner designed the table so it could be constructed in stages. At the bottom are four turned maple feet with round tenons that are glued into mortises in the stiles of the shelf section. Although the feet have lost height, they originally resembled those on several cupboards in the group. The shelf section follows the same plan as the trapezoidal storage compartments of the case forms. The joiner made the stiles pentagonal to allow for ninety degree joints with the rails and used the lower tenons of the pillars to secure the shelf (figs. 22, 24). The pillars (fig. 25) are similar to those on several other pieces attributed to this shop (see figs. 33, 43), and the small half-columns relate to those on the Staniford chest (fig. 1) and the Woodbury cupboard (fig. 8). With the exception of having a drawer, the upper section of the table is essentially the same as the shelf section below. Each leaf is made from a single piece of water-sawn oak over seventeen inches wide, and the lower one is attached with six large wooden pins (pegs). When open, the folding leaf is supported by a fly leg (fig. 26) with a turned baluster iden-

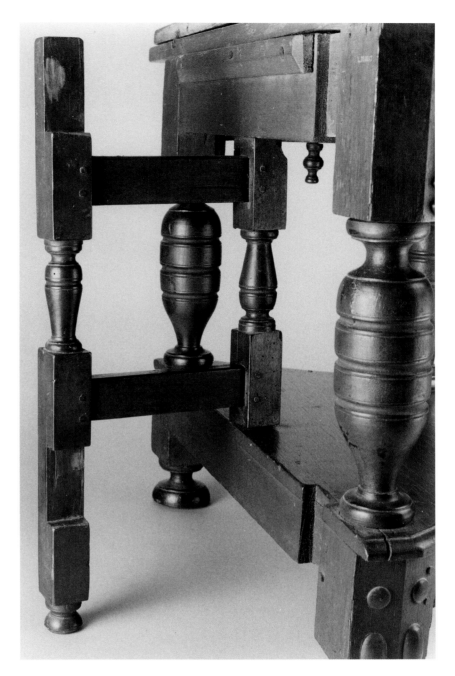

Figure 25 Detail of the right rear pillar of the leaf table illustrated in fig. 22. (Photo, Gavin Ashworth.) The pillars have tenons turned on both ends, exactly like those on cupboards in the Essex County group.

Figure 26 Detail of the fly leg of the leaf table illustrated in fig. 22. (Photo, Gavin Ashworth.)

tical to that on the pivoting post centered between the rear pillars. Although one might assume that the maker erred in inverting one of the balusters, joiners in this shop clearly considered either orientation to be correct.

Experimentation with Style and Structure
The furniture attributed to the Essex County shop is the most diverse and most "high concept" joinery from seventeenth-century America. Although the shop had developed two basic cupboard formats by the mid-1680s—one with storage compartments and drawers in the base and the other with one or two drawers and an open shelf in the base—no two examples are the same.

Figure 27 Cupboard, northern Essex County, Massachusetts, 1683. Oak, maple, and tulip poplar with oak and pine. H. 58¼", W. 49½", D. 20¾". (Private collection; photo, Gavin Ashworth.) The joiner used riven oak for the frame members and panels and water-sawn oak for the top boards of the upper and lower cases. Traces of bright vermilion paint—probably red lead—survive on the arcades of the upper case.

The cupboard illustrated in figure 27 is the earliest dated example with a storage compartment and drawers in the base. The interior of the lower storage compartment is divided into two sections by a riven oak panel captured in grooved slats nailed behind the center panel of the façade and at the rear of the cupboard. Although the lower portions of the feet and the pendants once present on the arcades of the upper compartment are missing, the pendants were smaller versions of the turnings on the stiles flanking the lower drawer (fig. 28). The case has never been disassembled, so the lower pillars are undoubtedly in their original positions.[31]

The turner's notion of form had evolved since he made the ornaments for the Woodbury and Appleton cupboards (figs. 8, 21). The large half-columns (figs. 29-31) have a series of dramatic thick-and-thin moves that characterize his work from 1683 to the 1690s. When he turned the pillars of the leaf table (figs. 22, 25), which are roughly contemporary with those of the cupboard shown in figure 27, he omitted the second base torus, so that the bottom of the baluster recurves or takes on an S-shape. This shape becomes even more pronounced on later turnings. The small half-columns flanking the upper drawer of the cupboard mirror those on the leaf table. On both pieces the applied turnings are single rather than paired.

Figure 28 Detail of the half-column to the left of the lower drawer of the cupboard illustrated in fig. 27. (Photo, Gavin Ashworth.)

Figure 29 Detail of the large half-columns to the left of the upper door of the cupboard illustrated in fig. 27. (Photo, Gavin Ashworth.)

Figure 30 Detail of the large half-column at the left rear corner of the upper storage compartment of the cupboard illustrated in fig. 27. (Photo, Gavin Ashworth.)

Figure 31 Detail of the large half-column adjacent to the left door of the lower storage compartment of the cupboard illustrated in fig. 27. (Photo, Gavin Ashworth.)

Figure 32　Detail of the upper right pillar of the cupboard illustrated in fig. 27. (Photo, Gavin Ashworth.)

Figure 33　Detail of the lower left pillar of the cupboard illustrated in fig. 27. (Photo, Gavin Ashworth.)

The base molding on the cupboard (fig. 27) echoes that on the Staniford chest (fig. 1) made five years earlier. The joiner used the same scratch-cutter, but his stock for the base molding of the cupboard was larger, producing a fascia at the bottom. Similarly, the arcades on the upper case are almost identical to those on the Woodbury cupboard, although the moldings on the spandrels are simpler than those on the jambs. This became a standard shop practice after 1680, probably because the joiners found the less complex cutter easier to control on the end-grain of the spandrel plaques.[32]

A different scratch-stock cutter produced the applied moldings on the doors and fixed center panel of the lower case. To accentuate the verticality of the panel, the joiner used a fenced rabbet or filister plane to cut a three-eighth-inch shoulder on the extra stock on the outer edge of the molding. A similar treatment appears on the two rectangular panels of the Appleton cupboard base (fig. 21), where the recessed shoulder has square-cut dentils. The upper door of the cupboard illustrated in figure 27 has applied moldings that differ from those on the lower doors and panel; however, all of the door frames have a simple ogee and fillet on their inside edges. The same scratch-stock moldings are also on the lower edge of the frieze and rail below the center drawer.

Figure 34   Base of a cupboard, northern Essex County, Massachusetts, 1685–1690. Oak and maple with oak. H. 38⅝", W. 46½", D. 20⅛". (Courtesy, Society for the Preservation of New England Antiquities, gift of Bertram K. and Nina Fletcher Little.)

Figure 35   Detail of the right pillar of the cupboard base illustrated in fig. 34.

The drawer fronts, rails, and muntins between the side panels have channel moldings with an ovolo element on each side. On both drawers, the channels are interrupted with mitered inserts with matching ovolos. The inserts terminating the channels cover the wrought nails used to attach the drawer fronts to the sides. Although the joiner cut the miters with a chisel, it is possible that he used a jig or die to expedite production and to ensure the accuracy of his work. The sheer number of inserts on pieces attributed to this Essex County shop suggests the use of a specialized setup. The joiners used these inserts to create rhythm and variety in their façades. These techniques were relatively simple, but their results were profound.

During the 1800s, James Lovell Little of Brookline, Massachusetts, collected the base of a cupboard (fig. 34) similar to the preceding example. Clarence Cook illustrated the fragment in *The House Beautiful* and noted that it was "found in a barnyard where it had for many years been given over to the hens … it was no easy matter to remove the traces of [their] … housekeeping." The base lacks several refinements present on the cupboard shown in figure 27 and may pre-date it. There is no soffit in the front jetty; the lower rails are decorated with a scratch bead rather than a base molding; the mitered inserts on the drawer fronts are not clustered to accentuate the three piers of the façade (center panel and flanking doors); and the applied molding on the center panel does not have a recessed shoulder.[33]

The half-columns on the stiles are similar to those on the preceding cupboard (fig. 27), but they appear to have been inverted during a restoration campaign. Both are attached with modern nails, and, like the larger half-columns and pillars below, they have paint that may mimic an original

Figure 36 Cupboard, northern Essex County, Massachusetts, 1683. Oak and maple. H. 58⅜", W. 46¼", D. 19¾". (Private collection; photo, Gavin Ashworth.) This is the earliest cupboard with a front jetty. It is shown prior to restoration in Sotheby's *Fine Americana and Silver,* New York, June 17, 1999, lot 187.

Figure 37 Detail of the large upper pillar at the right front corner of the cupboard illustrated in fig. 36. (Photo, Gavin Ashworth.)

Figure 38 Detail of the small half-columns to the left of the lower carved drawer of the cupboard illustrated in fig. 36. (Photo, Gavin Ashworth.) The back surfaces of the original turnings have marks from a water-powered saw, frame saw, and plane.

color scheme. Similar red and black paint survives on the half-columns and panels of a chest from this shop. The pillars (fig. 35) are also unusual in that they resemble those most often used for upper cases, and the profile of the front feet, which are integral with the stiles, is unique in this group.[34]

The most unprecedented case piece attributed to this shop is inlaid with the initials "AHP" and the date 1683 (fig. 36), making it contemporary with the cupboard illustrated in figure 27. Irving P. Lyon identified the original owners as Abraham and Hannah (Beamsley) Perkins, who were married at Ipswich in 1661. The Perkins cupboard is the only example made in one case, and it has no enclosed storage compartment. All three sections are fitted with drawers. The upper section has recessed sides and an overhanging head supported by four turned pillars (fig. 37) that rest on the mid-section containing the dated drawer. The cupboard has side jetties framed like those of the Woodbury example (fig. 8) and a short front jetty at the waist. The rail below the dated drawer extends forward about one-half inch from the stiles to create a slight overhang.[35]

The Perkins cupboard combines strong horizontal features—drawer fronts with varied ornament separated by rails with applied and integral moldings—with vertical elements — stiles, pillars (fig. 37), half-columns (figs. 36, 38), and pendants (fig. 39)—on alternating planes. With its molded channels and clusters of mitered inserts, the top drawer is very similar to that of the cupboard shown in figure 27. The third and fifth drawers below have a carved motif identical to that on the Staniford chest of drawers (fig. 1).

Figure 39 Detail of the left rear jetty pendant of the cupboard illustrated in fig. 36. (Photo, Gavin Ashworth.) The pendants on this cupboard are the boldest ones associated with this shop.

Figure 40 Cupboard, northern Essex County, Massachusetts, 1684. Oak and maple with oak. H. 53⅝", W. 48½", D. 20⅜". (Courtesy, Winter-thur Museum.) All of the oak secondary wood is riven. The perimeter moldings on the bottom drawer are missing, and the replaced knobs are not in the correct position. The lower stiles originally had half-columns on their front and side faces. The pendant appliqués of the arcades are missing and the glyphs decorating the imposts and plinths may be replacements. No other piece attributed to this shop has glyphs. The front feet match those of the Woodbury cupboard (fig. 8) and are integral with the stiles.

In its use of turned ornament, the Perkins cupboard is the most unified object from this shop. The design and placement of the appliqués and inserts give the façade a repetitive rhythm unparalleled in seventeenth-century American furniture. Because the case has been entirely disassembled, it is impossible to determine the original orientation of the pillars. Nevertheless, these turnings are related to others in the group (see figs. 10, 27, 32), differing primarily in the number of coved passages. Other features that distinguish the Perkins cupboard are its stepped dentil and astragal moldings.

Although four different sizes of half-columns appear on the cupboard, the form and sequence of their turned elements are basically the same and contribute to the façade's unified design. All of these appliqués are less than half-round because the turner glued the stock for each pair to a central core about three-sixteenths of an inch thick. Without a center core, the pressure of tightening the blank on the lathe could cause the work-piece to open up, snag the turner's tool, and tear or break. Stylistic concerns may also have prompted the turner to produce appliqués less than half-round.[36]

The cupboard illustrated in figure 40 has nine initials and dates one year later than the Perkins example. According to Irving P. Lyon, the original owners were Ephraim and Hannah (Eames) Foster of North Andover, who married at Ipswich in 1677. Like the cupboards shown in figures 36 and 47,

Figure 41 Detail of the back of the upper case of the cupboard illustrated in fig. 40.

Figure 42 Detail of the upper right pillar of the cupboard illustrated in fig. 40. The square shouldered pillars produced by this turner are exceptional, featuring dramatic transitions from thick to thin. They are usually found on upper cases and are the major forms in this shop's turning hierarchy. Tapered baluster-shaped pillars like those shown in fig. 43 are more commonly found on the lower sections of furniture from this shop.

Figure 43 Detail of the lower right pillar of the cupboard illustrated in fig. 40. These pillars are trapped between rails that have never been disassembled, thus their orientation must be correct. The pillars of the cupboard shown in fig. 27 display a similar orientation.

Figure 44 Detail of the large half-column to the right of the door of the cupboard illustrated in fig. 40.

the Foster example has an open base with a drawer. This design represents a significant departure from that of the Waters and Woodbury cupboards (figs. 8, 17).[37]

Like several other pieces in the group, the Foster cupboard has a storage compartment fitted with a shelf formed by an extension of the soffit boards. The back of the storage compartment (fig. 41) is comprised of scrub-planed,

Figure 46 Detail of the half-column to the right of the lower drawer of the cupboard illustrated in fig. 40.

tongue-and-groove boards that are set in grooves in the top rail and nailed to the lower, inner rear rail. This rail also supports the floorboards, which are set into grooves in the side rails and a rabbet in the front rail. To allow room for the groove, the joiner made the side rails taller than the front rail. This framing system required him to nail the floorboards to the rabbet and back rail before attaching the rear boards.

By the mid-1680s, the joiners in this shop had established a hierarchy for the major turnings on their case forms and routinely placed complex square-shouldered pillars (see fig. 42) over relatively simple baluster-shaped ones (see fig. 43). The maker of the Foster cupboard also used a hierarchical arrangement for his large half-columns (fig. 44). The most ornate ones are on either side of the storage compartment door, and the others diminish in complexity from front to back and top to bottom (figs. 44, 46). Boston half-columns based on the Tuscan order may have inspired the small examples flanking the upper drawer (fig. 45).

The large quantity of dated furniture attributed to this shop sheds light on the evolution of this turner's style. When he made the lower pillars for the Woodbury cupboard in 1680 (figs. 8, 10), his transition from the base of the baluster to the lower torus and fillet was quite abrupt. Four years later, the flow of his work had improved significantly. The lower pillars of the Foster cupboard, for example, have a cove molding above the torus that complements the S-shape of the baluster above (fig. 43). As the 1680s progressed, his resolution of these complex forms became increasingly graceful as his concepts and skills continued to develop.

A cupboard formerly owned by Boston collector Charles Hitchcock Tyler (fig. 47) shares several features with the Foster example. Although it

Figure 47 Cupboard, northern Essex County, Massachusetts, 1680–1690. Oak and maple with oak. H. 55½", W. 49⅛", D. 19⅞". (Courtesy, Museum of Fine Arts, Boston, bequest of Charles Hitchcock Tyler.) The half-columns were removed and repainted during an early restoration. Some may be in the wrong position and several are replaced. The lower pillars and half-columns on the center drawer lack the pronounced checks (from moisture loss) found on original turnings on the cupboards and are probably replacements.

Figure 48 Detail of the bracket on the cupboard illustrated in fig. 47. The bracket is attached with two wrought nails and has carving related to that on the drawer fronts of other pieces in the group.

Figure 49 Detail of the large half-columns to the left of the door of the cupboard illustrated in fig. 47.

Figure 50 Detail of the upper left pillar of the cupboard illustrated in fig. 47.

has the period initials "HEA" and the number "1" carved on the inner surface of the bottom rail, the original owner has not been identified. This is the only cupboard without surface arcades, suggesting that it was one of the least expensive examples made by this shop.[38]

The appliqués on the door and carved bracket (fig. 48) introduce a new element that became standard in this shop's production. These button-like ornaments are very uniform and appear to have been produced with a rotary cutter. The turned pendant that was originally fastened to the underside of the bracket is missing, but it probably resembled the period example on the leaf table (fig. 22).[39]

The turnings on the cupboard document the influence of Boston styles on Essex County furniture and link it to other pieces in the group. Boston turnings clearly inspired the Tuscan half-columns flanking the door (fig. 49), but the Essex County shop's interpretations are much more complex. The feet, pillars (fig. 50), and half-columns on the lower stiles (figs. 51) are sim-

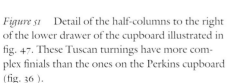

Figure 51   Detail of the half-columns to the right of the lower drawer of the cupboard illustrated in fig. 47. These Tuscan turnings have more complex finials than the ones on the Perkins cupboard (fig. 36).

ilar to the turner's earlier work, and the large half-columns at the back of the storage compartment (fig. 52) are related to those on the Perkins cupboard and the Capen chest of drawers (figs. 38, 53, 54).

Marked "IPC" and dated 1685, the Capen chest of drawers (fig. 53) is one of the most remarkable case forms attributed to this shop. Genealogical evidence suggests that the original owners were Rev. Joseph Capen (1658–1725) and his wife Priscilla Appleton (1657–1743) of Topsfield. They married about 1685 and lived in the Capen House, which has two summer beams dated 1683. Given the fact that Priscilla's brother John owned the case piece illustrated in figure 21, it is possible that the chest was part of the dower provided by her father, who was also named John.[40]

In terms of ornament, condition, and documentation, the Capen chest is one of the most important seventeenth-century examples made outside Boston. Gouge-carved moldings similar to those visible in figure 16 divide the façade into two distinct units—each comprised of two drawers flanked by pairs of large half-columns (fig. 54). The carved brackets (figs. 55, 56) are the most elaborate in the group. The center one is an inch shorter than the side brackets because it had a turned pendant similar to the original one on the leaf table (fig. 22).[41]

Figure 53 Chest of drawers, northern Essex County, Massachusetts, 1685. Oak and maple with oak. H. 35½", W. 44", D. 20½". (Courtesy, Brick Store Museum, Kennebunk, Maine, gift of Mrs. William Goedecke, Mrs. William Lamborn, and Mrs. Edwin E. Hooker; photo, Gavin Ashworth.) The brasses are modern and are not in the positions of the original knobs. Several ornaments are missing: two or three appliqués at each end of the second drawer from the top; two appliqués on the center plaque of the third drawer; four groups of three appliqués on the blank spaces between the plaques and carving on the bottom drawer. The latter ornaments resembled the pendants on the arcades of cupboards in the group.

Figure 54 Detail of the large half-columns to the right of the upper drawers of the chest of drawers illustrated in fig. 53. (Photo, Gavin Ashworth.)

Figure 55 Detail of the bracket on the chest of drawers illustrated in fig. 53. (Photo, Gavin Ashworth.)

Aside from the appliqués, all of the wood in the chest is oak. The top is comprised of four riven boards, several of which have a pronounced taper and may have come from a small tree. The ends of the case are framed with one horizontal panel over two vertical panels, and the back is framed with two pairs of superimposed vertical panels.[42]

Figure 56   Detail of the bracket adjacent to the right front foot of the chest of drawers illustrated in fig. 53. (Photo, Gavin Ashworth.)

Figure 57   Chest of drawers, northern Essex County, Massachusetts, 1685–1690. Oak and maple with oak and sycamore. H. 39¾", W. 41⅜", D. 20". (Courtesy, North Andover Historical Society, Samuel Dale Stevens Collection; photo, Gavin Ashworth.) The chest originally had four pairs of medium-sized half-columns on the stiles and small half-columns on the rectangular plaques of the drawers. The larger examples probably resembled those on the Capen chest (figs. 53, 54). The locks and brass escutcheons are old, but not original. They could not have been installed on the second and fourth drawers while the small half-columns were in place.

Two chests of drawers in the Essex County group have applied decoration similar to that on the Capen example. An example marked "TEP" (fig. 57) belonged to Samuel Dale Stevens (1859–1922), a North Andover collector who acquired most of his objects from local families rather than dealers. The date plaque is missing, but genealogical research strongly suggests that the original owners were Timothy Perkins (b. 1658) and Edna Hazen (b. 1667) of Topsfield, who were married in 1686. His father William (1607–1682) was minister of the Topsfield church and the predecessor of Joseph Capen. The presence of the Capen and Perkins chests in Topsfield is a significant index of this shop's reputation. During the seventeenth century, Samuel Symonds (1638–1722) dominated the market for turning and joinery in Topsfield and Rowley. He moved to Rowley from Salem in 1662 and remained active until his death.[43]

To insure correct placement of the drawers, the maker of the "TEP" chest marked them and the case with chisel cuts (fig. 58). The first and third drawers have rectangular panels with crossets formed by applied plaques and moldings (fig. 59), whereas the second and fourth drawers have V-shaped crossets (fig. 60) similar to those on the later cupboards (see figs. 66, 85). As on other pieces in the group, all of the moldings are oak.

Figure 58   Detail showing two of the four installation marks chiseled on the drawer sides of the chest of drawers illustrated in fig. 57. (Photo, Gavin Ashworth.)

Figure 59 Detail of the crosseted panel on the third drawer of the chest of drawers illustrated in fig. 57. (Photo, Gavin Ashworth.)

Figure 60 Detail of a V-shaped crosset on the second drawer of the chest of drawers illustrated in fig. 57. (Photo, Gavin Ashworth.)

Figure 61 Detail of the right front foot of the chest of drawers illustrated in fig. 57. (Photo, Gavin Ashworth.)

The feet on the "TEP" chest (fig. 61) differ from those associated with this shop in having an extra reel in the neck. Although their diameter is approximately the same as the stiles, the feet are separate components. Like all of the cupboards, the chest has stiles that are square in cross section. Boston chests may have inspired this feature, but they typically have feet turned from stock larger than the stiles. The patron who commissioned the "TEP" chest evidently specified turned feet and a base molding.[44]

Another chest (fig. 62) similar to the "TEP" example has rectangular stiles that extend to the floor and nail evidence indicating that it had a base molding and four pairs of half-columns similar to those illustrated in figure 53. Its water-sawn oak top (fig. 63) is over twenty inches wide, and several of the water-sawn sycamore drawer bottoms are approximately thirteen inches wide. Although the chest has lost all of its ornament, the drawers have deep scribe lines and scars indicating that the original moldings and plaques were identical to those on the "TEP" chest (figs. 57, 59). Quarter-inch chisel marks designate the positions of the plaques on the top drawer (fig. 64) and small gouge marks designate those on the third drawer. Numerical chisel marks also indicate the placement of the V-shaped plaques on the second and fourth drawers (fig. 65). Numbering systems for the identification and alignment of structural components are relatively common on seventeenth-century furniture, but little evidence of their use for applied ornament survives.[45]

Figure 62 Chest of drawers, northern Essex County, Massachusetts, 1685–1690. Oak with sycamore and oak. H. 39¾", W. 41⅛", D. 20¼". (Private collection; photo, Gavin Ashworth.) The sides of the drawers have numerical alignment marks like those on the chest illustrated in fig. 57.

Figure 63 Detail of the water-sawn interior surface of the top board of the chest of drawers illustrated in fig. 62.

Figure 64 Detail showing the position of the moldings on the upper drawer of the chest of drawers illustrated in fig. 62. (Photo, Gavin Ashworth.)

Figure 65 Detail showing the position of the moldings on the second drawer of the chest of drawers illustrated in fig. 62. (Photo, Gavin Ashworth.)

Monuments of Mannerist Design

By the late 1680s, this Essex County shop was producing the most elaborate and conceptually ambitious case furniture in British North America. A remarkable cupboard with the initials "IK" (figs. 66, 67) has long been considered a masterpiece of seventeenth-century design. Wallace Nutting illustrated it in *Furniture Treasury* and noted that it was from the estate of

Charles Paine of Weston, Massachusetts. In 1936, Paine's son John informed Irving P. Lyon that his great-grandmother, Hannah Farnham Sawyer Lee (1780–1865), was the earliest known owner of the cupboard. Her parents were Micajah and Sibyll (Farnham) Sawyer of Newburyport.[46]

The basic design of the Sawyer cupboard matches the description of a "chest of drawers & cupboard all in one" valued at £1.5 in the 1690 probate inventory of Robert Stone of Salem. These two-stage joined case forms with one (see fig. 66) or more tiers of drawers (see fig. 36) can be considered forerunners of the early baroque high chest. This is especially true of the Sawyer cupboard, which has the most advanced surviving drawer construction of any piece in the Essex County group (fig. 68). The third drawer

Figure 66   Cupboard, northern Essex County, Massachusetts, 1685–1690. Oak and maple with oak and pine. H. 58", W. 49⅛", D. 23". (Courtesy, Massachusetts Historical Society, gift of Mrs. J. B. Paine; photo, Gavin Ashworth.) This cupboard is the most intact example in the Essex County group. The bracket under the bottom rail is missing; there are minor losses and replacements of applied ornament; and the paint is relatively modern.

Figure 67   Detail of the central plaque, initials, half-column, and bosses on the bottom drawer of the cupboard illustrated in fig. 66. (Photo, Gavin Ashworth.) The incised initials are filled with mastic.

Figure 68   Detail showing the dovetails on four drawers of the cupboard illustrated in fig. 66. (Photo, Peter Follansbee.)

from the top, for example, has two dovetails at each corner. No other contemporary New England joined case piece has drawers with multiple dovetails at every corner. In the Anglo-American furniture making tradition, the use of multiple dovetails to join large boards is generally associated with the baroque style. English cabinetmakers such as John Brocas introduced this style in Boston about 1695.[47]

With its channel-molded frieze, complex door moldings, strong turnings, and triple arcades, the upper section of the Sawyer cupboard is one of the most elaborate attributed to this shop. The channel-moldings are punctuated with mitered inserts and bosses like those on the upper drawer of the Perkins cupboard (fig. 36), and the arcades are unique in having three arches each with elongated pendants on panels with applied bosses and triangular base plaques. The top of the Sawyer cupboard is also unusual in being made of water-sawn pine rather than oak. Considering the status and cost of this imposing object, the patron who commissioned it probably intended to cover the top with a cupboard cloth or cushions.[48]

The lower section of the Sawyer cupboard is similar to the base of the one illustrated in figure 27, but it has drawers between the pillars rather than a

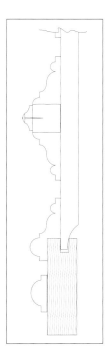

Figure 70 Drawing showing the construction of the door of the cupboard illustrated in fig. 66. (Drawing, Alan Miller; artwork, Wynne Patterson.)

Figure 71 Detail of the upper left pillar of the cupboard illustrated in fig. 66. (Photo, Gavin Ashworth.)

central panel flanked by two storage compartments. To alleviate the strong horizontal emphasis of the base and add variety to the façade, the maker of the Sawyer cupboard divided the ornament on the first, third, and fourth drawers into two sections and the second drawer into three sections. He accentuated the latter drawer's polyrhythmic effect by dividing each of its three sections into three with a carved lunette and trefoil motif. Whereas two integral reserves bisect the second drawer, thin plaques with half-columns divide the top, third, and fourth drawers. All of these components help balance the horizontal elements and create a strong vertical axis at the center of the lower case. The missing bracket pendant, originally nailed under the case, extended the visual line established by these components approximately four inches below the base molding. On the top drawer, the joiner positioned the raised plaques so their knobs would be aligned with the front corners of the trapezoidal storage compartment. By carefully sizing each component, he was also able to align the bosses on the horizontal inner plaques with the reserves and knobs trisecting the carved drawer below. These virtuoso details contribute to the rhythm and complexity of the façade and complement the vertical orientation of the stiles, pillars, and half-columns.[49]

It is difficult to determine why the joiners made such significant alterations to the decorative vocabulary previously used on drawer fronts. It is doubtful that many years separate the Sawyer cupboard from the Capen chest (fig. 53), given the similarity between their turned half-columns. The most plausible explanation for these changes is competition with Boston and Salem furniture. Like many Boston chests, the Sawyer cupboard has drawers with rectangular panels surrounded by broad chamfered moldings.

Although several of the moldings on the Sawyer cupboard match those on earlier pieces in the group, the joiner required new tools to produce a number of components. He apparently cut the waist molding with the same scratch-stock iron that produced the dentil molding on the Perkins cupboard (fig. 36), but varied the design by chopping out triangular segments rather than dentils separated by lunettes. In contrast, the production of the base molding (fig. 69) required several tools including conventional planes. The joiner used a hollow plane and a fenced rabbet plane to cut the astragal and fillet elements and a scratch-stock cutter to form the upper elements. This may have been the same hollow plane that produced the imbricated moldings on two chests of drawers in the group (figs. 16, 53). The same bold molding sequences appear on the cupboard door (figs. 66, 70). The joiner used the same astragal element on the rail between the second and third drawers to define the perimeter and two repeats of the base sequence for the inner moldings. To vary the effect, he rotated the inner repeat by ninety degrees. The outer application of base molding on the door became a "bolection" where it transits the junction of the frame and underlying panel. To complete the composition, he used five brass, drawer pull backplates to decorate the center plaque and corners of the frame.[50]

Because the Sawyer cupboard is built in two parts, the original orientation of the upper pillars is uncertain (fig. 71). This joiner's mannerist con-

Figure 72   Detail of the lower left pillar of the cupboard illustrated in fig. 66. (Photo, Gavin Ashworth.)

Figure 73   Detail of the small half-columns to the left of the center drawer of the cupboard illustrated in fig. 66. (Photo, Gavin Ashworth.)

Figure 74   Detail of the large half-columns to the left of the door of the cupboard illustrated in fig. 66. (Photo, Gavin Ashworth.)

cept of design and rhythm suggests that they may have been oriented in the opposite direction of the lower pillars (fig. 72) like the fly leg of the leaf table (fig. 26). The lower pillars have bold balusters with slender necks and pronounced collars. Their shape is more advanced than the corresponding pillars on the Foster cupboard (fig. 43), especially the areas where the baluster flows into the base and neck. The influence of Boston or Cambridge turning, manifest in the pillars of many earlier cupboards (see figs. 9, 10, 17), is barely discernable.[51]

The small half-columns flanking the upper drawer (fig. 73) are more elaborate versions of those on the Perkins cupboard (fig. 38), and the ones flanking the lower drawer (fig. 69) are similar to the pillars directly above (fig. 71) but are inverted. This reversal relates to the treatment of the inner and outer posts of the fly leg assembly of the leaf table (figs. 22, 26). The large half-columns on the front corners of the storage compartment (fig. 74) have capped urns like those on the Capen chest (figs. 53, 54).[52]

From an architectural standpoint, the most distinctive and structurally complex object attributed to the Essex County shop is a cupboard (fig. 75) that descended in the Weare family of Massachusetts and New Hampshire. The initials on the bottom drawer, added during a nineteenth-century restoration, refer to Meshech Weare (1713–1786), the first president of the New Hampshire congress after the Revolutionary War. Presumably, the original owner was his father, Nathaniel (1663–1755), who was born in Newbury and married Huldah Hussey in 1692 and Mary Wait in 1703.[53]

Figure 75   Cupboard, northern Essex County, Massachusetts, 1685–1690. Oak and maple with oak and pine. H. 61¾", W. 51¾", D. 21⅝". (Courtesy, Currier Gallery of Art, Manchester, New Hampshire, bequest of William G. Berry; photo, Gavin Ashworth.) The backboards of the upper section are replaced, the floorboards of the storage compartment are missing, and a new soffit seals the entire cornice. The latter replacement changed the height of the upper case, requiring the addition of small spacer blocks between the tops of the pillars and the cornice. The gothic door appears to have been added during the nineteenth century. Its arcade resembles those found on North Shore and Portsmouth furniture of the Federal period. The molding flanking the lunette carving on the top drawer is replaced and the third drawer and bottom drawer are completely new. The drawers originally had dovetails. Evidence suggests that the joints resembled those on the drawers of the Sawyer cupboard (fig. 66) and the example shown in figure 85. All of the moldings and appliqués flanking the carving and on the replaced center plaque of the fourth drawer are missing, and base molding is replaced. The moldings probably resembled those on the first, third, and fourth drawers of the Sawyer cupboard. The pendants, middle brackets and several half-columns, bosses, and pendant appliqués from the arcades are also missing.

The Weare cupboard has a recessed upper section with four pillars (fig. 76) and is similar in concept to the Woodbury and Perkins examples (figs. 8, 36). Its trefoil carving resembles that on the Sawyer cupboard (fig. 66), and the scrolled motif on the second and fourth drawers is a variation of that on the second drawer of the Staniford chest (fig. 1). Traces of bright red paint like that on the cupboard illustrated in figure 27 remain in the ground. The brackets are pierced rather than carved, but they have essentially the same profile as the one shown in figure 55.

The turnings on the Weare cupboard are most like those on the Sawyer example (fig. 66), but their hierarchy in the overall composition is more intricate. Like the orders in classical architecture, the pillars and appliqués descend in rank from top-to-bottom and front-to-back. One pair of the upper pillars (fig. 76) has two coves and a collared flange on its neck, whereas the other has three coves and no flange. Unfortunately, it is impossible to determine which design superceded the other because the upper pillars are removable and their original orientation is unknown. The same is true of the lower pillars (fig. 77), which could have been switched and/or inverted when the base was disassembled during a nineteenth-century restoration attempt. These pillars suggest that the Weare cupboard is

Figure 76 Detail of the right front pillar of the upper case of the cupboard illustrated in fig. 75. (Photo, Gavin Ashworth.)

Figure 77 Detail of the right front pillar of the lower case of the cupboard illustrated in fig. 75. (Photo, Gavin Ashworth.) The pillars at the rear have simple unadorned balusters.

Figure 78 Detail of a bracket fragment and the small half-columns to the right of the top drawer of the cupboard illustrated in fig. 75. (Photo, Gavin Ashworth.) The original brackets are tenoned into the front stiles and nailed to the lower edge of the front rail.

slightly later than the Sawyer example. Their thin necks and more pronounced curves are duplicated on later pillars in the group (see fig. 97).

As with the pillars, the complexity and location of the small half-columns denotes their "rank" in the overall design. The most elaborate ones (fig. 78), which are similar to those flanking the top drawer of the Sawyer cupboard, are on the façade, whereas simple Tuscan variants are on the sides. Other features linking these cupboards are the major half-columns on the upper case (fig. 79), small half-columns on the base (fig. 80), and front feet (fig. 81), although the turnings on the Weare example are slightly more detailed.[54]

The lower section of the Weare cupboard (figs. 82–84) is comprised of four distinct units, two of which extend to form jetties on the front and sides. The base, containing the drawer marked "MW," has wide side rails with channel moldings painted black and four turned feet (figs. 81, 82). Directly above is a recessed compartment with two drawers. The sides of the compartment consist of panels framed by stiles and channel molded rails. Both panels have applied moldings around the perimeter and turned bosses in the center. The front stiles are tenoned to interior struts in the base, and the back stiles are tenoned to the rear rail. Over this recessed compartment is a unit the same size as the base. It is supported by four turned pillars and sealed with riven oak soffit boards. The rear rail of this unit has mortises that engage tenons on the top of the recessed section's rear stiles. The only other

Figure 80 Detail of the small half-columns to the right of the bottom drawer of the cupboard illustrated in fig. 75. (Photo, Gavin Ashworth.)

Figure 81 Detail of the right front foot of the cupboard illustrated in fig. 75. (Photo, Gavin Ashworth.) The front feet are made of maple and tenoned to the oak posts. The rear feet are integral and have different turning sequences.

Figure 82 Detail of the back of the cupboard illustrated in fig. 75. (Photo, Gavin Ashworth.)

Figure 83 Drawing showing the framing of the side of the lower case of the cupboard illustrated in fig. 75. (Drawing, Peter Follansbee; artwork, Wynne Patterson.)

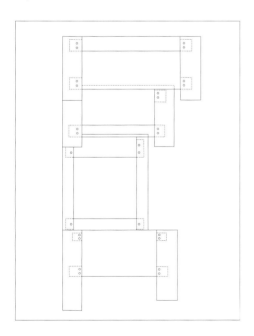

connection between these two units is the soffit boards, which are nailed to the side and front rails of the recessed compartment. The same structural features join the uppermost unit of the lower section to the one directly below. These details are most apparent on the rear façade (fig. 82).[55]

The jetties on the Weare cupboard are simplified versions of those occasionally found in seventeenth-century framed buildings. Architectural overhangs that protrude on the sides and front often receive additional support from an internal "dragon" beam. These diagonal beams extend from the interior framing and overshoot the corner post of the first story, providing support for the corner post of the second story. In contrast, nailed-in soffits stabilize many of the jetties on cupboards in the Essex County group.[56]

Although no New England building with a dragon beam survives, the Ross Tavern in Ipswich has jetties on all four sides. The original function of an overhanging second story is in dispute, but most scholars agree that, by the seventeenth century, it was primarily an aesthetic conceit. Architectural historian Abbott Lowell Cummings has observed that jetties most often appear on "ambitious dwellings" in the Massachusetts Bay region. He also notes that jetties were popular in New England from 1670 to 1690—the period when the Essex County shop flourished. Cummings' description of the evolution of architectural styles and patronage is certainly relevant to the furniture discussed here:

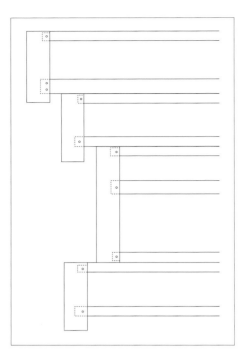

Figure 84 Drawing showing the framing of the front of the lower case of the cupboard illustrated in fig. 75. (Drawing, Peter Follansbee; artwork, Wynne Patterson.)

The earliest framed houses were added to almost as soon as they were finished, and the process of change and improvement went on continually, culminating in a "high" period at the end of the seventeenth century as the homes of ministers, merchants, and prosperous farmers blossomed forth with boldly projecting overhangs, pyramided gables, and ornamental brackets and drops.[57]

The cupboard illustrated in figure 85 is less complex than the Sawyer and Weare examples, but exceptional by contemporary New England standards. Given the fact that two pieces in the group belonged to members of the Perkins family, the initials "EP" on the bottom drawer are intriguing. During the seventeenth century, patronage often followed family lines.

On the "EP" cupboard, the joiner divided the top drawer into three sections using vertical plaques the same width as the stiles flanking the door of the storage compartment. To establish a visual link between the upper and lower sections of the cupboard, he made the carved panels approximately the same width as the arcades of the trapezoidal storage compartment and the geometric panels approximately the same width as the door. Other features reflect the maker's effort to balance various elements of the façade. The central plaques of the lower drawers, for example, establish a strong vertical line that alleviates the horizontal emphasis of the flanking panels. As on the lower case of the Sawyer cupboard (fig. 66), each drawer front is different but integrated in the overall composition.

Other features of the "EP" cupboard also have cognates in the group. The door is similar to the one on the Sawyer example, but the joiner omitted the large astragal (which appears on the rail between the second and third drawers) and used two repeats of the base molding mitered like the ones shown in figure 70. The surface arcades on the "EP" cupboard are identical to those on the Weare example (fig. 75), and the rear panel arrangement is similar to that of the Sawyer cupboard (fig. 66). On the "EP" cupboard, the maker used a single horizontal board for the lower case panel rather than a pair of panels.

The turnings on the "EP" cupboard differ only slightly from those on the Sawyer and Weare examples. The lower pillars (fig. 86) demonstrate the final form by this turner. He flattened the sides of the balusters, deepened and refined the curves of the necks, and made the collar flanges more pronounced. His upper pillars (fig. 87) are extrapolations of two on the Weare cupboard (figs. 76, 77), but with thinner necks and more prominent collar flanges. Similarly, the half-columns flanking the upper drawer of the "EP" cupboard (fig. 88) relate to those shown in figures 73 and 78. Like the Tuscan half-columns on either side of the bottom drawer (fig. 89), their placement is consistent with the ornamental hierarchy observed on other pieces in the group. The most complex appliqués on the "EP" cupboard are the large half-columns flanking the door. They have bold capped urns, a detail the turner introduced on the half-columns of the Capen chest of drawers (figs. 53, 54).

The base of a cupboard with turnings similar to those of the "EP" example is illustrated in the 1928 edition of Nutting's *Furniture Treasury* (fig. 90). It is initialed "SK" and belonged to Arthur W. Wellington of Weston, Mass-

Figure 86 Detail of the lower left pillar of the cupboard illustrated in fig. 85. (Photo, Gavin Ashworth.)

Figure 87 Detail of the upper left pillar of the cupboard illustrated in fig. 85. (Photo, Gavin Ashworth.)

achusetts, at the time of its publication. Nutting recognized the similarities between the base and other pieces now attributed to the Essex County group. He cited the Sawyer example in his caption and illustrated it and the "SK" and Foster cupboards on consecutive pages.[58]

The cupboard illustrated in figure 91 is the latest example with storage compartments in both the upper and lower cases. Like the Spaulding cupboard (fig. 27), it had a shallow shelf set in grooves in the top rear rail of the upper case and a panel that partitioned the compartment in the lower case. The floor of the upper case is comprised of riven oak boards. Unlike most of the boards on other examples, these fit into grooves in the lower side and rear rails. Typically, the rear rail is positioned below the floor and inside the back panel. The horizontal back panel on this cupboard is beveled on all edges and set into grooves in the rear frame. Although this design simplified the joinery, it appears only in this example.[59]

Client preference may account for the early design of this cupboard (fig. 91). Although possibly no more than ten years separate it and the cupboard shown in figure 27, the shop's decorative vocabulary had changed significantly. The pillars and appliqués (fig. 91) are more akin to those on the "EP" and "SK" examples (figs. 85, 90). Although the joiner used canted imposts for the jamb plinths on the arch between the lower doors, all of the other elements comprising the arch and the arcades on the storage compart-

Figure 88   Detail of the half-columns to the right of the upper drawer of the cupboard illustrated in fig. 85. (Photo, Gavin Ashworth.)

Figure 89   Detail of the half columns to the right of the lower drawer of the cupboard illustrated in fig. 85. (Photo, Gavin Ashworth.)

Figure 90   Base of a cupboard, northern Essex County, Massachusetts, 1685–1690. Oak and maple. Dimensions not recorded. (Wallace Nutting, *Furniture Treasury* [Framingham, Mass.: Old America Co., 1928], pl. 445.) The base molding and astragal element between the second and third drawers are repeated on other cupboards from the same shop (see fig. 66).

ment above are typical of the last phase of this shop's production. The curved spandrel moldings, which consist of three descending concave arcs, differ significantly from those on other arches in the group. Their irregular contours suggest that the joiner did not use a sweep. He also used a new scratch-stock cutter to make the perimeter moldings of the drawers.[60]

Figure 91 Cupboard, northern Essex County, Massachusetts, 1685–1690. Oak and maple with oak and pine. H. 58¾", W. 48½", D. 19⅜". (Museum of Fine Arts, Boston, gift of Maurice Geeraerts in memory of Mr. and Mrs. William H. Robeson.) The diamond-shaped applied frame on the upper door, knobs, and feet are replacements. The door probably had moldings similar to those on the door of the cupboard illustrated in figure 85, but in a diamond-shape configuration.

The joiner designed the cupboard with a molded lower rail rather than a base molding. For the stiles on either side, the turner made long half-columns with extra flanged collars on their finials. Like the pillars and half-columns above, these appliqués give the sides of the façade a strong vertical emphasis. The upper and lower pillars (figs. 92, 93) are very similar to those of the "EP" cupboard (figs. 85–87), but they have scored collar flanges. The half-columns flanking the upper drawer are narrow versions of those on the Sawyer and Weare cupboards (figs. 66, 75), and the large ones on the trapezoidal storage compartment (figs. 94, 95) differ only slightly from those on

Figure 92 Detail of the upper left pillar of the cupboard illustrated in fig. 91.

Figure 93 Detail of the lower left pillar of the cupboard illustrated in fig. 91.

Figure 94 Detail of the large half-columns to the left of the upper door of the cupboard illustrated in fig. 91.

the "EP" example (fig. 88). From a technical standpoint, the large half-columns on the lower case (fig. 96) are rivaled only by the most elaborate turnings on the Sawyer and "EP" cupboards (figs. 66, 88). With their complex base elements, compressed upper balls, and multiple collar flanges that increase in diameter from top to bottom, these half-columns are virtuoso examples of mannerist turning.

A square joined table (fig. 97) contemporary with these later cupboards descended in the Higgins family of eastern Massachusetts. In a letter dated June 24, 1937, Mrs. N. E. Bartlett informed Irving P. Lyon that the table

Figure 95 Detail of the large half-column on the right rear corner of the upper storage compartment of the cupboard illustrated in fig. 91.

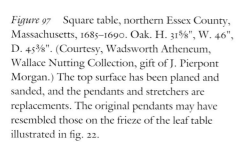

Figure 97 Square table, northern Essex County, Massachusetts, 1685–1690. Oak. H. 31⅝", W. 46", D. 45⅜". (Courtesy, Wadsworth Atheneum, Wallace Nutting Collection, gift of J. Pierpont Morgan.) The top surface has been planed and sanded, and the pendants and stretchers are replacements. The original pendants may have resembled those on the frieze of the leaf table illustrated in fig. 22.

formerly belonged to her husband's maternal grandfather Solomon Higgins, who found it in the basement of a house on Central Avenue in Andover. Since this location was adjacent to the site of the town's first meeting house, it is conceivable that the table was among the original furnishings of the church. Joiner Stephen Jaques may have made a communion table similar to it for the meeting house in Newbury.[61]

Although the legs of the Higgins table resemble the pillars on several of the Essex County cupboards, they are the only large-scale oak turnings associated with this shop. Making this table entirely from riven oak was a challenging process for the turner and joiner. The balusters of the posts are almost four inches in diameter, which constitutes nearly the entire quarter of a medium-sized tree. Contrary to popular belief, trees of moderate diameter were much easier to rive than extremely large ones. Although the maker could have saved wood by gluing up stock or making the legs in sections (see fig. 22), he turned the balusters and feet from a single piece of wood and painstakingly worked down the upper and lower squares that join the rails and stretchers. The leaf table illustrated in figure 22 has a swing leg with an integral baluster and foot (fig. 25), but the diameters of the turned elements are within the dimensions of the square stock.

Obtaining and extracting timber suitable for the rails presented a similar problem; their height and thickness required large boards and a substantial amount of hewing to achieve the desired shape. Because the joiner required a broad surface for nailing on the brackets and scrolled pendants, he used the widest portion of the rails at the bottom. This orientation is similar to that of the riven drawer fronts on several case pieces in the group. The boards comprising the top are less wedge-shaped and are approximately six inches wide. They are held together by mitered cleats pinned to each end. The underside of the top has four mortises that engage tenons cut on the outer corners of the four posts. This feature, which makes the top removable, may reflect the joiner's concern that the upper edges of the rails were too thin to receive pins. All other New England square tables have pinned tops.

Figure 98   Chest of drawers, northern Essex County, Massachusetts, dated 1692. Oak and maple with oak and pine. H. 40⅞", W. 45⅛", D. 18¾". (Private collection; photo, Gavin Ashworth.) The top is replaced.

The chest of drawers illustrated in figure 98 presents a stark contrast to the other examples in the group (figs. 1, 16, 53, 62, 67). It has simple moldings and plaques made of maple rather than oak and drawers that diminish in height from top to bottom. Given the date on the chest, this arrangement may reflect incipient influences of the new baroque style. If so, the influences were, at the most, superficial. The stiles have channel moldings with mitered inserts—a detail occasionally found on earlier Boston joined chests. Most of the construction features of the chest occur on earlier examples from the shop. The drawers are dovetailed at the front and nailed at the back, the interior has orientation and sub-assembly marks, and the ends have scratch-stock moldings and chamfers like those on the chests shown in figures 1, 16, and 53. The rear framing is somewhat simpler and consists of three horizontal rails between the rear stiles and two horizontal pine panels. This feature is probably a reaction to the availability of sawn versus riven timber rather than a modification of earlier construction practices.[62]

Context and Catalysts

With dates ranging from 1678 to 1701, the furniture in the Essex County group is clearly the product of a second- or third-generation shop tradition. New England furniture styles and patronage changed significantly between 1630 and 1700. During the first decades of the seventeenth century, immigrants from many provincial centers in England introduced the carved mannerist style. Rooted in Renaissance classical design, this style developed in northern Europe, arrived in the channel ports during the 1560s, and subsequently spread throughout England and her colonies. By the end of the sixteenth century, the carved style was being displaced in London by another phase of mannerism that had developed in Italy and Germany. This new style, characterized by the use of applied architectural ornament, matured in London during the late 1620s and arrived in Boston by the mid-1630s. Boston joiners and turners undoubtedly influenced furniture styles in surrounding counties, but to what extent and when remains unclear. Many case pieces from Plymouth Colony, Cambridge, Woburn, and Salem have ornamental details derived from Boston furniture, but most date from the last decades of the seventeenth century.[63]

Although a few details associated with the Essex County group have Boston precedents, the case pieces and tables discussed above have more in common with Parisian furniture from the last half of the sixteenth century. The Second School of Fountainbleau, which flourished from 1540 to 1590, had a profound impact on French regional traditions. The joiners in this school produced highly architectural forms such as display cabinets and one- and two-part *dressoirs* (fig. 99), which were the immediate antecedents of the seventeenth-century English cupboard (fig. 100). Many English ports traded directly with the continent and provided sanctuary for Protestant refugees who began leaving France during the mid-sixteenth century. Considering the period when the Second School of Fountainbleau flourished, it seems likely that Huguenot artisans played a pivotal role in transmitting Parisian styles to England.[64]

Figure 99   *Dressoir,* possibly Paris, 1590–1600. Illustrated in Edouard Baldus, comp., *Oeuvre de Jacques Androuet dit Du Cerceau* (1870), pl. 25. (Courtesy, Winterthur Museum.)

Figure 100   Base of a cupboard, England, 1625–1675. Oak and other unidentified woods. H. 37", W. 54", depth not recorded. Illustrated in Sotheby's, *Selected Pieces from the Cold Overton Hall Collections of Oak and Early Furniture,* London, October 10, 1986, lot 87.

The complex jetties on the most elaborate Essex County case pieces are unprecedented in British work. English cupboards from the West Country and the North Country occasionally have upper cases with cantilevered side rails, hanging posts, and turned pendants, but they display none of the compositional audacity of the Essex County cupboards. Parallels with contemporary jettied architecture in Ipswich and Newbury are also pertinent; however, the architectural and furniture joinery are not similar enough to establish a direct link.[65]

The earliest dated case pieces in the Essex County group are mature forms, which suggests that they are extensions of an earlier shop tradition—perhaps one established during the 1630s—or the products of a small group of immigrant artisans who arrived in Massachusetts during the 1670s. Neither explanation is conclusive because no Massachusetts antecedents for the group are known, and the artisans in this shop have not been identified. The extensive use of orientation and assembly marks similar to those on buildings suggests that the joiners may have done architectural work. New England woodworkers often practiced a variety of trades ranging from shipbuilding to lumbering.[66]

During the seventeenth century, ten families dominated the woodworking trades in Ipswich and Newbury. The Burnham, Norton, Roper, Strong, Waite, Wardell, Woodward, Rindge, Dennis, and Tilton traditions were in Ipswich, and the Chase-Follansbee, Titcomb, Parker, Jaques, Hale, Emery, Boynton, Lunt, Badger, and March traditions were in Newbury. A member of one of these dynasties almost certainly established the Essex County shop. These families competed on a variety of fronts, the most important of which involved large public projects such as the construction of meeting houses. On July 5, 1698, the residents of Newbury voted to build a new meeting house sixty feet wide, fifty feet deep, and over twenty-four feet high. To supervise the project, they hired Stephen Jaques (1661–ca. 1744), son of carpenter Henry Jaques (ca. 1618–1687) and brother-in-law of three other prominent Newbury woodworkers. An 1806 description of the meeting house notes:

> The roof was constructed with four gable ends, or projections, one on each side, each containing a large window, which gave light to the upper galleries. The turret was in the centre. The space within was open to the roof, where was visible plenty of timber, with great needles and little needles pointing downwards, to serve at once for strength and ornament. There were many ornaments of antique sculpture and wainscot.

The large and small "needles" were the ends of vertical beams, sawn or carved into pendants similar to those on house jetties and the cupboards in the Essex County group.[67]

Not to be outdone, the residents of Ipswich voted to build a new meeting house shortly thereafter. On November 11, 1698, they appointed a committee of prominent citizens and two carpenters —Captain Daniel Rindge, Jr. (ca. 1654–1738) and Abraham Tilton, Sr. (1638–1728)—to consider the size of the building and how to pay for it. Among the leaders were two members of the Appleton family, who were related to the owners of the cupboard base and chest of drawers illustrated in figures 21 and 53. Three days later, the committee recommended that the building be sixty feet wide, sixty-six feet long, and twenty-six feet to the eaves, and that the town commission Abraham Tilton, Sr. and his son Abraham Tilton, Jr. (1666–1756) to build the structure "provided they could have a convenient price." When the Tiltons responded that the project would cost £1,100, "Abraham Perkins . . . said that he would build it for nine hundred pounds. . . . And the Town . . . unanimously consented." Perkins' bid was clearly made on behalf of his son-in-law, Daniel Rindge, Jr. A prominent tradesman with strong ties to the regional elite, Rindge is the only woodworker linked directly to patrons of the Essex County shop. His father-in-law owned the cupboard illustrated in figure 21, and his daughter Hannah (1684–1749) married Thomas Staniford (1680–1740), whose parents commissioned the chest shown in figure 1. These connections make him a strong candidate for master of the Essex County shop.[68]

The Ipswich and Newbury meeting houses, which undoubtedly had ornamental structural details and furnishings, demonstrate that the mannerist impulse remained popular in Essex County during the late seventeenth and early eighteenth centuries and was only gradually replaced by the baroque style. Contrary to traditional assumptions, joiners accustomed to producing frame-and-panel forms did not stop practicing their trade when dovetailed board cases and elaborate veneers became popular. They simply adapted their styles and techniques to meet changing tastes. Indeed, some of the design features and construction details typical of the Essex County group—two-piece case forms with drawers in each section and dovetailed drawers—prefigure those associated with the baroque style. The cupboards, chests, and tables attributed to this shop are more than consummate examples of American joinery. They are the products of an extremely sophisticated woodworking tradition and a conduit linking the dominant styles of the sixteenth, seventeenth, and early eighteenth centuries.

1. For the Appleton family, see Robert F. Trent, *Historic Furnishings Report—Saugus Iron Works National Historic Site, Saugus, Massachusetts* (Harper's Ferry, W.Va.: National Parks Service, 1982), pp. 6–24.

2. William H. Sumner, "The Eliot Bureau," *New England Historic Genealogical Register* 9, no. 4 (October 1855): 329–33. Robert F. Trent and Peter Follansbee, "Repairs Versus Deception in Essex County Cupboards, 1830–1890," in *Rural New England Furniture: People, Place, and Production,* edited by Peter Benes (Boston: Boston University and the Dublin Seminar for New England Folklife, 2000), pp. 13–28. Clarence Cook, *The House Beautiful* (New York: Scribner, Armstrong, and Co., 1877), pp. 226–27, no. 72.

3. Irving Whitall Lyon, *The Colonial Furniture of New England* (New York: Houghton Mifflin Company, 1891), figs. 15, 16. Esther Singleton, *The Furniture of Our Forefathers* (New York: Doubleday, Page and Co., 1900–1901), pp. 168–69. Frances Clary Morse, *Furniture of the Olden Time* (1902; reprint and rev. ed., New York: Macmillan, 1936), p. 87. Trent and Follansbee, "Repairs Versus Deception," pp. 13–28.

4. Wallace Nutting, *Furniture Treasury,* 2 vols. (Framingham, Mass.: Old America Co., 1928), no. 211. Irving P. Lyon, "A Pedigreed Cupboard, Dated 1681 and Initialed IEA for John and Elizabeth Appleton of Ipswich, Massachusetts," *Old Time New England* 28, no. 4 (April 1938): 118–22; and Irving P. Lyon, "The Cupboard of Ephraim and Hannah Foster of North Andover, Massachusetts. Dated 1684, Analysis of Its Many Initials," *Old Time New England* 28, no. 4 (April 1938): 123–25. Irving P. Lyon, "The Oak Furniture of Ipswich, Massachusetts,

Part 1, Florid Type," *Antiques* 32, no. 5 (November 1937): 230–37; "The Oak Furniture of Ipswich, Massachusetts, Part 2, Florid Type, Miscellaneous Examples," *Antiques* 32, no. 6 (December 1937): 298–301; "The Oak Furniture of Ipswich, Massachusetts, Part 3, Florid Type, Scroll Detail," *Antiques* 33, no. 2 (February 1938): 73–75; "The Oak Furniture of Ipswich, Massachusetts, Part 4, The Small-Panel Type," *Antiques* 33, no. 4 (April 1938): 198–203; "The Oak Furniture of Ipswich, Massachusetts, Part 5, Small-Panel-Type Affiliates," *Antiques* 33, no. 6 (June 1938): 322–25; "The Oak Furniture of Ipswich, Massachusetts, Part 6, Other Affiliates: A Group Characterized by Geometrical Panels," *Antiques* 34, no. 2 (February 1939): 79–81. All of Lyon's *Antiques* articles are reprinted in *Pilgrim Century Furniture: An Historical Survey,* edited by Robert F. Trent (New York: Main Street/Universe Books, 1976), pp. 55–78.

5. Helen Park, "Thomas Dennis, Ipswich Joiner: A Re-examination," *Antiques* 78, no. 1 (July 1960): 40–44. Helen Park, "The Seventeenth-Century Furniture of Essex County and Its Makers," *Antiques* 78, no. 4 (October 1960): 350–55. Both of Park's articles are reprinted in Trent, ed., *Pilgrim Century Furniture,* pp. 84–94. Benno M. Forman, "The Seventeenth-Century Case Furniture of Essex County, Massachusetts and Its Makers" (master's thesis, University of Delaware, 1968). Benno M. Forman, "Urban Aspects of Massachusetts Furniture in the Late Seventeenth Century," in *Country Cabinetwork and Simple City Furniture,* edited by John D. Morse (Charlottesville: University Press of Virginia for the Winterthur Museum, 1970), pp. 1–33.

6. Forman, "The Case Furniture of Essex County," pp. 28–40. The versatility of British woodworkers is demonstrated in *Rural Economy in Yorkshire in 1641, being the Account Books of Henry Best, of Elmswell, in the East Riding of the County of York* (Durham, Eng.: George Andrews, 1857), pp. 153, 156:

> 1620, Apr 4. Agreed with Matthewe Carter, for paylinge the swyne stye with sawne ashe payles, to give him for his worke 9d. (per) yeardes, and hee is to sawe them, and to sawe the rayles and postes, and sett them in a groundsell, and rabbit them in to the rayle above; agreed also with him to pale the yearde, and hee is to sawe the rayles and postes, and to have 4d per yearde, for his labor. 1622

> Dec 13. Bargained with Matthewe Carter and John Carter his sonne, of Greate Driffeylde, carpenters, to digg upp a walnutt tree of myne, and to sawe it into 2 ynch and a half plankes, and the rest of the small peeces into such peeces as it is fittest for; and to make mee two chayres, one for my selfe, and the other a lesser, well turned and wrought, and I am to give them for doing these things above mentioned, workman like, 10s in money, a bushel of barley, and a pecke of oatmeale, and give them in money 3d for their godspenny.

7. *New England Begins: The Seventeenth Century,* edited by Jonathan L. Fairbanks and Robert F. Trent, 3 vols. (Boston: Museum of Fine Arts, Boston, 1982) 3: 531–32. Robert F. Trent, "The Emery Attributions," *Essex Institute Historical Collections* 121, no. 3 (July 1985): 210–20. *Old Town and the Waterside: Two Hundred Years of Tradition and Change in Newbury, Newburyport, and West Newbury, 1635–1835,* edited by Peter Benes (Newburyport, Mass.: Historical Society of Old Newbury, 1986), pp. 36, 40–41.

8. For the provenance of the Staniford chest, see Robert W. Skinner, Inc., *Fine Americana,* Bolton, Massachusetts, October 29, 1982, lot 214A. Additional information on this chest is in Winterthur Museum, object file, 1982.276. For the Reade, Lake, Winthrop, and Symonds intermarriages, see David Cressy, *Coming Over: Migration and Communication Between England and New England in the Seventeenth Century* (Cambridge, Mass.: Cambridge University Press, 1987), pp. 277–86. Rev. Hugh Peter was stepfather to the Reade sisters, having married their mother Elizabeth after Edmund Reade died. See Roger Thompson, *Mobility and Migration: East Anglican Founders of New England, 1629–1640* (Amherst: University of Massachusetts Press, 1994), pp. 152, 166, 196; and Walter Goodwin Davis, "Ancestry of John Lake, Husband of Margaret (Reade) Lake," *The New England Historical and Genealogical Register* 84, no. 335 (July 1930): 304–17.

9. The Harris and Staniford families lived near Thomas Dennis and witnessed several legal documents for him. These connections may explain why Thomas and Margaret Staniford commissioned Dennis to make them an expensive joined and carved chest the year of their marriage. Irving P. Lyon, "The Oak Furniture of Ipswich, Massachusetts," in Trent, ed., *Pilgrim Century Furniture,* p. 69. For the London and Boston chests, see Benno M. Forman, "The Chest of Drawers in America, 1635–1670: The Origins of the Joined Chest of Drawers," *Winterthur Portfolio* 20, no. 1 (spring 1985): 1–30; and Robert F. Trent, "The Chest of Drawers in America: A Postscript," *Winterthur Portfolio* 20, no. 1 (spring 1985): 31–48.

10. Benno M. Forman, "New Findings on the Vocabulary Chest," *Winterthur Newsletter* 25, no. 5 (September 1979): n.p.

11. No seventeenth-century scratch-stock is known. Joseph Moxon does not mention scratch-stocks specifically; however, his description of molding planes notes that: "if it be very hard Wood you are to Plane upon . . . [the angle of the blade to the sole of the plane] is set to 80 Degrees, and sometimes quite upright: So that these hard Woods, are, indeed, more properly said to be Scraped, than Planed" (Joseph Moxon, *Mechanick Exercises; or the Doctrine of Handy-works Applied to the Arts of Smithing, Joinery, Carpentry, Turning, Bricklaying* [3d ed., 1703; reprint, Mendham, N.J.: Astragal Press, 1994], pp. 73–74). Roubo illustrates examples constructed like a marking or cutting gauge, with an adjustable fence tightened by a wooden wedge (J. A. Roubo, *L'Art du Mensuisier,* 3 vols. [1769; reprint , Paris: Leonce Laget, 1977], 1: pl. 21, figs. 13–14). The Roubo version of the scratch-stock is discussed in Josef M. Greber, *The History of the Woodworking Plane,* translated by Seth W. Burchard (Delmar, N. Y.: Early American Industries Association, 1991), pp. 139–40. The authors thank Jay Gaynor for this reference and his insights on scratch-stocks. The 1675 inventory of Lynn, Massachusetts, joiner George Coall (Cole) listed two joynters, a fore plane, three smoothing planes, "2 Plans and revolving plains," four round planes, three rabbet planes, three hollow planes, and "9 Cresing plains" (W. L. Goodman, "Tools and Techniques of the Early Settlers in the New World," *Chronicle of the Early American Industries Association* 29, no. 3 [September 1976]: 40–51). Goodman notes that the creasing planes were most likely "side beads and reeds, and possibly . . . one or two ogees or ovolo[s]." It is possible that Coall's "cresing plains" may have been scratch-stocks and that seventeenth-century parlance did not distinguish scratch-stocks from molding planes with conforming soles. Modern scratch-stocks are shop-made, often from small scraps of wood and metal. Some seventeenth-century appraisers may have neglected to list scratch-stocks, whereas others may have referred to them generically (i.e. as "small tools" or "a lot of planes").

12. Sebastiano Serlio, *The Five Books of Architecture* (English edition, 1611; reprint, New York: Dover, 1982), bk. 1, ch. 1, fol. 9.

13. Edith Mannon, *Mobilier Regional* (Paris: Charles Massin, 1998), pp. 21–32; Jacqueline Boccador, *Le Mobilier Francais du Moyen Age a la Renaissance* (Paris: Monelle Hayot, 1988), passim; Jacques Thirion, *Le Mobilier du Moyen Age et de la Renaissance en France* (Pairs: Editions Faton, 1998), pp. 90–197.

14. Many New England joiners made drawers with grooved fronts to accept the beveled edges of bottom boards. Because Benno M. Forman and Richard Candee demonstrated thirty years ago that the New England sawmilling industry was up and running by the 1630s, one need not rely on technological determinism to explain the presence in these objects of water-sawn oak, sycamore, and pine. After all, the widespread use of riven oak and water-sawn pine in New England furniture was strictly tied to utility. The rarity of water-sawn hardwoods in early New England furniture, to say nothing of pit-sawn timbers of any species, does not make the Essex County shop tradition idiosyncratic. By the 1670s, supplies of oak timber were dwindling in coastal towns that were founded in the 1630s. The proximity of Ipswich and Newbury to sawmills on the Merrimac and Piscataqua Rivers may have influenced the use of water-sawn oak boards for the tops of cases, although the use of water-sawn sycamore is more difficult to explain.

15. The Sudbury communion table in the collection of the Wadsworth Atheneum is an exception. It was made from mill-sawn oak joists. For more on this table, see Robert F. Trent, "Joiners and Joinery of Middlesex County, Massachusetts, 1630–1730," in *Arts of the Anglo-American Community in the Seventeenth Century,* edited by Ian M. G. Quimby (Charlottesville: University Press of Virginia, 1975), p. 140. A Braintree, Massachusetts, chest in the collection of the Smithsonian Institution and a New Haven chest of drawers with doors in the collection of the Museum of Fine Arts, Boston, also have mill-sawn oak boards. These chests are illustrated and discussed in Peter Follansbee and John Alexander, "Seventeenth-Century Joinery from Braintree, Massachusetts: The Savell Shop Tradition" in *American Furniture,* edited by Luke Beckerdite (Hanover, N. H.: University Press of New England for the Chipstone Foundation, 1996), pp. 81–104, fig. 9; and Fairbanks and Trent, eds., *New England Begins,* 3: 524–25. For more on seventeenth-century mill sawing, see Benno M. Forman, "Mill Sawing in Seventeenth-Century Massachusetts," *Old Time New England* 60, no. 220 (April–June 1970): 110–30, and Richard M. Candee, "Merchant and Millwright—The Water Powered Sawmills of the Piscataqua," *Old Time New England* 60, no. 220 (April–June, 1970): 131–49. For wood processing, see Forman, "The Seventeenth-Century Case Furniture of Essex County," pp. 1–13. Robert F. Trent, "What Can a Chair and a Box Do for You?" *Maine Antique Digest* 15, no. 4 (April 1987); 10C–13C. The methods for converting trees into usable

timber differed between England and her colonies. By 1500, shortages of oak in metropolitan areas of England led to the importation of oak from Scandinavia and north Germany. This had political and military ramifications because the Royal Navy appropriated much of the wood, tar, and pitch that arrived in the "wainscot" and "mast" fleets. Wood purchased by the London building and furniture trades was reduced to panels, joists, and other units by pit sawing or frame sawing. Evidence suggests that oak or "wainscot" was imported in the form of great baulks, partly for ease of transport and partly to keep the wood slightly more moist than the ambient atmosphere (Trent, "The Chest of Drawers in America, 1635–1730: A Postscript," pp. 31–32, nt. 2). This moisture would have made the baulks easier to break up into manageable panels and scantling and possibly minimized warpage during the voyage. The downside of this practice was that moist wood was far heavier than drier stock. Timber obtained from the imported baulks was sawn from many different orientations in the tree, both radial (quarter-sawn) and tangential (plain-sawn). Often saw kerfs are visible on internal surfaces of English furniture. Conversely, almost no English furniture contains wood sawn in wind- or water-powered sawmills such as those frequently built by the Dutch. Apparently, English sawyers actively militated against such mills, and the savings in labor costs versus the expense of maintaining such elaborate machinery probably was not cost-effective in an English context. For more examples of this practice, see Rev. William Harrison, *A Description of England* (1577, 1587) as quoted in Victor Chinnery, *Oak Furniture: The British Tradition* (Suffolk, Eng.: Antique Collectors Club, 1979), p. 544: "Of all oke growing in England, the parke oke is the softest, and far more spalt and brittle than the hedge oke. And of all in Essex, that growing in Bardfield parke is the finest for joiner's craft: for oftentimes have I seene of their workes made of that oke so fine and faire, as most of the wainescot that is brought thither out of Danske, for our wainescot is not made in England."

16. For two examples of other New England shops that use alignment marks on their joinery, see Robert Blair St. George, "Style and Structure in the Joinery of Dedham and Medfield, Massachusetts, 1635–1685," in *American Furniture and Its Makers,* edited by Ian M. G. Quimby (Chicago: University of Chicago Press for the Winterthur Museum, 1979), pp. 1–46; and Follansbee and Alexander, "Seventeenth-Century Joinery from Braintree," p. 92.

17. Irving Whitall Lyon, *Colonial Furniture of New England,* fig. 16. When Lyon photographed the cupboard in 1886, he recorded but did not publish its family history. This history and the identification of Peter Woodbury as the probable original owner is included in Irving P. Lyon, "The Oak Furniture of Ipswich, Massachusetts" in Trent, ed. *Pilgrim Century Furniture,* pp. 72, 75.

18. Moxon, *Mechanick Exercises,* pp. 217–19, contains a lengthy description of a sweep:

I Had, soon after the Fire of London, occasion to lay Moldings upon the Verges of several round and weighty pieces of Brass: and being [without] . . . a Lathe of my own, I intended to put them out to be Turned: But then Turners were all full of Employment, which made them so unreasonable in their Prizes, that I was forc'd to contrive this following way to lay Moldings on their Verges. I provided a strong Iron Bar for the Beam of a Sweep. . . . To this Tool is filed a Tooth of Steel with such [moldings] . . . in the bottom of it, as I have intended to have . . . upon my work. . . . Then I placed the Center-point of the sweep in a Center-hole made in a square Stud of Mettal, and fixed in the Center of the Plain of the Work, and removed the Socket that rides on the Beam of the Sweep, till the tooth stood just upon its intended place on the Verge of the Work, and there screw'd the Socket fast to the Beam. To work it out, I employ'd a Labourer, directing him in his Left Hand to hold the Head of the Center-pin, and with his Right Hand to draw about the Beam and Tooth, which (according to the strength) he us'd, cut and tore away great Flakes of the Metall, till it receiv'd the whole and perfect Form the Tooth would make; which was as compleat a Molding as any Skillfull Turner could have laid upon it. Having such good Success upon Brass, I improv'd the invention so, as to make it serve for Wood also. And make a Plain-Stock with my intended Molding on the Sole of it, and fitted an Iron to that Stock with the same Molding the Sole had. Through the sides of this Stock I fitted an Iron Beam, to do the Office of the Beam I used for the Sweep, viz to keep the Plain always at what position I lifted from the Center (for thus the Iron in the Plain wrought about the Center, even as the Tooth in the Sweep (before rehearsed) and to that purpose I made a round Hole of about half an Inch Diameter near the end of the Iron: then in the Center of the Work I fixed a round Iron Pin, exactly to fit the said round Hole, putting the round Hole over the pin, and fitting the Iron onto this Stock commodious to work with. I used this Plain with both hands, even as Joyners do other Plains.

The cutter that Moxon added to the sweep to adapt a metal-scraping tool to wood was clearly a scratch-stock. If he had used a molding plane with a conforming sole curved to match the arc of the intended molding, the tool would not have been adjustable and would have produced only one fixed arc. The sweep blades used by the joiners in the Essex County shop and by many of their contemporaries cut clockwise and counterclockwise. This allowed them to avoid working against the grain in a 180-degree arc. It is possible that the "revolving planes" listed in George Coall's inventory (see nt. 11) were sweeps. Moxon's claim that he invented this tool is incorrect.

19. Susan Geib, "Hammersmith: The Saugus Ironworks as an Example of Early Industrialism," in Fairbanks and Trent, eds., *New England Begins,* 3: 352–60. The five iron firebacks are illustrated in entry no. 381, written jointly by Geib and Robert F. Trent.

20. For the Boston chest of drawers with doors, see Gerald W. R. Ward, *American Case Furniture in the Mabel Brady Garvan and Other Collections at Yale University* (New Haven, Conn.: Yale University Art Gallery, 1988), pp. 125–28. For more examples of composite appliqué arches and arcades on seventeenth-century New England furniture, see Patricia E. Kane, *Furniture of the New Haven Colony The Seventeenth-Century Style* (New Haven, Conn.: New Haven Colony Historical Society, 1973), nos. 8–11; Robert Blair St. George, *The Wrought Covenant: Source Material for the Study of Craftsmen and Community in Southeastern New England, 1620–1700* (Brockton, Mass.: Fuller Art Museum, 1979), nos. 17, 18, 54; Robert F. Trent, "New Insights on Early Rhode Island Furniture," in *American Furniture,* edited by Luke Beckerdite (Hanover, N. H.: University Press of New England for the Chipstone Foundation, 1999), fig. 7, p. 213; Robert F. Trent, "New England Joinery and Turning before 1700," in Fairbanks and Trent, eds., *New England Begins,* 3, no. 473; and Trent, "Joiners and Joinery of Middlesex County, Massachusetts, 1630–1730," figs. 2, 3, 5.

21. For an illustration of a 1666 English cupboard with rectangular rear stiles and toe-nailed side rails, see Margaret Jourdain, *English Decoration and Furniture of the Early Renaissance, 1500–1650* (New York: Scribners Sons, 1924), fig. 301. For the history of the Lawton cupboard, see Robert F. Trent, "The Lawton Cupboard: A Unique Masterpiece of Early Boston Joinery and Turning," *Maine Antique Digest* 16, no. 3 (March 1988): 1C–4C.

22. Luke Vincent Lockwood, *Colonial Furniture in America,* 3d. edition (New York: Charles Scribner's Sons, 1926), fig. 44. The chest of drawers belonged to Boston collector Dwight M. Prouty when Lockwood published it.

23. The side and rear façades of this chest are similar to those of the Staniford chest (fig. 1) in having two superimposed panels in each end and four in the rear. The Weare cupboard (fig. 75) has one drawer front made of sawn oak.

24. For Waters' alterations, see Nutting, *Furniture Treasury,* fig, 458; and Lyon, "The Oak Furniture of Ipswich, Massachusetts," in Trent, ed., *Pilgrim Century Furniture,* p. 73. For more on Waters, see Richard H. Saunders, "Collecting American Decorative Arts in New England–Part I: 1793–1876" in Trent, ed., *Pilgrim Century Furniture,* pp. 14–21; Elizabeth Stillinger, *The Antiquers* (New York: Alfred A. Knopf, 1980), pp. 72–73; and Trent and Follansbee, "Repairs versus Deception," pp. 13–28.

25. Trent, "The Joinery of Middlesex County," fig. 4. The Cambridge joiners made arch appliqués that differ from those on the Essex County cupboards. The arches on the Cambridge cupboards have rectangular imposts that are architecturally correct rather than tapered ones. Because the Cambridge arcades lack jamb and haunch moldings, they do not have the visual impact of their Essex County equivalents. Trent has suggested that the Cambridge shop may have purchased Boston turned ornament (Catalogue entry for the Cambridge cupboard in David Wood, ed., *The Concord Museum: Decorative Arts from a New England Collection* [Concord, Mass.: Concord Museum, 1996], pp. 1–2).

26. The authors thank furniture historian Victor Chinnery for pointing out the British cupboard base.

27. Sumner, "The Eliot Bureau," pp. 329–33; and Lyon, "A Pedigreed Cupboard," pp. 118–22. John Appleton and Elizabeth Rogers were married in Ipswich on November 23, 1681. See Clarence A. Torrey, *New England Marriages Prior to 1700* (Baltimore, Md.: Genealogical Publishing Co., 1977), p. 20. John Appleton's sister Priscilla married Rev. Joseph Capen of Topsfield, and they owned the chest of drawers illustrated in fig. 53. Lyon's article describes the most likely connection between the last known owner, Judge Daniel Gookin of North Hampton, New Hampshire, and John and Elizabeth Appleton. For more on the Appletons of Ipswich, see T. Frank Waters, *The Old Bay Road from Saltonstall's Brook and Samuel Appleton's Farm and A Genealogy of the Ipswich Descendants of Samuel Appleton* (Salem, Mass.: Salem Press Co., 1907), pp. 30–31.

28. In "The Eliot Bureau," pp. 329–30, Sumner reported:

> [The base] was in a dilapidated state. The top was split and broken, and the outside had been painted with red paint, over which there had been a coat of whitewash. At that time I had an ingenious carpenter, Mr. John Wilson, at work on my mansion house . . . and after his scraping off the paint and whitewash from the Cabinet, we saw that I had a rich and highly ornamented piece of furniture . . . with the initials I E A 1681 cut into the wood upon the centre of the door in front. Under my direction, Mr. Wilson attempted to restore it according to the original design, and make it a useful article. Such of the ornaments as remained, were taken off; the broken ones pieced out; and those, which were wanting, were turned and resupplied in the fashion of the old ones. The door was entire, and swung on a round stick or post, about one inch in diameter. This I divided in the centre and hung it on two pair of brass hinges, so that it opens in the middle, instead of on one side of it. The drawer over the door is about four inches in depth, and is almost the only part which remains entire in its original state. There were two shelves inside, which were split and so much defaced, that I removed them, in order to give room for ten shallow pine drawers, which I put in, for papers. I put a thick oak plank under the bottom, and supported it by two oak blocks, for the whole to rest upon. I had a handsome oak board, polished and placed on it, for a top, instead of the old one, which was split and broken. The projecting ornaments in front, on the drawer and door, were very much broken, but not so much so, that the fashion of them could not be discovered. I put locks upon it, and varnished the whole over, so that, like a restored painting, it resembles the original, the initials and date never having been touched.

For the Boston and New Haven chests of drawers with doors, see Fairbanks and Trent, eds., *New England Begins,* 3: 522–25. The Boston example is described and illustrated in detail in Ward, *American Case Furniture,* pp. 125–28. English examples illustrated and discussed in Chinnery, *Oak Furniture,* pp. 370–71, are similar in form and execution to the Boston example. Chinnery calls these "enclosed chest[s] of drawers."

29. Lyon, "A Pedigreed Cupboard," p. 121. In an undated letter to a Mr. Robinson of Harvard University, Lyon wrote: "Now a word of advice. The piece was outrageously reconstructed by . . . Sumner. It should be now restored to its original state under competent advice. Your own Philip L. Spaulding is eminently qualified to supervise this restoration and would do it with tender regard to proprieties." Spaulding owned the cupboard illustrated in fig. 27. The authors thank Sandra Grindlay, curator of Harvard University Art Museums, for making Lyon's letter available.

30. Nutting, *Furniture Treasury,* fig. 1011. Lyon recorded that the table was found in the Furness home in Manchester, New Hampshire, in 1921. See Lyon, "Oak Furniture of Ipswich Massachusetts," in Trent, ed., *Pilgrim Century Furniture,* p. 75. Little is known about the table before the late nineteenth century. The Appleton provenance associated with the piece is not entirely clear. In the 1920s, the table was purchased from a Mrs. Lily May (Appleton) Furness of Manchester. She was born in Hamilton, Massachusetts, in 1858, the daughter of George Appleton, Jr., and Esther Knowlton Annable of Ipswich. Tracing the table back in the direct patrilineal line of the Appleton family does not lead back to the original owners of the Appleton cupboard, but to a cousin. The 1920 Federal Census for Manchester lists James C. Furness and Lillie M. Furness. Her place of birth is listed as Massachusetts. Her death record identifies her as Lilly May Appleton who was born in Hamilton, Massachusetts, on January 17, 1858, the daughter of George Appleton, Jr. and Esther Knowlton Annable. Index to Massachusetts Birth Records, 1856–1860, vol. 114, p. 205.

31. The cupboard belonged to collector Philip L. Spaulding. The caption in Wallace Nutting's *Furniture Treasury* (1928) states that the cupboard is dated 1689 when it is actually dated 1683. An ash splint loop is attached to the backboard of the upper storage compartment with wrought nails. The date and purpose of this feature is unclear.

32. See caption for fig. 27: Ian C. Bristow, *Interior House-Painting Colors and Technology, 1615–1840* (New Haven, Conn.: Yale University Press, 1996), pp. 170–71.

33. The base appears in an 1896 photo of Little's house. See fig. 7 in Saunders, "Collecting American Decorative Arts in New England–Part I: 1793–1876," in Trent, ed., *Pilgrim Century Furniture,* p. 21. See Cook, *The House Beautiful,* pp. 226–27, fig. 72. The rear boards, which are most likely replacements, fit in a groove in the top rail, and are toe-nailed to the rear stiles. There is no groove in the inner edge of these stiles. The rear framing of the Perkins cupboard lacks these grooves as well.

34. Two related chests with one drawer have comparable red and black striped paint schemes. See Benes, ed., *Old Town and the Waterside,* p. 36; and Chinnery, *Oak Furniture,* p. 225, pl. 9.

35. Irving P. Lyon, "The Oak Furniture of Ipswich, Massachusetts," in Trent, ed., *Pilgrim Century Furniture*, pp. 67, 70. Francis Shaw (1855–1935) of Wayland, Massachusetts, owned the cupboard by the 1890s, and it eventually belonged to Mrs. B. A. Behrend, who corresponded with Lyon regarding the piece's history and restoration. When it was sold in 1999, it appeared in the same condition as shown in the photographs from Lyon's articles in the 1930s. It has since been restored, in an attempt to correct some of the earlier restoration work. For a discussion of the Perkins cupboard, see Sotheby's *Fine Americana and Silver,* New York, June 17, 1999, lot 187.

36. The authors thank Philip Ruhl for his experimentation with and insights on this half-column turning technique.

37. Lyon, "The Cupboard of Ephraim and Hannah Foster," pp. 123–25. According to Lyon's research, Hannah was born in 1661 and would have been sixteen when she married Ephriam. James Savage, *A Genealogical Dictionary of the First Settlers of New England,* 4 vols. (1860–1862; reprint, Baltimore, Md.: Genealogical Publishing Company, 1965), 2: 90, 187, also gives 1661 as her birth date.

38. Richard H. Randall, Jr., *American Furniture in the Museum of Fine Arts, Boston* (Boston: Museum of Fine Arts, Boston, 1965), fig. 22.

39. Charles Hummel, *With Hammer in Hand* (Charlottesville: University Press of Virginia for the Winterthur Museum, 1968), fig. 11 illustrates rotary button bits.

40. Descendants of the Bradstreet, Wildes, and Waite or Waitt families of Topsfield, Massachusetts, donated the chest to the Brick Store Museum in Kennebunk, Maine, in 1999. The chest probably passed from Joseph and Priscilla to their daughter Elizabeth Bradstreet (1691–1781); to her daughter Mary Wildes (1731–1810); to her son Sylvanus Wildes (1754–1829); to his daughter Elizabeth (1787–1853), who married William Waitt (1785–1817). The donors' grandmother stated that the previous owner of the chest was "Mrs Elizabeth Waite." This genealogy was compiled from *Vital Records of Topsfield, Massachusetts, to the End of the Year 1849,* 2 vols. (Topsfield, Mass: Topsfield Historical Society, 1903), 2: 208, 245; Douglas Wright Cruger, *A Wildes Genealogy: the Family of John Wild of Topsfield Massachusetts and His Descendants in Old Arundel, Maine* (Portland, Me.: privately printed, 1990), p. 7; Walter Goodwin Davis, *The Ancestry of Dudley Wildes 1759–1820 of Topsfield Massachusetts* (Portland, Me.: Anthoensen Press, 1959), pp. 1–36; and *The Capen Family: Descendants of Bernard Capen of Dorchester, Massachusetts,* compiled by Rev. Charles Albert Hayden (Minneapolis, Minn.: privately printed, 1929), pp. 20, 21, 36. For more on the Capens and their house, see Samuel Chamberlain and Narcissa G. Chamberlain, *The Chamberlain Selection of New England Rooms 1639–1863* (New York: Hastings House, 1972), pp. 46–47; Abbott Lowell Cummings, "Massachusetts and Its First Period Houses: A Statistical Survey" in *Architecture in Colonial Massachusetts,* edited by Abbott Lowell Cummings (Boston: Colonial Society of Massachusetts, 1979), p. 187.

41. The tip of a turned pendant two inches long (like that of the leaf table shown in fig. 22) would be exactly level with the bellies of the side brackets.

42. A chest marked "HT 1685" is contemporary with the Capen chest of drawers. The former, known as the "Brown" chest, has a history in the Chebacco section of Ipswich (now Essex). Its turned ornament suggests that the shop may have begun using medium-height large half-columns for chests with one drawer. Lyon, "The Oak Furniture of Ipswich, Massachusetts," in Trent, ed., *Pilgrim Century Furniture,* pp. 69, 71; and Helen Park, "The Seventeenth-Century Furniture of Essex County and Its Makers" also in Trent, ed., *Pilgrim Century Furniture,* pp. 91, 352, fig. 5.

43. Torrey, *New England Marriages Prior to 1700,* p. 572. These connections suggest that Timothy Perkins and Joseph Capen's father-in-law commissioned their chests from the same shop. Given the strong local tradition that the latter's daughter Priscilla abhorred the domestic arrangements provided by the church, it is possible that Timothy Perkins felt compelled to purchase a chest of drawers by the same maker as an oblique comment on the new minister's wife. Samuel Symonds' father John was the most important joiner in Salem. In 1682, Samuel made a ten-foot-long joined oak pulpit for the Topsfield meeting house, where he was a member of the congregation. For more on the Symonds family, see Forman, "The Seventeenth-Century Case Furniture of Essex County," pp. 44–46.

44. Roland B. Hammond, *The Collection of Samuel Dale Stevens (1859–1922)* (North Andover, Mass.: North Andover Historical Society, 1971), p. 1.

45. In a slight variation on the Capen model, the maker or makers framed the rear of the "TEP" chest with two horizontal panels over four vertical ones, and the example illustrated in fig. 62 with two horizontal panels over three vertical ones.

46. Dr. Micajah Sawyer and Sibyll Farnham were married in Newburyport on November 27, 1766. Hannah Sawyer was the second wife of Lt. George Lee, who was possibly born in Salem. See Nutting, *Furniture Treasury,* fig. 444. John B. Paine to Irving P. Lyon, November 24, 1936, Irving P. Lyon Papers, Collection 62, Joseph Downs Collection of Manuscripts and Printed Ephemera, Winterthur Museum. Thomas Amory Lee, "Old Boston Families No. 6, The Lee Family," *The New England Historic Genealogical Register* 76, no. 301 (July 1922): 197–223. Massachusetts Death Records 1861–1865, (microfilm) vol. 185, p. 164. *Vital Records of Newburyport, Massachusetts,* 2 vols. (Salem, Mass.: Essex Institute, 1911), 1: 344, 2: 424.

47. Boston or London case pieces with dovetailed drawers may have been a source for some of the drawer construction techniques used by the Essex County joiners during the 1680s and 1690s. All of the drawers except the third from the top have nails and one dovetail securing the sides to the front. The second and fourth drawers have rabbeted backs that are nailed to the sides. The back of the top drawer has one rabbeted and nailed rear corner and the other joined with a single dovetail. The third drawer, which is the deepest, has two dovetails and nails securing each corner. For information about London-trained joiners in seventeenth-century Boston and the arrival of Brocas, see Forman, "The Chest of Drawers in America," p. 21.

48. The top board of the base section is water-sawn oak. The 1661 inventory of Thomas Sallows of Salem lists "1 Court Cubbard 12s" and "1 Cushion for a Cubbard's head 1s" (*Probate Records of Essex County, Massachusetts, 1635–1681,* edited by George Francis Dow, 3 vols. [Salem, Mass.: Essex Institute, 1916–1920], 1: 418–19).

49. On the upper section, the joiner used three mitered inserts with bosses to divide the channel molding of the frieze. This design complements the vertical orientation of the stiles and half-columns of the storage compartment and resonates with the three bisected drawers of the lower case.

50. The maker of the Sawyer cupboard cut the channel moldings and edges of the arches and jambs with the same scratch-stock irons used on other examples in the group. The large astragal moldings, which appear to have been cut with a hollow plane and a fenced rabbet plane, are identical to those on the other cupboards that follow. On the first and third drawers of the Sawyer cupboard, the joiner made the inner edges of the chamfered moldings and plaques the same thickness. This enabled him to use the same scratch-stock moldings adjacent to either component. The joiner attached the backplates with brass upholstery nails. The pierced brass keyhole escutcheon on the door appears to be original, but the lock is replaced.

51. The back of the upper case is constructed like that of the Foster cupboard (fig. 40), but has a single water-sawn white pine board installed horizontally in the top of the frame. The joiner beveled the top edge and ends to fit into grooves in the rear stiles and upper rear rail, slid the panel in from below, and nailed it to the rear face of the lower rear rail. This rail, which supports the floorboards of the storage compartment, is positioned forward of the grooves for the back panel. The frame of the lower case has two white pine panels divided by a central muntin with edge moldings. The stiles and rails of the frame are chamfered. Although this is atypical of this shop, similar chamfering occurs on joined furniture from Plymouth Colony. See St. George, *Wrought Covenant,* p. 26, fig. 20A; and Peter Follansbee, "Unpacking the Little Chest," *Old Time New England* 78, no. 268 (Spring/Summer 2000): 5–23. The sides of the Sawyer cupboard's base have applied moldings around the panels, rather than scratch-stock edge moldings and chamfers on the frame like many other pieces in the group. Unlike all the other cupboards from this shop, the side panels of the upper case are horizontal. The drawer bottoms and floorboards of the storage compartment are riven oak and have V-joints. All of the other examples have either butt joints or tongue-and-groove joints. The Perkins cupboard is built as one case; however, it was completely disassembled, so its pillar orientation is not conclusive.

52. The Sawyer cupboard also has a variety of bosses. Large, turned oval bosses are on the stiles of the frieze and lower side panels of the base, and smaller turned ones are on the arcade panels and beneath the knobs of the carved drawer. Small round bosses made with a rotary cutter are on the upper stiles, arcade panels, and drawer plaques. All of the latter bosses are similar in diameter and cross-section except the ones on the top drawer, which have small central protrusions. The small half-columns on the upper rear stiles of the Sawyer cupboard are similar to the large half-columns on the Perkins cupboard, but the former have more collars.

53. Sybil Noyes, Charles Thornton Libby, and Walter Goodwin Davis, *Genealogical Dictionary of Maine and New Hampshire* (1928–1939; reprint, Baltimore, Md.: Genealogical Publishing Co., 1972), p. 364.

54. Small oval bosses are on the mitered inserts of the frieze rail, and larger ones are on the side corners of the upper stiles, side rails of the top drawer, and side panels of the lower case.

Irregularities in the ornament on the sides of the front stiles likely stem from the restoration.

55. The interior struts are joined to the front and rear rails of the base. Three oak boards form a shelf at the front and sides of the recessed compartment. The soffit boards on the unit above the compartment have beveled edges that fit into grooves in the front and side rails. This feature occurs on all of the Essex County cupboards with jetties.

56. For a description of dragon beams, see Abbott Lowell Cummings, *The Framed Houses of Massachusetts Bay, 1625–1725* (Cambridge, Mass.: Harvard University Press, 1979), pp. 55, 56. On the Weare cupboard, the soffit boards on the lower section engage the rails overhanging the sides and front. The boards at the sides extend front-to-back and those at the front extend side-to-side. The side boards provide the greatest stability because they fit into grooves in both the side and front rails. Framing members and pillars support some jetties (i. e., the jetty on the lower section of the cupboard illustrated in fig. 34) on furniture in the Essex County group. In fact, the cupboard shown in figure 34 never had a soffit in its framed overhang at the front.

57. Cummings, *Framed Houses of Massachusetts Bay*, pp. 13–15, 112, 113, 207. Cummings illustrates two pendants from house frames in Newbury (figs. 188, 189) and others from Topsfield and Hamilton (figs. 165 and 166.) The discussion and sketch of the Ross Tavern framing is on pp. 74–77. Evidence suggests that jettied house frames were not common in New England before 1650. For a 1657 building contract that includes a jettied second story, see Abbott Lowell Cummings, "Massachusetts Bay Building Documents, 1638–1726" in Cummings, ed., *Architecture in Colonial Massachusetts,* p. 193.

58. Nutting, *Furniture Treasury,* figs. 444–47.

59. The cupboard descended in the family of Mrs. Charles Sprague Sargent, whose husband founded the Arnold Arboretum.

60. Randle Holme, *Academie or Store house of Armory & Blazon* (1688; reprint, Menston, Eng.: Scholar Press, 1972), bk. 3, ch. 3, p. 100 refers to diamond-shaped decoration: "Arris Ways, is anything set or hung Diamond wise, having one corner of the square set upwards, the other downwards."

61. See caption for fig. 91: Only eight or nine New England square tables from the seventeenth century are known. Associated with either dining or reading and writing, they usually have riven oak bases and multi-board, oak tops. Some have maple frames. Despite their name, these tables were generally out of square by two or three inches. This example, however, is an exception. The top is 46" x 45⅜", and the base is 38⅛" x 37⅞". These dimensions are close enough to be regarded as square by New England joinery standards. Lyon Papers, box 7. For the history of the table attributed to Jacques, see Benes, *Old-Town and the Waterside*, p. 72. Higgins' sister married John L. Abbott.

62. Several one-drawer chests and an elaborate dressing box attributed to the Essex County shop have dates ranging from 1693 to 1701.

63. Forman, "The Chest of Drawers in America," pp. 9–15; and Fairbanks and Trent, eds., *New England Begins,* 3: 501, 522–24, 539–40. Although furniture historian Benno M. Forman believed that the shift from the carved phase of mannerism to the applied ornamental style began to during the 1660s in New England, recent research by Robert Trent suggests that it occurred much earlier. For Plymouth joinery, see St. George, *Wrought Covenant,* and Follansbee, "Unpacking the Little Chest." For Cambridge joinery, see Trent, "Joiners and Joinery of Middlesex County, Massachusetts, 1630–1730," pp. 123–148, and David Wood, ed., *Concord Museum,* pp. 1–2. For Woburn joinery, see David Wood, ed., *Concord Museum,* pp. 3–5. For Salem joinery, see Forman, "Seventeenth-Century Case Furniture of Essex County," pp. 41–55.

64. Parisian styles reached England through trade with the continent and the immigration of French Protestant artisans. The Huguenot diaspora began during the sixteenth century and increased after Louis XIV revoked the Edict of Nantes in 1685.

65. For West Country and North Country cupboards with cantilevered rails in the upper case, see Chinnery, *Oak Furniture,* pp. 486, 491–94.

66. In addition to houses and public buildings, furniture joiners occasionally worked on gristmills, fulling mills, sawmills, warehouses, wharves, and bridges. This was especially true of tradesmen residing near rivers or in the coastal regions of New England. Some furniture joiners also ventured into shipbuilding, block making, bridge building, coopering, pump making, dish turning, wagon making, and the production of ox yokes, whereas others did less specialized work such as fencing and making pipestave blanks for export to the West Indies and the wine islands.

67. For lists and genealogies of Ipswich woodworkers, see Forman, "Seventeenth-Century Case Furniture of Essex County"; Robert E. P. Hendrick, "John Gaines II and Thomas Gaines

I, Turners of Ipswich, Massachusetts" (master's thesis, University of Delaware, 1964); Susan Mackiewicz, "Woodworking Traditions in Newbury, Massachusetts, 1635–1745" (master's thesis, University of Delaware, 1981); Robert Tarule, "The Joined Furniture of William Searle and Thomas Dennis: A Shop Based Inquiry into the Woodworking Technology of the Seventeenth-Century Joiner" (Ph. D. diss., Graduate School of the Union Institute, 1992); and Susan Spindler Nelson, "The Life and Times of Capt. Abraham Knowlton, Joiner of Ipswich, Massachusetts, 1699–1751" (master's thesis, Boston University, 1998). Three tables, two joined cradles, and a joint stool, some of which have strong histories of ownership in Newbury, are attributed to the Jaques shop tradition. Mackiewicz, "Woodworking Traditions in Newbury, Massachusetts," pp. 1–39. The quote pertaining to the meeting house is on p. 30. *The First Parish, Newbury, Massachusetts 1635–1935,* edited by Eliza Adams Little and Lucretia Little Isley (Newburyport, Mass.: privately printed, 1935), p. 31. *Jaques Family Genealogy,* edited by Roger Jaques and Patricia Jaques (Decorah, Iowa: Anundsen Publishing Co., 1995), pp. 26, 33, 67.

68. Abraham Hammett, *The Hammett Papers: Early Inhabitants of Ipswich, Massachusetts 1633–1700* (Ipswich, Mass.: privately printed, 1880–1899), p. 246. George A. Perkins, *The Family of John Perkins of Ipswich* (Salem, Mass.: privately printed, 1889), p. 23.

Eleanore P. Gadsden

When Good Cabinetmakers Made Bad Furniture: The Career and Work of David Evans

▼ IN 1786 PHILADELPHIA cabinetmaker David Evans (1748–1819) faced the wrath of merchant Tench Coxe (1755–1824), an irate customer who wrote:

> My opinion of the furniture is that it has a great deal of sappy stuff in it, that it is very slight and thin, that the upholsterers work is bad, that it is patched in places much exposed to View, that it was made of unseasoned wood and badly put together. Under these circumstances I think Mr. Evans by no means entitled to the price of *well-made* furniture.

Coxe made these scathing remarks in a letter to a committee of arbitrators who had been assembled to resolve his four-and-a-half year dispute with Evans. The merchant's comments about the cabinetmaker's craftsmanship attacked the quality of his furniture and jeopardized his reputation and career in the process. What caused this private disagreement to escalate into an embarrassing public spat? How had a furniture transaction gotten so out of hand? And, how did the dispute affect the lives of the two men involved? The story behind this furniture is about more than a cabinetmaker's skills on trial. It is a tale of craftsmanship and ambition colliding with politics and economics in colonial Philadelphia.[1]

The details of Evans' career, and particularly his business transactions with Coxe, debunk time-honored myths of traditional craftsmanship in eighteenth-century America. Evans was first and foremost a businessman. His success depended on his craft skills and training as well as his commercial savvy and flexibility. During his career, Evans faced not only a typically fickle market, but also political revolution and all of its consequences. As a result, the social, political, and, most importantly, economic context in which he made furniture affected the furniture itself. Physical evidence from surviving pieces attributed to Evans and documentary evidence from his dispute with Coxe prove that even good cabinetmakers made bad furniture.

The Protagonists

David Evans was raised in a successful artisan family as a member of the Society of Friends, or Quakers. While previous scholars postulated that he was born in Gwynedd Township, Pennsylvania, the son of ship joiner and furniture maker Edward Evans, new evidence indicates otherwise. Born in 1748, Evans was the eldest child of Evan and Elizabeth Evans of Philadelphia. His grandfather and namesake, David Evans, owned a shop and tavern on Market Street at the "Sign of the Crown" where he lived with his wife, Elizabeth. The tavern keeper's will and probate inventory value his estate at

Figure 1 High chest by Henry Cliffton and Thomas Carteret, Philadelphia, Pennsylvania, 1753. Mahogany with tulip poplar, white cedar, and yellow pine. H. 95½", W. 44¼", D. 22½". (Courtesy, Colonial Williamsburg Foundation.)

£2032.6.42, an impressive amount for a member of the artisan class. The cabinetmaker's father was a successful cutler who also provided a high standard of living for his family. The administration papers for Evan Evans' estate list household goods including "Feather Beds, Tables, Chairs, a good eight Day Clock, a large Looking glass, and sundry other . . . Furniture" as well as "two good Milch Cows, a Chaise horse and Chaise, a considerable Quantity of Dung, Hay and Cord wood, some Rum Hogsheads, and Wine Pipes, with sundry other Things" and three years left on the term of a "likely servant Girl." His shop inventory included "a Waggon, two Carts, six draught Horses and their Geers, a Mare and Colt, a Sleigh, a Quantity of Cord wood, a Smiths Bellows, new Sickles, some Scale Beams, Iron and sundry Smith Tools, a Plough and Harrow, and sundry other Things." Evans' unexpected death in 1758 left Elizabeth with fine household furnishings, a shop full of tools, farm equipment, and livestock, but also an overwhelming amount of debt. She was forced to sell the estate to pay off their debtors, leaving the family without the luxuries to which they had become accustomed. Until that time, her son David had enjoyed a life of relative ease and financial security. The memory of this environment and its loss may have given him the incentive to strive for success and a life more comfortable than that of most artisans.[2]

The Evans family may have received some support from the Society of Friends. Records of the Philadelphia Monthly Meeting indicate that Elizabeth and her children, David, Rebecca, and Sidney, continued to be members after Evan Evans' death. Yet, on March 14, 1761, Elizabeth married Richard Gardiner who was not a Quaker. Shortly thereafter, the Philadelphia Monthly Meeting disowned her for disregarding the "Discipline Establish'd amongst Us, as to be marry'd by a Priest to a Person not in [our] Religious Fellowship." David Evans remained a Quaker, suggesting that he may have been an apprentice living outside Elizabeth's household at the time of her marriage.[3]

At some point during his teenage years, Evans began serving an apprenticeship with two cabinetmakers from his Quaker meeting, Henry Cliffton and James Gillingham. In exchange for Evans' labor and loyalty, Cliffton and Gillingham taught him the "art and mystery" of cabinetmaking, and provided him with room and board, some schooling, spiritual guidance, and, presumably, the skills to run a business.[4]

Cliffton and Gillingham were both accomplished, enterprising cabinetmakers. A cabriole leg high chest inscribed "Henry Cliffton/ Thomas Carteret/ November 15, 1753" is one of the earliest American examples with nascent rococo ornament (fig. 1). It and its matching dressing table have precisely finished primary and secondary surfaces, finely cut dovetails and mortise-and-tenon joints, and dustboards under the bottom drawers (figs. 2, 3). The dustboards in the dressing table and lower case of the high chest are supported by small strips of wood attached to the sides of the case and partitions separating the drawers. These and other construction details link both pieces to a much more elaborate high chest attributed to Cliffton and Carteret's shop (fig. 4). The latter example, which also appears to date from

the early to mid 1750s, has a large tympanum appliqué (fig. 5), bold flame finials, floral rosettes, and a massive central cartouche (fig. 6). More than any other carving on the chest, the exaggerated leaves and cabachon of the cartouche and tattered shell of the appliqué reflect the influence of British rococo style. The shell, in particular, has an amorphous, abstract quality reminiscent of London work from the late 1740s.

Cliffton's subsequent partner James Gillingham also kept abreast of prevailing London fashions. The latter's membership in the Library Company of Philadelphia gave him access to several British design books including Thomas Chippendale's *The Gentleman and Cabinet-Maker's Director* (1754). A Gothic side chair bearing Gillingham's printed label (fig. 7) is based on a design illustrated on plate 10 of the *Director*. As their apprentice, David Evans would have been trained to execute precise cabinetwork in the latest styles.

Figure 4 High chest attributed to Henry Cliffton and Thomas Carteret, Philadelphia, Pennsylvania, 1750–1755. Mahogany with tulip poplar, white cedar, and yellow pine. H. 94½", W. 45", D. 23⅝". (Chipstone Foundation; photo, Gavin Ashworth.)

Figure 5 Detail of the pediment of the high chest illustrated in fig. 4. (Photo, Gavin Ashworth.)

Figure 6 Detail of the center cartouche on the high chest illustrated in fig. 4. (Photo, Gavin Ashworth.)

Cliffton and Gillingham dissolved their partnership in August 1768, one year before Evans completed his apprenticeship. Although Evans undoubtedly learned his trade from both partners, evidence suggests that he remained with Cliffton and that their relationship played an important role in the young cabinetmaker's future career. Cliffton moved his shop to "Arch Street, opposite the gate of [the] Friend's burying ground" in 1770 and died the following year. Evans, who was twenty-three years old at the time, either inherited his master's shop and tools, or continued to operate the business for Cliffton's widow, Rachel. In 1773, Evans rented the land on

which this frame cabinet shop stood from Benjamin Loxley. The cabinet-maker signed a five-year lease for the "Lott of Ground in Arch Street opposite the Quaker Burial Ground gate" for £3.15 per year (fig. 8).[5]

The daily transactions of Evans' shop are recorded in three daybooks, the earliest of which contains furniture entries beginning in 1774. The dressing table illustrated in figure 9 is from his early period. Originally one of a pair, this relatively plain case piece was ordered by merchant Joseph Paschall for his sister Beaulah on July 16, 1774. Evans' daybook shows that he charged Paschall five pounds per table. A second dressing table has been attributed to Evans based on its similarity to the Paschall example (fig. 10). Both objects have the same basic proportions, fluted quarter columns, thumb-nail-molded drawers, side skirts cut from the same template, and similar front skirts. Their claw-and-ball feet are virtually identical, suggesting that the same specialist carved them.

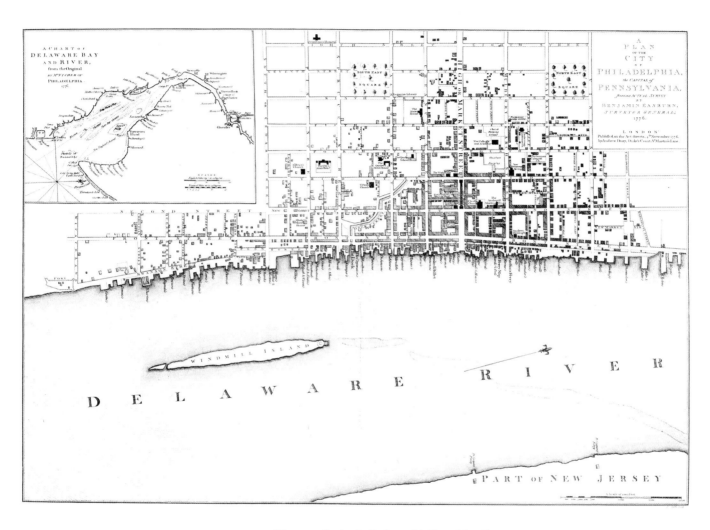

Figure 8   Benjamin Gasburn, "A Plan of the City
of Philadelphia, the Capital of Pennsylvania,"
London, 1776. 18⅞" x 24¾". (Courtesy, Winterthur Museum.)

Figure 9 Dressing table attributed to David Evans, Philadelphia, Pennsylvania, 1774. Mahogany with tulip poplar and white pine. H. 30½", W. 35⅛", D. 20½". (Courtesy, Philadelphia Museum of Art; bequest of Lydia T. Morris.) When she acquired this dressing table in 1774, Beaulah Paschall lived in two homes. The family townhouse, which she probably shared with her brother Joseph, was on Market Street in Philadelphia. Her country house, Cedar Grove, was in Frankford, Pennsylvania. She had inherited it from her mother, Elizabeth Coates Paschall. This dressing table and its mate were intended for one of these homes. The one shown here descended in the Paschall family to Lydia Thompson Morris, who gave it and other ancestral furniture of the Wistar and Morris families to the Philadelphia Museum of Art in 1932.

Figure 10 Dressing table attributed to David Evans, Philadelphia, Pennsylvania, 1773–1810. Walnut with tulip poplar and white pine. H. 31¾", W. 35½", D. 21½". (Courtesy, Philip H. Bradley Company; photo, Gavin Ashworth.)

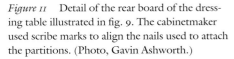

Figure 11   Detail of the rear board of the dressing table illustrated in fig. 9. The cabinetmaker used scribe marks to align the nails used to attach the partitions. (Photo, Gavin Ashworth.)

Figure 12   Detail of the interior construction of the dressing table illustrated in fig. 9. (Photo, Gavin Ashworth.)

Although some construction details on the tables are similar, others vary. Both case pieces have pinned (pegged) mortise-and-tenon joints, moldings attached with wrought finishing nails, and identical drawer construction. The techniques used to attach the drawer partitions, however, are quite different. The partitions of the dressing table illustrated in figure 9 are nailed to the backboard (figs. 11, 12), whereas those on the other example are glued and tenoned to the backboard. The shallow tenons are the full height of the partitions, and the joints are reinforced with wedges glued into the bottom of each mortise.

Despite these differences, both tables originated in Evans' shop. His daybooks indicate that at least twelve journeymen and apprentices worked for him in 1774 and 1775 alone. With so many different hands, construction methods must have occasionally varied from piece to piece. The size of Evans' work force, along with the high volume of orders recorded in his daybooks, indicate that he had a thriving business before the Revolutionary War, and the structure of the two dressing tables attests to the fine quality of his work.

The beginning of the Revolutionary War posed challenges to the young cabinetmaker as orders diminished and labor became scarce. Evans' business records, however, reveal that he prospered during this tumultuous period. His ability to adapt to changing political and economic circumstances by supplementing his income left him on solid financial ground. Although Evans' Quaker beliefs prevented him from enlisting, he supported and profited from the war effort by making camp chairs, cot bedsteads, and tent poles, as well as hundreds of staffs and ensign poles for flags and banners. He and his apprentices also received wages from the United States Quartermaster General for packing arms at the gunlock factory. During the British occupation of Philadelphia in the fall of 1777, Evans put his loyalties aside and hauled wood for "His Majesty." In short, he did whatever it took to survive.[6]

When Evans began his business relationship with Tench Coxe in 1781, he undoubtedly felt confident of his skills as a cabinetmaker, which had been proven before the war, and his ability to thrive in difficult times, which had been tested during the war. Coxe's experiences also gave him expectations of prosperity and success. He was born in Philadelphia on May 22, 1755, the son of William Coxe, a wealthy merchant, and grandson of Tench Francis, who had served as attorney general of the Province of Pennsylvania from 1741 to 1775. The young Coxe was groomed to continue his family's legacy of financial power and civic duty. Educated at the Academy College of Pennsylvania, he probably apprenticed with his father's firm, Coxe and Furman, before becoming a partner in 1776. Two years later, he married Catherine McCall, whose father Samuel was also a prominent merchant.[7]

Catherine died in 1778, and the firm of Coxe, Furman and Coxe disbanded two years later. Tench subsequently established his own mercantile firm and began to court his first cousin, Rebecca Coxe. By the time he commissioned Evans in 1781, his business had begun to rebound from the war. Like many ambitious merchants, Coxe had diversified his investments and supplemented his income by buying and selling land. The latter endeavor brought him together with Evans.[8]

The Contract

In January 1781, Evans paid Coxe £260 for a plot of land on the north side of Arch Street above Sixth Street, just three blocks west of the cabinetmaker's shop (fig. 8). Measuring twenty feet on Arch Street and one hundred and fourteen feet deep, the plot may have included a kitchen building. Later events suggest that Evans bought the land with the intention of building a new home for his expanding family. When negotiating the contract, Coxe had his family in mind as well. Widowed, but soon-to-be-engaged, Coxe may have foreseen a need for new household goods. He allowed Evans to pay half of the price of the land in furniture. Thus, Coxe extended a one-year cash credit to Evans for £65 and a two-year cash credit for £65. In exchange, Evans credited Coxe with £130 for future furniture orders.[9]

David Evans was not the only artisan with whom Coxe made such an agreement. On July 7, 1781, the merchant sold Philadelphia silversmith Edmond Milne a lot with a three-story brick building and a two-story brick kitchen on the west side of Sixth Street between Arch and Race Streets for £250. Coxe agreed to accept £150 of the total in silver, "the quality & prices to be good & merchantable & the fashion genteel, and to be delivered within four months from this date, at which Time conveyance shall be made valid & in due form of law." Coxe provided specifications for some of the work in a letter written two days later, adding that he wished "to have well finished plate in the plain stile generally used here." Coxe even noted that

Figure 13 Entry for December 29, 1781, David Evans Daybooks, Philadelphia, Pennsylvania, 1774–1812. (Courtesy, Historical Society of Pennsylvania.)

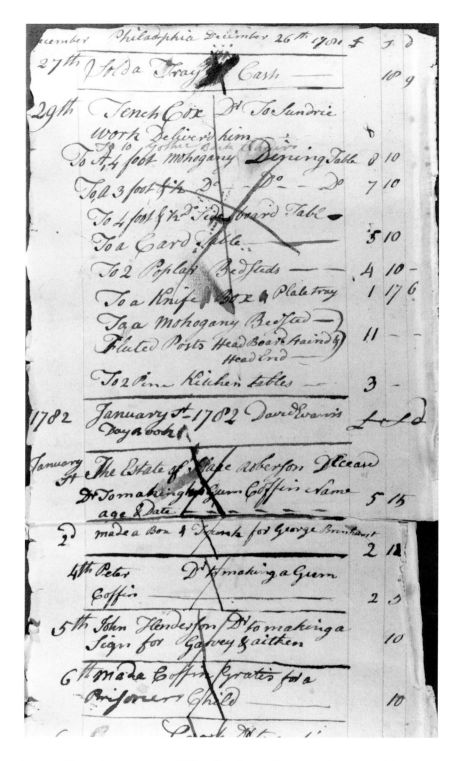

he would send a pattern to Milne for the coffeepot and teapot. It is possible that the merchant was equally involved in the design of his furniture, which may have exacerbated his later disappointment with Evans' work.[10]

The agreement between Coxe and Milne stipulated that the silversmith deliver £50 in cash at the end of four months and the remaining £50 in cash within the following four months "unless it shall be wanted in plate." Only when Milne delivered all of the silver could he take possession of the land. Although the contract between Coxe and Evans does not survive, it may have had similar provisions. The deed of transfer between the merchant and the cabinetmaker was not recorded until May 1, 1782, suggesting that Coxe received the furniture prior to conveying the land.[11]

The Transaction

Coxe evidently placed the order for his furniture in November, nine months after entering into the agreement with Evans. On December 29, 1781, the cabinetmaker described the forms required to fulfill his part of the transaction in his daybook (fig. 13). They included ten mahogany Gothic back chairs, two mahogany dining tables, a four-and-a-half foot mahogany sideboard table, a mahogany card table, two lowpost poplar bedsteads, a mahogany knife box, a "plate tray," a mahogany bedstead with fluted posts, a stained gum headboard and base board, and two pine kitchen tables. Later bills show that Evans also made Coxe a candle box and twelve walnut chairs with Gothic backs at the same time. The merchant required that the cabinetmaker deliver all thirty-four pieces in two months, in time to set up his house for his new bride.[12]

Because of the contract he had signed with Coxe, Evans could not refuse this large and demanding request. Despite the pressure, the cabinetmaker managed to finish the order in the prescribed time. Evans valued his work at £104 and delivered it to Coxe's home on January 24, 1782.[13]

The Complaint

When Coxe returned from his honeymoon in early March, neither he nor his bride was happy with the furniture Evans had delivered. Undated notes written in Coxe's hand record that "the dining Table [was] cracked & patched, & thin," and that the "walnut chairs [were] not peg'd." He noted that "the mahogy bedstead [was] ricketty, slender & without furniture to this day & without top rails" and "the sideboard table [was] patched in two places." To validate his complaints, and perhaps to publicly embarrass Evans, Coxe had all the furniture Evans had made for him (including several items made before and after the large order delivered in January) appraised on June 18, 1782, by two of Evans' fellow cabinetmakers, Francis Trumble and Thomas Affleck. These respected Philadelphia craftsmen determined that "several articles are not merchantable qualities" and that the value of the furniture was less than that charged. Evans valued all of the objects listed in the December entry in his daybook and subsequent bills at £154.17.6, which was more than he owed Coxe in exchange, whereas Trumble and Affleck concluded that the furniture was worth £105.18.[14]

After this evaluation, the intensity of Coxe's complaints diminished and he commissioned Evans to provide additional furniture for his new home. The cabinetmaker's sound reputation must have convinced Coxe that the inferior furniture was an anomaly. According to Coxe, Evans still owed the merchant £24.2 worth of furniture on their original contract, and Coxe evidently believed the cabinetmaker would fulfill his obligation in a satisfactory manner. During the next few years, Coxe placed several small orders with Evans. He purchased ten mahogany slat back chairs in May 1782, and in preparation for the birth of his first child in 1783, Coxe commissioned a large pine bureau table, a mahogany easy chair with a feathered cushion, and a mahogany cradle. Clearly wary of the merchant's anger, Evans wrote Coxe: "I have Strove my best to get a Cradle this morning but Could not If you will be Kind Enough, wait till 5th day I will have as good as a mahogany Cradle made & deliver'd at your House as I can possibly make & Will not Disappoint you by any means, but will work all night." No record of Coxe's response is known, but he subsequently complained that the slats of the ten mahogany chairs he ordered in 1782 were "very thin, sappy & the cross pieces among the feet all falling out." He also admonished Evans for the poor quality of the card tables he received in January 1782 and December 1783 which were "unseasoned and with one handle."[15]

There is no documentary evidence that Coxe attempted to rectify these problems until 1786, when his financial situation and Philadelphia's economy had reached "a very disagreeable condition." Once again, he and Evans disagreed over the value of the furniture that the cabinetmaker had made. Presumably Evans claimed that he had fulfilled, if not exceeded, his contractual obligations, whereas Coxe believed that the cabinetmaker's work was not worth "the price of well-made furniture."[16]

Rule of Court

In August 1786, Tench Coxe forced an end to his dispute with Evans. Perhaps sensitive to the Society of Friends aversion to legal proceedings, or possibly desiring to embarrass Evans into settling, Coxe entered a complaint with the Philadelphia Monthly Meeting. The Quakers, who frowned on the practice of maintaining debts, appointed Thomas Morris and William Garrigues to counsel Evans and help him find a solution to his situation. Shortly thereafter, all parties agreed to the appointment of an arbitration committee comprised of the complainant's and defendant's peers. The committee, which included "Messers. Bullock, Shields and Claypoole," had the disputed furniture appraised by Evans' former journeyman Jesse Williams and by George Claypoole, who may have been one of the arbitrators. Coxe submitted a letter reminding the committee of his complaints, and presumably Evans responded with his defense.[17]

Although the September 12, 1786 "award" was once in the Tench Coxe Papers of the Historical Society of Pennsylvania, the document is now missing. Judging from Evans' letter to Coxe four months later, the committee found in favor of the merchant, forcing the cabinetmaker to scramble for cash. On January 3, 1787, Evans wrote:

> Friend Coxe
>
> I did not receive an answer from Maryland till last week . . . my uncle . . . was to have been . . . in this City in December [but being sick] . . . he did not answer my letter but his wife did & think I am ill used as they have sent me no part of the money, I sent a letter to go by Richd Adams who is going to my uncles house & is to sett off as soon as the roads can be travelled I

Shall begg of him to Get me twenty five or thirty Pounds I have a Riding Chair which I mean to sell to make as much as Posibly I can . . . I have left no Stone unturned nor nothing that I can do to procure it but it Seems as if I could do nothing with regard to procuring the money as yet . . . . I will have it for you as Soon as posible but begg you will not Proceed against me with an Execution at this Encloment Season of the year.

Despite his efforts, Evans was unable to procure the money from his relatives. There is no evidence that Coxe ever filed suit, however, and Evans eventually paid off his debt.[18]

In Defense of Evans

From Coxe's complaints, Trumble and Affleck's criticism, and the arbitration committee's ruling, it appears that Evans made shoddy furniture. Yet, the cabinetmaker had exemplary training, ran a thriving cabinet shop before the Revolution, and even prospered during the war. Having proven himself to be a competent master and a good businessman, why did Evans endanger his reputation by providing Coxe with such bad furniture?

Several factors beyond Evans' control influenced the quality of his work. To fulfill his contractual obligation, he had to make Coxe thirty-four pieces of furniture in two months—an unrealistic goal for a small shop. In 1776, Evans made Philadelphia merchant Thomas Powell eleven pieces in three weeks, but he employed at least ten journeymen at that time. When Coxe placed his order in 1781, the cabinetmaker had only one documented journeyman, William Faries. Coxe's order also included forms more elaborate than those specified by Powell.[19]

The economic setbacks Evans suffered in 1781 also influenced his shop's production. His yearly income for that year was approximately £344, his lowest on record and substantially less than the £1857 he made in 1780. The tactics he pursued while the war raged in the Philadelphia region were not feasible in 1781. Evans could not procure lumber and other supplies for himself let alone to sell to fellow cabinetmakers, and the focus of the war had moved south along with the attendant jobs financed by the colonial government. Although Evans tried to increase his profits by collaborating with coachmakers George Way and George Bringhurst, the money he earned making "boxes to go behind a carriage" was insufficient to supplement the income from his declining cabinetmaking business.[20]

When Coxe placed his order in November 1781, Evans did not have the funds, materials, or labor to successfully complete the furniture required to fulfill the contract. The former must have informed the latter of his financial problems, for Coxe loaned Evans six pounds to buy materials on November 27 and another five pounds for materials that following January. With the British navy blockading Philadelphia's port, however, the proper woods, nails, hardware, and other supplies may not have been available. Some ship captains attempted to run the blockade to deliver cargoes of necessities or lucrative manufactured goods, but they would not have taken the risk for raw lumber. Evans probably had to scramble to find enough mahogany to complete Coxe's order. The merchant's objections to the thin

Figure 14 Dining table attributed to David Evans, Philadelphia, Pennsylvania, 1773–1810. Mahogany with oak, tulip poplar, and white pine. H. 28¼", W. 48", D. 59½". (Private collection; photo, Gavin Ashworth.) Like the dressing tables illustrated in figs. 9 and 10, the dining table has end rails with flattened stepped arches.

stock and sapwood in Evans' furniture suggest that the cabinetmaker elected to use bad materials rather than miss his deadline.[21]

Evans' situation failed to improve during the 1780s. After the Revolution, the city's merchants, entrepreneurs, and well-to-do consumers imported large quantities of furniture from England, France, and other countries. These imports saturated the market, which was just beginning to rebound from the effects of the war. At the same time, competition increased as many of the cabinetmakers that had abandoned their shops to fight returned home. Coxe's September 2, 1786 letter to the arbitration committee, which mentions "patches...much exposed to View" and furniture "perfectly unornamented" and "badly put together," indicates that Evans' sustained economic troubles continued to affect his craftsmanship.[22]

Repeat Offender

The dispute between Evans and Coxe demands a fresh examination of the surviving pieces attributed to the cabinetmaker's shop. Like the dressing tables illustrated in figures 9 and 10, a dining table (fig. 14) that reputedly descended in the Easby family of Philadelphia demonstrates that Evans' shop was capable of producing sturdy, well-designed furniture. The top of the table is comprised of three figured mahogany boards, and the stock selected for the legs is dense and free of knots. All of the joints are neat and tight despite years of use. Evans' daybooks record orders for forty dining tables made between May 1775 and September 1797, some of which were described as "clawfoot."

Figure 15 Armchair attributed to David Evans, Philadelphia, Pennsylvania, 1773–1795. Mahogany with white pine. H. 38", W. 23½", D. 18". (Private collection; photo, Gavin Ashworth.) The armchair is stamped "D.EVANS" on the inside of the rear rail and the underside of the slip seat.

The Easby table and closestool armchair shown in figure 15 are stamped "D.EVANS," the former on the flyrail and the latter on the rear rail, seat board, and slip seat. Both pieces reflect styles that originated in the 1740s and remained popular during the last quarter of the eighteenth century. Evans undoubtedly learned to produce these forms during his apprenticeship, and found them well suited to the tastes of conservative patrons and clients who preferred austere objects for secondary locations in their households.[23]

A card table commissioned by Edward Burd on April 4, 1788, exemplifies Philadelphia's version of the English "neat and plain" style (fig. 16). As British design book engravings attest, the taste for understated, classically correct furniture co-existed with the rococo. The neat and plain style was particularly suited to conservative Philadelphia Quakers, who eschewed the "vain arts and inventions of a luxurious world," but it also appealed to many other segments of the population. Wealthy Philadelphia patrons such as

Figure 16 Card table attributed to David Evans, Philadelphia, Pennsylvania, 1788. Mahogany with black walnut and tulip poplar. H. 29½", W. 35½", D. 17". (Courtesy, Philadelphia Museum of Art; photo, Gavin Ashworth.) This card table was one of a pair. The hardware is original.

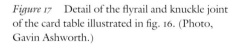

Figure 17 Detail of the flyrail and knuckle joint of the card table illustrated in fig. 16. (Photo, Gavin Ashworth.)

Figure 18 Detail of the flyrail and swing leg of the card table illustrated in fig. 16. (Photo, Gavin Ashworth.)

Charles Thompson often commissioned both simple and lavishly carved forms for the same household. Thompson owned one of the most elaborately carved sets of Philadelphia chairs as well as a neat and plain breakfast table purchased from David Evans in 1778.[24]

The gilded brass handles of the card table are unusual in having rococo bails and neoclassical post plates. Both sets of components were available from Birmingham brass manufacturers by the early 1770s, which suggests that they may have been part of Evans' stock before the war. Alternatively, the handles and post plates could have been among the British manufactured goods that flooded Philadelphia's marketplace after the war.[25]

Although the design of the card table is relatively sophisticated, its materials and construction display many of the shortcomings described by Coxe. The right rear leg has a large knot that caused the stock to warp, the inner

rail and flyrail are about one-third sapwood (figs. 17, 18), and both rails have worm damage that was present prior to construction. Evidence also suggests that Evans or one of his journeymen were working hastily and carelessly. The flyrail has an errant saw kerf where the maker began cutting the hinge segments in the wrong place, and the rabbet that allows the swing leg to engage the side rail has torn fibers from being chopped out too quickly. Instead of having knife-edge hinges like most contemporary card tables, the leaves of the table are joined with face-mounted butt hinges. Evans apparently had difficulty procuring or affording imported British hardware.

Figure 19   Tall clock case attributed to David Evans with an eight-day movement by David Rittenhouse, Philadelphia, Pennsylvania, 1789. H. 93", W. 23⅓", D. 12¾". (Courtesy, University of Pennsylvania Art Collection; photo, Gavin Ashworth.)

Figure 20   Detail of the hood of the tall clock case illustrated in fig. 19. (Photo, Gavin Ashworth.)

Figure 21 Detail showing the foot construction of the tall clock case illustrated in fig. 19. (Photo, Gavin Ashworth.)

As Evans struggled to repay Coxe in compliance with the arbitration committee's ruling, his income levels remained low. Consequently his cabinet shop continued to suffer from a lack of funds for materials and skilled labor. Furthermore, the construction of the card table indicates that the notion of eighteenth-century tradesmen painstakingly laboring over every piece is a romantic perspective, if not an outright myth. Despite Evans' training, skill, and business acumen, he continued to produce sub-standard furniture through most of the 1780s.

The cabinetmaker's declining business may have turned a corner in 1789. A "Large mahogany clock case" (fig. 19) commissioned by University of Pennsylvania Provost John Ewing on June 29 of that year is the most structurally advanced object attributed to Evans' shop. Built for an eight-day movement (fig. 20) made and donated by the university's astronomy professor and vice provost David Rittenhouse, the case is distinguished by having horizontally laminated foot blocks (fig. 21). Unlike the one-piece vertical blocks used by most colonial cabinetmakers, these "composite" supports shrank and expanded in the same direction as the foot faces and helped prevent the feet from cracking with seasonal changes in temperature and humidity. London cabinetmakers such as Giles Grendy began using horizontally laminated foot blocks by the early 1740s, but few of their American counterparts followed suite. As is the case with furniture attributed to the shop of Philadelphia cabinetmaker Jonathan Gostelowe, the occurrence of this blocking technique on the clock case suggests that Evans' workforce included at least one British-trained artisan.[26]

A tall clock case made for Evans' neighbor and regular client Jonathan Dickinson Sergeant (fig. 22) is similar to the preceding example. Both pieces have old-fashioned, square hoods with four Doric colonettes above a stepped ogee molding and waist doors with incurved top corners. Sergeant paid £3.10 less than Ewing, presumably because the university's case included a pitched pediment and fluted colonettes and quarter-columns.[27]

Consequences

David Evans' dispute with Tench Coxe and his subsequent financial problems marked a watershed in his career. During the late 1780s, the cabinetmaker shifted his focus from traditional furniture making to the mass production of coffins and Venetian blinds. As a result, Evans was able to employ semi-skilled laborers for his new venture, while maintaining a small workforce for cabinetwork. The University of Pennsylvania clock case dates from the period when Evans was revamping his shop.

By the end of the 1780s, Evans' financial situation began to improve. The stable market for coffins and the luxury market for Venetian blinds attracted a broad patronage. As a producer of luxury goods, his income and his status within the artisan community grew. He was able to provide fancy foods for his family and guests, fine schooling for his children, and secure his son an apprenticeship in the coveted apothecary trade. By 1800, Evans' new business was firmly established and only six percent of his income derived from cabinetwork. The professional embarrassment and economic prob-

Figure 22 Tall clock case attributed to David Evans with a thirty-hour movement by Benjamin Rittenhouse, Philadelphia, Pennsylvania, 1788. Dimensions and woods not recorded. (William MacPherson Hornor, *Blue Book: Philadelphia Furniture* [1931; reprint, Alexandria, Va.: Highland House, 1988], pl. III.) Benjamin Rittenhouse made the movement as a wedding present for Jonathan and Elizabeth (Rittenhouse) Sergeant. Elizabeth was Benjamin's niece.

lems Evans endured were catalysts for change and eventual prosperity. Ironically, Coxe speculated in land during the 1790s, lost all of his money, and eventually declared bankruptcy.[28]

Ultimately, the dispute between Evans and Coxe was far more complex than the protagonists, objects, and procedures that ultimately led to settlement. It involved the craftsman and merchant's businesses, their families, and the tenuous political and economic environment of post-war Philadelphia. Their story and Evans' career and work illustrate the importance of understanding the historical and personal contexts of material culture and invites scholars to reconsider traditional assumptions about period craftsmanship.

ACKNOWLEDGMENTS For assistance with this article, the author thanks Glenn Adamson, Gavin Ashworth, Luke Beckerdite, Wendy Cooper, Lynn Gadsden, Charles Hummel, Jack Lindsey, Jonathan Prown, Neville Thompson, and the private collectors of David Evans furniture.

1. Tench Coxe to Messrs. Bullock, Shields and Claypoole, September 2, 1786, Coxe Family Papers, 1638–1897, col. 2049, Historical Society of Pennsylvania (hereafter cited HSP). "Arbitration was frequently resorted to as a substitute for court proceedings in the eighteenth century," particularly among Quakers who "had an aversion to court proceedings." This usually involved a three-person committee formed to settle the differences in a commercial dispute. Each party selected one arbitrator, usually someone familiar with the business activity of the dispute, and both parties selected the third. Once the committee was chosen, each party submitted their grievances. The judgment of the arbitrators could be binding under a rule of court and enforced by law. The author thanks David W. Maxey, of Drinker, Biddle & Reath in Philadelphia and Bruce H. Mann, Professor of Law and History, University of Pennsylvania Law School, for information on arbitration proceedings.

2. Marriage certificate for David and Sarah Evans, November 22, 1775, Abington Monthly Meeting of Friends, Friends Historical Library, Swarthmore College. Obituary for David Evans, *Poulson's American Daily Advertiser,* January 3, 1820. Will of David Evans, September 27, 1745, file 47, bk. H, p. 80, Philadelphia County Wills, Office of the Register of Wills, Philadelphia, Pennsylvania (microfilm, Winterthur Library: Joseph Downs Collection of Manuscripts and Printed Ephemera). According to historian Gary Nash, fifty-five percent of artisans between 1681 and the late 1750s had estates valued at £51–£200 sterling, and twenty-five percent had estates valued at over £200 sterling. Nash described the latter group as having "a very comfortable standard of living." Gary Nash, "Artisans and Politics in Eighteenth-Century Philadelphia," in *The Craftsman in Early America,* edited by Ian M.G. Quimby (New York: W.W. Norton & Co., 1984), p. 66. *The Pennsylvania Gazette,* June 29, 1758. *The Pennsylvania Gazette,* May 25, 1758. Administration Papers of Evan Evans, May 23, 1758, file 32, bk. G, p. 122, Philadelphia City Archives.

3. Philadelphia Monthly Meeting of Friends, Membership List, 1759–1762, Friends Historical Library, Swarthmore College. Minutes of the Philadelphia Monthly Meeting, April 24, 1763, Friends Historical Library. "Gardner" was spelled "Gardiner" by Evans.

4. Evans' apprenticeship is documented in the receipt book of Philadelphia merchant Samuel Morris: "Received 1767 July 13th of Samuel Morris Esqr. the Sum of Five Pounds Ten Shillings in full for a Tea Table Recd. For my Masters Cliffton and Gillingham [signed] David Evans." Harrold E. Gillingham Papers, "Cliffton and Gillingham file," HSP. The author thanks Nancy Goyne Evans for this reference. It is unknown whether David Evans' mother arranged the apprenticeship after the early death of her husband in 1758, or if the Quaker Meeting took control of the situation, as was a common practice with fatherless children. Most apprenticeship contracts stipulated that the master teach the apprentice the "art and mystery" of the trade and provide room, board, and some schooling. Ian M.G. Quimby, *Apprenticeship in Colonial Philadelphia* (New York: Garland Publishing, Inc., 1985), pp. 1–25.

5. *Pennsylvania Chronicle*, August 6, 1770, as quoted in the Gillingham Papers, "Cliffton and Gillingham file," HSP. When their partnership ended, Gillingham left Cliffton's shop and opened his business on "Second-Street, a little below Dr. Bond's." *Pennsylvania Chronicle*, August 29, 1768, as quoted in the Gillingham Papers, "Cliffton and Gillingham file," HSP; David Evans' account with Benjamin Loxley, April 1, 1773, David Evans Daybooks, 1774–1812, 3 vols., Am 9115, HSP. Unless otherwise noted, all subsequent information on Evans and his career is taken from these daybooks. If a reference to a daybook entry in the text is accompanied by a full date, it will not be cited in the notes.

6. Evans Daybooks, December 10, 1776, January and February 1777 (back of vol. 1), HSP.

7. Jacob E. Cooke, "Introduction," Guide to the Coxe Family Papers, HSP.

8. Ibid.

9. Tench Coxe to David Evans, January 23, 1781, Philadelphia Land Deeds, bk. D, no. 4, p. 279, Philadelphia City Archives. In 1790, Evans began work on this house, using William Garrigues as a contractor. He kept detailed records of his transactions with various subcontractors, including bricklayers. Coxe Papers, April 24, 1786, HSP.

10. Tench Coxe to Edmond Milne, July 7, 1781 and Tench Coxe to Edmond Milne, July 9, 1781, Coxe Papers, reel 38, HSP.

11. Ibid.

12. Descriptions and details of the furniture come from both Evans' daybook entries for December 29, 1781, and the bills he sent to Tench Coxe (Coxe Papers, n.d. and May 14, 1774, HSP). Coxe had postponed the marriage until he received a valuable and profitable cargo from Europe. Coxe's aunt and soon-to-be mother-in-law, Rebecca, wrote to him:

> I was much surprised my Dear Sir at your fixing so early a day after Becky's return home as renders it impossible to get what things are absolutely necessary on the occation unless love shou'd add wings & you can find some quicker method . . . [the wedding items] must come at least a week beforehand in that case you shall have my Consent to compleat an Union. . . . I never had a thought of delaying the affair a day longer.

Coxe Papers, n.d. (probably 1781–1782), HSP.

13. Bill from David Evans to Tench Coxe, Coxe Papers, n.d., HSP.

14. Coxe Papers, n.d. (1781) (date given to document is incorrect); and June 18, 1782, HSP.

15. Evans Daybooks, February 27, 1783, HSP. David Evans to Tench Coxe, February 23, 1783, Coxe Papers, HSP; Coxe Papers, n.d. [1781], HSP. (Date given to document is incorrect.)

16. Tench Coxe as quoted in James F. Shepard, "British America and the Atlantic Economy," *The Economy of Early America: The Revolutionary Period, 1763–1790*, edited by Ronald Hoffman, et al. (Charlottesville: University Press of Virginia for the United States Capitol Historical Society, 1988), p. 23.

17. Minutes of the Northern District of the Philadelphia Monthly Meeting, August 22, 1786, Friends Historical Library, Swarthmore College. The names of the arbitrators are known only from Tench Coxe's letter of complaint, which was addressed to "Messers. Bullock, Shields and Claypoole." George Claypoole and Jesse Williams to Tench Coxe, August 30, 1786, Coxe Papers, HSP.

18. David Evans to Tench Coxe, January 3, 1787, Coxe Papers, HSP. On December 26, 1786, the Minutes of the Northern District of the Philadelphia Monthly Meeting reported that Evans had finally complied with the advice of Morris and Garrigues and the matter was considered closed.

19. Evans Daybooks (back of vol. 1), August 29, 1776, HSP: "Memorandum of work for Thos Powell to be done in 3 Weeks, 6 Chairs mohogany Gothic Back Price 11 a Beaurow Table 5. . 10 Card Table 3- Dining Table 4 . . 10 all Malbrough with 2 Tea Boards."

20. Although Philadelphia currency was inflated in 1780, Evans' earnings that year were significantly more than in 1781. Evans Daybooks, May 1781, HSP.

21. Coxe Papers, August 24, 1786, HSP.

22. Tench Coxe to Messrs. Bullock, Shields and Claypoole, September 2, 1786, Coxe Papers, HSP.

23. John and Elizabeth Cadwalader purchased elaborately carved rococo furniture for their principal rooms and conservative forms for secondary spaces. On August 27, 1770, William Savery billed them for walnut chamber tables, walnut chairs with leather and canvas bottoms, "rush bottom chairs," and other furnishings (Nicholas B. Wainwright, *Colonial Grandeur in Philadelphia: The House and Furniture of General John Cadwalader* [Philadelphia: Historical Society of Pennsylvania, 1964], pp. 37–60). The walnut chairs probably resembled the example illustrated in fig. 15.

24. Burd ordered a pair of card tables; the location of the matching card table is unknown. Although the table shown in fig. 16 has been taken apart and reassembled, the quality of its construction is evident. For design book engravings of neat and plain furniture, see Thomas Chippendale, *The Gentleman and Cabinet-Maker's Director* (1754), pls. 35, 46, 54, 60, 77, 85, 86, 96, 102. William Penn as quoted in Jack Lindsey, *Worldly Goods: The Arts of Early Pennsylvania, 1680–1758* (Philadelphia: Philadelphia Museum of Art, 1999), p. 21. William MacPherson Hornor, *Blue Book: Philadelphia Furniture* (1931; reprint, Alexandria, Va.: Highland House, 1988), pls. 225, 257.

25. Beatrice B. Garvan, *Federal Philadelphia, 1785–1825: The Athens of the Western World* (Philadelphia: Philadelphia Museum of Art, 1987), p. 20.

26. The London-trained artisan in Gostelowe's shop was Thomas Jones. Deborah M. Federhen, "Politics and Style: An Analysis of the Products and Patrons of Jonathan Gostelowe and Thomas Affleck," in *Shaping a National Culture: The Philadelphia Experience, 1750–1800*, edited by Catherine E. Hutchins (Winterthur, Del.: Winterthur Museum, 1994), pp. 283–311.

27. The clock case illustrated in fig. 22 descended in the Sergeant family. It is attributed to Evans based on oral tradition and its similarity to the case described in Sergeant's March 28, 1788 entry in Evans' daybook: "a Mohogany Clock Case, Square Head & corners" (Hornor, *Blue Book,* p. 129).

28. Cooke, "Guide to Coxe Family Papers," HSP.

Figure 1 Side chair, New York, 1660–1720. Cherry with unidentified secondary wood. H. 42", W. 18", D. 13½". (Private collection; photo, Helga Studio.)

Erik Gronning

Early New York Turned Chairs: A *Stoelendraaier's* Conceit

▼ OBJECTS OFTEN ILLUMINATE aspects of personal life rarely conveyed in historical documents. The *kast*, for example, has long been associated with Dutch settlers in early New York. In addition to being eminently useful for the storage of household textiles, these ubiquitous cupboard forms were a source of pride for their makers and symbols of wealth, order, and abundance for their owners. A large group of early turned chairs (see fig. 1) provides an alternative and possibly better perspective on New York's pluralistic society. Like early Boston and New York "leather chairs," these ornate seating forms show how artisans and consumers "engaged with their mental and material worlds."[1]

In the Netherlands, spindle-back chairs were typically made by *stoelendraaiers,* a specific class of artisan that specialized in the production of turned seating. David Wessels (1654–1678) is the only New York artisan identified as a *stoelendraaier;* however, twelve other *drayers,* "turners," and "chairmakers" worked there in the seventeenth century: Thomas Paulus (1669), Lourens Andrieszen van Boskerk (Buskirk) (1636–1694), Frederick Arentszen (Blom) (1654–1686), Arent Frederickszen Blom (1657–1709), Jacob Blom (1676–1731), Jacob Smit (1686), William Bogaert (1690–1703), Johannes Byvanck (1677–1727), Johannes Tiebout (1689–1728), Rutgert Waldron (1677–1720), Jan Poppen (1675–1689), and Albert Van Ekelen (1684).[2]

The earliest turners who arrived in New York came from different areas of northern Europe. David Wessels emigrated from Esens, East Friesland, Holland, an area adjoining western Germany; Lourens Andrieszen van Boskerk came from Holstein, Denmark; and Frederick Arentszen Blom was a native of Swarte Sluis, Overyssel, Holland. Frederick, however, did not immigrate directly from Swarte Sluis. When Lourens Andrieszen van Boskerk traveled to Amsterdam in 1654, he found Blom working for a turner and convinced him to immigrate to New York and serve a three-year apprenticeship. On July 23, 1656, Blom "without either words or reason . . . ran away from" van Boskerk and married Grietie Pieters. Although the master sued his apprentice for breach of contract, nothing came of the matter. During the ensuing years, van Boskerk, Blom, and Wessels lived near each other and interacted socially and professionally (figs. 2, 3).[3]

On March 24, 1662, Blom and Wessels complained that "some people come from out of the City asking for work or to make chair matting and are allowed to earn the wages." The petitioners noted that they were "Burghers" who paid city taxes and requested that the practice "be forbidden, for it prevents them [from supporting] . . . themselves and their families." Artisans

Figure 2   I. N. Phelps Stokes, *Redraft of the
Castello Plan of New Amsterdam in 1660*, New
York, 1916. Color gravure on paper. 14⅜" x
19¼". (Courtesy, J. Clarence Davies Collection,
Museum of the City of New York.)

Figure 3   Detail of the map illustrated in fig. 2, showing the residences of (*a*) Lourens Andrieszen van Boskerk, (*b*) Frederick Arentszen Blom, and (*c*) David Wessels.

often joined forces to oppose competition and secure contracts for large public projects. On April 27, 1702, the Council of the Colony of New York recorded payments to Frederick Blom's son Jacob and turner Rutgert Waldron for work done on the fort.[4]

The Bloms are the only documented family of seventeenth-century New York turners. As historian Joyce Goodfriend has noted, family and ethnicity were essential factors in determining occupation in that colony. Kinship allowed for the direct transmission and propagation of design and craftsmanship. Fathers often trained sons and left them tools and other property related to their trade. On March 23, 1711/12, turner Johannes Byvanck left his eldest son Evert all his tools and "wearing apparel," a great "Bilested chest," and £5. Evert may also have inherited an equally valuable asset—the good will of his father's patrons.[5]

Religion was another vehicle for the transmission of design and patronage. David Wessels and Lourens Andrieszen van Boskerk were Lutherans and often signed ecclesiastical documents together. Like many seventeenth-and eighteenth-century artisans, they probably met potential clients and made business contacts in their respective churches.[6]

Netherlandish Sources

The urban Dutch chairs illustrated in figures 4 and 5 are cognates for the seating produced by early New York turners such as Wessels and van Boskerk. Details shared by the European and American forms include low backs, tall urn finials, elliptical spindle and stretcher turnings, posts with ball and/or baluster elements, front posts with turned tops, and four turned feet. Rail and spindle backs like those on many Dutch chairs (see fig. 4) do not occur on New York seating, but are relatively common in other areas of Netherlandish settlement.[7]

Figure 4 Side chair, northern Netherlands, 1650–1700. Walnut with unidentified secondary wood. H. 40⅛", W. 18⅛", D. 15¾". (Courtesy, Rijksmuseum.)

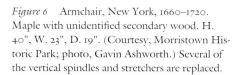

Figure 5 Side chair, northern Netherlands, ca. 1700. Rosewood and walnut with unidentified secondary wood. H. 37½", W. 18⅛", D. 14¾". (Courtesy, Rijksmuseum.)

Figure 6 Armchair, New York, 1660–1720. Maple with unidentified secondary wood. H. 40", W. 23", D. 19". (Courtesy, Morristown Historic Park; photo, Gavin Ashworth.) Several of the vertical spindles and stretchers are replaced.

The armchairs illustrated in figures 6 and 7 may represent the work of first generation New York *stoelendraaiers*. Both have massive arms that extend beyond the front posts (see fig. 8) and other turned components that are larger and more robust than those on related New York side chairs (see fig. 1). Furniture historians Robert Leath and John Bivins have documented the production of similar armchairs (see fig. 9) in northeast North Carolina and southeast Virginia—an area strongly influenced by Dutch and French styles during the last half of the seventeenth century.[8]

New York inventories provide little information regarding the design or use of early seating forms. During the seventeenth and early eighteenth centuries, appraisers typically referred to chairs by their woods, paint color, or upholstery material. Turned forms were usually described as having "matted," "flagged," or "rushed" seats. The 1686 estate inventory of former New York City mayor Cornelius Steenwyck lists rush-seated chairs in the "kitchen chamber." Contemporary records also document their use in "kitchen chambers," "great chambers," and bedrooms.[9]

Figure 7 Armchair, New York, 1660–1720. Maple, cherry, and ash with unidentified secondary wood. H. 50⅜", W. 23¼", D. 18¾". (Courtesy, Albany Institute of History and Art, Rockwell Fund; photo, Gavin Ashworth.) This chair reputedly descended in the Hendrickson family of Flatbush. With two tiers of back spindles and unusually complex post turnings, this chair is a superb example of the *stoelendraaier's* art. One arm and several spindles are replaced.

Figure 8 Detail of the left arm and front post of the armchair illustrated in fig. 6. (Photo, Gavin Ashworth.)

Figure 9 Armchair, probably southeast Virginia, 1670–1720. Cherry with unidentified secondary wood. H. 41¾", W. 23½", D. 23½". (Collection of the Museum of Early Southern Decorative Arts.)

Figure 10 Nicolaes Maes, *A Young Woman Sewing*, 1655. Oil on panel. 21⅜" x 17½". (Courtesy, Guildhall Art Gallery, Corporation of London.)

Seventeenth-century Netherlandish genre paintings frequently depict turned chairs in domestic settings. Nicolaes Maes' *A Young Woman Sewing* (fig. 10) shows a chair similar to the one illustrated in figure 4 adjacent to a *soldertien*, a low dias used to reduce drafts, whereas Hendrik van der Burch's *The Game of Cards* (fig. 11) portrays a mother and child seated on related spindle-back forms. Although most Dutch genre paintings were staged, many of the objects depicted in them were present in wealthy households. The kitchen of Petronella de la Court's (1674–1707) doll house (fig. 12) has a set of six miniature spindle-back side chairs (see fig. 13) similar to those in the aforementioned paintings. With their turned back rails and urn finials, these miniature forms are the closest parallels to the New York chairs illustrated here.[10]

At least twenty-five New York chairs with related turnings are known. Although these objects clearly represent the work of several different shops, all have spindles with ring and baluster turnings at the top and bottom and elliptical elements in the middle (see fig. 14). Some chairs have similar turnings on the rear posts (see fig. 1), but most have abbreviated sequences to compensate for differences in space and scale (see fig. 16). Tall urn-shaped

Figure 11   Hendrik van der Burch, *The Game of Cards,* 1660. Oil on canvas. 30½" x 26½". (Courtesy, Detroit Institute of Arts.)

Figure 12   Detail showing the kitchen of a doll house, Netherlands, 1674–1682. (Courtesy, Central Museum, Utrecht.)

Figure 14 Detail of the right finial and right rear
post and spindles of the chair illustrated in fig. 39.
(Photo, Gavin Ashworth.)

finials are another distinctive feature of chairs in this group. Similar finials also appear on many later slat-back chairs found in the vicinity of Bergen County, New Jersey, which suggests that at least one New York turner may have moved there during the eighteenth century.[11]

Most of the chairs in the New Netherland group are made of cherry, a wood rarely found in seventeenth-century American seating furniture. Cherry grew throughout the middle Atlantic region, and joiners from a variety of cultural traditions used it for case and table forms. Furniture historian Peter Kenny has shown that New York Dutch artisans used cherry for *kasten*, draw-bar tables, and gateleg tables. This tight grained wood was stable, easy to turn, and readily accepted stains and finishes, which undoubtedly appealed to *stoelendraaiers* desiring to simulate the exotic woods often found on urban Dutch chairs. The side chair shown in figure 1 has its original mahoganized surface, as do several contemporary New York draw-bar tables. Several chairs in the group probably had similar finishes or surfaces intended to resemble ebony.[12]

Other primary woods used in the construction of New Netherland turned chairs include walnut, maple, mulberry, and ebony. The example shown in figure 15 was thought to have European walnut components, but the microscopic wood identification may have been incorrect. Calcium oxalate crystals, which are present in the axial parenchyma of American black walnut but absent in European walnut, are not always visible in small samples. More importantly, the chair has stretchers made of hickory, an indigenous American wood that does not appear to have been exported to Britain or Europe. Court records indicate that early New York *stoelendraaiers* used

Figure 15 Side chair, New York, 1660–1720. Walnut with hickory. H. 30¹¹/₁₆", W. 16½", D. 13⅜". (Courtesy, Mabel Brady Garvan Collection, Yale University Art Gallery.)

black walnut for chairs and other turned forms. On May 1, 1666, Sieur Nicolaes Varlet sued Frederick Arentszen Blom for failing to make a black walnut spinning wheel. Seven years later Philip Johns complained that he had given Frederick Arentszen Blom "a parcel of Black walnut . . . for the makeing of . . . Chayres, which . . . the defendant sold . . . to another person."[13]

If the chair shown in figure 15 has European walnut components, that does not disprove its attribution. The Dutch were at the forefront of the international lumber trade, and exotic species such as ebony were available in New Amsterdam by 1644. Netherlandish chair makers often used ebony in conjunction with lighter woods such as walnut and rosewood, but they occasionally made seating entirely of a single exotic. A New York child's chair follows the latter practice in having ebony posts, rails, spindles, and stretchers (fig. 16).[14]

The cost of New York chairs similar to those illustrated here is difficult to determine because period references are scarce, and prices undoubtedly varied depending on the type of wood and complexity of the turnings. On November 11, 1657, Frederick Arentszen Blom purchased a house lot on Market Street in New Amsterdam from Teuis Tomassen van Narrden, who agreed to take three chairs valued at four guilders each as "part of the price." Two and a half years later, Blom appeared before the New Amsterdam Court arguing that Jan Janzen owed him eight guilders for two chairs. Janzen subsequently acknowledged the debt and offered "payment in plank." Blom's price of four guilders per chair appears moderate given the fact that fellow turners Lourens Andrieszen van Boskerk and David Wessels paid taxes of fifteen guilders and ten guilders respectively in 1655. Blom may also

Figure 16   Side chair, New York, 1660–1720. Ebony with red oak. H. 26", W. 15½", D. 14½". (Courtesy, Winterthur Library: Decorative Arts Photographic Collection.)

have produced case furniture. On September 27, 1661, Jan Jurriaansen Becker complained that his wife bought a chest of drawers from Blom for twenty-five guilders, whereas the latter asserted that he charged twenty-two guilders. Although it is impossible to determine if Blom made the chest, he probably turned balusters, spindles, and other ornaments for local joiners and carpenters.[15]

The Culture, Context, and Dating of New Netherland Spindle-Back Chairs
Although the English seized control of New Netherland in 1664, Dutch culture and influence persisted for over 150 years. The origins of this dominion can be traced to the Dutch West India Company's establishment of large land grants, or patroonships, in 1629. In exchange for their allegiance, the British Crown allowed many patroons to retain their vast estates under the British manorial system. This preserved much of the old social hierarchy, and ensured that the landowners and their progeny would retain considerable wealth, prestige, and political power.[16]

Late eighteenth-century *kasten* and jambless fireplaces are but a few of the many artifacts documenting the persistence of Dutch culture in the Hudson River Valley. Netherlandish traditions survived longer and more intact in rural areas, but even the wealthiest Dutch families who maintained residences in New York City had a reverence and respect for their origins. Furniture historian Lauren Bresnan has shown that their urban houses typically had English and Anglo-American furnishings, whereas their country residences often had family heirlooms as well as objects made by New York Dutch artisans. These patterns of production, consumption, and use have created confusion regarding the origin, date, and possible makers of New York spindle-back chairs.[17]

In the Netherlands, spindle-back chairs like those shown in the Maes and van der Burch paintings (figs. 10, 11) and the doll house of Petronella de la Court (fig. 12) were luxury furnishings typically commissioned by the wealthy and middle class. Immigrant *stoelendraaiers* probably discovered that their specialized craft could not sustain them or their family in the New World. To subsist, they had to expand their production. Frederick Arentszen Blom, for example, sold William Laurence "blocks and other turners worke" valued at fl. 1100 for the ship *James* in 1671. *Stoelendraaiers* who focused on the manufacture of turned seating needed to reside in densely populated areas where their work would be in higher demand. Bergen County, which some scholars considered the place of origin for the chairs discussed here, was an agricultural area settled by Dutch farmers who were unable to acquire land in Manhattan and western Long Island. During the seventeenth and early eighteenth centuries, this region was sparsely populated and unable to sustain a school of turning as large as that represented by this group of chairs. The only early *drayer* documented in northern New Jersey is Lourens Andrieszen van Boskerk, who moved from New Amsterdam to Minkakwa for religious reasons by 1664.[18]

Although most of the spindle-back chairs in the group probably represent the work of New York City *stoelendraaiers,* some may have been made in

Fort Orange (Albany), which grew from a trading post to a town of moderate size by the end of the seventeenth century. A side chair included in an exhibition of local "relics" at the 1886 Albany Bicentennial supports this hypothesis (figs. 17, 18). Alternatively, chairs like this example may have been made in New York and shipped up the Hudson River. On August 20, 1658, Frederick Arentszen Blom reported that his wife "had gone to Fort Orange with a parcel of chairs to procure beavers for them."[19]

Four of the chairs in the group have credible histories. The example illustrated in figure 19 descended in the family of Johannes De Peyster (1666–1711) of New York City, and the armchair shown in figure 7 descended in the family of Daniel Hendrickson, Sr. (d. 1728) who lived in Flatbush, Brooklyn. These historical associations and the close relationship between the earliest New York chairs and their European cognates suggest that most of the examples date from the late seventeenth and early eighteenth centuries. The finials on several of these chairs are similar to that of a weathervane (fig. 20) on the Sleepy Hollow Dutch Reformed Church which was built about 1685.[20]

Figure 19 Side chair, New York, 1680–1711. Cherry. H. 37", W. 19", D. 15¼". (Private collection; photo, Gavin Ashworth.)

Figure 20 Detail of the weathervane on the Dutch Reformed Church built in Sleepy Hollow, New York, in 1685. Unidentified metals. (Courtesy, Tarrytown Dutch Reform Church; photo, Gavin Ashworth.) This weathervane is a copy based on the original, which still survives in the church. Oral tradition maintains that the weathervane was presented to the church upon its completion.

Degraded versions of these finials appear on chairs made in New York and New Jersey as late as the twentieth century. The longevity and geographic distribution of this design is directly related to the settlement and cultural history of New York. After the English conquest, Dutch immigration dwindled significantly. By 1695, only twelve percent of New York's population consisted of first-generation Dutch emigrés. Time, distance, and isolation from Netherlandish design sources had a profound influence on regional furniture styles. During the late seventeenth century, many artisans and consumers of Dutch descent began embracing English fashions and cultural traditions. As noted, Dutch material culture did not disappear. Just as Netherlandish details appear on New York silver from the eighteenth century, northern European stylistic and structural features are common on

furniture made by second-, third-, and fourth-generation turners, joiners, and cabinetmakers working in the Hudson River Valley. Spindle-back chairs were eventually displaced by cheaper and less overtly continental slat-back forms, but certain turning sequences, such as the tall urn-shaped finial, remained fashionable from the seventeenth century to the twentieth century.[21]

New York *stoelendraaiers* undoubtedly produced both slat-back and spindle-back forms. The slat-back armchair illustrated in figure 21 has large urn finials, stretchers with elliptical turnings, and front posts with bold baluster, ring, and ball-shaped elements—details associated with the earliest spindle-back forms. Similarly, its shaped upper slat resembles those on surviving Dutch chairs (see fig. 5) as well as those depicted in seventeenth-century genre paintings (see fig. 22). Although one later slat-back chair

Figure 22 Detail of Pieter Cornelis van Slinge-landt, *Woman Making Lace with Two Children,* Netherlands, ca. 1679. Oil on panel. 18⅝" x 15½". (Courtesy, Guildhall Art Gallery, Corporation of London.)

Figure 23 Side chair, New York or northern New Jersey, 1730–1790. Maple with unidentified secondary wood. H. 38⅜", W. 18", D. 16". (Private collection; photo, Gavin Ashworth.)

shares this detail (fig. 23), most examples made between 1730 and 1800 have simple arched slats and components made of thinner stock (see fig. 24). Not surprisingly, the turnings on related eighteenth- and early nineteenth-century slat-back and spindle-back chairs from New York and northern New Jersey tend to be thinner and less detailed than corresponding elements on earlier examples.

Presumably, British influences began filtering into New York chairmaking traditions during the late seventeenth century. None of the earliest examples have rail-and-spindle backs, like the seating depicted in the Maes and van der Burch paintings (figs. 6, 7). All of the back components of the New York chairs are turned, as are those on most contemporary English and New England examples (see fig. 25). Although chairs made by *stoelendraaiers* in Holland and areas of Dutch influence often have fully turned backs, the absence of New York examples with rail-and-spindle construction may reflect a concession to British taste. An armchair (fig. 26) with a recovery history in Seatucket, Long Island, points out the difficulty of identifying specific Dutch and English features. Its finials and back spindles are modified versions of those on the earliest New York turned chairs, whereas its flat arms and pommels have precedents in Netherlandish, English, and New England work. A large group of seventeenth- and early eighteenth-century Dutch and New York slat-back armchairs have similar arms and pommels, as does a smaller group of contemporary turned great chairs attributed to the Boston-Charlestown area of Massachusetts.[22]

Figure 24 Side chair, New York or northern New Jersey, 1730–1790. Maple with unidentified secondary wood. H. 36¾", W. 19⅛", D. 16". (Courtesy, Staten Island Historical Society.)

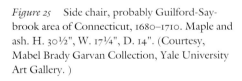

Figure 25 Side chair, probably Guilford-Saybrook area of Connecticut, 1680–1710. Maple and ash. H. 30½", W. 17¼", D. 14". (Courtesy, Mabel Brady Garvan Collection, Yale University Art Gallery.)

Several seating forms made in and around New York share details with the earliest spindle-back chairs, but also have features associated with other chairmaking traditions. The side chair illustrated in figure 27 has turned feet, front posts with compressed balusters, and spindles with elliptical elements in the center and balusters at the top and bottom. All of these features occur, albeit in slightly different form, on the more overtly Netherlandish forms exemplified by the chair shown in figure 1. The elongated balusters of the rear posts and peaked ball finials represent departures from the primary Netherlandish tradition, but all of these features have precedents in New England work. The finials and balusters of the rear posts are similar to those

Figure 26 Armchair, New York, 1670–1720. Maple with unidentified secondary wood. H. 40¾", W. 21⅜", D. 15⅝". (Courtesy, Society for the Preservation of Long Island Antiquities.)

Figure 27 Side chair, New York, 1680–1730. Maple with unidentified secondary wood. Dimensions not recorded. (Courtesy, Sotheby's.)

on chairs (see fig. 25) attributed to the Guilford-Saybrook area of Connecticut, which is just up the Long Island Sound from New York City. Related turnings are also on two child's chairs (figs. 28, 29), one of which is branded "RS" (fig. 28) for Robert Sanders (1705–1765) of Albany. Although some scholars have suggested that Sanders may have purchased the chair for his first child Maria (1749–1830), the style and workmanship of this object point to an earlier owner. It is much more likely that Robert's parents, Barent (1678–1757) and Maria (Wendell) (1677–1734), commissioned the chair. The other example descended in the Ten Eyck family of Albany. It appears to have replaced arms, stretchers, and back spindles and rails. Presumably, the original components were similar to those of the Sanders example.[23]

An unusual walnut side chair (fig. 30) with finials related to those on the preceding seating forms supports the idea that both high chairs (figs. 28, 29) were made in New York City during the early 1700s and subsequently transported up the Hudson River. With its ball-turned front and back posts and elliptically turned spindles and stretchers, this side chair clearly emanates from an urban Dutch tradition. Its proportions and turning sequences are

Figure 28   High chair, New York, 1680–1730.
Maple with unidentified secondary wood.
H. 35½", W. 14¾", D. 13½". (Courtesy, Albany
Institute of History and Art; photo, Gavin Ash-
worth.) The chair is branded "RS" on a back leg.
The footrest is a modern replacement.

Figure 29   High chair, New York, 1680–1730.
Unidentified woods; modern green paint. H. 37",
W. 23", D. 12½". (Courtesy, Albany Institute of
History and Art; photo, Gavin Ashworth.) The
back rails, stretchers, and arms may be replace-
ments.

Figure 30   Side chair, New York, 1680–1730.
Walnut with unidentified secondary wood.
Dimensions not recorded. (Courtesy, Issac
Royall House Museum.) The seat and seat rails
are replaced.

similar to those on the core group of New York chairs (see fig. 1), and, like
those forms, it would have complemented the high chests, dressing tables
(see fig. 31), and draw-bar tables found in upper class homes.[24]

Like the distinctive urn finial, some of the furniture forms introduced by
northern Europen *stoelendraaiers* persisted in the Hudson River Valley for
decades. This was particularly true of rural Dutch communities, which
tended to be more conservative and less influenced by new styles than their
urban counterparts. The side chair illustrated in figure 32 may be the product of a rural turner. It is slightly later than most of the related spindle-back
examples, and its turnings are much less refined in form and execution.

Figure 32 Side chair, New York, 1700–1740. Maple. H. 36½", W. 18¾", D. 15". (Private collection; photo, Gavin Ashworth.)

Figure 33 Side chair, New York, 1695–1730. Maple. H. 44¾", W. 19¾", D. 16". (Courtesy, Albany Institute of History and Art; photo, Gavin Ashworth.)

Regardless of their location or cultural background, *stoelendraaiers* had to accommodate their patrons' tastes. Urban turners also had to compete with imported caned, leather, and banister-back chairs from Britain and Boston. During the 1720s, the scions of first-generation *stoelendraaiers* began producing relatively inexpensive seating (see figs. 33, 34) that combined British and Anglo-American features—molded arched crests and multiple banister backs—with details found on early Netherlandish chairs—stretchers with elliptical elements and legs with compressed balls and turned caps and feet. The armchair shown in figure 35 is one of the most unusual cross-cultural hybrids. Its miniature spindles and rear post turnings clearly emanate from a New York turning tradition, whereas its banister back, crest, and pad feet reflect late baroque influences from England and New England.[25]

Figure 34 Side chair, New York, 1695–1730. Maple. H. 48", W. 18⅜", D. 13½". (Courtesy, Bergen County Historical Society.)

Figure 35 Armchair, New York, 1750–1780. Cherry. H. 47½", W. 26", D. 21½". (Courtesy, Metropolitan Museum of Art, gift of the Wunsch Americana Foundation.)

Markings, Sets, and Makers

As with Robert Sanders' high chair (fig. 28), several early New York spindle-back chairs are branded. Of the five known marks, the "HH" (fig. 36) and "RS" brands are conjoined in the typical Dutch manner, whereas the "HG" (fig. 37), "HR," and "A" are not. Four chairs with identical turnings are branded "HH" (see figs. 38, 39) and are clearly from the same set. The "A" brand is on a red mulberry chair published in Wallace Nutting's *Furniture Treasury* (1928) (fig. 40), and the "HG" brand is on a slightly larger pair made of cherry (fig. 41). A chair nearly identical to the ones marked "HG" was in the collection of Francis P. Garvan in 1931, but it was branded "HR" (fig. 42). The presence of two different brands on chairs that appear to be

Figure 36   Detail of the "HH" brand on the side chair illustrated in fig. 38.

Figure 37   Detail of the "HG" brand on the side chair illustrated in fig. 41. (Photo, Gavin Ashworth.)

Figure 38   Side chair, New York, 1660–1720. Cherry with ash. H. 35⅞", W. 18½", D. 15". (Courtesy, Bayou Bend Collection, Museum of Fine Arts, Houston, museum purchase with funds from the Houston Junior Woman's Club.)

Figure 39 Side chair, New York, 1660–1720. Cherry with ash. H. 34⅞", W. 18½", D. 15". (Courtesy, Historic Hudson Valley; photo, Gavin Ashworth.)

Figure 40 Side chair, New York, 1660–1720. Red mulberry. H. 35½", W. 17", D. 14¾". (Courtesy, American Museum in Britain.) The finials have lost their pointed tops.

Figure 41   Side chair, New York, 1660–1720.
Cherry with unidentified secondary wood.
H. 36⅛", W. 18¾", D. 14½". (Courtesy,
New Jersey State Museum).

Figure 42   Side chair, New York, 1660–1720.
Unidentified woods. H. 37", W. 18½", Depth
not recorded. (Anderson Art Galleries, *Francis
P. Garvan Collection,* January 8–10, 1931, lot 107.)

from the same shop suggests that the marks refer to owners rather than makers. Unmarked chairs with closely related turnings (figs. 1, 18, 43, 44) support this conclusion. The chair illustrated in figure 45, for example, has feet, finials, and leg turnings similar to those on the "HH" set.[26]

Documentary evidence suggests that Netherlandish spindle-back chairs were being made in New York by first-generation *stoelendraaiers* as early as the 1650s. Although most of the chairs illustrated here probably date from the last third of the seventeenth century, they are representative of the earliest

Figure 43 Side chair, New York, 1660–1720. Cherry with white oak. H. 34⅞", W. 17¾", D. 15¼". (Courtesy, Winterthur Museum.) The mate to this chair is illustrated in fig. 18.

Figure 44 Side chair, New York, 1660–1720. Cherry with unidentified secondary wood. H. 37⅜", W. 18⅛", Depth not recorded. (Private collection; photo, Gavin Ashworth.)

Figure 45 Side chair, New York, 1660–1720. Cherry with white oak. H. 34⅜", W. 18¾", D. 16⅛". (Courtesy, Winterthur Museum.)

turned seating produced in New Netherland. Journeymen and apprentices who learned their trade from first-generation *stoelendraaiers* continued to produce similar forms until changing tastes and competition from British and New England imports ultimately forced them to modify their styles. The persistence of this chairmaking tradition is a testament to the strength and vitality of Dutch culture and its adaptability to the changing political, social, and economic landscape of colonial New York.

ACKNOWLEDGMENTS For assistance with this article, the author thanks Gavin Ashworth, Roderic Blackburn, Elaine Clark, Meredith Cohen, Jet Pijzel-Dommisse, Judith Elsdon, Susan Finkel, Lori Fisher, Maxine Friedman, Mr. and Mrs. Dudley Godfrey, Jr., Sue Glyson, Mr. and Mrs. Arthur Goldberg, Joyce Goodfriend, Mr. and Mrs. Norman Gronning, Mr. and Mrs. Donald Hare, Kate Johnson, Neil Kamil, Peter Kenny, Sandra Markham, Joni Rowe, Frances Safford, John Shear, Kevin Stayton, Ruth Piwonka, Kevin Wright, and Mr. and Mrs. Fred Vogel. I am especially grateful to Shelley Farmer for her continued support and encouragement.

1. Wallace Nutting was the first furniture historian to illustrate New Netherland turned chairs (Wallace Nutting, *Furniture Treasury,* 3 vols. [1928; reprint, New York: Macmillan, 1966], 2: nos. 2085–86). More recent attempts to interpret these chairs are John T. Kirk, "Sources of Some American Regional Furniture, Part I," *Antiques* 88, no. 6 (December 1965): 798; John T. Kirk, *American Furniture and the British Tradition to 1830* (New York: Alfred A. Knopf, 1982), p. 235; and Benno M. Forman, *American Seating Furniture: 1630–1730* (New York: W. W. Norton, 1988), pp. 114–19. Peter Kenny, Frances Safford, and Gilbert T. Vincent, *American Kasten: The Dutch-Style Cupboard of New York and New Jersey, 1650–1800* (New York: Metropolitan Museum of Art, 1991), pp. 1–10. Neil D. Kamil, "Of American Kasten and the Mythology of Pure Dutchness," in *American Furniture,* edited by Luke Beckerdite (Hanover, N. H.: University Press of New England for the Chipstone Foundation, 1994), pp. 275–82. Neil D. Kamil, "Hidden in Plain Sight: Disappearance and Material Life in Colonial New York," in *American Furniture,* edited by Luke Beckerdite (Hanover, N. H.: University Press of New England for the Chipstone Foundation, 1995), pp. 191–249.

2. *Stoel* means chair and *draaier* means turner. The 1749 edition of *Sewall's Dutch Dictionary* lists *draaijer* and *wieldraaijer* for "turner." On July 17, 1664, David Wessels requested that the Orphanmaster Council allow Class Gerritsen to be his apprentice for five years to learn the trade of "stoeldraijen" (chair turning) and "laden maachen" (drawer making) *(The Minutes of the Orphanmasters of New Amsterdam, 1663–1668,* edited by Ken Stryker Rodda and Kenneth Scott [Baltimore, Md.: Genealogical Publishing Co., 1976], p. 12). *Year Book of the Holland Society of New York, 1900* (New York: Knickerbocker Press, 1900), p. 126. Thomas Paulus is described as a "drayer" in a record dated September 16, 1669 (A. J. F. Van Laer, *Minutes of the Court of Albany, Rensselaerswyck and Schenectady, Vol I: 1668–1673* [Albany, N. Y.: University of the State of New York, 1926], pp. 99–100); however, he may have been a baker (A. J. F. Van Laer, *Early Records of the City and County of Albany and the Colony of Rensslaerswyck,* 4 vols. [Albany, N. Y.: University of the State of New York, 1919], 3: 143). Berthold Fernow, *The Records of New Amsterdam from 1653-1674,* 7 vols. (1897; reprint, Baltimore, Md.: Genealogical Publishing Co., 1976), 1: 371; 7: 151; and "The Burgers of New Amsterdamn and the Freemen of New York 1675–1866" in *Collections for the New-York Historical Society for year 1885* (New York: By the Society, 1886), pp. 20, 63, 70, 71, 72, 73 list the following artisans and their trades: Lourens Andrieszen van Boskerk, "drayer," October 11, 1655; David Wessels, "chairmaker," April 13, 1657; Frederick Arentszen Blom, "drayer," February 11, 1658; Jacob Blom, "turner," August 9, 1698; Arent Blom, "blockmaker," September 6, 1698; William Bogaert, "turner," September 6, 1698; Johannes Byvanck, "turner," February 2, 1699; Johannes Tiebout, "turner," February 2, 1699; and Rutgert Waldron, "turner," February 3, 1699. Jacob Smit is described as a "turner," in Fernow, *The Records of New Amsterdam from 1653–1674,* 7: 48; and "New York Wills 1665–1707," in *Collections for the New-York Historical Society for year 1892* (New York: By the Society, 1892), p. 95. Turners Jan Poppen and Albert Van Ekelen are listed in Dean Failey, *Long Island is My Nation: The Decorative Arts and Craftsmen 1640–1830* (Setauket, N.Y.: Society for the Preservation of Long Island Antiquities, 1976), p. 283. English immigrant Henry Brasier (Brasar) (w. 1648–1689) referred to himself as a turner in his will (*Collections for the New-York Historical Society for year 1892,* p. 245), but other documents describe him as a carpenter.

3. *Council Minutes, 1652–1654: New York Historical Manuscript Series,* translated and edited by Charles Gehring (Baltimore, Md.: Genealogical Publishing Co., 1983), p. 172. *Iconography of Manhattan Island, 1498–1909,* edited by I. N. P. Stokes, 6 vols. (New York: Robert H. Dodd, 1915–1928), 2: 221. James Riker, *Revised History of Harlem: Its Origin and Early Annals* (New York: New Harlem Publishing Co., 1904), p. 128. Albert Van Ekelen served an apprenticeship

with Flatlands/Flatbush turner Jan Poppen (Failey, *Long Island is My Nation*, p. 283). Fernow, *The Records of New Amsterdam from 1653–1674*, 2: 144, 149.

4. *Minutes of the Orphanmasters of New Amsterdam, 1655–1663*, translated and edited by Berthold Fernow, 2 vols. (New York: Francis P. Harper, 1902–1907), 2: 132–33. Berthold Fernow, *Calendar of Council Minutes, 1668–1783* (1902; reprint, Harrison, N.Y.: Harbor Hill Books, 1987), p. 167.

5. Joyce D. Goodfriend, *Before the Melting Pot: Society and Culture in Colonial New York City, 1664–1730* (Princeton, N. J.: Princeton University Press, 1992), pp. 101–3. "Abstract of Wills, Vol. II, 1709–1723," in *Collections for the New-York Historical Society for year 1893* (New York: By the Society, 1893), p. 88. Failey, *Long Island is My Nation*, p. 283. For more on patronage in New York, see Simon Middleton, "The World Beyond the Workshop: Trading in New York's Artisan Economy, 1690–1740," *New York History* 81, no. 4 (October 2000): 381–416.

6. Arnold J. H. van Laer, *The Lutheran Church in New York: 1649–1772* (New York: New York Public Library, 1946), pp. 20, 21, 30, 31, 36–40. *The Andros Papers: 1674–1676*, edited by Peter R. Christoph and Florence A. Christoph (Syracuse, N. Y.: Syracuse University Press, 1989), p. 17. The Lutheran faith was poorly received in New York. Van Boskerk and Wessels frequently wrote home requesting aid.

7. Chairs with rail-and-spindle backs are common in southeast Virginia and northeast North Carolina, areas strongly influenced by Dutch and French culture. For more on such chairs, see Robert Leath, "Dutch Trade and Its Influence on Seventeenth Century Chesapeake Furniture," in *American Furniture*, edited by Luke Beckerdite (Hanover, N. H.: University Press of New England for the Chipstone Foundation, 1997), pp. 33–35. John Bivins and Forsyth Alexander, *The Regional Arts of the Early South: A Sampling from the Collection of the Museum of Early Southern Decorative Arts* (Chapel Hill: University of North Carolina Press for the Museum of Early Southern Decorative Arts, 1991), p. 21, n. 2. *Tolletjie* chairs from South Africa share numerous details with the New York spindle-back examples illustrated here. Two African chairs made of orangewood and dating ca. 1750 are in the Stellenbosh Museum in South Africa. For more on South African seating, see M. G. Atmore, *Cape Furniture* (Cape Town, South Africa: Citadel Press, 1965), pp. 61, 62, 91; Michael Baraitster and Anton Obholzer, *Cape Country Furniture* (Cape Town, South Africa: Struink Publishers, 1982), pp. 21–27, 92, 93; Michael Baraitster and Anton Obholzer, *Town Furniture of the Cape* (Cape Town, South Africa: Struink Publishers, 1987), p. 62; Richard Beatty, "Cape Dutch Design," *Colonial Homes* 10 (September-October, 1984): 86; William Fehr, *Treasures at the Castle of Good Hope* (Cape Town, South Africa: Howard Timmins, 1963), p. 113; and G. E. Pearse, *Eighteenth-Century Furniture in South Africa* (Pretoria, South Africa: J. L. Van Schaik, 1960), pp. 18, 22.

8. Leath, "Dutch Trade and Its Influence," pp. 33–35. Bivins and Alexander, *The Regional Arts of the Early South*, p. 21, no. 2.

9. For early New York inventories, see Ruth Piwonka, "New York Colonial Inventories: Dutch Interiors as a Measure of Cultural Change," in *New World Dutch Studies: Dutch Arts and Culture in Colonial America 1609–1776*, edited by Roderic H. Blackburn and Nancy A. Kelly (Albany, N.Y.: Albany Institute of History and Art, 1988), pp. 63–81; and Esther Singleton, *Dutch New York* (New York: Dodd, Mead & Co., 1909), pp. 81–103. For the Steenwyck inventory, see Peter M. Kenny, "Flat Gates, Draw Bars, Twists, and Urns: New York's Distinctive, Early Baroque Tables with Falling Leaves," in *American Furniture*, edited by Luke Beckerdite (Hanover, N. H.: University Press of New England for the Chipstone Foundation, 1994), p. 108. The 1711 inventory of Margareta Schuyler lists six *stoelen* (chairs) in the kitchen (Roderic H. Blackburn and Ruth Piwonka, *Remembrance of Patria: Dutch Arts and Culture in America, 1609–1776* [New York: Albany Institute of History and Art, 1988], p. 148).

10. Shirley Glubok, "The Dolls' House of Petronella de la Court," *Antiques* 137, no. 2 (February 1990): 489–501. S. Muller Jr. and W. Vogelsang, *Holländische Patrizierhäuser* (Utrecht, Holland: Verlag Von A. Oosthoek, 1909), pls. 5b, 11.7. Jet van Pizel, a specialist in seventeenth-century doll house furniture, provided this information.

11. Many slat-back chairs with tall, urn-shaped finials have been found in the Bergen County region of New Jersey. Consequentially, dealers and collectors began referring to these turnings as "Bergen County" finials.

12. For a New England joined chair made of cherry, see Peter Follansbee, "A Seventeenth-Century Carpenter's Conceit; The Waldo Family Joined Great Chair," in *American Furniture*, edited by Luke Beckerdite (Hanover, N.H.: University Press of New England for the Chipstone Foundation, 1998), pp. 197–214. Seventeenth-century, southern turned chairs made of cherry are illustrated in Luke Beckerdite, "Religion, Artisanry, and Cultural Identity: The

Huguenot Experience in South Carolina, 1680–1725," in *American Furniture,* edited by Luke Beckerdite (Hanover, N. H.: University Press of New England for the Chipstone Foundation, 1997), pp. 203–4; and Bivins and Alexander, *The Regional Arts of the Early South,* p. 21, no. 2. Kenny, Safford, and Vincent, *American Kasten.* Kenny, "Flat Gates, Draw-Bars, Twists, and Urns," pp. 106–35.

13. Patricia E. Kane, *300 Years of American Seating Furniture* (Boston: New York Graphic Society, 1976), pp. 32–33, fig. 5. This is the same chair illustrated in Nutting's *Furniture Treasury* (see n. 1 above). Varlet claimed that he had "delivered to the defendant in the year 1663 a tub of soap and as much black walnut, as would make a spinning wheel, for which he was then too deliver a spinning wheel as soon as possible, which he has not done." Fernow, *The Records of New Amsterdam from 1653–1674,* 5: 353–54, 6: 380.

14. Singleton, *Dutch New York,* pp. 81–82.

15. Stokes, *Iconography of Manhattan Island, 1498–1909,* 2: 247–48. Fernow, *The Records of New Amsterdam from 1653–1674,* 1: 367–75; 3: 363; 2: 327, 428; 3: 12, 147. Liber Deeds A: 217.

16. For a discussion of Dutch settlement in America, New Netherland's role as a commercial colony, and New Netherland landholding systems, see Blackburn and Piwonka, *Remembrance of Patria,* pp. 35–41, 43, 63–69.

17. These estates, originally referred to as patroonships, received manorial status under British rule. Kenny, Safford, and Vincent, *American Kasten.* Lauren L. Bresnan, "The Beekmans of New York: Material Posession and Social Progression" (master's thesis, University of Delaware, 1996).

18. Blom sued Laurence for non-payment on October 23, 1671 (Fernow, *The Records of New Amsterdam from 1653–1674,* 6: 339). Van Boskerk signed an Oath of Allegance at Bergen, New Jersey, on November 22, 1665 (Stokes, *Iconography of Manhattan Island,* 2: 221).

19. *Catalogue of Albany's Bicentennial Loan Exhibition at Albany Academy, July 5 to July 24, 1886* (Albany, N. Y.: Weed, Parsons, and Co., 1886), p. 136a. Fernow, *The Records of New Amsterdam from 1653–1674,* 2: 428.

20. Christie's, *Fine American Furniture, Silver, Folk Art and Decorative Arts,* New York, January 20, 21, 1989, lot 723. Sotheby's, *Important Americana,* New York, June 23, 24, 1994, lot 432. Howard James Banker, *A Partial History and Genealogical Record of the Bancker or Banker Families of America* (Rutland, Vt.: Tuttle Co., 1909), pp. 244–45, 280–82, 297–98. Waldron Phoenix Belknap, Jr., *The De Peyster Genealogy* (Boston, Mass.: privately printed, 1956), pp. 15, 16, 41, 42. Tammis K. Groft and Mary Alice Mackay, *Albany Institute of History & Art: 200 Years of Collecting* (New York: Hudson Hills Press, 1998), pp. 206–8. The armchair may have been turned by Jan Poppen of Flatlands/Flatbush. The author thanks Peter Kenny for information on the weathervane.

21. Michael Kammen, *Colonial New York: A History* (New York: Oxford University Press, 1996), p. 73. Goodfriend, *Before The Melting Pot,* pp. 42–43, 101–3. Betty Schmelz, Irene Fitzgerald, Catherine Marchbank, and Charles B. Szeglin, *T. R. Cooper's Chair Factory: Early Industry in Rural Schraalerburg* (Bergenfield, N. J.: Bergenfield Museum, 1985).

22. The author thanks Dean Failey for information on the armchair found in Setauket. For more on Dutch and New York turned armchairs with flat arms and pommels, see Forman, *American Seating Furniture,* pp. 122–23, 128–31.

23. Sotheby Parke-Bernet, *17th, 18th and Early 19th Century Furniture from Boston, Newport, Connecticut, New York, Philadelphia and Other Cabinet Making Centers,* New York, November 15–17, 1973, lot 915. For more on chairs from the Guilford-Saybrook area, see Patricia E. Kane, *Furniture of the New Haven Colony: The Seventeenth-Century Style* (New Haven, Conn.: New Haven Colony Historical Society, 1973), pp. 68–77. Blackburn and Piwonka, *Remembrance of Patria,* p. 191. Esther Singleton, *Furniture of Our Forefathers* (1900; reprint, Garden City, N. Y.: Doubleday, Page & Co., 1919), p. 252. A cradle with grisaille decoration (Blackburn and Piwonka, *Rememberance of Patria,* pp. 270-71, fig. 291) has finials similar to those on the related high chairs and side chairs (figs. 27–29). The festoons and figures on the cradle appear to be by the same hand that decorated two *kasten* (Joseph T. Butler, *Sleepy Hollow Restorations: A Cross-Section of the Collection* [Tarrytown, N. Y.: Sleepy Hollow Press, 1983], p. 73, no. 81; and Kenny et. al., *American Kasten,* p. 31). Although the board construction and somewhat naïve decoration of these pieces has led some scholars to suggest that they may have been made in the Albany region, the finials on the cradle and grisaille scheme on all three objects have parallels in New York City work. If the cradle was made in Albany rather than New York City, its finials may have been derived from those on early seating forms like the high chairs brought by

Sanders and the Ten Eycks. The author thanks Frances Safford and Peter Kenny for their thoughts on the grisaille decorated pieces.

24. Leigh French Jr., *Colonial Interiors: The Colonial and Early Federal Periods, First Series* (New York: Bonanza Books, 1923), pl. 13.

25. Neil D. Kamil's "Hidden in Plain Sight," pp. 223–25 illustrates chairs like those shown in figs. 33 and 34 and discusses their relationship to French turning and terminology. The chair shown in fig. 33 descended in the Pruyn family of Albany and is illustrated in Singleton, *Furniture of Our Forefathers,* p. 241. The Monmouth County Historical Society owns an armchair with a similar splat but lacking the spindles and pad feet.

26. For more on marks on New York furniture, see Roderic Blackburn, "Branded and Stamped New York Furniture" *Antiques* 119, no. 5 (May 1981): 1130–45. Nutting, *Furniture Treasury,* no. 2085. The chair illustrated in fig. 40 sold at auction in 1948 (Parke-Bernet Galleries, *Early Pennsylvania and Other Colonial Furniture,* New York, March 20, 1948, lot 185). Anderson Art Galleries, *Francis P. Garvan Collection,* New York, January 8–10, 1931, lot 107.

Figure 1 Desk-and-bookcase associated with John Goddard, Newport, Rhode Island, ca. 1761. Mahogany with maple, poplar, red cedar, white pine, and yellow poplar. H. 96½", W. 45¹³⁄₁₆", D. 26". (Courtesy, Museum of Art, Rhode Island School of Design; photo, Gavin Ashworth.)

Brock Jobe

The Lisle Desk-and-
Bookcase: A Rhode
Island Icon

▼ N O   A M E R I C A N   F U R N I T U R E   form has received more attention than the blockfront desk-and-bookcase with carved shells on the fallboard and bookcase doors (see fig. 1). As early as 1913, Luke Vincent Lockwood proclaimed that such examples "are probably as fine pieces of cabinet work as are found in the country." In *Colonial Furniture in America,* Lockwood offered the first substantive information on these distinctive objects, linking them to Rhode Island and suggesting a maker—Newport cabinetmaker John Goddard (1724–1785). Subsequent scholars have debated the accuracy of Lockwood's attributions to Goddard but remained steadfast in their admiration of the form. Collectors have long shared these sentiments. A six-shell, blockfront desk-and-bookcase commissioned by Nicholas Brown (fig. 13) holds the record for American furniture at auction.[1]

Today eleven examples of the form are known. Although all were once attributed to Newport, furniture scholars Wendy Cooper and Tara Gleason have convincingly tied two pieces to Providence. The remaining nine are the focus of this article. Because of its notable history and documentation, the desk-and-bookcase illustrated in figure 1 is a cornerstone for understanding the entire group. It descended in the Potter family of Kingston, and belonged throughout the late nineteenth century to the prominent Rhode Island antiquarian Thomas Mawney Potter (1814–1890). Potter's nephew later sold the piece to Arthur Lisle, who in 1927 loaned it to an exhibition at the Rhode Island School of Design.[2]

The show's curator, architect Norman Isham, delighted in the discovery of an inscription scratched into a small drawer behind the prospect door of the desk interior. According to Isham, the inscription stated: "Made by John Goddard 1761 and repaired by Thomas Goddard in 1813." In his mind, there was no reason to doubt the statement. "It was probably written," noted Isham, "by Mr. Potter at the time of the repairs by Thomas Goddard. If so, it may be taken as the truth." Two years later, in 1929, the editor of *Antiques* agreed that the inscription was authentic but credited authorship to Thomas Goddard rather than the owner. Careful examination of the interior drawers substantiates this claim. Three inscriptions, not one, appear— all in the same hand. On the backs of both the top and middle drawers are the words noted by Isham (fig. 4). But on the right side of the middle drawer is a far longer inscription: "Made by John Goddard 1761 and repaired / by Thomas Goddard his Son 1813 / Hea[l]th Officer of the Town of / Newport Appointed by the / Honr Town Council Members / Nicholas Taylor Esqr & my son T Topham" (fig. 5). The name T. Topham refers to

Figure 2 Detail of the bookcase interior of the desk-and-bookcase illustrated in fig. 1. (Photo, Gavin Ashworth.)

Figure 3 Detail of the desk interior of the desk-and-bookcase illustrated in fig. 1. (Photo, Gavin Ashworth.)

Figure 4 Infrared photograph of the inscription on the back of a drawer in the writing compartment of the desk-and-bookcase illustrated in fig. 1. (Courtesy, Society for the Preservation of New England Antiquities.)

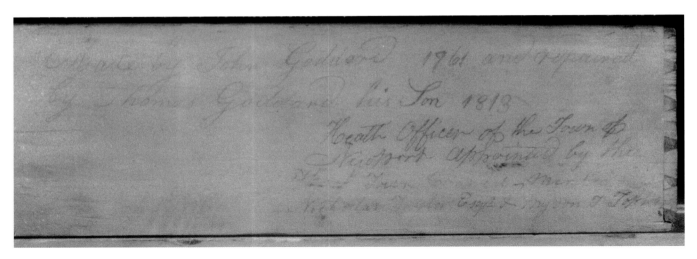

Figure 5 Infrared photograph of the inscription on the side of a drawer in the writing compartment of the desk-and-bookcase illustrated in fig. 1. (Courtesy, Society for the Preservation of New England Antiquities.)

Thomas Goddard's son-in-law Theophilus Topham who married Susan Goddard. Thomas Goddard's handwriting on documents dating from the 1820s resembles that on the desk, further confirming Thomas' authorship of the inscription. A reputable artisan in his own right, Thomas clearly took pride in his father's accomplishment and sought to perpetuate its record for posterity.[3]

John Goddard's forty-year career in cabinetmaking was one of the most successful in Newport. It began in the late 1730s, when his father, Quaker housewright Daniel Goddard, presumably apprenticed John and his brother James to joiner Job Townsend. The two young tradesmen later married Job's daughters, Hannah and Susannah, thus laying the groundwork for a cabinetmaking dynasty. John Goddard's earliest known work, a plain slant-front desk, bears the label "Made by John Goddard of Newport on Rhoad Island in New England in the year of our Lord 1745." The detailed reference to location suggests that Goddard intended the piece for export. Like his master, Goddard constructed standard desks with modest decoration for export to towns along the Atlantic coast. The true measure of his success, however, lay with his local clientele. Goddard's customers consisted of neighboring Quakers and prominent merchants, seamen, and governmental officials across the colony. The list of known patrons reads like a *Who's Who* of colonial Rhode Island: Governors Stephen Hopkins and Gideon Wanton, ship captain Anthony Low, and merchants John Banister, Aaron Lopez, Thomas Robinson, Jabez Bowen, and the Brown brothers—Nicholas, Joseph, John, and Moses—of Providence. Goddard's correspondence with the Brown family documents his production of such fashionable goods as a "Chest on Chest of Drawers & Sweld. front which are Costly as well as ornimental." Two desks probably made by Goddard in the early 1750s attest to his maturing skills, while an array of documented tables—side, tea, dining, and tilt-top—offer further proof of his keen sense of design.[4]

Such proficiency brought with it a degree of affluence. Tax records suggest that Goddard was Newport's wealthiest cabinetmaker throughout the 1750s and 1760s and second only to his cousin John Townsend in the 1770s. Like other craftsmen, he sometimes engaged in commercial ventures and became part owner of several vessels; however, cabinetmaking provided the bulk of his income throughout his long career. Ultimately his fortunes did decline, as did those of his neighbors, when British troops occupied Newport during the Revolution. At his death in 1785, he left an insolvent estate. Yet signs of his prosperity were still evident. His home on the waterfront along Easton's Point, adjacent to the present Robinson House, was a commodious structure, and behind it stood both a shop and small wharf (fig. 6)—the latter an ideal location to unload cargos of lumber or package furniture for export. The shop was, by New England standards, a large one. It contained five workbenches and a vast array of tools. His own sons manned

Figure 6 Jonas Bergner, John Goddard's house and shop, Newport, Rhode Island, before 1870. Watercolor on paper. (Courtesy, Newport Historical Society.)

several of these benches at various times. At least four of his and Hannah's sixteen children learned the trade of cabinetmaking. In his will, he left the shop and its contents to his sons Stephen and Thomas with the stipulation that they should complete the unfinished work for the benefit of their mother. John's workforce also included at least one slave (his cousin, John Townsend, had three slaves working with him in 1774), but he did not maintain an extensive network of journeymen like some Newport cabinet-

Figure 8 Detail of the interior of the desk-and-bookcase illustrated in fig. 7.

makers such as John Cahoone. Goddard and his Quaker kinsmen seem to have tightly controlled their craft environment, thus ensuring consistency in quality and design.[5]

Thomas Goddard (1765–1858) took over his father's shop and for many years worked in partnership with his brother Stephen. A respected tradesman and staunch Federalist, Thomas served in a number of town offices including health officer of the port, the role noted in his inscription. "He was an erect, fine-looking man, over six feet tall, and a man of great dignity," noted a great-grandson. Thomas outlived all of his siblings and, as the last of a generation, came into possession of many family items. Only one of these heirlooms can be identified today, but its presence alone offers intriguing insights. According to a late nineteenth-century reminiscence of the colonial Newport furniture trade, "John Goddard . . . adhered closely to the styles of Sir William Chambers, the brothers Adam, and Chippendale. . . . Goddard's copy of Chippendale's quarto volume of designs is now owned by a cabinet-maker in Newport." Although exaggerating Goddard's reliance on English design, the account is accurate in its reference to Thomas Chippendale's *The Gentleman and Cabinet-Maker's Director.* This particular volume (Museum of Fine Arts, Boston) bears Thomas Goddard's signature and presumably passed from John to his son. The elder Goddard apparently knew of English rococo styles but chose to ignore them. Instead, he and his counterparts throughout Newport developed distinctive versions of colonial design that mixed English, French, Boston, and local motifs in innovative ways.[6]

The most expensive objects produced by Newport cabinetmakers were desk-and-bookcases. The form served many purposes: a combination library, office, safe, and closet providing space for books, business accounts, and writing supplies, a surface for reading or writing, small lockable drawers for currency, jewelry, and other valuables, and larger drawers within the lower case for clothing or bedding. Desk-and-bookcases like the Lisle example (fig. 1) also reflected the wealth and status of their owners and marked them as educated and genteel men and women. Although many Newport cabinetmakers made the form, they did so infrequently. Between 1762 and 1778, Job Townsend, Jr. produced no more than six desk-and-bookcases, Benjamin Baker recorded the sale of a single example in surviving accounts during the 1760s and 1770s, and John Cahoone listed only two in the ledger he kept from 1749 to 1760. The cost of these forms exceeded the reach of all but the richest customers. Cahoone charged £200, Baker £300, and Townsend from £200 to £330. By comparison, a mahogany desk averaged about £85 and walnut or maple versions far less. Newport probate inventories for the years 1779 to 1790 list only twelve desk-and-bookcases. The town's cabinetmakers clearly made additional examples for export, but local patrons probably commissioned no more than sixty desk-and-bookcases during the entire second half of the eighteenth century. Within this small group, block-front forms with carved shells must have constituted only a small fraction of the total. The nine surviving examples could well represent the majority of those produced during this period. Fire, shipwrecks, and war undoubtedly accounted for some loss; however, the fact that these ornate forms were prized by their original owners and esteemed as family heirlooms encouraged their survival.[7]

At least fifteen Newport craftsmen were capable of producing this level of work during the 1760s. Among the Goddards and Townsends alone are nine candidates: John Goddard and his son Daniel (b. 1747); Job Townsend (1699–1765); Job Townsend, Jr. (1726–1778); the younger Job's brothers,

Figure 9 Desk-and-bookcase, Newport, Rhode Island, 1755–1770. Mahogany with chestnut, yellow poplar, red cedar, and white pine. H. 101¾", W. 43 ⅛", D. 26". (Courtesy, Museum of Fine Arts, Boston.)

Figure 10 Drawing showing detail of the interior of the desk-and-bookcase illustrated in fig. 9. (Artwork, Wynne Patterson.)

Edmund (1736–1810) and Thomas (1742–1827); Christopher Townsend (1701–1787); and Christopher's sons John Townsend (1733–1809) and Jonathan (1745–1773). In addition, another half dozen artisans had shops on Easton's Point late in the colonial era. A mid-nineteenth-century reminiscence of Newport noted that "the stores of David Huntington and Benjamin Baker were also on the Point; both these men were extensively engaged in manufacturing furniture, which they shipped to New York and the West Indies." Lesser known cabinetmakers included Benjamin Peabody, Constant Bailey, Walter Nichols, and Timothy Waterhouse. Such a concentration of cabinetmakers handicaps efforts to tie specific pieces to their makers. Collaboration by craftsmen within this group further complicates the issue of authorship. Job Townsend, Jr. engaged his brother Edmund to help make a "Large Mohogony Desk" for Nicholas Anderrese in 1767. Daniel Goddard signed the back of a drawer in a bureau table "Daniel Goddard His Draugh," suggesting that he designed the piece but may have worked with others to construct it. With numerous shops crowded into a small neighborhood and their owners often linked by kinship, joint productions clearly occurred.[8]

Four of the nine surviving shell-carved desk-and-bookcases have credible histories of ownership but lack documentation to connect original owners to specific makers. The first of the four (figs. 7, 8) belonged to Lodowick Updike II (1725–1804), a wealthy landowner along the western shore of Narragansett Bay in Rhode Island. A second desk-and-bookcase (figs. 9, 10) resided in the same area during the late eighteenth century. An early owner, James Helme, left this example to Elisha Reynolds Potter of South Kingstown, who in 1835 bequeathed it to his son Thomas Mawney Potter, one of Rhode Island's most noted antiquarians. By about 1870 Thomas Mawney Potter had purchased the Goddard desk-and-bookcase (fig. 1) as well, and for the next twenty years both examples stood in the Red House, Potter's home in Kingston. The last two examples descended in the Brown family of Providence, Rhode Island. According to family tradition, each of the four Brown brothers—Nicholas (1729–1791), Joseph (1733–1785), John (1736–1803), and Moses (1738–1836)—owned a version of this grand form. John's desk-and-bookcase descended in his family until sold in 1918 to collector Francis P. Garvan, who later gave it to Yale University (figs. 11, 12). Nicholas Brown's piece remained in his family for five generations (figs. 13, 14).[9]

The remaining four desk-and-bookcases have incomplete histories. Noted collector and antique dealer Charles Pendleton acquired one in the 1880s (figs. 15, 16, 17), which he later bequeathed, along with his entire collection, to the Rhode Island School of Design. His friend Richard Canfield, a notorious gambler and bon vivant, purchased another (figs. 18, 19), possibly in Providence, at about the same time. Canfield's attorney, furniture historian Luke Vincent Lockwood, orchestrated the sale of this piece to the Metropolitan Museum of Art in 1915. A third example (figs. 20, 21) turned up in Providence early in the twentieth century and was acquired by banker and art collector Marsden J. Perry. After his death, the piece was sold to collector Maxim Karolik, who presented it to the Museum of Fine Arts,

Figure 11 Desk-and-bookcase, Newport, Rhode Island, 1765–1785. Mahogany with cherry, chestnut, white pine, and yellow poplar. H. 106¾", W. 44¾", D. 24 ⅞". (Courtesy, Yale University Art Gallery, Mabel Brady Garvan Collection.)

Figure 12 Detail of the interior of the desk-and-bookcase illustrated in fig. 11.

Figure 13 Desk-and-bookcase, Newport, Rhode Island, 1765–1785. Mahogany with cherry, chestnut, and white pine. H. 113", W. 42½", D. 25". (Courtesy, Christie's.)

Figure 14 Detail of the interior of the desk-and-bookcase illustrated in fig. 13. (Courtesy, Israel Sack, Inc.)

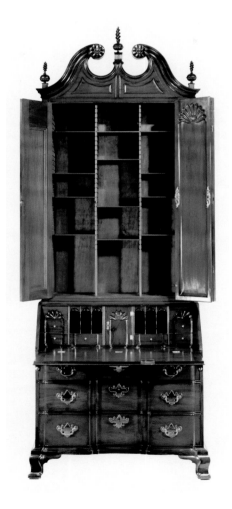

Figure 15 Desk-and-bookcase, Newport, Rhode Island, 1760–1770. Mahogany with maple, red cedar, white pine, and yellow poplar. H. 101", W. 45½", D. 27". (Courtesy, Museum of Art, Rhode Island School of Design; photo, Gavin Ashworth.)

Figure 16 Detail of the bookcase interior of the desk-and-bookcase illustrated in fig. 15. (Photo, Gavin Ashworth.)

Figure 17 Detail of the desk interior of the desk-and-bookcase illustrated in fig. 15. (Photo, Gavin Ashworth.)

Boston, in 1939. A final desk-and-bookcase (figs. 22–24) surfaced in London in the 1930s and subsequently returned to America twenty years later. In 1952 Miss Ima Hogg acquired the piece for her home, Bayou Bend, now a part of the Museum of Fine Arts, Houston.[10]

The design of these nine examples is remarkably consistent. At first glance, all appear to have originated in the same cabinet shop (see figs. 1–3). A blocked lower case of three drawers rests on a deep base molding and ogee bracket feet with the characteristic Newport cusp. The blocked panels on the drawer fronts continue upward onto the fallboard, terminating in large sculptural shells decorated with fluted centers. The blocking and shells on the bookcase echo that on the desk. Quarter-columns edge the corners of the case on all but one example. At the top, matching panels face the ogee pediment and, on some versions, they are enhanced with blocking. In addition, on five of the nine bookcases, the pediment is fully enclosed by a recessed panel behind the central opening and a full hood. Twisted "flame" finials complete the form. Inside the desk, the interior follows a standard Newport pattern with a shell-carved prospect door flanked by three pigeonholes with valance drawers above and blocked drawers below and to the side. On six of the desk-and-bookcases, a sliding panel in the writing surface allows access to the top drawer—a holdover from wells found on earlier desks. The overall formula is ornamental but integrated. The eye flows easily from the feet to the finials, drawn upward by the dramatic verticals created by the blocking and shells.[11]

Figure 18 Desk-and-bookcase, Newport, Rhode Island, 1760–1770. Mahogany with cherry, chestnut, red cedar, white pine, yellow pine, and yellow poplar. H. 99⅛", W. 44⅝", D. 25½". (Courtesy, Metropolitan Museum of Art, Rogers Fund, 1915.)

Figure 19 Detail of the interior of the desk-and-bookcase illustrated in fig. 18.

Figure 20 Desk-and-bookcase, Newport, Rhode Island, 1765–1785. Mahogany with cherry, chestnut, maple, white pine, and yellow poplar. H. 99", W. 39⅞", D. 23⅝". (Courtesy, Museum of Fine Arts, Boston, M. and M. Karolik Collection.)

Figure 21 Detail of the interior of the desk-and-bookcase illustrated in fig. 20.

Figure 22 Desk-and-bookcase, Newport, Rhode Island, 1755–1770. Mahogany with cedrela, chestnut, maple, poplar, red cedar, white pine, and yellow poplar. H. 99¾", W. 44½", D. 25½". (Courtesy, Museum of Fine Arts, Houston; Bayou Bend Collection, gift of Miss Ima Hogg.)

Figure 23 Detail of the bookcase interior of the desk-and-bookcase illustrated in fig. 22.

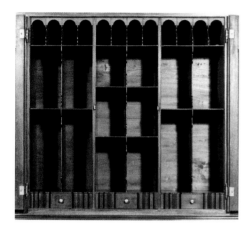

Figure 24 Detail of the desk interior of the desk-and-bookcase illustrated in fig. 22.

Figure 25 Drawing showing the construction of the lower case of the desk-and-bookcase illustrated in fig. 1. Adapted from Jeffrey P. Greene, *American Furniture of the 18th Century*. (Courtesy, Taunton Press).

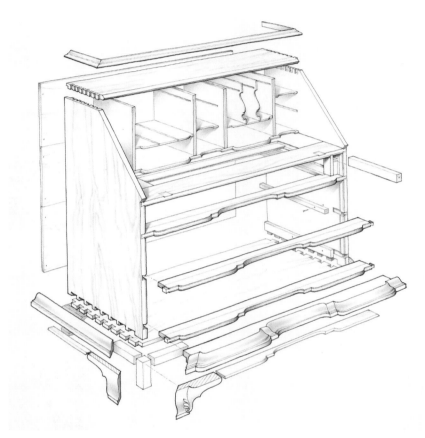

Within the case, the construction of each example also appears remarkably uniform (see fig. 25). Fine dovetails bind the top and bottom of the desk section to the sides. Base moldings are glued and nailed to the case; the front bracket feet are mitered at the corners and glued to the underside of the base moldings; and a vertical stump flanked by two horizontal blocks reinforces each foot (see fig. 26). At the back, the bracket foot is braced by a rear element with a curving diagonal outline. Again, a vertical stump and horizontal blocks support the foot. In addition, an applied strip with a beaded outer edge is sometimes nailed to the base molding between the feet.[12]

Shallow drawer dividers are dovetailed to the sides of the case (see fig. 27), and the joints are exposed rather than being covered by a thick strip of veneer as is often the case in Boston or Salem furniture. The dividers and narrow strips of wood nailed to the case sides support the drawers. The lowest divider hangs almost an inch above the case bottom—a practice that also varies from Massachusetts custom, which eliminates this divider and places the lowest drawer directly on the bottom of the case. Thin blocks nailed to the case sides at the back serve as drawer stops. The waist molding is glued and nailed to the top of the desk section; on many Newport high chests and chests-on-chests, the waist molding is attached to the upper case.[13]

The hinged fallboard opens onto two narrow supports that slide out at the upper corners of the case. Occasionally the top edge of the support is gouged to accommodate the shell on the fallboard. The corners of the top drawer are notched to fit around the supports, a standard Newport trait. As a result, the drawer front overlaps the sides, and the two parts are joined in a distinctive manner. Each drawer side is fastened to the front with a vertical sliding dovetail, rather than the typical column of dovetails. The lower two drawers, however, follow the standard method. The well within the interior also conforms to established Newport practice. Exposed dovetails secure the front board of the writing surface. Behind this surface,

Figure 26 Detail of the foot construction of the desk-and-bookcase illustrated in fig. 1. (Photo, Gavin Ashworth.)

Figure 27 Detail of the lower case interior of the desk-and-bookcase illustrated in fig. 1. (Photo, Gavin Ashworth.)

Figure 28 Detail of the dovetail joints for a valance drawer and a larger drawer in the desk interior of the desk-and-bookcase illustrated in fig. 1.

six-inch-wide boards extend to the back of the case and form a frame for the well. These boards taper at the back and rest on a brace that fits into mortises in the case sides. The cover for the well slides in slots cut in the frame.

The drawers in the desk interior are assembled in typical Newport fashion (see fig. 3). Both the small valance drawers above the pigeonholes and the larger drawers flanking the pigeonholes are joined at the corners with fine dovetails (fig. 28). The drawer bottoms are glued into the rabbeted edges of the sides and back. But at the front, the sides are set into a groove on the valance drawers and glued to a rabbet on the other drawers. The recessed arch on each valance drawer appears to have been made with a jig, possibly a double-edged scratch stock mounted on an arbor. Half of a scribed "X" denoting the center of the drawer front is usually visible on the back (see fig. 29).

The large exterior drawer fronts are cut from solid mahogany boards and frequently backed by a thin block of mahogany or cedrela behind the concave section (see fig. 30). This allowed the maker to use thinner stock for the front and still provide room for a lock. The dovetailing at the corners of the drawers is precise, but not as fine as some Newport work. The drawer bottoms are typically made of three or four butt-jointed and glued boards with the grain oriented front to back. Each bottom is nailed to the rabbeted edge of the front and flush edge of the sides and back. Runners are fastened along the edges of the bottom. The drawer sides are rounded along the top edge, and the back is cut with a slight chamfer.

The upper case is essentially a dovetailed box with an attached cap (see fig. 31). Wedge-shaped glue blocks secure the pediment façade, pediment back, and cornice molding to the top of the case; the hood, usually thin white pine or yellow poplar boards, is nailed to the upper edges of the pediment to strengthen the unit and enclose it. Quarter-columns at the corners on all but one example create pockets within the sides of the case. These pockets, as well as the top and bottom of the bookcase, are covered by slender boards that form a tight liner for the interior. At the back of the case, three or four lap-jointed vertical boards are nailed to the rabbeted edges of the top and sides. The upper case typically sits on support blocks mounted on top of the desk.[14]

The construction of the desk fallboard and bookcase doors (see fig. 32) follows a consistent pattern on all nine desk-and-bookcases. Each fallboard is comprised of a single board with cleated ends. The convex blocking and convex shells are glued to the front, and the concave shell is carved in relief. In some cases, the blocking is curved to fit neatly against the lower edge of the shell. On the Lisle desk-and-bookcase (fig. 1) and three other examples, however, the blocking and shell are squared off and butt-jointed. The doors also follow the same pattern. The center door is made of a solid board carved with recessed blocking and a relief-carved shell. Each outer door consists of a joined frame, in which the rails are tenoned through the stiles. The blocked panel is glued to the surface of the frame, and that joint is reinforced by an ogee molding set within the edges of the frame. The shell is glued to the upper rail. Unlike the fallboard where two methods are used to join the

Figure 29 Detail of the rear surface of a valance drawer in the desk interior of the desk-and-bookcase illustrated in fig. 1.

Figure 30 Detail of an applied block on the rear surface of an exterior drawer front of the desk-and-bookcase illustrated in fig. 1.

Figure 31 Drawing showing the construction of the upper case of the desk-and-bookcase illustrated in fig. 1. Adapted from Jeffrey P. Greene, *American Furniture of the 18th Century.* (Courtesy, Taunton Press.)

blocking and the shell, the decoration on the doors required only one technique. The blocking always slips tightly against the curved lower edge of the shell. If the two were butt-jointed, the vertical-grained panel and horizontal-grained shell would be visually disturbing. By fitting the panel tightly against the carving of the shell, the juncture is less obvious.[15]

With so many similarities in design and construction among the nine block and shell desk-and-bookcases, it is tempting to attribute them to a single maker. Closer scrutiny, however, suggests that they are the products of at least four different shops. Three desk-and-bookcases (figs. 11–14, 20–21) appear to be from the same shop that produced an unusual clothes press, chest-on-chest (both in the collection of the Chipstone Foundation), and bureau table. All six objects share many distinctive traits. The desk-and-bookcases have open bonnets with rosettes decorated with two rows of stylized petals and plain bookcase interiors with adjustable shelves. All of the other examples have fixed shelves and adjustable partitions. The finials on the three desk-and-bookcases also have deeply cut twisted flames, rather than shallow ones. On the bookcase doors, the quarter-columns are framed

Figure 32 Drawing showing the construction of the desk fallboard and bookcase door of the desk-and-bookcase illustrated in fig. 1. Adapted from Jeffrey P. Greene, *American Furniture of the 18th Century.* (Courtesy, Taunton Press.)

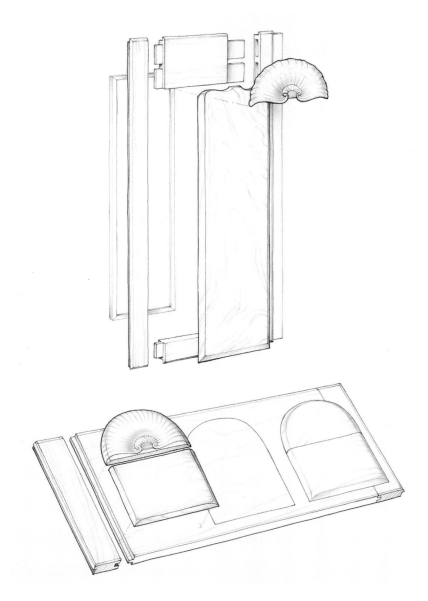

Figure 33 Detail of a quarter-column on the desk-and-bookcase illustrated in fig. 11.

at the top and bottom with a peculiar sequence of double-beaded turnings (fig. 33). In addition, two of the pieces in this subgroup have roughly carved triangular insets at the upper corners of each door, suggesting that the area may have been gilded or covered with a brass spandrel. The carved shells on the desk and doors are also readily distinguishable from those on the other block and shell pieces; the centers of the shells are broader and more crowded with flutes (fig. 34).[16]

The writing compartments of the three desk-and-bookcases have valance drawers with cherry linings and blocked and shell-carved drawers with white pine frames, backs, and bottoms. The makers of the other pieces used a single wood—usually red cedar or mahogany— for all the interior drawers. All of the valance drawers of the three desk-and-bookcases have one dovetail at each corner, whereas those of the other examples often have two

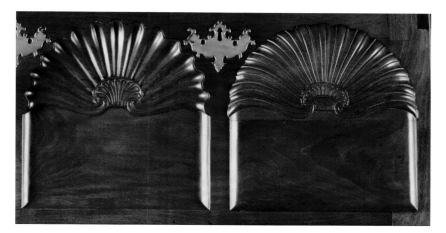

Figure 35 Detail of the interior of the lower case of the desk-and-book-case illustrated in fig. 11.

Figure 36 Detail of the carved shells on the fall-board of the desk-and-bookcase illustrated in fig. 1. (Photo, Gavin Ashworth.)

small dovetails. None of the writing compartments of the desk-and-book-cases in this subgroup have wells, but two have writing slides and two have full dustboards in the lower case (fig. 35)—features rarely seen on Newport furniture. The fallboard supports on all three pieces are cherry faced with mahogany, and the partition separating each support from the top drawer extends to the back of the case. The other desk-and-bookcases have mahogany supports and a shallow partition between the supports and drawer. Finally, the exterior drawers on all of the case pieces in the subgroup differ from the norm. Their bottom boards are chestnut with the grain run-ning side-to-side rather than pine or yellow poplar with the grain oriented front-to-back. The chestnut boards are set into grooves in the front and sides and nailed to the back. Although this technique is common in New England furniture of the late eighteenth century, it differs noticeably from the drawer construction of the other desk-and-bookcases.[17]

Within this small cluster of six related pieces, four have histories in Provi-dence. John and Nicholas Brown commissioned the desk-and-bookcases illustrated in figures 11–14, and Providence collector Marsden Perry owned

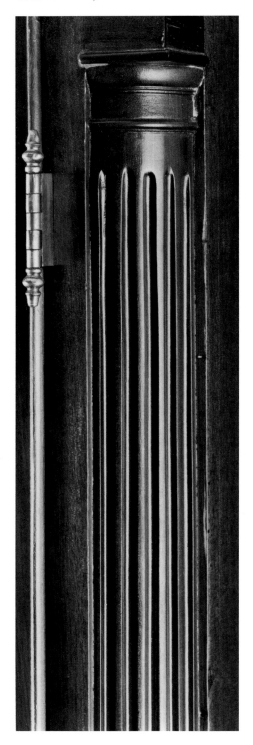

Figure 37 Detail of the pediment, doors, and a finial on the desk-and-bookcase illustrated in fig. 1.

Figure 38 Detail of a quarter-column on the desk-and-bookcase illustrated in fig. 1. (Photo, Gavin Ashworth.)

the other example (figs. 20, 21). The bureau table in this subgroup descended in the Bowen family, and the chest-on-chest reputedly belonged to the Brown brothers' cousin Sarah Brown and her husband Jabez Bowen. Members of the Brown and Bowen families patronized both Newport and Providence craftsmen. In 1763, John Goddard made a tea table and common chairs for Jabez Bowen and a bureau table for Moses Brown. After receiving an order for a case of drawers from Bowen, Goddard wrote Moses Brown "there is a sort which is called a Chest on Chest of Drawers & Sweld. Front which are Costly as well as ornimental. thou'l Plese to let me know friend Bowens minde that I may Conduct accordingly." Newport furniture of this type probably served as a design source for Providence artisans who made similar forms for the Browns, Bowens, and other prestigious local families.

Although it is tempting to speculate that the chest-on-chest mentioned in Goddard's letter is the one that reputedly belonged to the Bowens, there is insufficient evidence to support that conclusion. If this piece and the three related desk-and-bookcases could be attributed to Goddard, it would refute the inscription on the Lisle desk-and-bookcase. The construction of the Lisle piece and the furniture in the subgroup that includes the chest-on-chest is too different to ascribe these objects to the same maker.[18]

In many respects, the Lisle desk-and-bookcase (fig. 1) stands alone in the group. It is the only piece that has shells with diapering in the center (fig. 36), and its unique finials have an inverted urn with reeding (fig. 37) rather than a ball-shaped urn with fluting. Although the authenticity of these finials has been questioned, x-radiography indicates that they are original and unaltered. The quarter-columns on the Lisle piece also differ from those on the other desk-and-bookcases in having a one-half-inch gap separating the rounded ends of the fluting from the capital (fig. 38). Typically the end of the fluting extends to the capital (see fig. 43). The interior of the

Figure 39 Detail of a removable side panel in the bookcase interior of the desk-and-bookcase illustrated in fig. 1.

Figure 40 Detail of the front foot of the desk-and-bookcase illustrated in fig. 1. (Photo, Gavin Ashworth.)

bookcase has removable side panels secured with spring latches. These latches, which were discovered during conservation in 1985 (fig. 39), do not occur on any other piece in the group. Similarly, the feet are singular in shape and ornament (fig. 40). A few Newport case pieces with carved feet are known, but none have leaves drawn and modeled like those on the Lisle desk-and-bookcase.[19]

Two desk-and-bookcases (figs. 7, 15) are visually quite similar to the Lisle example, but they appear to have originated in a different shop or are collaborative products involving the maker of the Lisle piece and another cabinetmaker. The shells and quarter-columns present the most noticeable variations. On the desk-and-bookcases illustrated in figures 7 and 15, the fluted centers of the shells nearly match (figs. 41, 42) and the quarter-columns have identical bases and capitals that project beyond the corner post of the case (see fig. 43). The quarter-columns on the desk-and-bookcase shown in figure 15 are slightly larger and have seven flutes rather than five.[20]

The bookcase sections of the pieces in this small subgroup (figs. 7, 8, 15, 16) also have similar interiors, although the one shown in figures 7 and 8 has lost its sliding partitions, which probably resembled those on the other example. In their original configuration, both interiors echoed that of the Lisle bookcase (figs. 44, 45). The secondary woods in all three bookcases are also the same: red cedar for the interior linings and case back; yellow poplar for the pediment back and hood; and maple for the top and bottom of the case. Most Newport cabinetmakers would have used chestnut in one or more of these positions.

The panels lining the sides of all three bookcase sections slid into grooves (see fig. 39). On the bookcase illustrated in figures 7 and 8 and the Lisle example, the panels are still removable. The partitions of the Lisle bookcase and the example shown in figure 15 are also removable and have notched numbers on their top edge. On the latter example, the partitions are numbered vertically in columns and then horizontally. Thus, the top left partition has a single notch, the middle left has two notches, and so forth. On the Lisle bookcase, however, the partitions are numbered horizontally along the top row, then the middle row, and finally the bottom. The technique of cutting the notches with a chisel is consistent, but the application varies. Clearly the makers of both pieces were familiar with each other's work.

The desk sections of the three pieces are also related (figs. 1, 3, 7, 8, 15, 17). In every case, the lower edge of the convex shells on the lid is squared off and butts against the blocking (figs. 41, 42); on all but one of the other six desk-and-bookcases, the blocking is shaped to fit neatly against the scalloped lower edge of the shell (see fig. 34). The overall construction of each desk—secondary woods, dovetailing of the case, and fabrication of the dividers, drawer supports, and feet—is similar. Unfortunately the desk-and-bookcase illustrated in figure 7 has replaced drawer linings and feet, but its intact structural features match those of the Lisle (fig. 1) and Pendleton (fig. 15) examples and confirms its relationship to them. The dovetails on the exterior drawers of the Lisle and Pendleton desk-and-bookcases differ only

Figure 41 Detail of the carved shells on the fallboard of the desk-and-bookcase illustrated in fig. 7.

Figure 42 Detail of the carved shells on the fallboard of the desk-and-bookcase illustrated in fig. 15. (Photo, Gavin Ashworth.)

Figure 43 Detail of a quarter-column on the desk-and-bookcase illustrated in fig. 15. (Photo, Gavin Ashworth.)

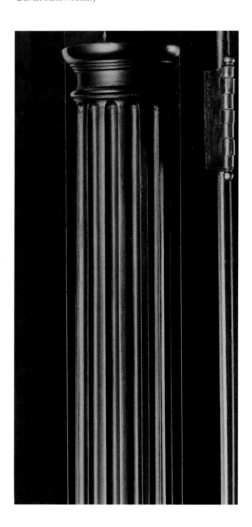

slightly (figs. 46, 47). The pattern and angles of the pins and tails match, but the joints on the Lisle drawers are coarser and have extended saw kerfs. Such comparisons reinforce the theory that the makers of these pieces were associated in some way.

The last three desk-and-bookcases (figs. 9, 10, 18, 19, 22–24) share several features, and the one illustrated in figure 22 is the most ornate in the group. It has pigeonholes with arched valances, ogee-shaped drawer fronts (fig. 23), and carved shells capped with incised arches—details that occur on Newport desk-and-bookcase interiors from the 1750s. The desk-and-bookcase shown in figures 18 and 19 lacks these early features, but is otherwise similar. It and the example illustrated in figure 22 have fixed bookcase partitions with identical profiles (which also resemble the profiles of the partitions in the desk sections) and a single bead on the edge. In contrast, the partitions in the Lisle (fig. 2) and Pendleton (fig. 16) bookcases have double-beaded edges and are removable like those on other pieces in the group. The design of the bookcase interiors illustrated in figures 19 and 23 is also related.[21]

Several features in the desk sections of these two objects (figs. 18, 22) reinforce the connection between them. Most of their secondary woods are the same, and the use of true poplar (also called cottonwood or aspen) for the exterior drawer sides and chestnut for the drawer dividers is distinctive. The applied blocking on the fallboards is scalloped to fit neatly against the lower

Figure 44 Detail of the bookcase interior of the desk-and-bookcase illustrated in fig. 1. (Photo, Gavin Ashworth.)

edge of the convex shells, and the design, modeling, and finishing of the carving is virtually identical. Both sets of applied shells have sixteen large lobes and nine small petals in the center. In addition, the center petal in each shell is convex whereas the others are fluted. The feet of the two desk sec-

Figure 47 Detail of the dove-tailed joint for an exterior drawer of the desk-and-book-case illustrated in fig. 15.

Figure 46 Detail of the dovetailed joint for an exterior drawer of the desk-and-bookcase illustrated in fig. 1.

tions are also similar. The scroll along the inside edge of each front face lacks the pronounced tip seen on feet of the other desk-and-bookcases in the group. These distinctive features are signatures of a particular shop—one that at this point remains unidentified.

Although clearly related to the desk-and-bookcases illustrated in figures 18 and 22, the last example in this study (figs. 9, 10) is the most unusual. It lacks quarter-columns on the bookcase section and has carved shells with open centers in the writing compartment, feet with a reverse-curved scroll beneath the characteristic Newport cusp, and only one finial. Other differences are less obvious. The convex blocking on the drawer fronts and front strip of base molding is applied rather than cut from the solid as on every other desk-and-bookcase in the group. Furthermore, deep gouge cuts outline the shells on the doors and fallboard, a detail far more prominent on this example than on any other from the group. Such idiosyncrasies suggest that the maker had little familiarity with the form at the time he made this desk-and-bookcase and that, when constructing the piece, he had to develop his own solutions for the blocking and shell carving.[22]

Based on its pediment design, the desk-and-bookcase shown in figure 9 appears to be an early example by the maker of the Lisle piece (fig. 1). Both objects have tympana with book-matched panels rather than the stepped ones found on other bookcases in the group. Other structural features, however, link the desk-and-bookcase illustrated in figure 9 with the examples shown in figures 18 and 22. Two of these pieces (figs. 9, 18) have chalk inscriptions in the same florid script on the backs of their exterior drawers (numerals in one case, letters in another) and shells with stop-fluted centers on their bookcase doors. Although these shared details suggest that all three pieces originated in the same shop, they fail to provide conclusive proof.

None of the desk-and-bookcases in this survey has survived in pristine condition. The inscriptions on the Lisle piece refer to three separate restoration campaigns including one in 1879 when the desk was "scraped & varnishd." Another example (fig. 7) has replaced feet, new exterior drawer linings, waist moldings, and finials and lacks its original bookcase partitions. The feet of nearly every desk-and-bookcase in the group have been removed at least once for repair, and the hardware on several of these objects has been replaced. In addition, all of these pieces have been cleaned on several occasions, and most currently have twentieth-century shellac finishes. The most conspicuous alterations occurred on the desk-and-bookcase illustrated in figure 22. When photographed in England during the 1930s, it had carved panels in the pediment, applied moldings on the case sides, leafage on the base molding, and gadrooning on the feet (fig. 48).[23]

During the middle of the eighteenth century, Newport cabinetmakers created what subsequently became an icon of American furniture—the six-shell, blockfront desk-and-bookcase. The similarity of the nine examples documents the presence of a rigid, tightly controlled aesthetic. Unlike Boston or Philadelphia cabinetmakers who offered their clients a wide range of options for specific forms, Newport furnituremakers had a limited vocabulary. Their patrons preferred a few specific designs, and craftsmen continued to provide them for decades.[24]

Within this established format for block and shell desk-and-bookcases, minor variations do occur, which make it possible to subdivide the group. Three of these objects (figs. 11, 13, 20) clearly represent the work of one shop. The design of their shells, layout of their bookcase interiors, and overall construction are remarkably consistent. The two Brown family pieces (figs. 11, 13) may well be the latest in the entire group; the simplicity of their bookcase shelving, lack of a well, and commanding scale suggest a date no earlier than the late 1760s. The Pendleton desk-and-bookcase (fig. 15) and the example shown in figure 7 constitute a second subgroup. The craftsman who made these pieces appears to have been associated with the maker of the Lisle desk-and-bookcase (fig. 1). One maker may have trained the other,

Figure 48 Photograph showing the desk-and-bookcase illustrated in fig. 22 prior to conservation. (Courtesy, Robert W. Symonds Collection, Visual Resources, Winterthur Library.)

and the two may have worked collaboratively on at least one of these three desk-and-bookcases. A third subgroup includes the desk-and-bookcases illustrated in figures 18, 22, and possibly 9, although the last is enigmatic enough to make any conclusion about its origin somewhat problematic. If the example illustrated in figure 9 is by the same maker, it was likely his first attempt at the form. In light of this analysis, these nine desk-and-bookcases represent the output of at least four, and possibly five, Newport shops.

Although the desk-and-bookcases can be separated into groups, the identities of the cabinetmakers that made them remain a mystery. During the 1760s and 1770s, Newport supported more than a dozen cabinetmaking establishments, the most prominent of which was John Townsend's. Although his furniture ranks at the summit of Newport work, he does not appear to have been involved in the production of any of the surviving desk-and-bookcases. None of the block and shell examples are constructed like the desks documented and attributed to Townsend's shop, nor do they have the assembly marks that he typically wrote in pencil or chalk.

Job and Christopher Townsend are better candidates for at least some of the six-shell desk-and-bookcases. These brothers were the progenitors of Newport's most important cabinetmaking shops, and ambitious straight-front desk-and-bookcases by both men survive. Although neither of the documented examples by Job and Christopher share enough features with any of the six-shell blockfronts to warrant an attribution, the relationships between certain subgroups suggest the involvement of at least one multi-generational shop tradition. If the inscription on the Lisle example could be verified, one could postulate that the desk-and-bookcases illustrated in figures 7 and 15 represent the work of John Goddard's master and father-in-law Job Townsend or another cabinetmaker trained by the latter craftsman. Job trained his sons Job, Jr., Thomas, and Edmund, and may have taken apprentices in addition to Goddard.[25]

Regrettably, John Goddard's construction of the Lisle desk-and-book-case cannot be proven at this time. He remains a likely candidate, but three plain desks, supposedly made by him, do not share enough features with the Lisle piece to link the desk-and-bookcase to this noted cabinetmaker. Given the great expense of the Lisle desk-and-bookcase and other pieces in the group, it is surprising that none are signed by the maker or by an early owner. Aside from Thomas Goddard's remarks and a few notations by later repairmen, the inscriptions on the nine objects are limited mostly to marks designating drawer order or partition locations. These desk-and-bookcases, therefore, remain difficult to document and deserve further study as part of a larger analysis of all Rhode Island case furniture.

ACKNOWLEDGMENTS I am grateful to the following individuals for their research assistance, critical comments, and access to objects during the preparation of this article: Luke Beckerdite, Allan Breed, Michael Brown, Ralph Carpenter, Linda Eppich, Jeffrey Greene, Morrison Heckscher, Patricia Kane, Alexandra Kirtley, Thomas Michie, Michael Moses, Peter Obbard, Michael Podmaniczky, Ron Potvin, and Gerald Ward.

1. Luke Vincent Lockwood, *Colonial Furniture in America,* 2d ed., 2 vols. (New York: Charles Scribner's Sons, 1913), 1:246. The Brown desk-and-bookcase brought $12.1 million (Christie's, *The Magnificent Nicholas Brown Desk and Bookcase,* New York, June 3, 1989). A Newport desk-and-bookcase signed by Christopher Townsend brought $8,250,500 in 1999 (Sotheby's, *Important Americana: Furniture and Folk Art,* New York, January 16–17, 1999, lot 704).

2. Wendy A. Cooper and Tara L. Gleason, "A Different Rhode Island Block-and-Shell Story: Providence Provenances and Pitch-Pediments," in *American Furniture,* edited by Luke Beckerdite (Hanover, N. H.: University Press of New England for the Chipstone Foundation, 1999), pp. 162, 176. The attribution of these two objects to Providence was first suggested in Michael Moses, *Master Craftsmen of Newport* (Tenafly, N. J.: MMI Americana Press, 1984), p. 303. For the provenance of the Lisle desk-and-bookcase, see Christopher P. Monkhouse and Thomas Michie, *American Furniture in Pendleton House* (Providence, R.I.: Museum of Art, Rhode Island School of Design, 1986), p. 96.

3. Norman M. Isham, "John Goddard and his Work," *Bulletin of the Rhode Island School of Design* 15, no. 2 (April 1927): 23. Homer Eaton Keyes, "The Frontispiece," *Antiques* 15, no. 4 (April 1929): 277. For further information about Thomas Goddard, see Mabel Munson Swan, "John Goddard's Sons," *Antiques* 57, no. 6 (June 1950): 448–49.

4. The best early accounts of John Goddard are Walter A. Dyer, "John Goddard and his Block-Fronts," *Antiques* 1, no. 5 (May 1922): 203–8; Isham, "John Goddard and his Work," pp. 14–24; and Keyes, "The Frontispiece," pp. 275–77. For a biography of Goddard, see Michael Moses, *Master Craftsmen of Newport,* pp. 195–200. For information about the history of Goddard's shops, see Ron M. Potvin, "Furniture Makers on the Point, A Selected List of Sites," (unpublished research report, Newport Historical Society, 1999), p. 5. The Goddard desk in the collection of the Chipstone Foundation is illustrated in Oswaldo Rodriguez Roque, *American Furniture at Chipstone* (Madison: University of Wisconsin Press, 1984), pp. 56–59. The application of labels on furniture made for export is discussed in Margaretta M. Lovell, "'Such Furniture as Will Be Most Profitable,' The Business of Cabinetmaking in Eighteenth-Century Newport," *Winterthur Portfolio* 26, no. 1 (Spring 1991): 44–48. It is interesting to note that the Goddard desk at Chipstone has replaced backboards made of yellow pine, suggesting that the object may have been shipped to the South in the eighteenth century and later repaired there. The correspondence between Moses Brown and John Goddard is quoted in Moses, *Master Craftsmen of Newport,* p. 196, and Goddard's two desks from the 1750s are illustrated on pages 201–2 of the same volume.

5. Inventory of John Goddard, August 1, 1785, Newport, Wills and Inventories, Newport City Hall, I: 267–68. Wendell Garrett, "The Goddard and Townsend Joiners of Newport, Random Biographical and Bibliographical Notes," *Antiques* 121, no. 5 (May 1982): 1154. Lovell, "'Such Furniture as Will Be Most Profitable,'" pp. 50–51. Jeanne Vibert Sloane, "John Cahoone and the Newport Furniture Industry," in *New England Furniture: Essays in Memory of Benno M. Forman,* edited by Brock Jobe (Boston: Society for the Preservation of New England Antiquities, 1987), pp. 93–95.

6. Dyer, "John Goddard and his Block-Fronts," p. 208. George Champlin Mason, *Reminiscences of Newport* (Newport, R.I.: Charles E. Hammett, Jr., 1884), p. 50. Goddard's copy of Chippendale's *Director* is housed in the Prints, Drawings, and Photographs Department at the Museum of Fine Arts, Boston.

7. For additional information on uses for desks and desk-and-bookcases, see Gerald W. R. Ward, *American Case Furniture in the Mabel Brady Garvan and Other Collections at Yale University* (New Haven, Conn.: Yale University Art Gallery, 1988), pp. 343–44; and Brock Jobe and Myrna Kaye, *New England Furniture: The Colonial Era* (Boston: Houghton Mifflin Company, 1984), pp. 226–28. In his daybook, Job Townsend, Jr. never specifically bills any client for a desk-and-bookcase. However, it is possible that the "large" mahogany desks or especially expensive desks in his accounts were desk-and-bookcases. His typical charge for a true desk ranges from £50 to £90 during the 1760s and 1770s. The price of his large mahogany desks exceeded £200 and on one occasion amounted to £330. See Martha H. Willoughby, "The Accounts of Job Townsend, Jr." in *American Furniture,* edited by Luke Beckerdite (Hanover, N. H.: University Press of New England for the Chipstone Foundation, 1999), pp. 133–61. On December 26, 1765, Benjamin Baker billed a customer £300 for a mahogany "full [head] desk," which must have been a desk-and-bookcase; his account book lists no other items that could be interpreted as a desk-and-bookcase. See Ron Potvin, "Transcript of Furniture Recorded in the Account Book of Benjamin Baker, 1761–1790" (unpublished research report, Newport Historical Society, n.d.). Cahoone's two desk-and-bookcases included a mahogany example cost-

ing £200 in 1756. His ledger documents only his credit sales from 1749 to 1760 (Sloane, "John Cahoone and the Newport Furniture Industry," pp. 94, 99). I am grateful to Alexandra Kirtley for her survey of Newport inventories for the years 1779 to 1790. Of the 200 inventories she examined, 125 included a total of 142 desks and twelve desk-and-bookcases. Of the twelve, five are identified as mahogany, one as maple, one as walnut, and five lack any designation. The results of Kirtley's research are on file at the Winterthur Museum.

8. For lists of Newport craftsmen working in the 1760s, see Garrett, "The Goddard and Townsend Joiners of Newport," pp. 1153–55; and Sloane, "John Cahoone and the Newport Furniture Industry," p. 116. Thomas Hornsby, "Newport, Past and Present," *Newport Daily Advertiser,* December 8, 1849. Job Townsend, Jr. and Edmund Townsend jointly billed Nicholas Anderrese £330 for the "Large Mohogony Desk" on February 28, 1767 (Willoughby, "The Accounts of Job Townsend, Jr.," p. 144). For illustrations and a discussion of the Daniel Goddard bureau table, see Moses, *Master Craftsmen of Newport,* pp. 265, 271–72, 291–92.

9. For more on the desk-and-bookcase illustrated in fig. 7, see Nancy E. Richards and Nancy Goyne Evans, *New England Furniture at Winterthur, Queen Anne and Chippendale Periods* (Winterthur, Del.: Winterthur Museum, 1997), pp. 439–42. Potter family records are ambiguous regarding the histories of the two desk-and-bookcases. An 1836 account book at the Pettaquamscutt Historical Society records the settlement of the estate of Elisha Reynolds Potter. According to the accounts, Potter left a "high desk (formerly James Helme's)" to his son Thomas Mawney Potter. Presumably this is the example (fig. 9) that later passed back into the Helme family, who gave it to the Museum of Fine Arts, Boston (see Richard H. Randall, Jr., *American Furniture in the Museum of Fine Arts, Boston* [Boston: Museum of Fine Arts, 1965], p. 84). Debra Anne Hashim to Michael Brown, March 26, 1980, object file for 40.790, Art of the Americas Department, Museum of Fine Arts, Boston. In a family note of about 1870, Potter's second desk-and-bookcase is briefly described as: "High book case writing desk in study Dr. P [otter] bought in Newport." William D. Miller, "An Early Rhode Island Collector," *Walpole Society Note Book 1935* (Hartford, Conn.: Walpole Society, 1935), p. 45. Christopher Monkhouse and Thomas Michie proposed that this was the one later owned by Arthur Lisle (see Monkhouse and Michie, *American Furniture in Pendleton House,* pp. 17, 96–99). In addition to the two block and shell desk-and-bookcases, Potter also owned a third Newport desk-and-bookcase and a block and shell bureau table, probably the one now in the Museum of Art, Rhode Island School of Design (Monkhouse and Michie, *American Furniture in Pendleton House,* pp. 84–85). Moses Brown's example burned in a fire, and the nine-shell desk-and-bookcase owned by Joseph Brown represents the work of a Providence cabinetmaker. The latter example's design clearly follows a Newport model, but in its details (such as the layout of the desk interior) it stands apart. The Brown family presented the piece to the Rhode Island Historical Society, and since the 1960s it has been displayed in the John Brown House. For information about the Brown family examples, see Ward, *American Case Furniture in the Mabel Brady Garvan and Other Collections at Yale University,* pp. 339–44; Moses, *Master Craftsmen of Newport,* pp. 328–29; Christie's, *The Magnificent Nicholas Brown Desk and Bookcase;* and John T. Kirk, *American Furniture, Understanding Styles, Construction, and Quality* (New York: Harry N. Abrams, 2000), pp. 154–61. In 1989, to raise funds for the John Nicholas Brown Center for the Study of American Civilization, the family consigned this desk-and-bookcase to Christie's. The desk-and-bookcase remains in private hands.

10. For the collecting careers of Pendleton, Canfield, and Perry, see Elizabeth Stillinger, *The Antiquers* (New York: Alfred A. Knopf, 1980), pp. 113–21; and Monkhouse and Michie, *American Furniture in Pendleton House,* pp. 20–30. For catalogue descriptions of the desk-and-bookcases owned by Pendleton, Canfield, and Perry, see Monkhouse and Michie, *American Furniture in Pendleton House,* pp. 97–99; Morrison H. Heckscher, *American Furniture in the Metropolitan Museum of Art, II, Late Colonial Period: The Queen Anne and Chippendale Styles* (New York: Metropolitan Museum of Art and Random House, 1985), pp. 282–85; and Edwin J. Hipkiss, *Eighteenth-Century American Arts, The M. and M. Karolik Collection* (Cambridge, Mass.: Harvard University Press, 1941), pp. 30–32. Ima Hogg's desk-and-bookcase is discussed in David B. Warren, Michael K. Brown, Elizabeth Ann Coleman, and Emily Ballew Neff, *American Decorative Arts and Paintings in the Bayou Bend Collection* (Houston, Tx.: Museum of Fine Arts, Houston in association with Princeton University Press, 1998), pp. 73–75.

11. The Helme desk-and-bookcase (fig. 9) is the only one without quarter-columns. The two pieces with book-matched panels in the pediment are the Lisle and Helme examples (figs. 1, 9). All of the others display raised panels with applied blocks. The five desk-and-bookcases with

enclosed pediments are shown in figs. 1, 7, 9, 18, 22. In addition, the five previous pieces and the Pendleton example (fig. 15) have wells in the desk interior.

12. Typically the beaded strip (fig. 17) on the base molding is present only at the front, not at the sides. Sometimes, as was the case with the Lisle desk-and-bookcase (fig. 26), it was added to the sides at a later date.

13. For a comparison of standard Boston case construction to that of Newport, see Margaretta Markle Lovell, "Boston Blockfront Furniture" in *Boston Furniture of the Eighteenth Century* (Boston, Mass.: Colonial Society of Massachusetts, 1974), pp. 81–89, especially figs. 58, 59. For information on the application of the waist molding to the upper case in Newport furniture, see Jobe and Kaye, *New England Furniture: The Colonial Era*, pp. 174–75. Of the block and shell desk-and-bookcases, only the one illustrated in fig. 7 has a waist molding attached to the upper case. In this instance the molding is a replacement and has been incorrectly installed.

14. During conservation of the desk-and-bookcase shown in fig. 7, the board at the center of the hood was removed revealing the original wedge-shaped blocks securing the pediment to the top of the bookcase. At the same time, conservators were able to slide out the panels along the sides of the interior of the bookcase. Behind the panels, they discovered "secret" pockets, one of which contained a packet of eighteenth-century needles.

15. The squared-off, butt-joined blocking and shells appear on the fallboards of the Lisle desk-and-bookcase (fig. 38) and examples shown in figs. 9, 41, and 42.

16. For illustrations of the bureau table, clothes press, and chest-on-chest, see Moses, *Master Craftsmen of Newport*, p. 332; and Roque, *American Furniture at Chipstone*, pp. 2–3, 29–31. Also see Cooper and Gleason, "A Different Rhode Island Block-and-Shell Story: Providence Provenances and Pitch-Pediments," pp. 173–74.

17. The linings of the valance drawers within the Lisle desk-and-bookcase (fig. 1) and examples illustrated in figs. 7, 9, 22 are constructed entirely of red cedar. The maker of the desk-and-bookcase shown in fig. 18 used mahogany for the sides and back of the valance drawers but continued the standard practice of using red cedar for the drawer bottoms.

18. The ties between Providence patrons and Newport craftsmen are presented in Cooper and Gleason, "A Different Rhode Island Block-and-Shell Story: Providence Provenances and Pitch-Pediments," pp. 168–184, 195–97. The Goddard-Brown correspondence is quoted and discussed in Moses, *Master Craftsmen of Newport*, pp. 196–97.

19. The x-radiograph of the finial is pictured in Monkhouse and Michie, *American Furniture in Pendleton House*, p. 98. Although the finial is intact and old, it remains problematic for this desk-and-bookcase. Double-reeded urns are not associated with furniture from the early 1760s, but rather with the following two decades. It is possible that these finials are one of the "repairs" made by Thomas Goddard in 1813. A bureau table signed by John Goddard's son Daniel has feet with leaf carving, but the work is clearly not by the same hand that carved the feet of the Lisle desk-and-bookcase. Moses, *Master Craftsmen of Newport*, pp. 141, 265, 291–93.

20. The bold, seven-fluted quarter-columns on the Pendleton desk-and-bookcase (fig. 15) resemble columns of similar scale on a bureau table signed by Daniel Goddard. Furthermore, the design of the shells on the two pieces is similar. This prompted Michael Moses to attribute both objects to "Daniel Goddard's family" in *Master Craftsmen of Newport*, pp. 271–72. Although this connection may well be correct, the ambiguity of the Daniel Goddard inscription prevents this author from attributing the Pendleton desk-and-bookcase (fig. 15) and the example shown in fig. 7 to Daniel Goddard at this time.

21. A desk labeled by John Goddard and dated 1745 (Roque, *American Furniture at Chipstone*, pp. 56–59) and a desk-and-bookcase signed by Christopher Townsend (Sotheby's, *Important Americana: Furniture and Folk Art*, January 16–17, 1999, lot 704) have arches above the pigeonholes. The shaped drawer fronts within the bookcase of fig. 22 are reminiscent of those in the same location on the aforementioned Christopher Townsend desk-and-bookcase. The incised arches surrounding the carved shells on the corner drawers of the desk-and-bookcase shown in fig. 22 are related to those framing shells on early Newport dressing tables. For images of Newport dressing tables, see Roque, *American Furniture at Chipstone*, pp. 38–39; and Moses, *Master Craftsmen of Newport*, p. 41. Although Newport craftsmen continued to employ each of these features—arches above the pigeonholes, shaped drawer fronts in the desk interior, and incised arches around the carved shells—well into the 1760s, the combination of them here suggests a date in the 1750s for this particular desk-and-bookcase.

22. Feet similar to those on the desk-and-bookcase illustrated in fig. 9 are on a blockfront chest of drawers at the Museum of Fine Arts, Boston (Moses, *Master Craftsmen of Newport*, p. 311), and a privately owned desk shown in the seminal exhibition of Newport furniture

organized by Ralph Carpenter in 1953 (see Ralph E. Carpenter, Jr., *The Arts and Crafts of Newport, Rhode Island, 1640–1820* [Newport: Preservation Society of Newport County, 1954], p. 75).

23. Furniture historian Charles Montgomery examined the desk-and-bookcase shown in fig. 22 in the shop of Stair and Company in London in July 1952. He subsequently sent photos of it to his colleague Joseph Downs, who expressed his concerns. "The carving in the pediment and around the base and feet," Downs wrote, "left me quite skeptical, as it seemed quite out of period with the rest of the design, and I would guess it was somewhat later than the original work." Despite Downs' reservations, Montgomery purchased the desk for the Winterthur Museum. The museum's founder Henry Francis du Pont declined to keep the piece and traded it to antiques dealer John Walton the following September. New York cabinetmaker Ernst Peterson restored the desk-and-bookcase for Walton. He scraped away the carving on the pediment, base molding, and feet; removed the moldings on the sides, and refinished the exterior surface. By November 1952, Walton had sold the desk-and-bookcase to Miss Ima Hogg for Bayou Bend. For a complete history of the piece and its restoration, see Alexandra Kirtley, research report, object folder for B.69.22, Bayou Bend, Museum of Fine Arts, Houston. The author is grateful to Ms. Kirtley for sharing her findings.

24. Gerald W. R. Ward, "'America's Contribution to Craftsmanship': The Exaltation and Interpretation of Newport Furniture," in *American Furniture,* edited by Luke Beckerdite (Hanover, N. H.: University Press of New England for the Chipstone Foundation, 1999), pp. 225–27, 237–44.

25. A desk-and-bookcase with Job Townsend's label is in the Museum of Art, Rhode Island School of Design (see Moses, *Master Craftsmen of Newport,* pp. 254, 257; Monkhouse and Michie, *American Furniture in Pendleton House,* pp. 94–96). Among Christopher Townsend's signed furniture is a flat-topped high chest and a dramatic desk-and-bookcase with silver hardware. Both were discussed in Luke Beckerdite, "The Early Furniture of Christopher and Job Townsend," in *American Furniture,* edited by Luke Beckerdite (Hanover, N. H.: University Press of New England for the Chipstone Foundation, 2000), pp. 15–22. Two of the three documented desks by John Goddard are illustrated in Moses, *Master Craftsmen of Newport,* pp. 201–2; the third appears in Roque, *American Furniture at Chipstone,* pp. 56–59. These three examples vary considerably in their individual details. Even in such related features as the shape of the feet on the two pictured by Moses, the craftsmen used different templates in sawing them out.

Figure 1   George Washington Felt, *View of Court House Square*, Salem, Massachusetts, 1810–1820. Oil on wood panel. 35" x 52". (Courtesy, Peabody Essex Museum; gift of B. F. Brown.)

*Dean Thomas
Lahikainen*

A Salem Cabinet-makers' Price Book

▼ IN DECEMBER 1999, the Peabody Essex Museum purchased an unrecorded cabinetmakers' price book published in Salem, Massachusetts, in 1801. Titled "Articles of the Salem Cabinet-Maker Society, Associated June 26, 1801," the booklet is the first document to give a formal voice to one of the most important centers for furniture production during the Federal period. Since 1915, numerous scholars have attempted to chronicle various aspects of Salem's furniture making industry, relying largely on receipts, shipping manifests, and craftsmen's account books. Additional documentation has come from objects bearing labels or brands of owners or makers. With many aspects of work from this complex urban center yet to be explored, the "Articles of the Salem Cabinet-Maker Society" provides an accurate snapshot of the industry at a pivotal moment in its development and establishes a useful framework and period terminology to aid further study.[1]

The booklet contains twenty numbered pages; the first six state the twelve articles or rules governing the new society, along with the names of the sixteen founding members. The second part contains twelve pages listing various forms of furniture along with the price for making and retailing each. Seventeen other American or English cabinet and chairmakers' price books, in either manuscript or printed form, predate the Salem example. These include price books from Providence, Rhode Island (1756), London (1788, 1793, and 1797), Philadelphia (1772, 1786, two in 1794, 1795, and two in 1796), Hartford, Connecticut (1792), New York (1796 and 1800), Hatfield, Massachusetts (1796 and 1797), and Norwich, England (1801). Each one represents an attempt either by the masters or journeymen to regulate prices and the standards of work within their craft community. Most list the rate journeymen will be paid on a piecework basis for making various furniture forms, while two list only the retail prices. A number of these agreements also established a forum to handle disputes between members. Indeed, several urban American price books were the direct outgrowth of labor disputes between journeymen and masters. As decorative arts historian Charles Montgomery noted, price books "chart a key development in the emergence of labor from its vassal-like beginnings to its present day position of power. They mark the organization of labor and document its demands, the acceptance of arbitration and reach agreement based on a piecework system for remuneration."[2]

The most influential price book was *The Cabinet-Makers' London Book of Prices, and Designs of Cabinet Work*, published in 1788 and revised in 1793 and

1803. Comprehensive in scope, it was the first to contain engraved illustrations that helped spread knowledge of London furniture forms and a common neoclassical design vocabulary. This publication had a direct influence on several other price books, including those published in Philadelphia and New York. Surviving price books from the smaller centers such as Providence, Hartford, and Hatfield are more original in their content and arrangement, reflecting more closely local preferences and practices. The "Articles of the Salem Cabinet-Maker Society" falls into this latter group, for it owes little to the London version or any other previously published price book. It appears to be an entirely original document accurately reflecting the needs and activities of the most prominent group of master cabinetmakers in Salem in 1801.

Like the first edition of the *Cabinet-Makers' London Book of Prices,* the "Articles of the Salem Cabinet-Maker Society" does not list prices for chairmaking. London craftsmen maintained separate price books for cabinetmaking and chairmaking until 1802, reflecting the clear division that existed between the cabinetmaking, carving, and chairmaking trades. The absence of chairs in the Salem book suggests that a similar situation existed there, more so perhaps than in other American cities. Chairs outnumbered all other forms shipped from Salem between 1790 and 1810. The few surviving documents relating to the town's chairmaking industry, however, provide no evidence of any formal organization or price list. Nevertheless, historical references document business relationships between chair makers and cabinetmakers. Some cabinetmakers bought chairs for inventory or took them as consignments for venture cargo shipments. Elijah and Jacob Sanderson, for example, formed a partnership with cabinetmaker Josiah Austin and purchased painted seating from the Burpee Chair Manufactory, Micaiah and Edward Johnson, Isaac Stone, and James C. Tuttle.[3]

By 1801, Salem merchants had successfully revived the town's maritime economy by establishing new trade routes to the Far East. With unprecedented profits resulting from daring voyages to uncharted territories, Salem's merchant class ushered in an era of unsurpassed prosperity that transformed the community. There was a dramatic increase in opportunities for employment as local industries expanded, especially in the areas of shipbuilding, house construction, and furniture making. Artisans came from surrounding communities, more distant coastal towns, southern New Hampshire, and a few were natives of England and Ireland. Furniture historian Margaret Clunie documented only three cabinetmakers active in Salem between 1770 and 1780, but by 1801 there were at least twenty-one. A majority were born and trained elsewhere, including most, if not all, of the members of the Salem Cabinet-Maker Society. They were part of a town population that had grown by 1800 to just under ten thousand inhabitants, making Salem the sixth largest city in the United States.[4]

This expansion coincided with the introduction of the "antique" or neoclassical taste in architecture and furniture. The style received its first significant expression in 1793 with the construction of the Nathan Read house designed by Salem architect and carver Samuel McIntire. At least six other three-story townhouses were built during the next eight years. Newly arrived cabinetmakers and chair makers found work furnishing these residences as well as public buildings constructed during the same period. A view of the center of town painted about 1810 (fig. 1) provides an image of this prosperity, showing a number of the new buildings along Court Street (now Washington Street) where cabinetmakers Samuel Frothingham, Samuel Cheever, and many of their contemporaries lived and worked. There were also opportunities to supplement local custom orders by producing furniture for the burgeoning venture cargo trade. Rev. William Bentley observed that many of these artisans had attained "wealth by other means than the slow gains of its [native born] inhabitants." Shipping manifests listing furniture transported from Salem rose from five in 1789 to forty in 1800, the most in a given year. By the turn of the century, the industry had reached a point where some attempt at regulation was desirable.[5]

The establishment of the Sanderson-Austin partnership in 1779 was a watershed in the development of Salem's furniture export trade. The firm employed many cabinetmakers, journeymen, and apprentices, as well as carvers, gilders, turners, and upholsterers on a piecework basis. They sent large shipments of furniture on speculation to the southern states, the East and West Indies, the Madeiras, South America, Africa, and more distant ports, including those in India. Not surprisingly, the names of all three men appear at the top of the list of the founding members of the Salem Cabinet-Maker Society, a clear indication of the central role they must have played in forming that organization.[6]

Although all of the other cabinetmakers on the list appear to have operated their own shops, many were relatives, former employees, or associates of Austin and the Sandersons. Richard Austin was Josiah's brother and Daniel Clarke was a nephew and former employee of the Sandersons. William Hook (fig. 2), the youngest member of the Salem Cabinet-Maker Society, came from Salisbury, Massachusetts, and worked for both Jacob Sanderson and Edmund Johnson before setting up his own shop in 1800. The names of many other members appear in the Sandersons' business records from the 1790s, underscoring the cooperative rather than competitive nature of the town's cabinetmaking trade.[7]

Salem artisans often joined forces to purchase materials, assemble large venture cargos, and share the cost and risk of shipping. In 1795, George W. Martin, William Appleton, Josiah Austin, and the Sandersons bought a large quantity of mahogany and hired Col. Israel Hutchinson to cut the logs into planks. The following year, the Sandersons, Austin, and William Appleton purchased the schooner *Olive Branch*, undoubtedly for use in the furniture export trade. Most cooperative efforts involved venture cargo, such as Daniel Clarke, Edmund Johnson, Nehemiah Adams, and Josiah Austin's shipment of furniture to Surinam in 1799.[8]

This cooperative and entrepreneurial spirit led to the founding of the Salem Cabinet-Maker Society in June of 1801. The governing rules were simple, straightforward, and democratic. Membership was open to anyone "generally accepted" to be a "master-cabinet-maker"—a designation deter-

Figure 2 John Christian Rauschner, *William Hook,* ca. 1809. Colored wax. H. (frame) 6½". (Courtesy, Peabody Essex Museum; photo, Mark Sexton.)

mined by a vote of the entire membership. The society met in March, June, September, and December. Missing a meeting, tardiness, neglecting to bring one's copy of the price book, and failure to adhere to set prices were offenses punishable by fines. It was the clerk's duty to record any changes agreed upon by vote directly into each member's book. Anticipating this practice, Joshua Cushing left a generous space between each entry when he printed the book. In the copy illustrated here, clerk Daniel Clarke recorded the first change on September 22, 1801, when the society voted to make the fine for deviating from the prices the cost of making the piece of furniture.[9]

The other articles in the price book established arbitration procedures to settle potential grievances between members and between masters and their apprentices. Members were required to report any apprentice attempting "to leave his master or in any manner to injure him" and were forbidden from harboring runaways. Court cases and newspaper notices indicate that disputes over apprentices were a persistent, albeit infrequent, problem. In 1798, Elijah Sanderson sued B. Radson for causing one of his apprentices to leave. Three years later, Edmund Johnson offered a thirty-dollar reward for information leading to the return of two nineteen-year-old apprentices. He warned all persons against "harboring or trusting said runaways" and cautioned "masters of vessels … against carrying them to sea as they would avoid the penalty of the law." The time invested in training apprentices and the cost of housing, feeding, clothing, and educating them was considerable. Rewards typically varied depending on an apprentice's skill and time served.[10]

The last twelve pages of the "Articles of the Salem Cabinet-Maker Society" list the retail and journeyman's prices for thirty different furniture forms, half of which were available with less expensive woods, design features, and ornamental details. With only sixty-four separate entries, the price book documents a narrow range of neoclassical forms popular within the community. It is much smaller than the Philadelphia and London publications, both of which have 346 entries.

Evidence suggests that Salem tradesmen and consumers began embracing the neoclassical style during the last quarter of the eighteenth century. Bookseller John Jenks, for example, advertised the first edition of George Hepplewhite's *The Cabinet-Maker and Upholsterer's Guide* (1788) in 1791. Designs from this book, the *Cabinet-Makers' London Book of Prices*, and Thomas Sheraton's *The Cabinet-Maker and Upholsterer's Drawing Book* (1793) clearly influenced Salem production. Some of the newer forms illustrated in these publications—sideboards, window stools, commodes, and washstands—are mentioned in the Salem price book, whereas many others are not. Conspicuously absent are references to work tables, chamber or dressing tables, drawing tables, pier tables, mixing tables, urn stands, bidets, knife boxes, dressing boxes, tea caddys, trays, bottle boxes, and other forms known to have been made in the city.[11]

Documentary evidence suggests that Salem furniture makers made few of the aforementioned objects prior to 1801. Margaret Clunie's survey of 109 shipping manifests submitted between 1790 and 1810 lists twenty-two forms that generally match entries in the price book but makes no mention of a "work table." The earliest use of that term in Salem is August 1807, when the Sandersons paid Samuel McIntire three dollars for "Reeding & Carving 4 legs for [a] Worktable." During the eighteenth century, few American cabinetmakers attempted to compete with their British counterparts in the manufacture and sale of looking glasses, dressing boxes, and other objects with mirrored components. The first reference to a dressing box being made in Salem is 1809.[12]

The retail price of objects listed in the "Articles of the Salem Cabinet-Maker Society" is between three and three-and-one-half times the cost of making the piece. Research by Charles Montgomery suggests that large cabinet shops in other urban centers evidently worked on similar profit margins during the early nineteenth century. Labor determined most of the cost. As the price book reveals, a card table that retailed for fourteen dollars required approximately four days of labor at one dollar per day.[13]

The society clearly monitored the prices of all objects commonly produced by its members and on several occasions altered them. Ink notations in the Peabody Essex copy record the lowering of prices for the mahogany chair frame and press bed in December 1801 and for an easy chair frame, fire screen, and wash stand in June 1802. The largest number of changes was voted at the September 1802 meeting, when the society agreed to offer a fully painted cradle for six dollars and lowered prices for the larger "secretary & bookcase" and all variations of the bureau and lady's secretary. These forms were among the most popular export items, but there is no indication of what prompted the changes. The last changes recorded in the book occurred on December 6, 1803, when the members voted to raise the price of several bedsteads and to add a pembroke table and coffins to the list.

The brevity of the entries for each form is unusual, especially when compared with those in contemporary price books, which usually describe material, structural, and decorative options and the cost for each. It is possible that the society's members were so familiar with each other's work and the demands of their consumers that it was unnecessary to include too much detail. During the late eighteenth century, Salem cabinetmakers almost invariably used square tapered legs for tables, whereas their counterparts in other American cities and London had a more varied repertoire. The earliest reference to turned and reeded legs in Salem is 1803.[14]

Entries for certain forms allude to the specialization that existed in Salem's furniture making community. Carving was "excluded" from the price of the sofa, mahogany chair, window stool, and bedstead with "swelled pillars," which implies that the patron determined the type and amount of ornament, and that most cabinetmakers subcontracted carving to specialists. The same was true of "painting." This generic reference probably encompassed a variety of treatments including faux surfaces, *trompe l'oeil*, and gilding. The terms "superior quality," "best quality," and "another quality" are more difficult to access, but in some instances they also refer to decoration. The "superior quality" cabinet, for example, was "inlaid and decorated in every part" and had an elaborate "checkered cock bead round the doors."

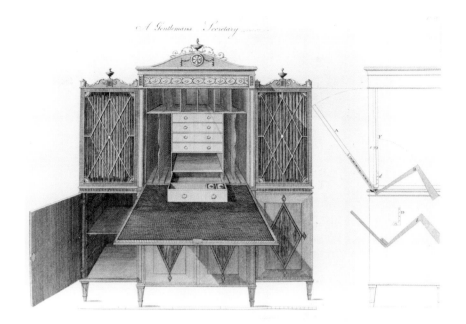

Figure 3 Gentleman's secretary, Salem, Massachusetts, 1795–1805. Mahogany with pine. H. 96⅜", W. 72⅛", D. 20¼". (Courtesy, Museum of Fine Arts, Houston; gift of Miss Ima Hogg.)

Figure 4 Design for a "Gentleman's Secretary" illustrated on plate 52 of Thomas Sheraton's *The Cabinet-Maker and Upholsterer's Drawing Book* (1793). (Courtesy, Winterthur Museum Library: Printed Books and Periodical Collection.)

All of the entries in the "Articles of the Salem Cabinet-Maker Society" are transcribed below. Each has been numbered to simplify future reference and annotated to establish the cultural, historical, and artistic context of the form described.

PRICES of FURNITURE, and JOURNEYMEN'S PRICES for MAK-ING, established by the Society June 26th, 1801:—To be altered at the discretion of the Majority.

[1] CABINET, of a superior quality, with circular doors, inlaid and dec-orated in every part, to be made with a cock bead round the doors, drawers and head———dolls. 120
Making———dolls. 40

[2] Ditto, finished with circular doors———115
Making———37

[3] Ditto, of another quality, with diamond doors———110
Making———34

The first three entries describe a "cabinet" or gentleman's secretary, the most expensive form in the price book and one long associated with Salem. More than a dozen examples have survived including one of "superior qual-ity" with husks, stringing, and "check'd" inlay (fig. 3). An amendment at the end of the price book notes that the term "check'd" should precede "cock bead" in the first entry.[15]

Although no European prototype for the archetypal Salem cabinet is known, several features typical of this form have parallels in British design books. The lower section (see fig. 3) is similar to that of a gentleman's sec-retary illustrated on plate 52 of Sheraton's *Drawing Book* (fig. 4), whereas the pediment resembles that of a "wing" clothes press shown on plate 3 of the *Cabinet-Makers' London Book of Prices* (fig. 5). Gothic cornice moldings related to the one shown in the latter engraving also occur on Salem "cabi-nets" and other case forms.[16]

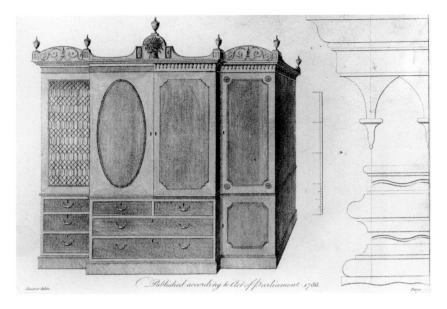

Figure 5   Thomas Shearer, design for a "Wing Clothes Press," illustrated on plate 3 of the Society of Upholsterers, *Cabinet-Makers' London Book of Prices* (1788). (Courtesy, Winterthur Museum Library: Printed Books and Periodical Collection.)

Figure 6   Gentleman's secretary attributed to Edmund Johnson, Salem, Massachusetts, 1795–1812. Mahogany and satinwood with pine. H. 88", W. 67½", D. unrecorded. (Courtesy, Sotheby's.)

The term "circular doors" in the first and second entries probably refers to curved glazing bars like those on the upper doors of the gentleman's secretary illustrated in figure 3, rather than oval panels of veneer like those on the lower doors. This glazing pattern appears on a group of doors illustrated on plate 27 in the *Cabinet-Makers' London Book of Prices*. The term "diamond doors" in the third entry refers to the crossed glazing bars found on many Salem examples, including one with a pediment very similar to that shown in the *Cabinet-Makers' London Book of Prices* (fig. 6).

The earliest documented Salem gentleman's secretary was made by Nehemiah Adams before 1798. Because of their high cost, these forms are rarely found in venture cargo manifests. Elijah Sanderson shipped "two cases Containing One cabinet... $250" to Batavia in 1804, and William Appleton exported "two cases . . . [containing] one cabinet . . . $120" in 1805. A few of the cabinets mentioned in period documents may have been library bookcases, although only one Salem example is currently known.[17]

> [4] WARDROBE, of the best quality, scrole head, 70
> Making———18
>
> [5] Ditto, of another quality, with square head, 60
> Making———17

No Salem wardrobe from the Federal period is known, which suggests that high chests and chest-on-chests were the preferred forms for storing clothes. Most American examples are from cities and towns in the Middle Atlantic region and the South. Their popularity in the South, which was a major venture cargo destination for Salem cabinetmakers and merchants, may explain why the wardrobe form is listed in the price book. The terms "square head" and "scrole head" refer to plain and broken-scroll pediments respectively.[18]

> [6] SECRETARY & BOOK-CASE, best quality, with a swell'd front———70
> Making———23
>
> [7] Ditto, of the best quality, with straight front, scrole head, crossband doors, decorated with dentals, &c———63
> Making———19
> [in ink] Voted Sept 21st 1802———60
> [Making]———18
>
> [8] Ditto, straight front, with pediment head, 60
> Making———18

Secretary-and-bookcases were among the most popular furniture forms made in Salem. With its "swell'd front," "scrole head," carved volutes, and urn ornament, the example illustrated in figure 7 is more elaborate than any of the variants described in the price book. The façade of the secretary drawer is embellished with an applied astragal molding (or "bead") forming a rectangle with ovolo corners, a detail found on the doors and drawers of case pieces shown in many British design books (see fig. 5). String-inlaid versions of this design are even more common on Salem furniture. A secretary-and-bookcase bearing the label of William Appleton (fig. 8) represents

Figure 7　Secretary-and-bookcase, Salem, Massachusetts, 1795–1800. Mahogany with pine. H. 91½", W. 45", D. 23". (Courtesy, Peabody Essex Museum, bequest of Mrs. Arthur West; photo, Mark Sexton.)

the "straight front" form described in the second entry. The frieze decoration, consisting of interlaced stringing with a central diamond motif, occurs on case pieces by several different Salem cabinetmakers. A small secretary-and-bookcase attributed to William Appleton (Peabody Essex Museum) is a good example of the less expensive "pediment head" form. Lacking any decoration, it has lozenge-shaped door mullions and a simple pediment with plinths.[19]

Figure 8   Secretary-and-bookcase with the label of William Appleton, Salem, Massachusetts, 1795–1804. Mahogany and pine. H. 99½", W. 42", D. 24½". (Courtesy, Winterthur Museum.) An inlaid scroll volute similar to those on this example is illustrated in a design for a bookcase on plate 1 of the Society of Upholsterer's *Cabinet-Makers' London Book of Prices*.

[9] BOOK-CASE, with scroll head and glass doors, 28
Making———8

No Salem bookcase matching the description in the price book is known, nor do any references to "bookcases" appear in shipping manifests other than as the upper unit of a cabinet, secretary, or desk. Cabinetmaker Mark Pitman made two sets of grain-painted bookcases with "square" or "pediment" heads and glass doors on the upper and lower cases (Ropes Mansion, Peabody Essex Museum). Harvard divinity student Joseph Orne paid Pitman twenty-four dollars for making the earlier set on February 17, 1816.[20]

[10] SIDE-BOARD, sash-corner'd, with a secretary drawer, decorated, crossbanded and finished, 60
Making———18

[11] Ditto, scolloped front, with a secretary drawer, decorated and finished———57
Making———17

[12] Ditto, scolloped front, without a secretary drawer, decorated and finished———50
Making———15

The 1788 edition of Hepplewhite's *Cabinet-Maker and Upholsterer's Guide* was the first British design book to illustrate sideboards (see fig. 9), but the form was fashionable in London earlier. Like virtually all of their American counterparts, Salem cabinetmakers did not begin producing sideboards until after the Revolution. The earliest reference to the form is November 1797, when Daniel Clarke charged Nathaniel Ropes eighteen pounds for a mahogany example with a serpentine or "scalloped front" (fig. 10). Later Salem sideboards (see fig. 11) typically have stringing, husks, and other inlaid motifs, and some are fitted with a secretary drawer, an unusual feature mentioned in all three sideboard entries in the price book. Sideboards with "sash corners" had additional drawers and were slightly more expen-

Figure 9   Design for a "Side Board" illustrated on plate 29 of the second edition of George Hepplewhite's *Cabinet-Maker and Upholsterer's Guide* (London, 1789). (Courtesy, Winterthur Museum Library: Printed Books and Periodical Collection.)

Figure 10   Sideboard made by Daniel Clarke, Salem, Massachusetts, 1797. Mahogany with pine. H. 37¾", W. 68½", D. 28". (Courtesy, Peabody Essex Museum, gift of Eliza and Mary Ropes; photo, Mark Sexton.) This sideboard differs from the design illustrated in fig. 9 in having a cabinet with two doors beneath the center drawer.

Figure 11   Sideboard bearing the label of Edmund Johnson, Salem, Massachusetts, 1800–1810. Mahogany with pine. H. 39½", W. 63½", D. 26¼". (Private collection; photo, Decorative Arts Photographic Collection, Winterthur Museum.)

sive than those with serpentine fronts. Salem cabinetmaker Nathaniel Safford made one of the former (fig. 12) for John and Elizabeth Gardner in 1805.[21]

[13] DESKS, swelled, the front and fall finiered, 40
Making———13

[14] Ditto, swelled, solid front———40
Making———11

[15] Ditto, straight front, the front, fall, top and seatboard finiered———30
Making———9

[16] Ditto, straight front and solid———30
Making———8

[17] Ditto birch, straight front———15
Making———7.50
[in ink] birch Desk———18

[18] Ditto, travelling, of the common quality, 7
Making———2

After chairs, desks were the most numerous form exported from Salem. The term "swelled" in the first two entries probably refers to the shape described today as "oxbow." Desks with shaped façades typically had fall fronts. Salem cabinetmakers made them well into the nineteenth century,

Figure 12   Sideboard attributed to Nathaniel Safford, Salem, Massachusetts, 1805. Mahogany with pine. H. 42", W. 69", D. 26". (Private collection; photo, Mark Sexton.)

even though fall-front forms were less fashionable than case pieces with secretary drawers. A desk attributed to Elijah Sanderson (fig. 13) conforms to the description in the initial entry, although the price book provides no information on the design of the foot. This is perplexing given the price difference between straight bracket, ogee, and claw-and-ball feet. Veneering (presumably in mahogany) added to the cost, whereas the use of native

Figure 13   Desk attributed to Elijah Sanderson, Salem, Massachusetts, 1780–1800. Mahogany and pine. H. 43⅜", W. 45", D. 23". (Courtesy, New England Historic Genealogical Society.)

Figure 14 Desk by Edmund Johnson, Salem, Massachusetts, ca. 1800. Cherry with pine. H. 45", W. 21", D. 42¼". (Courtesy, Peabody Essex Museum; gift of F. J. Bradlee.)

Figure 15 Dwarf clock with movement by Samuel Mulliken II, Salem, Massachusetts, 1790–1796. Mahogany with pine; brass. H. 36⅜", W. 11¾", D. 7". (Courtesy, Peabody Essex Museum; photo, Mark Sexton.)

woods reduced it. The straight-front desk with veneered façade, fall, top, and seatboard (floor of the writing compartment) cost twice as much as a comparable form in birch. Although the only native wood mentioned in the desk entries is birch, Salem cabinetmakers occasionally used cherry. A simple cherry desk bearing the label of Edmund Johnson (fig. 14) is representative of the "gentleman's writing desks" mentioned in many shipping manifests. The last and least expensive entry is for traveling desks. The only surviving example (Peabody Essex Museum) is a simple box with brass carrying handles, a slanted lid, and storage compartment partitioned for bottles and writing implements. Mark Pitman charged Elizabeth Ropes eight dollars for it on June 6, 1812.[22]

> [19] CLOCK-CASE, mahogany, glazed and finished, 30
> Making———9

This entry probably refers to a "Roxbury case," a modern designation for the type commonly found with movements marked by the Willard family of Grafton. Most of these cases have brass fluted quarter-columns on the waist and a hood with pierced fretwork and three plinths.[23]

A dwarf clock owned by Captain Henry Prince is the only documented Salem clock made between 1790 and 1820. It has a movement marked by Samuel Mulliken II (1761–1847), who worked in the town from 1790 to 1796 (fig. 15). His sister Mary married Elijah Sanderson. Mulliken probably made movements for cases by his brother-in-law and many of Elijah's contemporaries. Although a few watchmakers worked in Salem during the late eighteenth and early nineteenth centuries, no other clockmaker is recorded in Salem until the 1820s.[24]

Salem cabinetmakers clearly produced tall clock cases for local patrons as well as for the export trade. In 1795, Daniel Clarke charged "4-15-0" for "making 2 clock cases and turning the moldings for same." Eight years later, Elijah Sanderson shipped several cases with eight-day movements to Brazil. Most eight-day movements in such clocks were British or comprised of imported parts assembled by regional clockmakers. Jacob Sanderson purchased a "warrented Patent time piece" from Simon Willard in 1804 and

Figure 16 Design for a "Commode" illustrated on plate 78 of the third edition of George Hepplewhite's *Cabinet-Maker and Upholsterer's Guide* (1794). (Courtesy, Winterthur Museum Library: Printed Books and Periodical Collection.)

Figure 17 Commode, Salem, Massachusetts, 1800–1810. Mahogany with pine. H. 40", W. 55", D. 32". (Courtesy, Christie's.)

Figure 18 Commode with carving attributed to Samuel McIntire, Salem, Massachusetts, 1800–1805. Mahogany with pine. H. 43¼", W. 65¾", D. 28¼". (Courtesy, Decorative Arts Photographic Collection, Winterthur Museum.)

three clocks from Levi Hutchins in 1807.[25]

[20] COMMODE, common circular, five feet in length, 60
Making———20

[21] Ditto, different sizes, in proportion

Hepplewhite's design for a demi-lune commode (fig. 16) served as the inspiration for several Salem examples. Some have drawers and cabinets arranged like those in the engraving (fig. 17), whereas others have a different configuration. The most elaborate Salem commode (fig. 18) has four graduated drawers, the top of which has carving attributed to Samuel McIntire. In 1802, Jacob Sanderson charged Captain John Derby sixty dollars for making a "mahogany Commode with secretary draw" and an additional twelve dollars to pay "Mr. Fuller's bill for varnishing." Salem inventories indicate that commodes were used in bedchambers for the storage of linens. Many have sliding trays rather than shelves to facilitate this function. In 1799, the appraisers of Elias Hasket Derby's estate listed a "mahogany Commode" valued at fifty dollars in his best second-floor northwest bedchamber and noted that it contained a "Damask Table Cloth & 18 Napkins" of equal value.[26]

[22] LADY'S SECRETARY, with a frieze, head-moldings, and bracket feet———35
Making———11
[in ink] Voted Sept 7th 1802———30
[Making]———10

[23] Ditto, with legs, decorated and finished, 30
Making———9.50
[in ink] Voted Sept 7th 1802———25
[Making]———8

Given the variety of small writing desks made in Salem during the Federal period, it is surprising to find only these two brief entries for this form. The distinguishing features are the hinged fall and two sliding supports that form the writing surface when open. The retail cost of each lady's secretary is exactly one-half that of the larger secretary-and-bookcases discussed earlier. A lady's secretary that descended in the West family of Salem (fig. 19) has "head-moldings" and "bracket feet" (undoubtedly a reference to what are today called "French feet"), two details mentioned in the first entry. The door mullions and skirt and foot shape may have been inspired by a design for a "secretary and bookcase" in Hepplewhite's *Cabinet-Maker and Upholsterer's Guide* (fig. 20). Several Salem secretaries conforming to the description in the second entry are known. The most common variant has three drawers in the lower section and short tapered legs.[27]

Figure 19 Lady's secretary, Salem, Massachusetts, 1800–1810. Mahogany with pine. H. 61¼", W. 38", D. 29¼". (Courtesy, Peabody Essex Museum; bequest of Mrs. Arthur West.)

Figure 20 Design for a "Secretary and Bookcase" illustrated on plate 44 of the third edition of George Hepplewhite's *Cabinet-Maker and Upholsterer's Guide* (1794). (Courtesy, Winterthur Museum Library: Printed Books and Periodical Collection.)

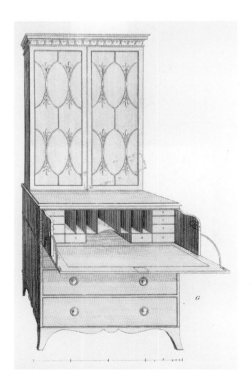

The lack of references to tambour doors is surprising since they are common on Salem secretaries, particularly the type described in the second entry. Also called writing tables or tambour tables, this form was fashionable in Salem by 1797. A desk with the branded initials of Elijah Sanderson illustrates one of the most common designs with a solid central prospect door and cabinets on either side (fig. 21). Shipping manifests frequently list lady's secretaries. Jacob Sanderson sent six valued at $243 to the Madeiras and the West Indies in 1806.[28]

[24] BUREAU, with canted corners, of best quality, finiered, decorated and crossbanded, 27
Making———9
[in ink] Voted Sept 7th 1802———25
[Making]———8

[25] Ditto, with a scolloped front, and decorated, 25
Making———8
[in ink] Voted Sept 7th 1802———24
[Making]———7/50

[26] Ditto, with a circular front, and decorated, 25
Making———7

[in ink] Voted Sept 7th 1802———23
[Making]———6/50

[27] Ditto, with straight front, and decorated, 20
Making———5.50
[in ink] Voted Sept 7th 1802———18
[Making]———5

[28] Ditto, birch———11
Making———5
[in ink] Voted Sept 21st 1802———10
[Making]———5

Chests of drawers with canted corners were popular in Salem by the 1780s. Six examples made between 1785 and 1800 have ogee feet related to those on a magnificent chest-on-chest made for Elizabeth Derby West in 1796. One

Figure 22 Circular front bureau, Salem, Massachusetts, 1795–1813. Mahogany and birch with pine. H. 37½", W. 41", D. 21½". (Courtesy, Peabody Essex Museum; gift of Francis and Miriam Shaw.) The chest descended in the family of Salem merchant Aaron Waite.

is completely in the rococo style, but the others have a modicum of neo-classical details. A chest in a private collection has a case and top with a modest cant, straight bracket feet, and a simplified inlaid decoration characteristic of later work. More numerous are examples of "scalloped" or serpentine-front bureaus, including one with straight bracket feet and the label of Thomas Needham. Many circular or bow front chests have also survived. A mahogany and birch veneered chest (fig. 22) that descended from merchant Aaron Waite of Salem is a sophisticated interpretation of the drop-panel form usually associated with Portsmouth. Waite was a frequent client of the Sandersons. In 1796, he paid them twenty-five dollars for a "mahogany Buro."[29]

[29] DINING-TABLES, by the set, to be 4½ feet wide, and to spread 8 feet in the square, with two semi-circular ends of 2 feet in width, which adds 4 feet to the length—the spreading of the whole extent to be 12 feet in length, and 4½ in breadth———60
Making———12

[30] Other sizes to be regulated in proportion.

[31] Ditto, common kind, spreading 4 feet square, 14
Making———3

[32] Ditto, birch, spreading 4 feet square———7
Making———3

Figure 23 Dining table, eastern Massachusetts, 1795–1815. Birch. H. 28", W. 47½", D. 46". (Courtesy, Peabody Essex Museum; gift of Charles Cotting, Jr.)

No documented Salem dining tables matching the first description have been identified, but they are mentioned in both three- and four-part forms in shipping invoices. On January 18, 1802, Jacob Sanderson sent "one sett mahogany dining tables varnished, four tables in the sett" valued at $116 to the West Indies on the brig *John*. Approximately seven years later, Elijah Sanderson exported a set of three tables valued at fifty-five dollars on the brig *Venus*. A drop-leaf table that descended in the Cotting family (fig. 23) conforms to the description in the last entry.[30]

> [33] CARD-TABLE, of the best quality, sash-cornered— — —14
> Making— — —4
>
> [34] Ditto, of best quality, circular, 12
> Making— — —3.33
>
> [35] Ditto, birch, or pine without painting— — —4
> Making— — —2

During the late eighteenth and early nineteenth centuries, Salem cabinet-makers made vast numbers of card tables for the local market and for export. Although the entries in the price book list only two shapes—"sash-cornered" and "circular"—furniture historian Benjamin Hewitt's study of card tables suggests that Salem cabinetmakers produced a variety of "square" tables as well as examples with elliptic fronts and serpentine ends. The first entry refers to a square table with ovolo corners, a shape Sheraton called "sash plan corners." A card table bearing the label of Thomas Needham (Yale University Art Gallery) is a conservative interpretation of this form.[31]

Most documented Salem card tables have panels of contrasting veneer on the skirt. An oval set within a mitered panel is one of the most common treatments. Salem craftsmen also used patterned inlay on the edges of the leaves and skirt. Round card tables inlaid with an oval fan or patera in the center of each section of the apron were especially popular between 1795 and 1800. This treatment appears on several tables made by Samuel and William Fiske (see fig. 24) and a table made by member George Whitefield Martin, while in partnership with Robert Choate in Concord, New Hampshire. In 1796, the Sandersons charged Aaron Waite of Salem twenty-four dollars for a pair of round card tables "with in Laid work."[32]

As the last entry indicates, painted tables cost one-third the price of a mahogany table. In 1808, Thomas Hodgkins charged $2.50 for "making a pine card table" for Jonathan Prince. Specialists such as William Gray and

Figure 24 Card table attributed to William and Samuel Fiske, Salem, Massachusetts, 1795–1800. Mahogany with pine. H. 28½", W. 35¾", D. 19½". (Courtesy, Peabody Essex Museum; bequest of Mrs. Isabel Newcomb.)

Figure 25 Night table made by Elijah Sanderson, Salem, Massachusetts, ca. 1800. Mahogany with pine. H. 29½", W. 25¾", D. 19". (Private collection; photo, Peabody Essex Museum.)

William Luscomb did the decorative painting. The latter charged Capt. Jacob Sanderson "0-9-3" for "painty a Card Table" in November 1801.[33]

> [36] NIGHT TABLE, of the common kind, 2 feet 4 inches high, and 2
> feet deep, without the pan ———12
> Making———4

Both Hepplewhite and Sheraton illustrated designs for night tables—small cabinets designed to conceal a chamberpot, basin, or pan. The more elaborate examples also contain compartments for a wash basin and other toiletries. A night table bearing the initials of Elijah Sanderson is one of the few documented Salem examples (fig. 25). Its dimensions are similar to those in the entry, and its form conforms to the description "common kind." The folding lid, which consists of two hinged panels, resembles the one on the right in plate 82 of Hepplewhite's *Cabinet-Maker and Upholsterer's Guide* (fig. 26). In 1808, Thomas Hodgkin charged four dollars for making "a corner night table" for the Sandersons.[34]

> [37] [in ink] Dec 6th 1803
> Voted Pembroke Tables 3 ft long & be $14

It is unclear why pembroke tables were not included in the initial printing of the price book. Small tables with folding leaves were popular much earlier, although some may have been referred to as "square," "breakfast," "folding," "leaf," or "tea" tables. An early example (Winterthur Museum) has several labels of Elijah and Jacob Sanderson. Its serpentine top and fluted Marlboro legs suggest a date in the 1780s; however, Charles Mont-

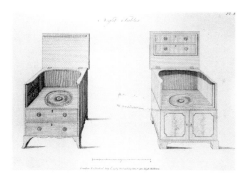

Figure 26 Designs for "Night Tables" illustrated on plate 82 of the third edition of George Hepplewhite's *Cabinet-Maker and Upholsterer's Guide* (1794). (Courtesy, Winterthur Museum Library: Printed Books and Periodical Collection.)

Figure 27 Pembroke table, possibly Salem, Massachusetts, 1795–1810. Mahogany with pine. H. 28", W. 33½", D. 33½". (Courtesy, Peabody Essex Museum.)

Figure 28 Quarter table, probably Maryland, 1795–1810. Mahogany with pine and tulip poplar. H. 32¾", W. 32¾", D. 22⅞". (Courtesy, Winterthur Museum.)

gomery speculated these features may have remained an option through the end of the century. The neoclassical table illustrated in figure 27 has a similar top, tapered legs, and string-inlaid drawer. This model is probably more representative of the price book entry than the Sanderson example. In 1802, Capt. John Derby purchased a veneered pembroke table from Jacob Sanderson for fourteen dollars.[35]

> [38] QUARTER-TABLE, of the best quality, decorated, 19 inches demi-circular———6
> Making———1.50

This entry probably describes a small corner table similar to the one illustrated in figure 28. Such tables were designed to fit snugly into the corner of a room and used for a variety of household functions including serving food and beverages. The cost cited in the price book is half that of a round card table. No Salem quarter-tables are known, but other triangular forms—corner sideboards, washstands, and night tables—are relatively common.[36]

> [39] SLAB-TABLE, without painting———3
> Making———1

Although the period term "slab table" generally refers to a rectangular table with a marble top, the amounts cited in the price book indicate a different form, possibly a simple folding table or an ironing board. An object conforming to this entry is described in the *Cabinet-Makers' London Book of Prices* under dining tables: a "four foot flap or slab, the top 3 inches wide, hung with a rule joint to the flap. With 2 fram'd brackets to support ditto, to fix against a wall." The kitchen in Elias Hasket Derby's mansion had a "folding board" valued at three dollars in 1799, and John Chandler charged Aaron Waite three dollars for "Making a folding board" in 1813. Waite's folding board was probably an ironing board, since Chandler billed him for "two closehorses" and a number of small kitchen items at the same time.[37]

A few Salem tables with faux marble tops are known including a pier or dressing table used by George Washington at Joshua Ward's home in 1789 (fig. 29). The top has a realistically marbleized surface and the frame and legs are grain-painted to imitate mahogany. In 1790, Salem painter William Gray painted a table "marble" for Joseph Sampson. Approximately six years later, he charged Dr. Edward A. Holyoke "1-25-0" for "painting a table mahogy & marble."[38]

[40] KITCHEN TABLE, with a drawer———3
Making———1.50

Many common kitchen tables from the early nineteenth century survive, but no documented Salem example is known. Most kitchen tables found in or near the town are pine and maple and have an overhanging rectangular top with "bread board" ends, square tapered legs with beaded edges, and a single drawer with a wooden pull. The frame and legs are usually painted, but the top is often left unfinished. Inexpensive tables were among the most popular export items.[39]

[41] STAND, mahogany, oval, to turn up———5
Making———1.50

An oval-top candlestand that descended in the Peirce-Nichols family of Salem (fig. 30) is one of the most successful interpretations of this popular

Figure 29 Table, Salem, Massachusetts, ca. 1789. Pine; black, brown, white, and ochre paint. H. 30¼", W. 42", D. 22¼". (Courtesy, Peabody Essex Museum; gift of Ellen Chever.)

Figure 30   Stand, Salem, Massachusetts, 1795–1805. Mahogany. H. 30½", W. 24", D. 15½". (Courtesy, Peabody Essex Museum; gift of Mrs. George Nichols.)

form. It is attributed to Salem based on its history and the similarity of its pillar to that on an earlier stand by William King. Several more elaborate candlestands with satinwood veneer and "check'd" inlay may also have been made there. Evidence suggests that Salem cabinetmakers routinely purchased pillars for stands and other three-legged forms from turners. The Sandersons purchased turned "stand pillars" from Jonathan Gavet and Daniel Clarke in 1801. The following year, Clarke charged them twenty-five cents for a single pillar.[40]

> [42] FIRE-SCREEN, of the common kind———8
> Making———2
> [in ink] Voted June 1st 1802 without flap leaf———7.5
> [Making]———1.6

Several Salem fire screens with a folding shelf or "flap leaf" to support a candlestick survive. The shield and shelf usually have a brass ring with a tension clip that engages the pole and allows the user to adjust the height. The example illustrated in figure 31 probably pre-dates the price book. It has pillar turnings similar to those on a candlestand made by John Gavet in 1784.[41]

On December 24, 1802, Jacob Sanderson paid Thomas Hodgson two dollars for making a fire screen. Three days later, Sanderson charged John Derby eight dollars for the same piece, which he described as a "Fire Screen with a leaf to sett candlestick on." Plate 93 of Hepplewhite's *Cabinet-Maker and Upholsterer's Guide* illustrates designs for three "Pole Fire Screens," one with a "pillar-and-claw" base similar to the example shown in figure 31.[42]

Figure 31   Firescreen, Salem, Massachusetts, 1795–1805. Mahogany. H. 59¾", W. 17½", D. 17½". (Courtesy, Peabody Essex Museum; bequest of George Rea Curwen.)

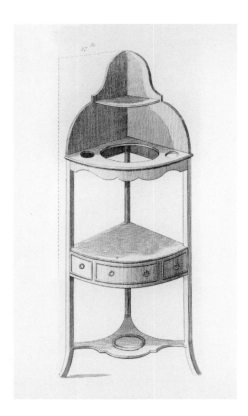

Figure 32 Design for a "Corner Basin Stand" illustrated on plate 42 of Thomas Sheraton's *Cabinet-Maker and Upholsterer's Drawing Book* (1793). (Courtesy, Winterthur Museum Library: Printed Books and Periodical Collection.)

Figure 33 Corner washstand, Salem, Massachusetts, 1800–1815. Mahogany with pine. H. 41", W. 14½", D. 14½". (Courtesy, Peabody Essex Museum; photo, Mark Sexton.)

[43] WASH-STAND, circular, of the common kind, 9
Making———3.50
[in ink] Voted June 1st 1802———8
[Making]———3

[44] Ditto, square———6
Making———2

The first entry refers to a corner basin stand, an object Hepplewhite considered "very useful . . . as it stands in a corner out of the way." Sheraton also published designs for this form (see fig. 32), one of which resembles an example (fig. 33) Lydia Kimball received from her uncle, Captain Joseph White. Although the maker of her stand is not known, similar ones are documented to Salem cabinetmakers Nehemiah Adams and William Hook.[43]

The stand mentioned in the last entry was probably neoclassical in style, but square basin stands were fashionable decades earlier. Hepplewhite published three variations on plate 84 of the *Cabinet-Maker and Upholsterer's Guide,* two with a lower shelf and drawer and one with a cabinet and drawer. The designs on the right and left have folding lids to conceal the basin, a feature found on one example attributed to Salem.[44]

During the late eighteenth and early nineteenth centuries, the terms "basin stand" and "wash stand" were used interchangeably. Lydia Waite purchased "1 bason stand" for "2-8-0" from William Appleton in 1796. Six years later, the Sandersons began exporting "wash hand stands," although they do not appear to have been in great demand as venture cargo until 1810. Like some of their contemporaries, the Sandersons purchased certain components for these forms from specialists. Turner Jonathan Gavet sold them parts for washstands in 1801.[45]

[45] CRADLE, mahogany— — —12
Making— — —3

[46] Ditto, cedar— — —8
Making— — —3

[47] Ditto, pine, without painting— — —4
Making— — —1.5
[in ink] Voted Sept 21st 1802 painted complete— — —5

The board cradles illustrated in figure 34 were probably made in Salem about the same date, given the similarity of various design and construction features. The more elegant mahogany example descended from George and Elizabeth Leach Watson who were married on June 14, 1801. On both cradles, dovetails join the footboard to the sides, whereas nails secure the bottom, rockers, and elements of the hood. The double-arch treatment on the side of each hood is identical, and both sets of rockers end in a modified volute. The Watson cradle retains its brass carrying handle on the footboard and back of the hood, a convenient feature no longer on the pine example. Entries in the price book suggest that the pine cradle cost half as much as the mahogany one.

Figure 34　Cradles, Salem, Massachusetts, 1790–1810. (left) Mahogany with pine. H. 29", L. 40", W. 21½". (right) Pine; blue-green paint. H. 31", L. 40", W. 20". (Courtesy, Peabody Essex Museum; [left] gift of Mr. and Mrs. Joseph K. Elliot.)

Figure 35 Sofa, possibly by Nathaniel Safford, with carving attributed to Samuel McIntire, Salem, Massachusetts, ca. 1805. Mahogany with unidentified secondary woods. H. 38½", L. 83", D. 33". (Private collection; photo, Mark Sexton.)

[48] SOFA FRAME, with a mahogany top-rail, excluding the carving——22
Making (the moulding to be finished)———6.50

[49] Ditto, without mahogany top———20
Making———5

Most documented Salem sofas contemporary with the price book have scrolled arms and serpentine or "commode" backs. Similar features are shown on sofas in eighteenth-century design books including the third edition of Thomas Chippendale's *The Gentleman and Cabinet-Maker's Director* (1762). Elizabeth Derby West owned one of the most elaborate Salem sofas (Museum of Fine Arts, Boston), whereas her relatives, John and Elizabeth West Gardner, purchased a slightly less ornate example for their new home in 1805 (fig. 35). Both sofas have a molded crest rail and a carved center ornament and arms. In 1801, Samuel McIntire charged Jacob Sanderson "1.7.0" for "carving [a] Sofa and working the top rail."[46]

As the last entry indicates, sofas "without [a] mahogany top" were also fashionable. In 1799, Salem upholsterer William Lemon shipped "two Mahogany sofas stuffed in Russia Sheetg [with] Copperplate furniture covers fring'd and bound" on the ship *John* bound for Surinam. While receipts show that the Sanderson firm made sofas in the 1790s, probably for local clients, sofas do not appear on their surviving shipping invoices until 1805. In April, Elijah Sanderson sent six sofas valued at one hundred dollars each on the ship *Exeter*.[47]

[50] EASY CHAIR FRAME———7
Making———2.50
[in ink] Voted June 1st 1802———6
[Making]———2.50

Figure 36 Easy chair, Salem, Massachusetts, ca. 1800. Mahogany. H. 48", W. 27½", D. 21". (Courtesy, Peabody Essex Museum, bequest of George Rea Curwen; photo, Mark Sexton.)

Figure 37 Design for an "Easy Chair" illustrated on plate 15 of the second edition of George Hepplewhite's *Cabinet-Maker and Upholsterer's Guide* (1789). (Courtesy, Winterthur Museum Library: Printed Books and Periodical Collection.)

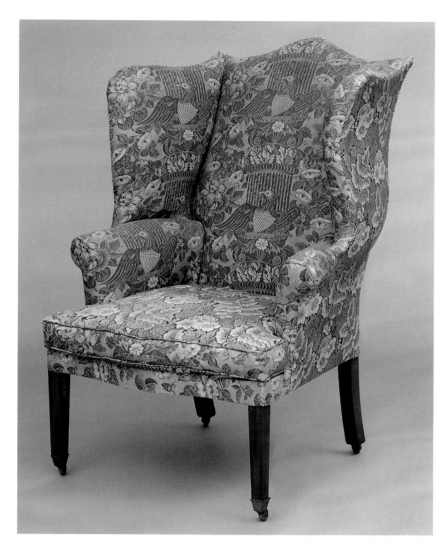

Although no easy chair has been documented to a specific Salem cabinet-maker or chair maker, an example that descended in the George Rea Curwen family (fig. 36) was probably made there about 1800. The contours of the cheeks and crest are similar to those in Hepplewhite's design for a "Saddle Check, or easy chair" (fig. 37). References to easy chairs are rare in shipping manifests, suggesting that most were commissioned by local consumers. Merchant Aaron Waite's large order for furniture from the Sandersons in 1796 included "1 Easy chair stuft" valued at twelve dollars. Five years later, upholsterer Jonathan Bright charged $8.50 for "Stufing" an easy chair.[48]

> [51] MAHOGANY CHAIR, finished with drapery back, &c. excluding
> the carving———6
> Making———2
> [in ink] Voted December 1st 1801———5.50
> [Making]———2

This entry probably refers to a high-back upholstered armchair with a carved crest. Several examples from Salem are known, including a matching pair in the Winterthur Museum and the one illustrated in figure 38. The term

Figure 38 Armchair, Salem, Massachusetts, 1795–1805. Mahogany with unidentified secondary woods. H. 43½", W. 23", D. 19½". (Courtesy, Peabody Essex Museum; gift of George Rea Curwen.)

"drapery back" refers to the carved swag on the crest rail. The shape of the crest was adapted from a sofa design on plate 35 in Sheraton's *Cabinet-Maker and Upholsterer's Drawing Book*, and the sloping arms and turned supports were derived from the chair shown on plate 6, number 3, of *The London Chair-Makers' and Carvers' Book of Prices* (1802).[49]

[52] LOLLING-CHAIR FRAME, with mahogany arms — — —5
Making — — —2

Inventories attest to the popularity of lolling chairs in Salem and indicate that most were used in parlors in pairs. Many of those shipped as venture cargo had muslin upholstery and slipcovers. Upholsterer William Lemon sent four mahogany lolling chairs "with copperplate furniture covers, Fring'd and bound with cotton lace" valued at twenty dollars each on the ship *John* bound for Surinam in 1799. No lolling chair can be documented to a specific Salem maker, but many have local histories. A chair that

Figure 39 Lolling chair, Salem, Massachusetts, ca. 1805. Mahogany with unidentified secondary woods. H. 42", W. 24", D. 21". (Private collection; photo, Peabody Essex Museum.)

descended from John and Elizabeth Gardner (fig. 39), the original owners of the Gardner-Pingree House, represents one of the most popular designs. The couple purchased several pieces of furniture for their new house from cabinetmaker Nathaniel Safford in 1805.[50]

[53] WINDOW-STOOL FRAME, excluding the carving———6
Making———2

Many mahogany window stools are attributed to Salem, including a set of four that remain in their original location in the parlor of the Peirce-Nichols House (fig. 40). The carved details have parallels in Hepplewhite's designs (see fig. 41) and echoed features in the room, which was remodeled under the direction of Samuel McIntire in 1801. Hepplewhite commented that "the size of the window stools must be regulated by the size of the place where they are to stand." This may explain why the form does not appear on any venture cargo lists.[51]

Figure 40 Window stool with carving attributed to Samuel McIntire, Salem, Massachusetts, 1801. Mahogany with unidentified secondary woods. H. 26", W. 44½", D. 14¾". (Courtesy, Peabody Essex Museum, gift of the estate of Charlotte Nichols; photo, Mark Sexton.)

[54] BEDSTEAD, mahogany, swelled pillars, excluding the carving, fluting and sacking, 16
Making (to be finished, the sacking put in, &c.)———4

[55] Ditto, birch, excluding the sacking———12
Making (finished as above)———4

[56] Ditto, mahogany field, excluding the sacking, 18
Making (finished as above)———4.50
[in ink] Dec 6th 1803 if all the parts mahogany $20

[57] Ditto, birch field, excluding the sacking, 12
Making (finished as above) 4.50
[in ink] Dec 6 1803———14

[58] Ditto, press———6
Making———2.50
[in ink] Voted Dec 1st 1801———5
[Making]———2.50

[59] Ditto, cot, excluding the sacking———3
Making———1.50

[60] Ditto, low post———3
[in ink] Dec 6th 1803———3.50

During the late eighteenth and early nineteenth centuries, Daniel Clarke, Jonathan Gavet, and Nathaniel Safford invoiced the Sandersons for turning pillars for high- and low-post beds and urns for field beds. On October 7, 1800, Nathaniel Safford received three dollars for "two set[s] of highbedstead pillars." The Sandersons subcontracted most of the carving on bedsteads

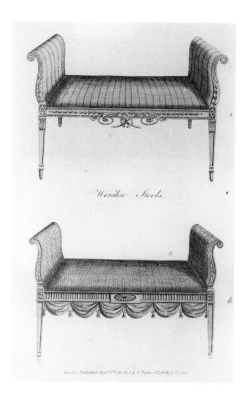

Figure 41 Designs for "Window Stools" illustrated on plate 19 of the third edition of George Hepplewhite's *Cabinet-Maker and Upholsterer's Guide* (1794). (Courtesy, Winterthur Museum Library: Printed Books and Periodical Collection.)

Figure 42 Detail of a bed post with carving attributed to Samuel McIntire, 1801–1811. Mahogany. H. 76", W. 4", D. 4". (Courtesy, Peabody Essex Museum, gift of the estate of Charlotte Nichols; photo, Mark Sexton.)

and other forms to Samuel McIntire. Two of the most ornate posts attributed to McIntire's shop are on a bedstead made for Jerathamiel Peirce (fig. 42). A bedstead originally owned by George and Elizabeth Watson is less elaborate, but more typical of Salem production (fig. 43). Family tradition maintains that it survived a fire at their house in 1801. The bed retains its original painted cornice with floral and leaf swags, tassels, and central landscape panels in shades of brown, orange, yellow, and pink. On June 5, 1804, Samuel Page paid Jacob Sanderson six dollars for a "bedcornish & Painting same." Bed cornices are often mentioned in the accounts of fancy chair makers. Richard Austin received $4.50 for "Painting & Gilding [a] set [of] Cornishes" for Mrs. Rodgers' bed in October 1805.[52]

Figure 43 Bedstead, Salem, 1795–1801. Mahogany and maple with pine. H. 87", W. 57", D. 79". (Courtesy, Peabody Essex Museum, gift of Deborah J. Elliot: photo, Mark Sexton.)

Figure 44 Folding cot, probably Salem, Massachusetts, nineteenth century. Maple, pine, iron, and canvas. H. 25", W. 79", D. 55". (Courtesy, Peabody Essex Museum; photo, Mark Sexton.)

Figure 45 *Luxe et Indigence*, France, ca. 1818. Engraving. Dimensions not recorded.

Cots were the least expensive sleeping form listed in the price book. In 1804, Joshua Howard made one for Capt. Andrew Tucker, charging $1.75 for the frame, two dollars for labor, and six dollars for "10 yds Russia Duck." Six years later, Frederick Breed paid Jacob Sanderson's estate $3.50 for "a Cott bedsted" and an additional $3.50 for the canvas bottom. A nineteenth-century folding cot found in the attic of the Gardner-Pingree House in Salem (fig. 44) consists of two chamfered square rails supported by two sets of crossed legs with stretchers. The joints are marked with Roman numerals and secured with wooden pegs. The position of the legs is adjustable using either of two holes at the center of the legs and a removable peg. The end of each rail is bound with a narrow metal band next to which is a half-

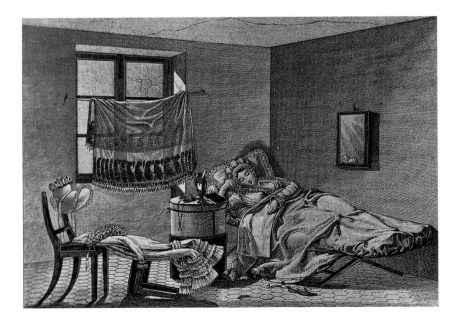

Figure 46 Sea chest, probably Salem, Massachusetts, 1811–1830. Pine; gray paint. H. 18¾", W. 49½", D. 18". (Courtesy, Peabody Essex Museum, gift of the Reverend George D. Latimer; photo, Mark Sexton.) This chest belonged to Capt. Charles Hoffman of Salem.

inch round hole presumably to secure a frame for curtains or a canopy. The sleeping platform consists of two pieces of coarse canvas sewn together down the middle with each outer edge permanently embedded into the rail using glue and a wedge of wood. A French engraving from about 1818 shows a cot of similar construction being used in a garret chamber (fig. 45).[53]

> [61] SEAMAN'S CHEST, 4 feet, without painting, 6
> Making———2

Several seaman's chests from Salem are known, most of which are comprised of six boards and have massive corner dovetails and a hinged lid. The chest owned by Captain Charles Hoffman of Salem (fig. 46) has the traditional rope beckets on either side for carrying. The plain unpainted interior has a narrow covered till to one side. Other examples have additional features such as a small drawer below or partitions to secure bottles.

> [in ink] Voted Dec 6th 1803
> That the price of the large size
> [62] Mehogany Coffin be———$20
>
> [63] Cedar Ditto———14
>
> [64] Pine ditto———4

The Sanderson firm was probably producing coffins by 1789, when they imported fifty-three cedar logs from Charleston, South Carolina. Salem cabinetmakers preferred that wood for coffins, the interiors of small drawers, and cradles. Thomas Hodgkins' account with the firm mentions only three coffins between July and December 1808. In August and November, he made pine coffins for two dollars each. References to coffins in business papers often give the name of the deceased or an agent of their estate. Decorative painter Robert Cowan charged the Sandersons $3.33 1/3 for a "Coffin Plate Lettered & Clasp for Mrs. Dana" in 1803, and Hodgkins' account mentions a "coffin for Mr. Clark" in July 1808. Although coffins for children are not specifically mentioned in the price book, they were undoubtedly less expensive than comparable examples for adults. Michele Felice Corne's *The Death of William* depicts a child's example commissioned by the Webb or Luscomb family of Salem (fig. 47).[54]

The clerk of the Salem Cabinet-Maker Society made the last notations in the price book on December 6, 1803. Earlier that year, nine members had joined forces to send fifty cases of mahogany furniture valued at over $5,000 to Brazil. Although this venture was consistent with the society's mission to create "important advantages" for its members, Elijah Sanderson's instructions to supercargo Jeremiah Briggs suggests that external and internal forces were undermining the price agreement:

> It often happen that furniture shipped by different people on board the same vessel is invoiced at different prices some higher and some lower of the same kind and quality and sometimes there is a difference in the goodness of the work and stock and when the whole is sold together at a particular rate for the invoice and all of the different invoices together, it is a disadvantage to those whose furniture put a lower rate is of a quality to

Figure 47 Michele Felice Cornè, *The Death of William*, Salem, Massachusetts, ca. 1807. Watercolor on paper. 19½" x 15". (Courtesy, Peabody Essex Museum; deposit of Mrs. Nathaniel S. Sanders.) The deceased was a member of the Webb or Luscomb family of Salem.

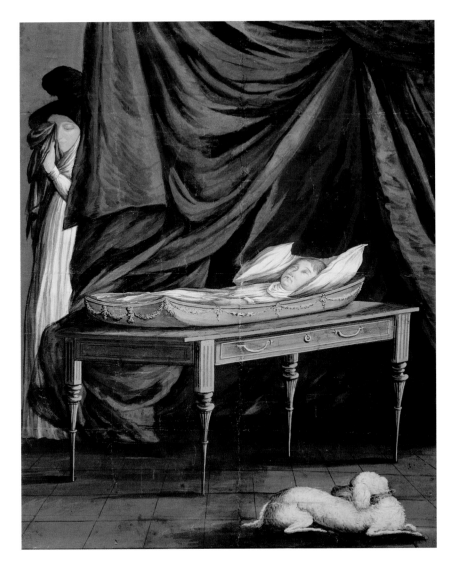

have it sold together—therefore I wish you to sell mine by itself—not to mix it in a bargin with others and let me have the benefit of the sale of my own—you will find that my furniture is all marked with a brand E.S. on the back of each piece besides the mark on the case.

Given the competitive and entrepreneurial nature of Salem's cabinetmaking trade, it was inevitable that competition with non-members would arise.[55]

The Sandersons' business began to unravel following Jacob's death in 1810 and ended amid bitter lawsuits when the restructuring failed. The furniture industry had suffered during the embargo of 1807 and the War of 1812. During this period, many cabinet and chair makers went bankrupt, and the furniture export trade all but vanished. In 1811, Rev. William Bentley admonished artisans involved in speculative ventures, many of whom had joined new religious organizations that challenged the supremacy of older established churches in town:

A strange deficiency of honesty among the officers of the Churches which have professed great zeal for conversions. Deacons S[anderson, Elijah] and L[amson] are added to the list of fraudulent bankrupts, & B[urpee] A[mes] is abroad upon the public courtesy. . . . Salem has been unhappy in the wretches designated for these offices. . . . The failures of the speculators have strongly fallen upon the enthusiastic leaders of little Sects. Deacons Batchelder, Saunderson, Meservy, Safford, Adams, Palfrey, Lamson. . . . None of these have been natives of Salem or well informed men, but thrusting themselves from mechanic employment's into mercantile affairs & venturing largely upon credit, breaking embargo laws, & and making promises have plunged themselves into the greatest evils.[56]

For many members of the Salem Cabinet-Maker Society, economic misfortune extracted a much larger toll. In 1810, Eziekiel Goodnow and George Martin died at the early ages of thirty-six and thirty-nine respectively. The following year, Edmund Johnson was lost at sea while overseeing his own declining business. Samuel Cheever committed suicide in 1818. Other members who had drifted into town during its prosperous days moved on and found opportunities elsewhere. Jonathan Marston, for example, settled in Maine in 1812 and became a lumber dealer. Salem's furniture industry eventually recovered and expanded in the ensuing decades under the leadership of a new generation of artisans, who presumably had not been members of the earlier society. They found a new voice for their collective interests in the founding of the Salem Charitable Mechanic Association in 1817, electing cabinetmaker Thomas Needham as their first president.[57]

1. The Phillips Library (hereafter cited PL), Peabody Essex Museum (hereafter cited PEM), purchased the booklet from Cambridge, Massachusetts, bookseller Charles B. Wood III, who acquired it at auction (Swann Gallery, *Printed and Manuscript Americana Featuring Western Americana*, New York, December 2, 1999, lot 463). A bibliography of previous works is included in Margaret Burke Clunie, "Salem Federal Furniture" (master's thesis, University of Delaware, 1976), pp. 304–10.

2. Charles Montgomery, *American Furniture: The Federal Period* (New York: Viking Press, 1966), pp. 19–26, 488–89; Martin Eli Weil, "A Cabinetmaker's Price Book," *Winterthur Portfolio* 13 (1979): 175–92; and Benjamin Hewitt, et al., *The Work of Many Hands: Card Tables in America, 1790–1820* (New Haven, Conn.: Yale University Press, 1982), pp. 46–47. Montgomery, *American Furniture*, p. 19.

3. Clunie, "Salem Federal Furniture," p. 302. Although Edmund Johnson was primarily a cabinetmaker, he occasionally sold chairs. In the October 31, 1800, *Salem Gazette*, he advertised "mahogany furniture, and Windsor Chairs of all kinds at the lowest cash prices." For more on Windsor chair makers in Salem, see Nancy Goyne Evans, *American Windsor Chairs* (New York: Hudson Hills Press, 1996), pp. 365–69. Mabel Munson Swan, *Samuel McIntire and the Sandersons: Early Salem Cabinet Makers* (Salem, Mass.: Essex Institute, 1934), p. 29. Some cabinetmakers, such as Daniel Clarke, advertised cabinetmaking, chair making, and carving.

4. Richard J. Morris, "Wealth Distribution in Salem, Massachusetts, 1759–1799, the Impact of the Revolution and Independence," *Essex Institute Historical Collections* 114 (1978): 101; and James Duncan Phillips, *Salem and the Indies: The Story of the Great Commerical Era of the City* (Boston: Houghton Mifflin, 1947), pp. 224–30. Clunie, "Salem Federal Furniture," p. 14.

5. Fiske Kimball, *Samuel McIntire, Carver: The Architect of Salem* (Salem, Mass.: Essex Institute, 1940), p. 71. *The Diary of William Bentley, D.D., Pastor of the East Church, Salem, Massachusetts*, 4 vols. (1905–1914; reprint, Gloucester, Mass.: Peter Smith, 1962), 4: 55. Clunie, "Salem Federal Furniture," p. 300.

6. Swan, *Samuel McIntire and the Sandersons*, pp. 1–3. The Sandersons were originally from Watertown, and Austin was originally from Charlestown. Austin's association with the Sandersons may explain his brother Richard's membership in the Cabinet-Maker Society. Richard Austin was primarily a chair maker, and membership was generally limited to master cabinetmakers.

7. Clunie, "Salem Federal Furniture," p. 23. See also Margaret B. Clunie, "Furniture Crafts-

men of Salem, Massachusetts in the Federal Period," *Essex Institute Historical Collections* 113 (1997): 191–203.

8. See the appendix for biographical information on the founding members. In the initial printing, the name of Edmund Johnson was left off the list, probably in error, so the printer pasted a new list in a slightly different order over the original listing. Daniel Clarke, who served as first clerk of the Salem Cabinet-Maker Society, worked as a cabinetmaker and carver in Boston prior to 1794 and as a journeyman for the Sandersons in 1794. The Sandersons purchased ebony from William Appleton in 1799. Clunie, "Salem Federal Furniture," pp. 29, 30, 48.

9. Two officers were elected at the December meeting, a moderator to run the meetings and a clerk to record all transactions.

10. Swan, *Samuel McIntire and the Sandersons*, pp. 13, 26.

11. Jenks advertised copies of the first edition of Hepplewhite's *The Cabinet-Maker and Upholsterer's Guide* (1788) in 1791 and 1792. The copy he advertised in 1794 could be the first or second (1789) edition. For more on these copies and the importation of design books into Salem, see Barbara Jobe, "Importation of Books into Salem, Massachusetts: 1783–1799," unpublished research paper, 1972, p. 5, PL, PEM. Jacob Sanderson's 1810 inventory lists three copies of Hepplewhite's design book (Swan, *Samuel McIntire and the Sandersons*, p. 55).

12. Clunie, "Salem Federal Furniture," p. 302. Clunie notes that the 109 surviving manifests are incomplete for the period mentioned, thus her analysis only points to the relative popularity of each form. Her list includes the following forms and number of references to each: basin stands (3), bureaus (23), cabinets (3), cabinet-bookcases (2), candlestands (2), card tables (39), clock cases (9), chairs (1,231), chests (6), desks (177), desk and bookcases (1), lady's secretaries (6), light stands (4), lolling chairs (10), night tables (1), pembroke tables (7), secretaries (6), secretary-bookcases (19), sideboards (8), sofas (4), stands (25), and tables (80). Swan, *Samuel McIntire and the Sandersons*, p. 19. A work table made by Philadelphia cabinetmaker Robert McGuffin in 1808 is illustrated and discussed in David L. Barquist, *American Tables and Looking Glasses in the Mabel Brady Garvan and Other Collections at Yale University* (New Haven, Conn.: Yale University Press, 1992), pp. 290–93. An invoice dated November 21, 1809, for furniture shipped by Elijah Sanderson on the schooner *Neutrality* includes three lady's dressing boxes valued at six dollars each. Sanderson Papers, (hereafter cited SP), PL, PEM. Imported knife boxes, tea caddys, trays, and bottle boxes were readily available in Salem. American cabinetmakers usually found it more profitable to sell British examples than to produce their own interpretations.

13. Montgomery, *American Furniture*, p. 23.

14. The two entries for a lady's secretary, for example, are the only ones describing feet. One entry mentions "bracket feet" and the other "legs." The entries for desks indicate a demand for older designs, but they do not specify options such as claw-and-ball feet and ogee bracket feet. Swan, *Samuel McIntire and the Sandersons*, pp. 9, 13–14, 31. Turned legs are not mentioned in invoices submitted by Samuel McIntire, Daniel Clarke, and Jonathan Gavet to the Sandersons between 1801 and 1803.

15. Checkered cock beading occurs on several elaborate case pieces made in Salem during the late eighteenth and early nineteenth centuries. See Jonathan Fairbanks and Elizabeth Bates, *American Furniture, 1620 to the Present* (New York: Richard Marek Publishers, 1981), p. 199, for a magnificent chest-on-chest with checkered cock beading made for Elizabeth Derby West in 1796.

16. Richard H. Randall, Jr., *American Furniture in the Museum of Fine Arts, Boston* (Boston: By the museum, 1965), p. 96, fig. 67.

17. Clunie, "Salem Federal Furniture," p. 147. Invoice for Elijah Sanderson, August 4, 1804, SP, PL, PEM. Waite Family Papers, PL, PEM. Clement E. Conger and Alexandra W. Rollins, *Treasures of State: Fine and Decorative Arts in the Diplomatic Reception Rooms of the U.S. Department of State* (New York: Harry N. Abrams, 1991), p. 79.

18. John Bivins, "The Convergence and Divergence of Three Stylistic Traditions in Charleston Neoclassical Case Furniture, 1785–1800," in *American Furniture*, edited by Luke Beckerdite (Hanover, N. H.: University Press of New England for the Chipstone Foundation, 1997), pp. 47–105.

19. Margaret Burke Clunie, Anne Farnam, and Robert Trent, *Furniture at the Essex Institute* (Salem, Mass.: Essex Institute, 1980), p. 31.

20. Ropes Family Papers, PL, PEM.

21. Ibid. A sideboard (acc. 137,782) with a secretary drawer and string and husk inlay is in the collection of the Peabody Essex Museum. Dean Lahikainen, "The Gardner-Pingree House,

Salem, Massachusetts," *Antiques* 137, no. 3 (March 1990): 721, 724. Sideboards with reeded legs are not mentioned in cabinetmakers' receipts until 1808 (Swan, *Samuel McIntire and the Sandersons*, p. 22).

22. James B. Bell and Cynthia Dunn Fleming, "Furniture from the Atkinson-Lancaster Collection at the New England Historic and Genealogical Society," *Antiques* 113, no. 5 (May 1978): 1082. For other examples with "swell'd" façades, see Brock Jobe and Myrna Kaye, *New England Furniture, The Colonial Era: Selections from the Society for the Preservation of New England Antiquities* (Boston: Houghton Mifflin, 1984), pp. 230–38. Ropes Family Papers, PL, PEM.

23. Philip Zea, Robert Cheney, and Caroline F. Sloat, eds., *Clock Making in New England, 1725–1825: An Interpretation of the Old Sturbridge Village Collection* (Sturbridge, Mass.: Old Sturbridge Village, 1992), pp. 38–40.

24. Theodore R. Crom, "An American Beauty: The Samuel Mulliken II, Salem, Mass., Dwarf Clock," *National Association of Watch and Clock Collectors Bulletin* 37, no. 299 (December 1995): 756–61. Other members of the Mulliken family had connections in Salem. Samuel's brother Joseph worked as a watchmaker there in the early 1790s, and his brother, John, sent two clocks as venture cargo with the Sandersons in 1799 (Swan, *Samuel McIntire and the Sandersons*, pp. 2, 8, 14). Benjamin Balch, a member of the Newburyport clockmaking family, began working as a watchmaker in Salem in 1796. Edmund Currier is documented as a clockmaker in David R. Proper, "Edmund Currier Clockmaker," *Essex Institute Historical Collections* 91, no. 4 (October 1965): 281–88. Henry Wyckoff Belknap, *Artists and Craftsmen of Essex County, Massachusetts* (Salem, Mass.: Essex Institute, 1927), pp. 84–108.

25. Swan, *Samuel McIntire and the Sandersons*, pp. 9, 14. Swan, *Samuel McIntire and the Sandersons*, p. 8. Belknap, *Artists and Craftsmen of Essex County*, pp. 84–108. Swan, *Samuel McIntire and the Sandersons*, p. 8. Simon Willard to Jacob Sanderson, November 21, 1804, SP, PL, PEM.

26. Swan, *Samuel McIntire and the Sandersons*, p. 37. Inventory of Elias Hasket Derby, October 7 , 1799, Derby Family Papers, PL, PEM.

27. Elijah Sanderson made a lady's secretary similar to the one shown in fig. 19 for his daughter Sally. A photograph of the piece is in the Sanderson Papers, PL, PEM. Montgomery, *American Furniture*, no. 190.

28. *Museum of Fine Arts, Boston, Bulletin* 81 (1983): 39. Swan, *Samuel McIntire and the Sandersons*, p. 12.

29. Conger and Rollins, *Treasures of State*, p. 179; and Brock Jobe, et al., *Portsmouth Furniture: Masterworks from the New Hampshire Seacoast* (Hanover, N.H.: University Press of New England for the Society for the Preservation of New England Antiquities, 1993), p. 108. Christie's, *The Collection of Mr. and Mrs. James L. Britton*, New York, January 16, 1999, lot 605. The chest with the modest cant is illustrated in Bivins, "The Convergence and Divergence of Three Stylistic Traditions," p. 88, fig. 34. Another example is published in Israel Sack, Inc., *American Furniture from Israel Sack Collection* 3 (January 1970): 580, no. 1353. Related examples from other centers influenced by Salem include a chest by Langley Boardman discussed in Jobe, *Portsmouth Furniture*, p. 106. The Needham chest appears in Dean A. Fales, Jr., *Essex County Furniture: Documented Treasures from Local Collections, 1660–1860* (Salem, Mass.: Essex Institute, 1965), fig. 28. The Waite receipt is cited in Swan, *Samuel McIntire and the Sandersons*, p. 36.

30. A set of three tables (ca. 1800), probably from the Portsmouth-Salem area, is in the Strawbery Banke collection. Each section has tapered legs with simple inlay. The dimensions are close to those given in the first table entry in the price book. For an illustration of the set, see Northeast Auctions, *New Hampshire Auction*, Portsmouth, N. H., November 6–7, 1999, lot 857. Invoices dated January 18, 1802, and December 25, 1809, SP, PL, PEM.

31. Montgomery, *American Furniture*, no. 294. Hewitt, *The Work of Many Hands* , p. 133.

32. Hewitt, *The Work of Many Hands*, pp. 116, 131. Receipt dated July 7, 1796, SP, PL, PEM.

33. Swan, *Samuel McIntire and the Sandersons*, p. 22.

34. Ibid.

35. Montgomery, *American Furniture*, p. 347. Swan, *Samuel McIntire and the Sandersons*, p. 22. A receipt dated May 20, 1796, is in the Waite Family Papers, PL, PEM.

36. Montgomery, *American Furniture*, no. 355. Corner sideboards attributed to Salem are illustrated in Israel Sack, Inc., *American Furniture from Israel Sack Collection* 2 (April 1965): 767, no. 311 and 3 (September 1971): 773, no. 3322. The Peabody Essex Museum has a Salem corner washstand, acc. no. 102937.8.

37. Inventory of Elias Haskett Derby, October 7, 1799, Derby Family Papers. Receipt dated October 20, 1813, Waite Family Papers, PL, PEM.

38. Ledger of William Gray, 1750–1819, PL, PEM.

39. Examples appear in Skinner's, *American Furniture and Decorative Arts*, Bolton, Massachusetts, August 12, 2000, lots 57, 64, 328.

40. Israel Sack, Inc., *American Furniture from Israel Sack Collection* 2 (April 1965): 305, no. 744. Randall, *American Furniture in the Museum of Fine Arts, Boston*, no. 108; Conger and Rollins, *Treasures of State*, p. 206; and Montgomery, *American Furniture*, p. 389. Swan, *Samuel McIntire and the Sandersons*, pp. 19, 31.

41. For related fire screens, see Dean A. Fales, Jr., *Furniture of Historic Deerfield* (New York: E. P. Dutton, 1976), p. 163; and Montgomery, *American Furniture*, no. 203. The Gavet stand is pictured in Randall, *American Furniture in the Museum of Fine Arts, Boston*, no. 106.

42. Swan, *Samuel McIntire and the Sandersons*, pp. 20–21.

43. Hepplewhite, *Guide*, p. 15. Randall, *American Furniture in the Museum of Fine Arts, Boston*, nos. 101, 137; and Clunie, "Salem Federal Furniture," p. 237.

44. For earlier examples, see pl. 55 in the third edition of Thomas Chippendale, *The Gentleman and Cabinet-Maker's Director* (1762). Peabody Essex Museum, acc. no. 132, 787.

45. Receipt, William Appleton to Lydia Waite, March 1796, Waite Family Papers, PL, PEM. Invoice for the schooner *Sally*, March 30, 1802, SP, PL, PEM. Swan, *Samuel McIntire and the Sandersons*, p. 31.

46. Clunie, "Furniture Craftsmen of Salem," p. 199. The West sofa is illustrated in Fairbanks and Bates, *American Furniture, 1620 to the Present*, p. 217. The McIntire receipt is cited in Swan, *Samuel McIntire and the Sandersons*, p. 18.

47. Although square-back sofas with turned legs are illustrated in Thomas Sheraton's *Cabinet-Maker and Upholsterer's Drawing Book* (1793), the form did not become popular in Salem until around 1810. In that year, Lucy Hill purchased a fully carved version from Nehemiah Adams for sixty-seven dollars. Upholsterer Jonathan Bright charged her nineteen dollars for "Stufing" it and an additional twelve dollars for making a cushion (Nancy Cooper, "Samuel McIntire, Carver; Nehemiah Adams, Maker," *House Beautiful* 69 [1931]: 394–95). Shipping manifest, April 25, 1805, SP, PL, PEM.

48. Swan, *Samuel McIntire and the Sandersons*, pp. 33, 36.

49. Montgomery, *American Furniture*, p. 165.

50. Clunie, "Salem Federal Furniture," p. 199. Lahikainen, "The Gardner-Pingree House, Salem, Massachusetts," p. 721.

51. Montgomery, *American Furniture*, p. 263. *Elegant Embellishments: Furnishings from New England Homes, 1660–1860*, edited by Penny J. Sander (Boston: Society for the Preservation of New England Antiquities, 1982), p. 53. Hepplewhite, *Guide*, p. 4.

52. Swan, *Samuel McIntire and the Sandersons*, pp. 31, 37. Two other documented Salem bedsteads are at the Peabody Essex Museum. One was made by Jacob Sanderson for Aaron Waite in 1807 (Clunie, Farnam, and Trent, *Furniture at the Essex Institute*, p. 38). The other, which bears the label of Thomas Needham, is illustrated in Fales, *Essex County Furniture*, no. 27. A Salem field bed, 1801–1810, is pictured in Sotheby's, *Important Americana, Furniture, Folk Art and Decorations*, New York, October 15, 1999, lot 83; and Northeast Auctions, *New Hampshire Weekend Americana Auction*, Portsmouth, N. H., March 3–4, 2001, lot 949. Swan, *Samuel McIntire and the Sandersons*, p. 28.

53. Gideon Tucker Family Papers, vol. 2, p. 96, PL, PEM. Sanderson Papers, PL, PEM.

54. Swan, *Samuel McIntire and the Sandersons*, pp. 6, 22–23. Mark Pitman charged twenty dollars for a mahogany coffin and five dollars for a silver plate for "Miss Abigail Ropes" in 1839 (Nathaniel Ropes Papers, PL, PEM). Salem cabinetmakers do not appear to have exported coffins.

55. Swan, *Samuel McIntire and the Sandersons*, p. 9.

56. Clunie, "Salem Federal Furniture," p. 300. *Diary of William Bentley*, 3: 51–52. The sects included Baptists, Methodists, Free-Will Baptists, and Adventists. See Phillips, *Salem and the Indies*, p. 202.

57. Gary Kornblith, "From Artisans to Businessmen: Master Mechanics in New England, 1789–1850" (Ph.D. diss., Princeton University, 1983), p. 177.

Appendix A

NEHEMIAH ADAMS was baptized in Ipswich, Massachusetts, on April 16, 1769, and died in Salem on January 24, 1840. He married Mehitable Torry of Boston in 1802. He purchased his shop on the corner of Newbury and Williams Streets in Salem in 1796. It burned down on April 3, 1798. Adams was briefly in partnership with Benjamin Adams and Thomas Russell Williams in 1804. The former was active in the venture cargo trade and was a part owner of three vessels, including the brig *Unicorn* in 1804 (with the Sandersons). Documented furniture includes a labeled gentleman's secretary (Winterthur Museum) and a suite of furniture made for Lucy Hill Foster in 1810.

SOURCES: Ethel Hall Bjerkoe, *The Cabinetmakers of America* (Garden City, N.Y.: Doubleday, 1957), p. 20; Henry Wyckoff Belknap, *Artists and Craftsmen of Essex County, Massachusetts* (Salem, Mass.: Essex Institute, 1927), p. 23; Margaret Burke Clunie, "Salem Federal Furniture" (master's thesis, University of Delaware, 1976), p. 140; Essex County Registry of Deeds, 159: 232; A. Frank Hitchings, *Ship Registers of the District of Salem and Beverly, Massachusetts, 1789–1900* (Salem, Mass.: Essex Institute, 1906), pp. 62, 86, 191; Fiske Kimball, "Salem Furniture Makers II, Nehemiah Adams," *Antiques* 24, no. 6 (December 1933): 218–20; Charles Montgomery, *American Furniture: The Federal Period* (New York: Viking Press, 1966), no. 181; and Nancy Cooper, "Some Documented Salem Furniture," *House Beautiful* 69, no. 4 (April 1931): 280–81.

WILLIAM APPLETON was baptized in Ipswich, Massachusetts, on June 30, 1765, and died in Salem on September 23, 1822. He probably apprenticed with his father, William. The younger Appleton's shop was on Essex Street by 1794, and near the Sun Tavern on the corner of Liberty and Charter Streets from 1795 until 1804. He purchased a house and land on Market Street in 1798. He was a part owner of the snow *Fanny* with the Sandersons and the schooner *Olive Branch* with Josiah Austin and the Sandersons. Documented pieces include a lady's tambour desk (Winterthur Museum) and a labeled secretary-and-bookcase (Winterthur Museum).

SOURCES: Bjerkoe, *Cabinetmakers of America,* p. 29; Belknap, *Artists and Craftsmen of Essex County,* p. 26; Clunie, "Salem Federal Furniture," pp. 153–56; Essex County Registry of Deeds, 164: 172; Hitchings, *Ship Registers of the District of Salem and Beverly,* pp. 59, 136; Clunie, "Salem Federal Furniture," p. 154; and Montgomery, *American Furniture,* no. 178.

JOSIAH AUSTIN was born in Charlestown, Massachusetts, on April 27, 1746, the son of Josiah Austin (b. 1719) and Mary Austin. He died in Salem on November 5, 1825. His brother Richard was a chair maker. Josiah moved to Medford in 1775 and was in Salem by 1779 when he joined with the Sandersons to establish a cooperative furniture export business. He was a part owner of the schooner *Olive Branch* in 1796 with the Sandersons and William Appleton. Josiah was one of the surveyors of boards, plank, and timber for the town of Salem in 1799. In 1803, his son Josiah died at sea in the schooner *Friendship* that was owned by fellow society members. No documented furniture by him is known.

SOURCES: Daniel Austin, Austin manuscript genealogy, Phillips Library, Peabody Essex Museum; Bjerkoe, *Cabinetmakers of America*, p. 32; Clunie, "Salem Federal Furniture," p. 157; Hitchings, *Ship Registers of the District of Salem and Beverly*, p. 136; and Brock Jobe and Myrna Kaye, *New England Furniture, The Colonial Era: Selections from the Society for the Preservation of New England Antiquities* (Boston, Mass.: Houghton Mifflin, 1984), p. 232.

RICHARD AUSTIN was baptized in Charlestown, Massachusetts, on July 1, 1744, the son of Josiah and Mary and brother of Josiah. He married Isabel Symonds in Salem in 1797 and died of consumption in Salem on April 20, 1826. He was primarily a chair maker. No documented furniture by him is known.

SOURCES: Daniel Austin, Austin manuscript genealogy; Bjerkoe, *The Cabinetmakers of America*, p. 32; and Belknap, *Artists and Craftsmen of Essex County, Massachusetts*, p. 26.

SAMUEL BARNARD was born in Watertown, Massachusetts, on July 22, 1776, the son of Major Samuel Barnard and Elizabeth Bond. He died in Watertown on June 14, 1858. He was in Salem by May 30, 1799, when he married Elizabeth Cook. He was a part owner of the schooner *Friendship* in 1802 with Edmund Johnson, George W. Martin, and Jonathan Marston. Barnard shipped furniture in 1805 on the schooner *Good Intent* with other members of the society. A card table branded "S.B." (Yale University Art Gallery) has been attributed to him.

SOURCES: Benjamin Hewitt et al., *The Work of Many Hands: Card Tables in America, 1790–1820* (New Haven, Conn.: Yale University Art Gallery, 1982), p. 136, no. 19; Hitchings, *Ship Registers of the District of Salem and Beverly*, p. 67; David L. Barquist, *American Tables and Looking Glasses in the Mabel Brady Garvan and Other Collections at Yale University* (New Haven, Conn.: Yale University Art Gallery, 1992), pp. 188–91.

SAMUEL CHEEVER was born in Manchester, Massachusetts, on March 12, 1756. He was the son of the Reverend Ames Cheever, the town's minister, and his fourth wife, Sarah Davis. Samuel hung himself on May 14,

1818, and left an estate valued at $1,420.80. He was in Salem by March 29, 1787, when he married Anna Ropes (d. 1799). He took his second wife Hannah Clark on May 10, 1800. Samuel purchased his shop at the end of Court Street from cabinetmaker and merchant Henry Rust in 1796. No documented furniture by him is known.

SOURCES: Bjerkoe, *Cabinetmakers of America,* p. 62; Belknap, *Artists and Craftsmen of Essex County, Massachusetts,* p. 33; John T. Hassam, *Ezekiel Cheever and Some of His Descendants* (Boston: David Clapp and Son, 1879), pp. 36–37; and Essex County Registry of Deeds, 159: 268.

DANIEL CLARKE was born in Braintree, Massachusetts, on March 14, 1768, and died in Salem on March 30, 1830. He was the son of Captain Peter Clarke and Hannah Clarke. In October 1794, he moved from Boston to work for the Sandersons for whom he did carving, turning, and cabinetmaking. Clarke established his own shop on Essex Street opposite Cambridge Street in 1796. On February 11, 1800, he moved to Chestnut Street near Summer and Norman Streets. He married Mary Sanderson in 1803. A sideboard made by him for Nathaniel Ropes in 1797 is in the Ropes Mansion (Peabody Essex Museum).

SOURCES: Belknap, *Artists and Craftsmen of Essex County, Massachusetts,* p. 33; Bjerkoe, *Cabinetmakers of America,* p. 65; and Clunie, "Salem Federal Furniture," p. 161.

EZEKIEL GOODNOW was born in Princeton, Massachusetts, on October 27, 1774. He married Sophia Farrington in Salem on December 20, 1801, and died before December 25, 1810, when his wife advertised for the administration of his estate. No documented furniture by him is known.

SOURCES: Belknap, *Artists and Craftsmen of Essex County, Massachusetts,* p. 43.

WILLIAM HOOK was born in Salisbury, Massachusetts, on February 19, 1777, and died in Roxbury, Massachusetts, on May 15, 1867. He was apprenticed at the age of fourteen to John Swett in Salisbury. He came to Salem in 1796 and worked for Edmund Johnson for two years and then the Sandersons for one year before opening his own shop at Essex and Court Streets in 1800. He married Abigail Greenleaf in 1800. He moved his shop to Federal Street in 1803, to Marlborough Street in 1804, and to Essex Street in 1818. Documented pieces include furniture made for his sister in 1809 (Museum of Fine Arts, Boston), a chest of drawers and dressing glass made in 1818 (Peabody Essex Museum), and a suite of furniture made for Capt. George Hodges in 1819. Hook's business papers are in the Phillips Library of the Peabody Essex Museum.

SOURCES: Belknap, *Artists and Craftsmen of Essex County, Massachusetts,* p. 48; Bjerkoe, *Cabinetmakers of America,* pp. 128–29; Clunie, "Salem Federal Furniture," pp. 169–83; Fiske Kimball, "Salem Furniture Makers III, William Hook," *Antiques* 25, no. 4 (April 1934): 144–46; Richard H. Randall, Jr., *American Furniture in the Museum of Fine Arts, Boston* (Boston: by the museum, 1965), nos. 37, 49, 99, 101; Clunie, "Salem Federal Furniture," pp. 177–82.

EDMUND JOHNSON was the son of Edward Johnson (1722–1799) a Lynn, Massachusetts, "shop joiner." He died at sea before July 19, 1811. He was in Salem by 1793 when he married the widow Betsy Smith. He purchased property on Federal Street at Bickford from the estate of cordwainer John Bullock in 1798. He had a shop at River and Federal Streets in 1796 and subsequently moved to Essex Street. Very active in the export trade, he was a part owner of the schooner *Friendship* with George W. Martin, Jonathan Marston, and Samuel Barnard in 1802 and a half owner of the schooner *Theoda* in 1803. Labeled pieces by Johnson include a gentleman's secretary (Winterthur Museum), a slant top desk (Peabody Essex Museum), a lady's tambour desk, a sideboard, a tambour desk, and a pair of knife boxes.

SOURCES: Belknap, *Artists and Craftsmen of Essex County, Massachusetts,* p. 50; Bjerkoe, *Cabinetmakers of America,* p. 135; Clunie, "Salem Federal Furniture," pp. 184–91; Essex County Registry of Deeds, 165:19; Hitchings, *Ship Registers of the District of Salem and Beverly,* pp. 67, 183; Montgomery, *American Furniture,* no. 179; Dean A. Fales, Jr., *Essex County Furniture: Documented Treasures from Local Collections, 1660–1860* (Salem, Mass.: Essex Institute, 1965), nos. 22–23; Winterthur Museum Decorative Arts Photographic Collection, 71.3513; *Antiques* 65, no. 6 (June 1954): 466–68; Fales, *Essex County Furniture,* nos. 20, 21.

JONATHAN MARSTON was born in Hampton, New Hampshire, on May 13, 1777, the son of farmer Elisha Marston. Jonathan died in Machiasport, Maine, on March 12, 1862. He married Sarah Holt in Salem on July 5, 1801. The following year he was a part owner of the schooner *Friendship* with Edmund Johnson, George W. Martin, and Samuel Barnard. His brother Morrill Marston (1785–1831) was in business in Salem around 1805. Jonathan moved to Machiasport about 1812 where he kept a store and engaged in the lumber business with his brother Elisha. No documented furniture by him is known.

SOURCES: Hitchings, *Ship Registers of the District of Salem and Beverly,* p. 67; Nathan W. Marston, *The Marston Genealogy in Two Parts* (South Lubec, Maine: by the author, 1888), pp. 143–44.

GEORGE WHITEFIELD MARTIN was born on March 5, 1771, in Marblehead, Massachusetts, and died in Salem on January 5, 1810. He was in partnership with Robert Choate (b. 1770) in Concord, New Hampshire, from 1794 to 1796. Martin moved to Salem by April 11, 1797, when he married Sally Bullock. Through his wife's family he acquired land and a shop on Federal Street next to Edmund Johnson. In 1802, Martin was a part owner of the schooner *Friendship* with Edmund Johnson, Samuel Barnard, and Jonathan Marston. His tools and shop on Federal Street were sold at auction on June 19, 1810. A card table with the label of Choate and Martin (New Hampshire Historical Society) is the only documented piece by him.

SOURCES: Belknap, *Artists and Craftsmen of Essex County, Massachusetts,* p. 58; Bjerkoe, *Cabinetmakers of America,* p. 150; Clunie, "Salem Federal Furniture," pp. 198–99; Hewitt et al., *Work of Many Hands,* p. 118; Hitchings, *Ship Registers of the District of Salem and Beverly,* p. 67; Hewitt et al., *Work of Many Hands,* no. 3.

FRANCIS PULCIFER was born in 1771 (possibly in Ipswich, Massachusetts) and died on June 24, 1823, in Salem. He married four times: Hannah Trask (1792), Martha Hodgkins (1806), Hannah Haskell (1814), and Lydia Lakeman (1816). Pulcifer was in business with Samuel Frothingham on Church Street until he moved to Court Street in 1795 when the partnership dissolved. Four years later, he purchased property on Williams Street from watchmaker James Dalrymple. Pulcifer was active in the venture cargo trade. No documented furniture by him is known.

SOURCES: Belknap, *Artists and Craftsmen of Essex County, Massachusetts,* p. 65; Bjerkoe, *Cabinetmakers of America,* p. 180; Clunie, "Salem Federal Furniture," pp. 213–14; Essex County Registry of Deeds, 165: 183.

ELIJAH SANDERSON was born in Watertown, Massachusetts, on October 10, 1751, and died in Salem on February 18, 1825. In 1781, he married Mary Mulliken whose brother Samuel was a clockmaker. With his brother Jacob and Josiah Austin, Elijah started a cooperative furniture export business in 1779. Their firm employed many of the town's cabinetmakers, journeymen, turners, carvers, gilders, and upholsterers. The partners owned the schooner *Olive Branch* with William Appleton in 1796, the snow *Fanny* with Appleton in 1799, and the brig *Unicorn* with Nehemiah Adams in 1804. Documented furniture by him includes a desk-and-bookcase branded "ES," a slant-top desk (New England Historic Genealogical Society), a night table, a branded lady's tambour desk, a labeled (with Jacob Sanderson) desk-and-bookcase (Diplomatic Reception Rooms, U.S. Department of State), a card table (with Jacob Sanderson) with painted initials (Winterthur Museum), and a labeled (with Jacob Sanderson) pembroke table (Winterthur Museum). His business papers are in the Phillips Library of the Peabody Essex Museum.

SOURCES: Belknap, *Artists and Craftsmen of Essex County, Massachusetts,* p. 68; Bjerkoe, *Cabinetmakers of America,* pp. 189–90; Clunie, "Salem Federal Furniture," pp. 216–20; Hitchings, *Ship Registers of the District of Salem and Beverly,* pp. 59, 136, 191; Mabel M. Swan, *Samuel McIntire, Carver and the*

Sandersons, Early Salem Cabinetmakers (Salem, Mass.: Essex Institute, 1934); Winterthur Museum Decorative Arts Photographic Collection, 88.472; Swan, *Samuel McIntire and the Sandersons,* opposite p. 32; Fales, *Essex County Furniture,* no. 37; Winterthur Museum Decorative Arts Photographic Collection, 70.279; Clement E. Conger and Alexandra W. Rollins, *Treasures of State: Fine and Decorative Arts in the Diplomatic Reception Rooms of the U.S. Department of State* (New York: Harry N. Abrams, 1991), no. 121; Montgomery, *American Furniture,* nos. 300, 322.

JACOB SANDERSON was born about October 20, 1757, in Watertown, Massachusetts, and married Katherine Harrington of Watertown in 1781. He died in Salem in December of 1810. In partnership with his brother Elijah, he was a part owner of three vessels (see above). Documented furniture by him includes a bed cornice (Peabody Essex Museum), two tables (Winterthur Museum), and pieces jointly labeled with Elijah Sanderson (see above). His business papers are in the Phillips Library of the Peabody Essex Museum.

SOURCES: Belknap, *Artists and Craftsmen of Essex County, Massachusetts,* p. 68; Bjerkoe, *Cabinetmakers of America,* p. 190; Clunie, "Salem Federal Furniture," pp. 220–26; Hitchings, *Ship Registers of the District of Salem and Beverly,* pp. 59, 136, 191; Margaret Burke Clunie, Anne Farnam, and Robert Trent, *Furniture at the Essex Institute* (Salem, Mass.: Essex Institute, 1980), no. 34. Montgomery, *American Furniture,* nos. 300, 301.

ROBERT WALLIS was born about 1764 and died in Salem on October 2, 1824. He married Mary Polly Aveson in the town on December 13, 1787. The following year, he purchased land and buildings on Essex Street from the estate of Mary Ford. No documented furniture by him is known.

SOURCES: Vital Records of Salem, Massachusetts, 4: 430, 6: 302; Essex County Registry of Deeds, 147: 275.

Appendix B

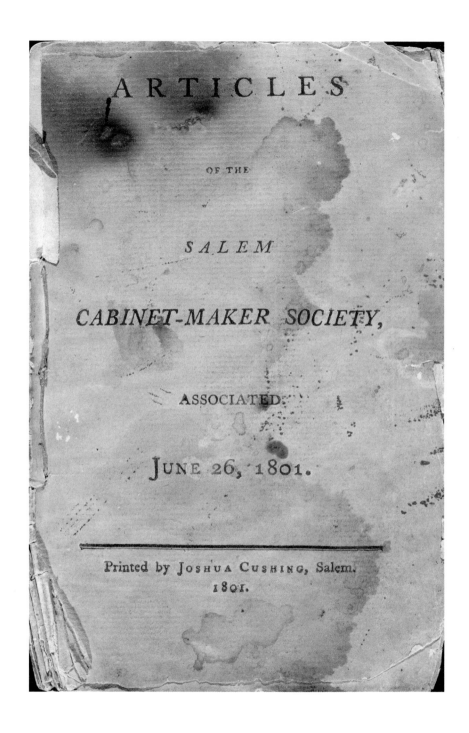

ARTICLES, &c.

WHEREAS it is contemplated many important advantages may refult from the inftitution of a fociety, we the fubfcribers, feveral cabinet-makers in Salem, do hereby agree to form ourfelves into a company, by the name of THE SALEM CABINET-MAKER SOCIETY; and, for the good order of the fame, do affent to and adopt the following articles, viz.

I.

THE fociety fhall meet four times in a year, viz. the firft Tuefday in December, March, June and September, at fuch an hour and place as the moderator fhall appoint.

II.

A MODERATOR fhall be chofen at each annual meeting, in December, who fhall be empowered to direct the clerk to call a fpecial meeting, as occafion may require, and who fhall be addreffed by each member who has any thing to offer for the confideration of the fociety.

III.

A CLERK fhall be chofen at each annual meeting, in December, who fhall be held to ferve until another is chofen in his ftead, whofe bufinefs fhall be, to warn each member to attend every meeting, one day at leaft previous thereto, by leaving a printed ticket at his dwelling—to keep a fair journal of the votes and tranfactions of the fociety, to be produced at the requeft of any member for his infpection and perufal—to receive and keep a juft account of all fines and forfeitures incurred by the breach of any

laws

laws that are or may be established by the society for the benefit thereof—and to collect and pay the reckoning at every meeting. In case of neceſſary abſence, he shall engage some other perſon to ſerve in his ſtead; and for each and every neglect he shall be fined at the diſcretion of the society in a ſum not exceeding four dollars. And he shall be allowed and paid four dollars in full for his ſer-vices.

IV.

The clerk shall call the roll at one half hour from the time of meeting; and any member, hav-ing been duly warned, being tardy, shall forfeit twelve and a half cents; and for total abſence twenty-five cents.

V.

Any perſon who is duly conſidered and generally accepted as a maſter cabinet-maker, by applying to the society, and ſigning his name to this inſtitu-tion, as a teſtimony of his aſſent to be governed thereby, shall be admitted as a member, by ballot, at a ſtated meeting, and shall pay to the clerk, for the uſe of the society, one dollar, which shall entitle him to every benefit reſulting therefrom, and shall receive a printed copy of theſe articles, together with the prices of furniture, &c.

VI.

If any diſpute ſhould ariſe between any two or more members, that may be conſidered as relative to the cabinet buſineſs, either party shall have a right to lay the same before the society, and claim their opinion thereon, by a vote or a committee.

VII.

If any member shall have any difficulty with any one or more of his apprentices, he may, by applying to the moderator for the purpoſe, call a
special

special meeting for their assistance and advice thereupon. And if it shall come to the knowledge of any member, of an apprentice making attempts to leave his master, or in any manner to injure him, he shall immediately acquaint his master thereof; and no member shall receive or harbour an apprentice who leaves or may be attempting to leave his master, until he has first consulted him, and obtained his full consent and approbation therefor.

VIII.

Each member shall keep a printed copy of this institution, and produce it at each quarterly meeting, on penalty of forfeiting twenty-five cents.

IX.

Any member who shall neglect or refuse to observe these articles, or to adhere to any and every law, forfeiture, assessment or penalty which is or may be established by the society, or shall absent himself four meetings successively, he shall be fined at the discretion of the society, or shall be excommunicated as an unworthy member: *Provided, nevertheless*, that nothing in these articles shall be so construed as to debar any member from offering his plea for the violation of them, and making his appeal to the judgment of the society.

X.

Any one or more of these articles may be obliterated, altered or erased, and new ones introduced, by the assent of two thirds of the members present at a special meeting which may be called for that purpose.

XI.

All laws, regulations and establishments which shall from time to time be resolved on by the society shall be accurately recorded in the clerk's book, and every law respecting forfeitures shall be established blifhed after having the affent of two thirds of the whole number of the members prefent; and every other fubject that may come before the fociety fhall be governed by the majority: but, in cafe of difpute, no law fhall become eftablifhed without paffing two fucceeding quarterly meetings, unlefs the majority fhall confift of more than two thirds of the whole number of the members prefent.

XII.

EACH member hereby jointly and feverally agrees and binds himfelf, not only by his honour, but by every forfeiture and penalty that may from time to time be levied by the fociety, ftrictly to adhere to thefe articles, together with the prices of furniture that are now or may be hereafter eftablifhed, and firmly to uphold this inftitution: in teftimony whereof we do hereunto fubjoin our names.

Jofiah Auftin	Edmund Johnfon
Elijah Sanderfon	George W. Martin
Jacob Sanderfon	Daniel Clarke
Samuel Cheever	Samuel Barnard
Robert Wallis	Jonathan Marfton
William Appleton	Richard Auftin
Nehemiah Adams	William Hook
Francis Pulcifer	Ezekiel Goodnow

PRICES *of* FURNITURE, *and* JOURNEY-
MEN's PRICES *for* MAKING, *eftablifhed by
the Society* JUNE *26th,* 1801 :—*To be altered at the
difcretion of the Majority.*

CABINET, of a fuperior quality, with circular
    doors, inlaid and decorated in every part, to
    be made with a cock bead round the doors,
    drawers and head - - - - *dolls.* 120
    Making - - - - - *dolls.* 40

DITTO, finifhed with circular doors - - 115
    Making - - - 37

DITTO, of another quality, with diamond doors
    110
    Making - - - 34

WARDROBE, of the beft quality, fcrole head,
70

Making - - - - 18

DITTO, of another quality, with fquare head, 60
Making - - - - 17

SECRETARY & BOOK-CASE, beft quality,
with a fwell'd front - - - 70
Making - - - - 23

DITTO, of the beft quality, with ftraight front,
fcrole head, crofsband doors, decorated with
dentals, &c. - - - - 63
Making - - - 19

DITTO, ftraight front, with a pediment head, 60
Making - - - 18

BOOK-CASE, with fcroll head and glafs doors,

              28

 Making   -   -   -   8

SIDE-BOARD, fafh-corner'd, with a fecretary
  drawer, decorated, crofsbanded and finifhed,

              60

 Making   -   -   -   18

DITTO, fcolloped front, with a fecretary drawer,
  decorated and finifhed   -   -   -   57
  Making   -   -   -   17

DITTO, fcolloped front, without a fecretary drawer,
  decorated and finifhed   -   -   -   50
  Making   -   -   -   15

DESKS, fwelled, the front and fall finiered, 40
Making - - - 13

DITTO, fwelled, folid front - - 40
Making - - - 11

DITTO, ftraight front, the front, fall, top and feat-
board finiered - - - - 30
Making - - - 9

DITTO, ftraight front and folid - - 30
Making - - - 8

DITTO, birch, straight front   - -   15
   Making   - - -   7.50

birch Desk —   10

DITTO, travelling, of the common quality,   7
   Making   - - -   2

CLOCK-CASE, mahogany, glazed and finished,
                                          30
   Making   - - -   9

COMMODE, common circular, five feet in length,
                                          60
   Making   - - -   20

DITTO, different sizes, in proportion

LADY'S SECRETARY, with a frieze, head-
mouldings, and bracket feet - - 35
Making - - 11
Voted Sept. 7th 1802 - 10 - 30

DITTO, with legs, decorated and finished, 30
Making - - 9.50
Voted Sept. 7th 1802 - 8 - 25

BUREAU, with canted corners, of the best qua-
lity, finiered, decorated and crofsbanded, 27
Making - - 9
Voted Sept. 7th 1802 - 8 - 25

DITTO, with a fcolloped front, and decorated, 25
Making - - 8
Voted Sept. 7th 1802 - 7/50 - 24

DITTO, with a circular front, and decorated, 25
Making - - 7
Voted Sept. 7th 1802 - 6/50 - 23

DITTO, with a ftraight front, and decorated, 20
Making - - - 5.50
Voted Sept. 7th 1802 - 5 - 18

DITTO, birch - - - 11
Making - - 5
Voted Sept. 21st 1802 - 0 - 10

DINING-TABLES, by the set, to be 4½ feet
wide, and to spread 8 feet in the square, with
two semi-circular ends of 2 feet in width,
which adds 4 feet to the length—the spreading of the whole extent to be 12 feet in length,
and 4½ in breadth - - - 60
Making - - 12

Other sizes to be regulated in proportion.

DITTO, common kind, spreading 4 feet square, 14
Making - - 3

DITTO, birch, spreading 4 feet square - 7
Making - - 3

CARD-TABLE, of the beſt quality, faſh-corner-
ed   -   -   -   -   14
Making   -   -   4

DITTO, of the beſt quality, circular   -   12
Making   -   -   3.33

DITTO, birch, or pine without painting   -   4
Making   -   -   2

NIGHT TABLE, of the common kind, 2 feet
4 inches high, and 2 feet deep, without the
pan   -   -   -   -   12
Making   -   -   4

Dec.ʳ 6ᵗʰ 1803
Votes Pembroke Tables 3 ſt long &c &c 14

QUARTER-TABLE, of the best quality, decorated, 19 inches demi-circular - - 6
Making - - 1.50

SLAB-TABLE, without painting - 3
Making - - 1

KITCHEN TABLE, with a drawer - 3
Making - - - 1.50

STAND, mahogany, oval, to turn up - 5
Making - - - 1.50

FIRE-SCREEN, of the common kind - 8

Making - - 2

Voted June 1st 1802 without Flap Leaf £ 1 67 5

WASH-STAND, circular, of the common kind,

9

Making - - 3.50

Voted June 1st 1802 3 ~ 8

DITTO, square - - - - 6

Making - - 3

CRADLE, mahogany   -   -   12
   Making   -   -   3

DITTO, cedar   - - - - -   8
   Making   -   -   3

DITTO, pine, without painting   -   -   4
   Making   -   -   1.50

[handwritten: Viler Sep. 21. 1802 painted complete 6]

SOFA FRAME, with a mahogany top-rail, excluding the carving   - - -   22
   Making (the moulding to be finished) 6.50

DITTO without mahogany top   - -   20
   Making - - - -   5

EASY-CHAIR FRAME - - - 7
Making - - - 2.50

Voted June 1st 1802 - 0 : 6

MAHOGANY CHAIR, finished with drapery
back, &c. excluding the carving - 6
Making - - - - 2

Voted December 1st 1801 . 0 - 5/50

LOLLING-CHAIR FRAME, with mahogany
arms - - - - - - 5
Making - - - 2

WINDOW-STOOL FRAME, excluding the
carving - - - 6
Making - - 2

BEDSTEAD, mahogany, ſwelled pillars, excluding the carving, fluting and facking,   16
   Making (to be finiſhed, the facking put in,
    &c.) - - - 4

DITTO, birch, excluding the facking - 12
   Making (finiſhed as above) 4

DITTO, mahogany field, excluding the facking, 18
   Making (finiſhed as above) 4.50

t ed. 6th 1803 if all the poſt mehogany   *20*

DITTO, birch field, excluding the facking, 12
   Making (finiſhed as above) 4.50

Dec. 6 1803   *14*

DITTO, preſs - - 6
   Making - - 2.50

ted Dec. 1st 1801 . .0 . . 5

DITTO, cot, excluding the facking - - 3
   Making - - 1.50

DITTO, low poſt - - - 3
   Making - - 1.50

Dec. 6th 1803 . . . . . . 3/50

SEAMAN'S CHEST, 4 feet, without painting,

6

Making - - - 2

☞ IN the defcription of the firft article of furniture read, " to be made with a check'd cock bead
round the doors," &c·

Voted Sept. 22d 1801
That the penalty for deviating
from the foregoing prices shou'd be
a forfiture of the price of making
the article deviated upon be it
more or lefs
Attest
Danl Clarke Cler

Voted Decr 6th 1803
That the price of the largersize

Mehogony Coffins be — 20

Cedar Ditto — 14

Pine Ditto — 4

Figure 1 Chest, probably Columbia County,
New York, 1775. Pine. H. 18¼", W. 52½", D. 20".
(Courtesy, New York State Museum, Albany,
New York.)

Peter M. Kenny

Two Early Eighteenth-Century *Schränke:* Rare Survivals of the German Joiner's Art in the Hudson River Valley

▼ LITTLE IS KNOWN ABOUT the material culture of the Germans who immigrated to New York from the Rhine River Valley, an area known as the Palatinate since its occupation by the Roman Empire. In the realm of furniture, only a small group of painted chests has been linked to this distinct ethnic group (see figs. 1, 2). Most of these examples, however, represent the work of second- and third-generation descendants of the original Palatine settlers. Only a few are eighteenth century, and none are dated earlier than 1773. Thus, there is reason to celebrate the discovery of two eighteenth-century *schränke* made in the Hudson River Valley (figs. 3, 4). Even more exciting is the strong possibility that both of these quintessential German furniture forms are the products of a first-generation Palatine joiner in the vanguard of German settlers sent to New York in 1709/10.[1]

The first Palatines in New York arrived in 1708. Led by Rev. Joshua Kocherthal, a small party of forty-one settlers from Landau near Mannheim disembarked in New York City in December of that year and stayed on through the winter. The following year, the colonial governor made provisions for the Palatines to settle fifty-five miles north of the city on the western bank of the Hudson. There they established the settlement of Newburgh. Kocherthal received five hundred acres for a glebe plus an additional two hundred fifty acres for his family, whereas the heads of the other families received fifty acres each. Among this group of Palatines was a joiner who may have made both *schränke*.[2]

Figure 2 Chest, Schoharie County, New York, 1778. Pine. H. 20½", W. 47½", D. 21½". (Courtesy, Metropolitan Museum of Art.)

Figure 3 Schränk, Dutchess or Ulster County, New York, 1715–1740, Maple with white pine and yellow pine. H. 83¼", W. 76¾", D. 29". (Courtesy, Ulster County Historical Society; photo, Gavin Ashworth.)

Figure 4 Schränk, Dutchess or Ulster County, New York, 1715–1740, Maple with white pine and yellow pine. H. 76", W. 76", D. 29⅛". (Private collection; photo, Gavin Ashworth.) The iron drawer pulls are replacements based on the originals on the *schränk* illustrated in fig. 3.

In immigrating to New York, Kocherthal's group preceded the mass exodus from the Rhine Valley that began in 1709. The Palatinate had been in an almost constant state of conflict from the onset of the Thirty Years War (1618–1648) through the War of the Spanish Succession (1701–1714). According to genealogist and historian Henry Z. Jones, Jr., the families of the New York immigrants had endured decades of suffering and dislocation as well as relentless taxation by whatever local prince had jurisdiction over their particular village or township. In his estimation the catalyst for the exodus was the severe winter of 1709. Throughout southern Germany, frigid temperatures ravaged crops, fruit trees, and vines thus destroying any hope for subsequent harvests. According to one observer, "the oldest people here could not remember a worse [cold]. . . . Almost all mills have been brought to a standstill. . . . Many cattle and humans, . . . even the birds and the wild animals in the woods froze." Enticed by British propaganda devised to lure settlers to the Crown's colonies in the New World, many Palatines began leaving their homeland the following spring. Most traveled up the Rhine to Rotterdam then on to London, where they were welcomed and sustained by the British government until plans could be made for their dispersal to the colonies.[3]

The massive scale of the Palatine exodus and the desperation, anxiety, and anticipation felt by many immigrants are reflected in the writings of Ulrich Simmendinger who left Germany in 1709. After spending several years in America, he returned home and published a brief account of the Palatine immigration and a register of the names and locations of the families that remained in New York. Simmendinger's account is both emotional and factual:

> In the year 1709, when in consequence of the most golden promises of the English letters, many families departed from the Palatinate, and the districts of Zweibruecken, Hesse-Cassel, and also Waldeck, down the Rhine to England. . . . As joyful as was the entrance upon our journey out of Wurtemburg, so sorrowful and sad the same suddenly became when in Rotterdam 1,000 souls were recalled and ordered back, the Queen having given new orders prohibiting the entrance of more immigrants. This pretext discouraged from their intended journey at that time more than 3,000 of the Catholic religion, who returned home rather than change faith at the demand of the Queen."[4]

Given the deteriorating and increasingly desperate social and economic conditions throughout southern Germany, it is hardly surprising that the Crown's propaganda campaign, which included the circulation of pamphlets that portrayed the American colonies as a land of unparalleled opportunity, proved to be so successful. During the spring and summer of 1709, nearly 13,000 Palatines arrived in London. To feed and house the immigrants, British officials distributed 1,600 tents and set up encampments at Blackheath, Greenwich, and Camberwell (see fig. 5). Sickness and death stalked the crowded camps, and many of the weak, very young, and elderly died from fevers and contagious diseases. At first the Palatines were looked upon with a mixture of wonder and pity, but many poor Londoners became resentful and fearful that the immigrants would take their jobs and reduce wages. Although axe- and hammer-wielding mobs periodically attacked the

Figure 5 Title page from *The State of the Palatines, For Fifty Years past to this present Time* (1709) showing the Palatines soon after their arrival in England encamped outside London at Camberwell or Blackheath. (Courtesy, Houghton Library, Harvard University.)

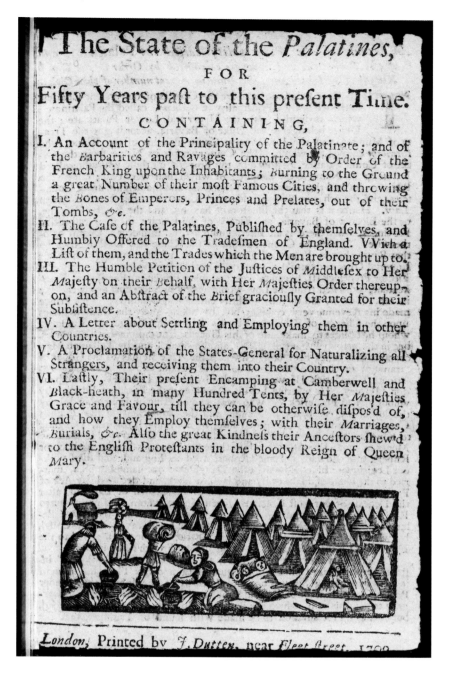

The State of the *Palatines,*
FOR
Fifty Years paſt to this preſent Time.
CONTAINING,

I. An Account of the Principality of the Palatinate; and of the Barbarities and Ravages committed by Order of the French King upon the Inhabitants; Burning to the Ground a great Number of their moſt Famous Cities, and throwing the Bones of Emperors, Princes and Prelates, out of their Tombs, &c.

II. The Caſe of the Palatines, Publiſhed by themſelves, and Humbly Offered to the Tradeſmen of England. With a Liſt of them, and the Trades which the Men are brought up to.

III. The Humble Petition of the Juſtices of *Middleſex* to Her Majeſty on their Behalf, with Her Majeſties Order thereupon, and an Abſtract of the Brief graciouſly Granted for their Subſiſtence.

IV. A Letter about Settling and Employing them in other Countries.

V. A Proclamation of the States-General for Naturalizing all Strangers, and receiving them into their Country.

VI. Laſtly, Their preſent Encamping at Camberwell and Black-heath, in many Hundred Tents, by Her Majeſties Grace and Favour, till they can be otherwiſe diſpos'd of, and how they Employ themſelves; with their Marriages, Burials, &c. Alſo the great Kindneſs their Anceſtors ſhew'd to the Engliſh Proteſtants in the bloody Reign of Queen Mary.

London, Printed by *J. Dutten,* near *Fleet Street.* 1709

encampments, the Palatines defended themselves vigorously. One early account describes an occasion when a small group of drunken Englishmen "made some [disparaging] Reflections upon the Receiving of these People into the Kingdom; which, being heard by one of the Palatines, he gave a hint to his Companions, and they all immediately came into the Room and beat the persons in a very rude and inhuman manner." Whether any of the feisty Palatines involved in this brawl ever made it to colonial New York is uncertain, but those who did most certainly possessed a similar fighting spirit.[5]

By late 1709, the British government realized that the Germans had to be dispersed to alleviate mounting tensions in London. As Simmendinger

noted, the Crown sent approximately 1,000 unfortunate souls back to Rotterdam and, eventually, on to Germany. Some of their more fortunate counterparts settled in England and Ireland, whereas others set sail for the English plantations in Jamaica, the West Indies, and the American colonies. Approximately 650 Germans settled near Bath, North Carolina, where they joined the Swiss settlement established by Christoph Baron von Graffenreid, but most immigrated to the middle Atlantic colonies.[6]

A quarter of the Palatines who sojourned in London went to New York under a plan devised by the Earl of Sunderland and endorsed by Governor-Elect Robert Hunter (fig. 6). They envisioned Protestant settlements that would serve as a bulwark against French encroachment and as a source for naval stores manufactured from the native pines of the Hudson River Valley. The Palatines agreed to remain in the service of the Crown until they repaid all the expenses incurred for their transportation and settlement, and the British government agreed to give each settler forty acres free from taxes and quit rents for seven years once payment had been made.[7]

The Palatines bound for New York boarded eleven ships in December 1709 but did not leave port until the following April. Nearly a fifth died in

Figure 7 Robert Livingston, attributed to Nehemiah Partridge, New York, 1718. Oil on canvas. 50" x 40". (Private collection; photo, Gavin Ashworth.) The painting is inscribed "AETAT 64 1718."

passage owing to their unhealthy diet and the spread of typhus. Upon their arrival that summer, the Palatines established a camp at Nutten (Governor's Island) in New York's harbor, a safe distance from the general populace which was anxious over the arrival of 2,000 diseased immigrants. To achieve the goals underlying the Earl of Sunderland's plan, Governor Hunter purchased 6,000 acres on the east side of the Hudson from Robert Livingston (figs. 7, 8), Commissioner of Indian Affairs. Simmendinger noted:

> Since we were all in duty bound to live upon the grace of the Queen and under her services, we camped for a time near the City of New York, until, away from there, and about fifteen miles south of Mr. Livingston's tract, we began to erect cabins, which everyone fashioned according to his own invention and architecture. During this time—because it was planned to seize Canada or New France . . . whose inhabitants were mostly savages— equipment, bread and other necessities of life were provided for us, but as the campaign did not succeed as expected, after our return march certain work which consisted in the burning of tar was demanded of us, which was carried on with much labor for two years, yet with no special and evident profit to the Governor. Thereupon each received his freedoms to the extent that he might seek his own piece of bread in his own way within the

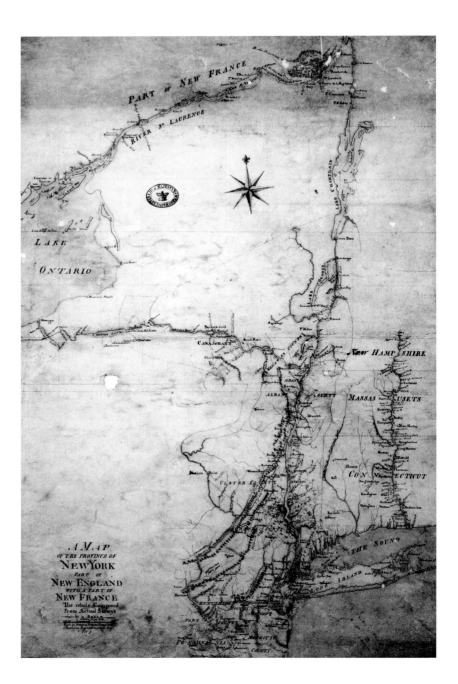

Figure 8 Frances Pfhister, *A Map of the Province of New York, Part of New England, with Part of New France,* 1759. (Courtesy, Public Records Office, London.) The area of detail shows Livingston Manor, East Camp, and Rhinebeck. The circles on the map indicate later Palatine settlements at Schoharie and Canajoharie.

Province until the Queen should again need our services and we, prepared for the first call, could be assembled together. I, for my part, returned once more to the aforesaid New York, lived about four years on the long island, a half hour distant, and in the village of Brooklyn situated there, and sought sustenance by various labors among honest people.[8]

Although enlightening, Simmendinger's account hardly describes the wretched existence of the Palatines' first years in the Hudson Valley or the Crown's ineptitude in helping them produce naval stores. In selling Hunter a portion of his land, Livingston sought to promote growth in and around his manor. Prior to the sale, he shrewdly arranged to have himself appointed as the colony's inspector of the Palatines and procured the contract for providing them with bread and beer. Despite his well-laid plans, Livingston had problems from the start. Because he was unable to get enough grain to make sufficient quantities of bread and beer, the Palatines nearly starved the first winter. The colonial government's failure to provide an experienced manager to supervise the production of naval stores exacerbated the problems at East Camp. By the spring of 1711, some of the Palatines were planning to escape to Schoharie, west of Albany (fig. 8). The leaders of this small clandestine group were under the mistaken impression that the Queen had acquired land for them there from the Indians. A concerned Robert Livingston appealed to Governor Hunter for help in dealing with the Palatines. Hunter visited East Camp and tried to rally the Germans to their assigned task but was unsuccessful and subsequently intervened with the militia. Shortly thereafter, Hunter admitted that the effort to produce naval stores was a failure and terminated the program.[9]

Although their settlement was in shambles, the Palatines had fulfilled their obligations to the Crown by 1712. Some became tenants on Livingston's manor or remained as squatters on the original tract known today as Germantown, but nearly half moved to the New York City vicinity, the Schoharie Valley, New Jersey, and Pennsylvania the following year. Many of the Germans remained together after leaving East Camp. Those who moved south to the Beekman Patent in northern Dutchess County established the settlement of Rhinebeck.

One of the *schränke* (fig. 4) reportedly descended in the female line of Palatine families from Rhinebeck, most recently the Travers. The other *schränk* (fig. 3) probably belonged to a first-generation German settler in the vicinity of Rhinebeck, Germantown, or Livingston Manor. Dr. John Paul Remensnyder of Saugerties, New York, who donated the piece to the Ulster County Historical Society, stated that he purchased the *schränk* on the "other side of the River," presumably in southern Columbia County or northern Dutchess County.[10]

The Remensnyder *schränk* (fig. 3) has traditionally been mistaken for a *kast*, a Netherlandish cupboard form common in the Hudson Valley. It and the nearly identical Traver family example provide a unique opportunity to examine the work of an early Palatine joiner. Formal analysis of these two objects may facilitate the identification of other furniture made by members of this largely forgotten cultural group and illuminate their contributions to early New York material culture.

Like *kasten* in Netherlandish households (fig. 9), *schränke* (fig. 10) were the principal forms for storing textiles and clothing in the Teutonic countries from the late Renaissance until the late eighteenth century. The Remensnyder *schränk* is a type known in Germany as a *kleiderschränk* (clothing cupboard). This form typically has an interior arrangement consisting of an open area with pegs for hanging clothes in one half, and a shelved section for storing folded garments or textiles in the other (fig. 11). The Traver *schränk* differs in having a single compartment with full-width shelves like New York *kasten* (fig. 12). This arrangement was designed for the storage of bed linens, tablecloths, and other textiles associated with the dowries or

Figure 9 Kast, possibly Rotterdam or Amsterdam, Netherlands, 1680–1690. Walnut veneer on oak. H. 90", W. 89 ¾", D. 31 ¾". (Private collection; photo, Gavin Ashworth.) This elaborate Dutch baroque kast is one of seven owned in New Netherland and colonial New York. It descended in the family of Robert Livingston (fig. 7). His father, Rev. John Livingston (1603–1672), was a Scottish minister active in Scotland's struggle for independence from England. John was exiled to Rotterdam in 1663, where his son Robert was born, reared, and educated. Robert and his wife Alida Schuyler

Van Rensselaer (1656–1727) may have purchased this *kast* after their marriage in 1679. Under the applied moldings on the right side panel is inscribed what appears to be the name *"Myndert banta,"* possibly the maker, along with layout lines for cutting miters in the applied moldings.

outsets that women brought to their marriages. German examples fitted in this manner are referred to as *wäscheschränke,* or linen cupboards. No New York *kast* with a *kleiderschränk* interior is known, and Pennsylvania German *schränke* with *wäscheschränk* arrangements are rare. The interior of the Traver family *schränk* may reflect acculturation on the part of the Palatines into the Hudson River Valley's predominantly Dutch culture.

If the dates assigned to the New York *schränke* are accurate, as their style, construction, and workmanship suggests, they are the products of a first-generation Palatine joiner and document the direct transfer of southern German baroque design. The urban antecedent for these objects is the Frankfurt *nasenschränk* or "nose cupboard" (fig. 10). The latter term derives

Figure 10 Nasenschränk, Frankfurt, Germany, ca. 1700 (Courtesy, Historisches Museum, Frankfurt am Main.)

Figure 11 Interior view of the *schränk* illustrated in fig. 3. (Photo, Gavin Ashworth.) Both of the horizontal shelves on the right side are modern, but the cleats for the original shelves are still in place. The *schränk* illustrated in fig. 4 was originally made with two full-width shelves. It is likely that the patron specified this arrangement since it represents a departure from the norm.

from the proboscis-like knobs at the tops and bottoms of the quirk moldings on the front corners, which on this baroque behemoth are nearly as large as organ pipes. Made for farming families in provincial settings, the Traver and Remensnyder *schränke* are simpler evocations of this sophisticated and visually complex urban form. They aspire to the grandeur of their high-style counterparts in several ways. Both have enormous, dynamically curved cyma base moldings, which unlike those on the *nasenschränk,* are fitted with drawers at the front. The quirk moldings on the corners of New York *schränke* are minuscule versions of those on Frankfurt examples, but

Figure 13 Detail of the locking system on the *schränk* illustrated in fig. 3. (Photo, Gavin Ashworth.) The large faceted end of the through-tenon and the thin wedge at the top lock the cornice substructure to the paneled side. The locking system on the *schränk* illustrated in fig. 4 is identical except the tenon is elliptical rather than faceted at the top. The individual components of the locking system are coded with the incised Roman numerals I–III and the Arabic numeral 4.

Figure 14 Isometric drawing of the *schränk* illustrated in fig 3. (Drawing by Dan Kershaw.)

Figure 15 Detail of the drawer bottom of the *schränk* illustrated in fig. 3. (Photo, Gavin Ashworth). The drawer bottoms of the *schränk* illustrated in fig. 4 are secured with rosehead nails instead of wooden pins.

Figure 16 Details showing the (left) wedged dovetails of the *schränk* illustrated in fig. 4 and (right) unwedged dovetails of the one illustrated in fig. 3. (Photo, Gavin Ashworth.)

they clearly reference the same baroque detail. To simulate the opulent visual effect of exotic veneers, which are common on urban German *schränke,* the New York joiner used pigmented varnishes. Remnants of what appears to be stylized rosewood graining remain on the cornice of the Remensnyder *schränk* (fig. 3). The Traver family example has a faux curly maple surface over an original varnish that may have been grained like that of the Remensnyder *schränk*.[11]

The construction of the New York *schränke* also relates to early eighteenth-century German work. Both pieces have locking systems (see figs. 13, 14) that secure the cornice and base to the center section and allow the *schränke* to be disassembled and moved more easily from place to place. Other Germanic details are the wooden pins (pegs) securing the thick pine bottoms of the drawers (fig. 15) and wedged dovetail joints of the drawer frames (fig. 16). The joiner also drove a wedge into the tenon of each foot piercing the bottom of the case.[12]

Like most New York *kasten,* the Remensnyder and Traver *schränke* have massive cornices. The cornices on the *kasten* are comprised of a single, wide molded board angled to extend out at the top, whereas those on the *schränke* are comprised of several narrow molded boards. One similarity between the

Figure 17 Detail of the cornice and architrave moldings on the *schränk* illustrated in fig. 3. (Photo, Gavin Ashworth.)

Figure 18 Detail of the cornice and architrave moldings on the *schränk* illustrated in fig. 4. (Photo, Gavin Ashworth.)

Figure 19 Detail of the foot and base molding on the *schränk* illustrated in fig. 3. The spline in the front corner has fallen out of the saw kerfs in the miter. The ebonized surface of the turned feet is original, and contrasts with the red-brown paint on the case. (Photo, Gavin Ashworth.)

Figure 20 Detail of the foot and base molding on the *schränk* illustrated in fig. 4. The original ebonized surface of the feet is visible under the later yellow ochre paint. (Photo, Gavin Ashworth.)

moldings on the *schränke* and *kasten* from the Elting-Beekman shops that flourished in the vicinity of Kingston, just across the Hudson River from Rhinebeck, is the use of splines to reinforce the miter joints (figs. 17, 18). The joiner responsible for the *schränke* also used them to help prevent the large miters of the base section from separating (figs. 19, 20). Kingston *kasten* (see fig. 12) usually have only one spline at the very top of the cornice because the front and side molding are comprised of a single board, whereas the New York *schränke* have multiple splines. The use of splines on Ulster County *kasten* is difficult to explain, since similar forms from other areas of New York do not have them. It is possible that a Palatine journeyman introduced them to the Elting-Beekman tradition. Although one hesitates to ascribe too much influence to Germanic joiners during the early 1700s, the impact of one or two individuals cannot be discounted, particularly in rural areas where furniture makers were relatively scarce.[13]

Not surprisingly, only a few artisans can be identified as possible makers of the *shränke*. A house carpenter could have made the pieces, but their

Figure 21 *Wäscheschränk*, probably New York City, 1715–1740. Cherry with yellow poplar and red gum. H. 82¾", W. 78½", D. 27". (Private collection; photo, Gavin Ashworth.) The drawer handles are replaced. Filled holes and outlines from backplates on the drawer fronts suggest that they may have had baroque brass handles.

Figure 22 Drawings of *schränke* by (left) J. I. Frantzner and (right) J. A. Beyerle, Mainz, Germany. (Courtesy, Kunstbibliothek, Staatliche Museen zu Berlin.) The Frantzner drawing is dated 1697 and the Beyerle drawing is dated 1708.

complex construction is much more typical of a furniture joiner. One of the most intriguing candidates is joiner Melchior Gülch (also referred to as Gilles or Hilg), who arrived in New York in 1708 and subsequently settled at Newburgh, about twenty miles south of Rhinebeck on the west side of the Hudson. When the Kocherthal party sailed for New York in October 1708, Gülch and his family had stayed behind because his wife was sick with "a cancer of the breast." Frau Gülch soon succumbed to the illness, and Melchior petitioned for transportation to New York the following April. His arrival

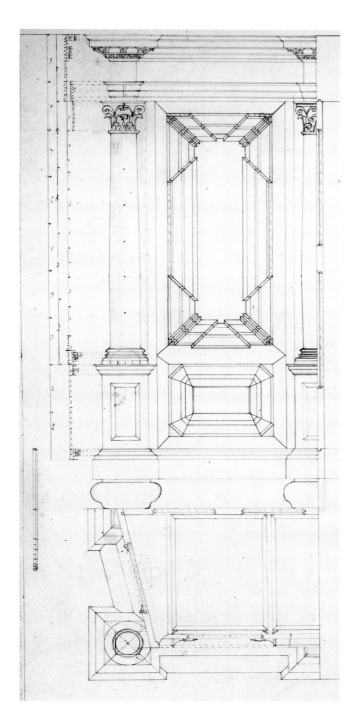

Figure 23 Detail of a door panel of the *wäscheschränk* illustrated in fig. 21. (Photo, Gavin Ashworth.)

caused some dissention when he landed at Newburgh with his children Magdelena and Heinrich, who were about twelve and ten years old respectively. Although Gülch was the only joiner in Kocherthal's party, the settlers at Newburgh claimed his tools by common division. On April 29, 1710, Gülch sought to block the division. His petition stated that the tools were a gift intended for use by him, his son, and his apprentice. The latter may have been Isaac Türck, the only single man in the Kocherthal party. Either Türck or young Heinrich Gülch are also possible makers of the *schränke*.[14]

The elder Gülch was clearly a well-established resident of Ulster County by 1717, when he appeared as "Gullis, the German joiner" in a list of land grants. Two years earlier a man described as "Melgert the joyner," perhaps the same individual, lived in the precinct of Highland on the west bank of the Hudson River just opposite Poughkeepsie in Dutchess County. If either of these men was Melchior Gülch, he moved closer to Rhinebeck and Kingston at an early date.[15]

The English Board of Trade's lists of "poor Germans lately come over from the Palatinate into the kingdom" taken at St. Catherines, Walworth, and Debtford in May and June of 1709 simplifies the process of identifying and locating Palatine tradesmen who immigrated to New York. These documents provide detailed demographic information on the first 6,000 Palatines who arrived in England earlier that year. Of the 1,232 adult males included in the total, only twenty-one were described as joiners, and only two appear on later government lists as New York immigrants: Peter Dinant, aged thirty-nine in 1709, and Peter Pfuhl, aged forty-eight. Dinant's household included seven family members prior to his departure, but only four survived the journey to New York. His daughter Susanna was baptized at the Kingston Reformed Church on October 28, 1711. Although nothing is known about Dinant's career as a joiner, he must also be considered a candidate for the maker of the Traver and Remensnyder *schränke*. His church affiliation in Kingston might indicate that he lived there and had contact with tradesmen in the Elting-Beekman shops.[16]

Born in Nider-Rammstadt in Darmstadt, Peter Pfuhl married widow Anna Sophia in the West Camp Lutheran Church in Ulster County north of Kingston on September 27, 1710. He was still at West Camp on April 19, 1713, when his daughter Anna Catharina was baptized in the same church. By 1716, he had moved to Raritan, New Jersey, on Newark Bay. The New York City Lutheran Church Book documents the baptism of three of Pfuhl's children between 1716 and 1721.[17]

Although joiners were undoubtedly among the approximately 7,000 Germans not included in the Board of Trade's initial lists, it is doubtful that many more furniture makers immigrated to New York and worked in the Hudson River Valley. Given the fact that Pfuhl only resided in the Kingston vicinity between 1710 and 1716, one of the Gülchs, Melchior's apprentice, or Peter Dinant become the most likely candidates for maker of the Traver and Remensnyder *schränke*.

The massive *wäscheschränk* illustrated in figure 21 may also represent the work of a Palatine joiner. Its early German baroque design and gum secondary wood points to New York as the probable place of origin. Like many late seventeenth- and early eighteenth-century *schränke* from the Rhine River port Mainz and other parts of Germany (see fig. 22), the example shown in figure 21 has doors with complex applied moldings (fig. 23). The joiner used a scratch-stock cutter to produce the moldings, which must have been an arduous task considering their size and profile. This may indicate a production date before 1720, when dedicated molding planes of this size became more widely available. The dramatic geometry of the moldings may have been derived from seventeenth- and eighteenth-century fortress plans.[18]

No other American *wäscheschränk* like the one illustrated in figure 21 is known. Its drawer construction (fig. 24) is fairly typical of New York baroque cabinetwork, but the dovetails at the corners of the frames are not wedged and the bottoms are not pinned as one might expect on such an

Figure 24 Detail of a drawer from the *wäscheschränk* illustrated in fig. 21. (Photo, Gavin Ashworth.)

overt Germanic form. The large cornice is comprised of multiple parts as on the Traver and Remensnyder *schränke,* but there are no splines reinforcing the miters. One unusual feature of the cornice is its blind-dovetailed frame, which forms the fascia just below the uppermost cyma recta. This detail does not occur on any other seventeenth- or eighteenth-century New York case pieces, and could, if discovered in other furniture, help establish a link between the *wäscheschränk* and related work by Germanic (or Anglo) artisans in New York and other colonies such as Pennsylvania.

The quality and sophistication of the *wäscheschränk's* construction far exceeds that of the Traver and Remensnyder *schränke,* and appears to represent a different German tradition. The maker of the *wäscheschränk* was undoubtedly a joiner or cabinetmaker whose patrons were upper middle class burghers and merchants, whereas the joiner responsible for the Hudson Valley *schränke* probably produced furniture and architectural components for a predominantly rural clientele. The latter class of patrons had neither the means, nor necessarily the desire, to fill their homes with furniture in the latest style.

The workmanship in the upriver *schränke* is charmingly direct, if not somewhat coarse, as evidenced by their maker's failure to scrape away the marks left from the hollow and round planes he used to form the large, ogee-curved bases and the fielded door panels. The joiner may have assumed that surface irregularities would be concealed by the grain-painted decoration.

Given the fact that painted pine dower chests are the only other Palatine case forms found in New York, it is possible that most of the German joiners who immigrated were from a class of furniture makers similar to the *witwerkers* of the Netherlands. These artisans specialized in the production of relatively simple forms made of soft, light-colored woods that were invariably painted. The joiner who made the Traver and Remensnyder *schränke* used maple for the primary wood. This would have been a logical choice for a rural Germanic *witwerker* who wanted to add durability to two ambitious forms.[19]

In contrast, the sophisticated style and construction of the New York *wäscheschränk* suggest that its maker worked in a large town or urban area. Joiner Christian Hartman, who is listed as a freeman in 1715, is the only Germanic furniture maker documented in New York City during the dates assigned to this imposing form. Unfortunately, his name does not appear in the lists of Palatines prepared by the Board of Trade, the Hunter Subsistence Lists, or in the Simmendinger Register. Other Hartmans are recorded, however, including a Johann Hermann and a Peter. A "master Chrisitan Hartman, citizen and carpenter" appears in an early reference in a Frankfurt churchbook. He was a sponsor of the baptism of Anna Elizabeth Bergman (b. 1707), whose parents Andreas and Anna Sibylla immigrated to New York with other Palatines in 1709. Regrettably, it is impossible to determine if he is the same Christian Hartman who worked in New York City.[20]

One can only speculate about the work of urban Palatine joiners such as Christian Hartman, but it is probably safe to assume that they had to adjust their styles to accommodate prevailing New York tastes and cabinetmaking traditions, which turned increasingly to London by the mid-eighteenth century. With their tulip poplar sides, competent dovetailing, and lipped fronts, the drawers of the *wäscheschränk* differ little from those in other New York baroque case forms. The acculturation of immigrant artisans probably occurred more rapidly in the cosmopolitan environs of New York City than in the rural Hudson River Valley. But even in the latter region, interaction with artisans with Dutch, French, and English backgrounds, intermarriage with people from other ethnic groups, and the contingencies of frontier life probably helped transform the furniture making traditions of the few Palatine German joiners who survived the debacle on Livingston Manor. The products of these artisans represent another of the myriad ingredients that make New York baroque furniture such an appetizing stew.

ACKNOWLEDGMENTS The author thanks Luke Beckerdite for suggesting that he publish these New York *schränke,* and Gavin Ashworth for his superb photography. Others who have helped in the preparation of this article include Roderic Blackburn, Dennis Bakoledis, Dean Failey, Amanda Jones, Neil and Madeline Kamil, Nancy Kelly, Noe Kidder, Wolfram Koeppe, Leslie Lafever-Stratton, Jack Lindsay, Mr. and Mrs. Henry Livingston, William E. Lohrman, Kim Orcutt, Steve Regan, Donna Reston, John Scherer, and Alvin Sheffer.

1. The area known to the English-speaking world as the Palatinate is referred to as the *Pfalz* in Germany. Geographically the Palatinate comprises two regions of Germany, the Rhenish or Lower Palatinate (Ger. *Rheinpfalz* or *Niederpfalz*) and the Upper Palatinate (Ger. *Oberpfalz*). The Rhenish Palatinate extends from the left bank of the Rhine and borders in the south on France and in the west on Saarland and Luxembourg. Traditionally, it has been an agricultural area, famed for its wines, and the majority of the Palatines who came to New York were from this geographic region. The Upper Palatinate is a district of northeast Bavaria on the right bank of the Rhine, separated in the east from Czechoslovakia by the Bohemian Forest. The name of the two regions came from the office known as count palatine, a title used in the Roman, Byzantine, and Holy Roman empires and elsewhere, notably in England, Hungary, and Poland (*The New Columbia Encyclopedia* [New York and London: Columbia University Press, 1975]). The only other published works on New York Palatine furniture are by Mary Antoine de Julio, whose research focuses on painted chests. See Mary Antoine de Julio, *German Folk Arts of New York State* (Albany, N.Y.: Albany Institute of History and Art, 1985), pp. 3–17; and Mary Antoine de Julio, "New York German Painted Chests," *Antiques* 127, no. 5 (May 1985): 1156–1165. In her essay and article de Julio provides the name of only one possible maker, a Johannes Kniskern, who by family tradition is said to have made identical chests for his twin daughters. She does not present conclusive evidence, however, that Kniskern was a joiner.

2. Walter Knittle, *Early Eighteenth Century Palatine Emigration* (Baltimore, Md.: Genealogical Printing Company, 1965), pp. 41–42.

3. Henry Z. Jones, Jr., *The Palatine Families of New York, A Study of the German Immigrants Who Arrived in Colonial New York in 1710*, 2 vols. (University City, Ca.: By the author, 1958), 1: ii. Knittle, *Early Eighteenth Century Palatine Emigration*, p. 3. Jones, *The Palatine Families of New York*, 1: iii.

4. Ulrich Simmendinger, *Warhoffte und glaubwürdige Verzeichnüss jeniger Personen; welche sich ano 1709 aus Teutschland in Americam oder neue welt begeben,* translated by Herman Vesper (1717; reprint, St. Johnsville, N.Y.: L. D. MacWethy, 1934), p. vii. The "golden promise of the English letters" probably refers to the so-called "Golden Book" which the British government circulated throughout southern Germany before 1709. This book depicted British North America as the promised land. For more on the "Golden Book" see Jones, *The Palatine Families of New York,* 1: iv.

5. Knittle, *Early Eighteenth Century Palatine Emigration*, pp. 71, 72.

6. Jones, *The Palatine Families of New York,* 1: xii. For more on Graffenreid, see J. Russell Snapp's entry in John A. Garraty and Mark C. Carnes, *American National Biography* (New York and Oxford, Eng.: Oxford University Press, 1999), pp. 370–71. Snapp states that Queen Anne offered to pay £4,000 to transport 1,000 Palatines to North Carolina. Graffenreid ultimately settled about 650 in 1710.

7. Jones, *The Palatine Families of New York,* 1: xii.

8. Simmendinger, *Warhoffte und glaubwürdige Verzeichnüss jeniger Personen,* pp. vii–viii.

9. Ruth Piwonka, *A Portrait of Livingston Manor 1686–1850* (New York: Friends of Clermont, 1986), pp. 30–33; and Jones, *The Palatine Families of New York,* 1: xiii–xvi. A smaller number of Palatines involved in the naval stores project settled directly across the Hudson from Livingston Manor at a place called West Camp. Some of these West Camp settlers moved back across the Hudson onto the Beekman Patent when the project collapsed and settled in and around Rhinebeck with their fellow countrymen from East Camp.

10. The author thanks William E. Lohrman and Steve Regan for bringing the *schränk* illustrated in fig. 4 to his attention, and Dennis Bakoledis for information pertaining to its history (Dennis Bakoledis to Peter Kenny, February 15, 2000.) The author also thanks Nancy Kelly of Rhinebeck, New York, who interviewed Mrs. Ada Harrison, whose sister Muriel Goodwill and brother-in-law Harold Goodwill consigned the *schränk* for auction in 1995. According to Mrs. Harrison, the *schränk* belonged to her grandparents, William Rynders and Samantha Traver. Samantha was the daughter of Stephen L. Traver. Mrs. Harrison told Mrs. Kelly that the *schränk* was a marriage gift to daughters in her family. If this tradition is correct, Samantha would have received the *schränk* from her mother Rosina Mead Traver (1826–1902). Rosina's mother was Elizabeth Pink Mead (m. 1804), who may have inherited the *schränk* from her mother Catharina Holsapple. Given the probable date of the *schränk*, it may have originally belonged to Susanna Link who was born at Livingston Manor on February 27, 1734, or her mother. This genealogical information is derived from inscriptions in a bible owned by Mrs. Ada Harrison. Conversation between the author and Amanda Jones, Director, Ulster County Historical Society, Marbletown, New York, April 10, 2000.

11. The current owner of the Traver family *schränk* had the surface analyzed by Chris Shelton, Conservator of Furniture and Painted Surfaces at Bayou Bend, Houston, Texas. This analysis confirmed that the *schränk* was originally coated with a reddish varnish. Over this surface is a later grain-painted layer in imitation of curly maple, which may have been applied in the late eighteenth or early nineteenth century. A later nineteenth-century varnish is the uppermost layer. Letter from the owner of the *schränk* shown in fig. 4 to Peter M. Kenny, April 13, 2000. Original microscopy samples and infrared photographs of the surfaces were made available to the author.

12. For more on Germanic construction characteristics, particularly wedged dovetails and pinned drawer bottoms, see Benno M. Forman, "German Influences in Pennsylvania Furniture," in *Arts of the Pennsylvania Germans* (New York and London: W.W. Norton & Company, 1983), p. 123, fig. 71; pp. 158–59, fig. 98.

13. For the Elting-Beekman makers of Ulster County, see Peter M. Kenny, Frances Gruber Safford and Gilbert T. Vincent, *American Kasten, The Dutch-Style Cupboards of New York and New Jersey, 1650–1800* (New York: Metropolitan Museum of Art, 1991), pp. 23–26. Jan Elting (1632–1729), progenitor of the Elting family of furniture makers at Kingston, was from the province of Drenthe, which borders Germany in the northeastern part of the Netherlands. It is possible that he introduced the wedging, pinning, and splining techniques manifest in Ulster County *kasten*. Many *kasten* from the Elting-Beekman shops have wooden pegs, or "trunnels" (tree-nails) as they are sometimes called, securing the paneled front stiles to the sides and the backboards to the back edges of interior shelves and the sides.

14. Knittle, *Early Eighteenth Century Palatine Emigration*, pp. 39, 42, 243.

15. Nathaniel B. Sylvester, *History of Ulster County, New York* (Philadelphia: Everts and Peck, 1880), p. 30. *The History of Ulster County, New York*, edited by Alphonso T. Clearwater (Kingston, N.Y.: W. J. Van Deusen, 1907), p. 71.

16. The English Board of Trade Lists of 1709 are reprinted in *New York Genealogical and Biographical Records*, vol. 40 (1909), 49–54, 93–100, 160–67, 241–48 and vol. 41 (1910), 10–19. In addition to the twenty-one joiners, ninety carpenters are listed. Although carpenters often made case furniture, the sophisticated style and construction of the *schränke* suggest that they are the products of furniture joiners. Accordingly, only members of the latter trade have been researched in the course of this study. The men who compiled the lists for the British government understood the distinction between the two trades. For more on Dinant, see Jones, *The Palatine Families of New York*, 1: 171.

17. Jones, *The Palatine Families of New York*, 2: 728–29.

18. New York dealer Morgan MacWhinnie purchased the *schränk* at C. G. Sloan and Company in Washington, D. C. on October 3, 1982 (lot 1517) and advertised it in the March 1985 issue of *Maine Antique Digest*. The author thanks the owner for information pertaining to the auction and Frances Gruber Safford for sharing her correspondence with Morgan MacWhinnie and her notes on the *schränk*. The author also thanks Alan Miller for his observation that the applied moldings on the door panels and drawer fronts were made with a scratch stock rather than a plane. Wolfram Koeppe, my colleague in the department of European Sculpture and Decorative Arts at the Metropolitan Museum, theorized that the molding designs on this piece and many German *wäscheschränke* may derive from fortification plans.

19. For *witwerkers*, see T.H. Lunsingh Scheurleer, "The Dutch and Their Homes in the Seventeenth Century" in *Arts of the Anglo-American Community in the Seventeenth Century*, edited by Ian M. G. Quimby (Charlottesville: University Press of Virginia, 1974), pp. 14–15. Scheurleer states that the *witwerkers* became part of the Josefs Guild of furniture makers in Amsterdam in the late seventeenth century. According to him many artisans came to Amsterdam from Belgium and Germany in the seventeenth century and were incorporated into the Josefs Guild.

20. *The Burghers of New Amsterdam and the Freemen of New York 1675–1866, in Collections of the New-York Historical Society for…1885* (New York: By the Society, 1886), p. 94. Jones, *The Palatine Families of New York*, 2: 1156.

Betty C. Monkman. *The White House: Its Historic Furnishings and First Families*. Washington, D.C: White House Historical Association, 2000; New York: Abbeville Press, 2000. 320 pp.; 260 color and 35 bw illus., catalogue, bibliography, index. $65.00.

The White House: Its Historic Furnishings and First Families was published in celebration of the 200th anniversary of the building's first occupancy by a president and his lady. In November 1800, a reluctant yet steadfast Abigail Adams joined her husband at the nation's new presidential residence, which had been under construction for eight years, in the then-stark, nascent federal city, thereby becoming the first first lady to try to make this house a home. It was not easy. Abigail found half the rooms unplastered, and many of them "vastly deficient in furniture." In this informative and eminently readable book, Betty C. Monkman, the White House curator, chronicles the successive efforts of presidents and their ladies over the next two hundred years as each in turn "struggled, made do, accomplished, enjoyed." The special significance of the first lady's role in this endeavor is acknowledged throughout the book and signaled in the foreword where six former first ladies capsulize and personalize the extraordinary experience of living in the White House. While there have been many books written on the President's House, there had been none which focused on the decorative arts. The objective of this volume, therefore, is to put on display the White House decorative arts collection: French, English, and American furniture, ceramics, glass, metals, lighting devices, clocks, and textiles; while also chronicling the legacy of the successive first families in gathering and building that collection.

To discover and disclose the history of White House furnishings has been a complex task: constant change has been the two-hundred-year leitmotif. Any generations-old house would typically reflect the permutations of evolving taste and technology, but add to that the vicissitudes of enforced change of occupancy every four to eight years. Monkman mines and unravels the entanglements of history and art, people and pieces, as she provides the historical context for examining the decorative arts in this collection.

For those who have been to the White House, or wish to tour again at leisure, or to prepare for an upcoming visit, this volume offers much. The book brings the reader in close to individual pieces and also opens up the rooms for which they were intended—in both their historical and present-day demeanor. Though the state rooms are featured, the reader will have the privilege of visiting more private spaces such as the "Queens' Bedroom," the "Queens' Sitting Room," or the "Lincoln Bedroom." (This latter would perhaps benefit from the affectionate hand of a "Victorianist," for the room lacks the ambiance, the easy layered comfort of its earlier years. One longs to see the éclat of snow-white pillow shams against the polished mahogany headboard and the billowing drama of the original purple satin and gold lace bed hangings.)

The success of the book is in part due to its clear organizing principle. Seven chapters are divided chronologically in an interweaving of art historical styles and presidential administrations. In tandem with presidents, one moves from late eighteenth- and early nineteenth-century neoclassicism to the revival styles of the Victorian era to the colonial revival of the early twentieth century, and, in the second half of that century, back to the neoclassicism of the earliest White House years. Along the way, individual pieces in the collection are examined: the specifics of manufacture, details of their original acquisition, their role in the furnishing vision of the time, and their political and cultural context. Each chapter concludes with a pictorial essay on one of the state rooms or other topic particularly relevant to that chapter. Chapter one, for example, looks at "The President's House in the Early Years, 1789–1814," encompassing the administrations of Washington through Madison. The pictorial essay visually narrates the evolution of the exterior design of the President's House from James Hoban's final design of 1793 through the building's torching by the British in 1814 and beginning reconstruction. Because of this fire and other transformations of time, few actual White House furnishings survive from the earliest years, but the collection boasts numerous pieces—silver, furniture, porcelains, a presentation saber, etc.—with presidential associations which have been acquired in part from descendants of these first presidents. These objects are easy to study in the stunning, close-up, full-color photography of Bruce White which liberally illumines each chapter. An exuberance of Parisian gilded bronze, gilded wood, polished mahogany, and glittering silver fills the pages of chapter two, "French Taste at its White House Zenith, 1817–1829," which pays tribute to James Monroe's extensive efforts to refurbish the President's House with furnishings and settings that would convey the dignity and grandeur of this resilient, powerful country. Monroe ordered many of the finest pieces for the (red) Oval Room, now the Blue Room, which was the main drawing room where the president and first lady received guests and where foreign dignitaries presented their credentials. Visitors at the time were awed by this "most splendid room," "designed to impress upon foreign ministers a respect for the government." The pictorial essay for chapter two, therefore, chronicles the evolution of décor in this singularly important Oval or Blue Room, from the earliest known image, an engraving published in the *United States Magazine* of 1856, through stereoscopic views of 1870 during the Grant administration, and on through photographs taken in 1900, 1903, 1995, and ultimately a 1999 photograph of its current dignified grandeur.

Each chapter is rich in documentation. In researching chapter two, to give just one example, Monkman turned to government records in the National Archives including records of the House of Representatives, Congress, Treasury Accounts; records of the General Accounting Office, vouchers, and early appraisals; contemporary newspapers; the James Monroe Papers at the New York Public Library; period correspondence; travel accounts; journals; letter-books; and more recent published scholarship on specific pieces, decorative arts styles, and history. Two hundred years of quarrelsome voices provided the author with lively documentary material, for such a contentious combination as fiscal expenditure, the arts, democracy, and politics always will offer tentative peace at best and more often outright hostilities. A well-intentioned George Washington, at home in the then-presidential residence in New York City, was admonished for living in an aristocratic manner, though the French minister found that same house "squalid." John Quincy Adams took the heat and the barbed rhymes of a "poet" for indulging in a secondhand billiard table, while Martin Van Buren was skewered by his political opponents for his "regal" life style, and Northern newspapers launched a war-era attack on Mary Todd Lincoln's shopping trips and purchases "while her sister women scraped lint, sewed bandages."

The care of these collections—from the earliest years of leaking roofs to the ongoing uneasy balance between public and private, ceremonial and curatorial—has always been a concern. Four months after Benjamin Henry Latrobe supplied James Madison with elegant Greek klismos chairs with fine saber-cut legs for the Oval Room, Latrobe noted that three had been broken by men leaning back in them—a violation of no surprise to anyone who has studied American genre painting or listened to the remonstrances of British and European travelers in early nineteenth-century America, who were shocked by these tasteless Yankees and their perverse and persistent habit of tilting back in chairs. The public's embrace of the President's House has not always been gentle. The depredations on the glass and chinaware during Andrew Jackson's tumultuous "democratic" inaugural reception are legendary, but over the years many more souvenir hunters have stuffed their pockets with tassels and fringes, fabric swatches and gilded ornaments. Open to the public since 1801, this celebrated house, home, office, entertainment center, historical stage, and art museum, today receives more than a million visitors a year. This extraordinary wear and tear on furnishings has of course necessitated regular refurbishing of the rooms. As early as 1797, when George Washington left office, Congress authorized the disposition of "decayed presidential furnishings" through local auctions, and regular sales of outmoded, shabby, unfavored furnishings continued on a regular basis until 1903. The collection today, therefore, is made up of historical government purchases of the nineteenth and early twentieth century, former White House pieces which have been returned, decorative arts associated with the first presidents, and objects which have been donated by an American public intent on ensuring that the White House have a significant collection of American decorative arts.

One of the many interesting sub-themes of the book is the rising historical consciousness that helped to stem this disposal of and increase the regard for White House furnishings. In the 1890s first lady Caroline Harrison began to assemble surviving examples of porcelain from the various state dining services. Some thirty years later Grace Coolidge brought together the first advisory committee to study state room history, and in 1929 Lou Hoover, wishing to learn more about various pieces, instigated the first concerted effort to study historical White House furnishings. The real benchmark, of course, came with Jacqueline Kennedy's many-pronged initiative to bring America's history to life in the President's House. The final chapter, "A Museum Evolves from a Collection," gives ample evidence of the far-reaching philosophical and physical changes that her enlightened stewardship set in motion. Under her direction many of the state rooms were returned to early nineteenth-century neoclassical splendor, and the final pictorial essay, "Important [furniture] Acquisitions 1961–2000," underscores the stunning success with which that aspect of her mandate has been met. Further, with President and Mrs. Kennedy's guidance and encouragement, Congress passed legislation in 1961 to establish the museum character of the public rooms and created a curatorial position. That same year the White House Historical Association was organized to publish educational materials on the White House. This volume is one example of the many worthy projects which have emanated from that curatorial chair and Historical Association.

The White House: Its Historic Furnishings and First Families includes an informative "Catalogue of Illustrated Objects" by Assistant Curator William G. Allman, and an encompassing introduction by Wendell Garrett. The large-scale format of the volume, the glossy white paper, and the generosity of excellent photographs by Bruce White make this an elegant production worthy of its topic. But it is more. It is a model for integrating history and the arts. Betty Monkman deserves special credit not only for this clear yet complex interweaving, but for sustaining a lively, engaging narrative while at the same time incorporating so much significant documentation, and for her masterful organization of this multifaceted material. This will be a rich resource for students of the decorative arts, those interested in the history of interior design, and political and cultural historians alike. And patriotic Americans can simply take pride in this handsome volume that visually and verbally portrays two hundred years of achievement in this "symbol of a nation."

Elisabeth D. Garrett
Cornish, New Hampshire

Rosemary Troy Krill with Pauline K. Eversmann. *Early American Decorative Arts, 1620–1860: A Handbook for Interpreters*. American Association for State and Local History Book Series. Walnut Creek, Cal.: AltaMira Press, 2001. xii + 299 pp.; numerous bw illus., index. $80.00; $39.95 pb.

This extremely useful book is based on *Handbook for Winterthur Interpreters: A Multidisciplinary Analysis of the Winterthur Collection,* a formidable, five-hundred-page document funded by a 1987 grant from the National Endowment for the Humanities. Published in 1992, the *Handbook* is the most recent in a long line of collection guides written since Winterthur opened to the public as a museum in 1951. Designed specifically as a textbook for Winterthur docents-in-training, it is an interpretive guide rather than a source of specific information about the more than 85,000 objects in Winterthur's decorative arts collections. It is an interesting and, to my mind, commendable reflection of a national trend toward more visitor-oriented interpretation in that, whereas earlier Winterthur docent textbooks were written solely by curators, the creation of the *Handbook* also involved staff members of Winterthur's Education, Public Programs, and Visitor Service Division as well as various advisory committees and consultants.

The stated purpose of *Early American Decorative Arts, 1620–1860: A Handbook for Interpreters* is to "expand the benefits of the NEH grant to interpreters in many historic houses and museums by publishing the book more widely" (p. viii). Its authors, Rosemary Troy Krill and Pauline K. Eversmann, were, respectively, the Project Coordinator and Project Director for the *Handbook*. Both are museum educators employed at Winterthur.

Part One of the book is general in theme, examining ways in which decorative arts might be interpreted and providing social, economic, and cultural context. The evolution of interpretation from simply supplying object-specific information to offering insight and understanding as well—responding to the interests and questions of a range of visitors—is discussed, with reference to current techniques and theories. Although there is nothing particularly groundbreaking here, the concise compilation and summation should be useful even to those familiar with the material.

The chapters in this first section are carefully and thoughtfully organized and resist the temptation to overwhelm the reader with detail. The initial chapter, "Looking at Objects," is designed to help visitors look closely through analysis of material, color, texture, line, ornament, scale, proportion, and volume. "Understanding Style" broadens the examination by asserting that stylistic comprehension requires more than memorizing a list of visual characteristics. Issues of society and culture in a given period play a role as well. There is considerable discussion of terminology, differentiating among current art historical names for styles (mannerist, early baroque), traditional ones (Jacobean, William and Mary) and those used by dealers and collectors. According to the book, different visitors are comfortable with different names for things and interpreters should use those that communicate most clearly to their audience. In my experience, terminology is best avoided altogether as much as possible, as visitors become focused on getting it right and have a hard time moving on to more salient matters. However, the authors do try to make sense of style names by explaining how each one gives different information about the period in which the style flourished (for example, federal and early classical revival).

The chapters titled "Making and Marketing Objects" and "Owning Objects" provide the kind of context that brings objects alive for visitors and is often limited in verbal and written discussions of decorative arts for a general audience (although this is less true now than a decade ago). Issues outlined include trade, settlement patterns, occupations and incomes, merchants and payments, production of goods, labor, population, industrialization, transportation, families, education, and religion.

Each chapter has an extensive bibliography. For example, "Owning Objects" (a ten-page essay) offers ninety-six bibliographic references and "Making and Marketing Objects" fifty-two. Although undeniably valuable, these bibliographies might seem overwhelming to many interpreters.

Prioritization—beginning with a list of the five or six most cogent works—would have been more helpful and created less anxiety in docents at the less-specialized venues than Winterthur that the book purports to serve.

Part Two comprises eighteen chapters focusing on different types of decorative arts objects—six chapters on high-style furniture (organized chronologically), and one each on Windsor furniture, clocks, ceramics, glass, silver, pewter, iron and copper, paintings, prints, textiles, needle-work, and floor coverings. Each chapter follows the same format, structured according to the sections laid out in Part One. Although written for the novice student, the chapters are given added usefulness by the inclusion of footnotes and a bibliography that is prioritized (as those in Part One might profitably have been) into "Standard Sources" and "Additional Sources."

A characteristic example of the sections in Part Two is "Furniture in the Federal or Early Classical Revival Style" (pp. 99–126). It begins with a reassuring catalogue of stylistic characteristics—the all-important foundation that every docent looks for. The next section, "Thinking about the Federal Style," is typically brief, clear, and thorough, demonstrating the qualities of discipline and rigorous editing that are the hallmarks of this book. Discussed in only three pages are classicism, neoclassicism, the contributions of Robert Adam, George Hepplewhite, and Thomas Sheraton, how the style made its way to the United States, major makers in this country, the decreased importance of regional differences, and more. I could not think of an essential point that was not touched on.

"Making and Marketing Federal Furniture" explains cabinetmaking techniques, evolution from craft to industry, the publication of price books, the period's increase in consumption and decrease in British mercantilism, venture cargo, and the relationship between craftsman and customer and between master and journeyman. The final section, "Living with Federal Furniture," explores the what and why of the new forms and domestic spaces that evolved in the federal period.

Even within the restraints imposed by the enormous amount of material covered, one almost never gets the sense of "this is the fact, believe it." Instead, statements are footnoted and backed up with evidence—quotes from journal entries and inventories, a close look at a pattern book, description of a particular shop, or the history of an individual piece, etc. This approach not only gives the "fact" additional credence but also enlivens it. In such a careful and thorough volume, the absence of a glossary is surprising. Most terms are defined within the text, but often only once. This somewhat undermines one of the great virtues of the book, which is that every chapter is an individual entity that can be used effectively on its own. Providing definitions within the text sometimes makes for awkward passages, and the information might better have been given in a glossary. This sentence is an example: "Steamed or bent wood in fancy chairs and lamination (pieces of wood glued together in a like-grain direction for flexibility and alternating grain for strengthening rounded corners of tables) to construct the curves on federal-style furniture were two new techniques that were widely employed" (p. 105). Line drawings of furniture with the different parts identified would also have been useful.

On a more general level, the authors might have evaluated more closely the differences in requirements, expectations, and even psychological make-up between docents at Winterthur and those at less specialized institutions. The book is a superb work of reference, but as a self-described "handbook for interpreters," it might well feel intimidating and overly demanding for docents at historic houses and art museums. For a handbook, there is too little filtering of information, establishment of hierarchies, and guidance.

However, the virtues of this volume far outweigh its few limitations. The format is no-nonsense and serviceable; illustrations are minimal but carefully chosen to make a point and captioned with additional material. Current scholarship is effectively summarized and synthesized. The writing is clear, matter-of-fact, and not condescending. There is no fluff; every sentence, shaped for lucidity, has something to say and builds informatively on the one that precedes it. And, as mentioned before, each chapter stands alone, making it an easily accessible source of reference.

The amount of well-ordered and well-written information in this slim book is remarkable. Although it may not comfortably serve as a handbook for docents beyond Winterthur, it is unquestionably an invaluable reference work for everyone that lectures on or writes about American decorative arts in a museum setting.

Gilian Ford Shallcross
Museum of Fine Arts, Boston

Peter Benes, editor. *Rural New England Furniture: People, Place, and Production*. The Dublin Seminar for New England Folklife Annual Proceedings 1998. Boston: Boston University Scholarly Publications, 2000. 256 pages; 113 bw illus., maps, bibliography. $25.00.

How useful is a set of printed papers from a conference? Like an exhibition catalogue after the exhibit is dismantled, such a volume serves as a compendium of the ideas expressed and at least some of the images presented. But the process of editing the papers into a comprehensive whole capable of standing on its own can be long and arduous. Some papers will never be revised; others may seem peripheral or unrelated to the whole. At best, the papers will offer complementary perspectives on the topic, stimulate further discussion, and serve as a milestone of research on the subject.

Rural New England Furniture: People, Place, and Production gives a more accurate picture of the original conference than many such reports by actually including a copy of the conference program, listing papers and conference activities, and printing abstracts of the papers which are not in the final publication. A useful bibliography compiled by Gerald W. R. Ward, similar to that which readers of *American Furniture* have come to expect in each volume, is here focused on the region of the conference subject. This reviewer, who did not attend the conference in question, examines the transfer from spoken sessions to printed papers and evaluates their lasting value in published form.

The Dublin Seminar for New England Folklife has been sponsoring conferences and publishing the conference reports on a wide variety of traditional subjects since 1976; this is the first time, however, that the overall topic has been furniture. The introduction to this volume by Robert Trent, a member of the program committee for the conference, presents an unusually frank discussion of the lively debate engendered by the designation of the topic of rural New England furniture. The conference organizers were forced to reexamine what "folklife" and "rural" mean when mass-produced furniture is concerned. The group also had to confront the long-established tendency of the seminar to ignore almost everything created after 1830. It is indeed refreshing to see work about New England which covers the nineteenth century, dips into the twentieth, and even mentions practices recalled by recently retired furniture workers (p. 135). Perhaps symbolic of this shift toward greater emphasis on more recent times and quantity production, the striking cover photograph—of a horse cart loaded with chairs—dates from about 1900.

In the editing process the papers were reorganized and the sections reconfigured, strengthening the whole but occasionally confusing the reader, as with Trent's own paper (written with Peter Follansbee) on furniture made in the colonial revival period using seventeenth-century construction techniques and style. In the conference, it was presented last. In the anthology, it leads off under the heading "The Seventeenth Century." Yet in the book's introduction Trent argues that "the paper embodies a shift in our perceptions of the nineteenth century" (p. 8). This would seem to indicate it should be classified under the nineteenth century, if indeed it is to be categorized by a period at all rather than by the subject of reproductions. Evidently, the editing phase also allowed for revised thinking and refinement of terminology: the Trent-Follansbee article appeared on the conference program as the sole paper under the heading "Furniture Fakes." The revised published essay stresses "[a]bove all, the five revival cupboards should not be called 'fakes'. . . . The fakery resides in Waters's having marketed the objects as period, which is fraud" (p. 27).

An obvious benefit of attending the conference is the opportunity to view all the images meant to accompany each talk. The book format has, one supposes, necessitated a reduction in the number of illustrations available, but the presence of footnotes partially makes up for this. Thus, though the Perkins cabinet is not shown in the text (p. 23), a footnote guides the reader to an illustration in another source. Less happily, in a later essay, a portrait by Robert Peckham of the Timothy Doty family, depicting many family possessions, is described in detail but not shown (pp. 112–13). It is also difficult to follow the intricacies of construction details of at least six separate cabinetmaking shops when only full overall shots of four chests are illustrated in David F. Wood's essay "Cabinetmaking Practices in Revolutionary Concord: New Evidence." Footnotes serve another purpose in linking text to references to other works and previous studies and creating a network of scholarship to guide future directions of research, something that would have interrupted the straightforward narration of a spoken paper.

Trent may overstate the case in saying "[s]urely the lament that the New England furniture industry was eclipsed by nationally-recognized factories in Jamestown, New York; Grand Rapids, Michigan; and High Point, North Carolina, is grossly inaccurate" (p. 12). From the point of view of numbers of furniture pieces produced—there are few statistics of large annual production in these papers—this may actually be accurate. But certainly the wealth of information here illuminates a previously little-understood field and examines seldom-discussed auxiliary crafts such as cane and rush seating in addition to the more frequently studied style, construction, and attribution to shop or craftsman.

Two papers consider aspects of Shaker furniture: the identification of objects produced at the Enfield community, and the influence of Shaker women's textile production on the development of a unique form, the sewing desk. Studies of the products of late eighteenth- and nineteenth-century cabinetmakers and small shops are the main focus of the papers. Readers will also find much interesting information about women, American Indians, and prison inmates as furniture workers; the organization of family-run businesses; and a case study of an itinerant cabinetmaker who practiced another profession at the same time.

Is this book about New England furniture useful for those not directly involved in New England studies? Yes, for several reasons. New England furniture has been widely dispersed through family migration and sale, some of it ending up in museum collections in other regions. There are also tantalizing mentions of New England workers migrating to Pennsylvania, Kentucky, and Illinois. And it is instructive to find studies of New England shop practices contemporary with the development of furniture production in other parts of the United States, and to see in New England a slow transition from handmade, one-of-a-kind pieces to mass production taking place during most of the nineteenth century, a process which was accelerated in places where settlement and the development of manufacturing occurred later. It is noteworthy that those giving papers included the expected curators and academics, but also a professional furniture maker, an educator, an historic preservation worker, and interested amateurs, including collectors. All these groups should also find the volume of interest.

Anne Woodhouse
Missouri Historical Society

John T. Kirk. *American Furniture: Understanding Styles, Construction, and Quality.* New York: Harry N. Abrams, 2000. 236 pp.; 57 color and 194 bw illus., 7 line drawings, bibliography, index. $39.95.

John T. Kirk is one of few aestheticians with the kind of hands-on woodworking experience that allows him to describe how the qualities of wood affect furniture design and provide clues about its authenticity. His love for the materials and tools that make furniture enables him to address construction details and surfaces of domestic furnishings as historical artifacts as well as works of art. For Kirk, the artisanry that defines an object's beauty is derived both from the intrinsic qualities of its materials, and from the design iconography and historical references that traditionally dominated the furniture analyses of connoisseurs who preceded him.

Kirk's gift has been described as the "ability to see furniture and to communicate his understanding of form and ornament to others." His breakthrough text published in 1970, *Early American Furniture: How to Recognize, Evaluate, Buy and Care for the Most Beautiful Pieces—High Style, Country, Primitive, and Rustic,* was "not a documentary history of furniture styles, construction, or makers, but rather a primer on how to evaluate the proportions and organization of an object, how to assess the role of small details, and how to recognize the various sources on which an object is based." An update of Kirk's introduction to furniture study was long awaited in academic circles, as collectors, dealers, and material culture teachers have become more sophisticated in their knowledge of the styles and cultural contexts of objects. New furniture collectors in particular have sought a comprehensive text on decorative arts connoisseurship that might serve as a portal to more specialized works.[1]

Kirk has taught extensively since the publication of *Early American Furniture,* primarily at Boston University and Sotheby's. Unlike many non-teaching furniture historians and scholars, he has endured years of the naïve, probing, and know-it-all questions that emerge from classrooms. He taught students to examine objects from the ground up, and to think critically about how various components of an object were intended to fit together. He could appear taciturn and reclusive in the university environment, and he was intolerant of academic nonsense. Yet as a teacher he was patient, deeply thoughtful, Socratic, and often amusing in his presentations and insights. His slide comparisons and photocopied readings focused on eclectic interpretations of design sources, and his knowledge of how small regions of England influenced the emergence of regional characteristics in America enabled students to think clearly about the genealogy of early American design. He taught students to be thorough researchers, and to look hard at, and to really *see,* objects for their formal aesthetic qualities, and for their internal design and construction details. A quarter century of classroom discourse has shaped the questions addressed in *American Furniture: Understanding Styles, Construction, and Quality.*

Perhaps the only work comparable to Kirk's exploration of aesthetics in *American Furniture* would be Albert Sack's *New Fine Points of Furniture— Early American* (1993). Sack provides numerous illustrations of his "Good, Better, Best, Superior, Masterpiece" hierarchy of aesthetic criteria for judging comparable furnishings, but his text does not introduce an overall paradigm for assessing quality in types of objects outside those he presents. There are virtually no references in Sack to larger cultural, economic, or aesthetic influences, and he does not delve into construction details, materials, influences, or rural and vernacular forms. Kirk takes a noble and largely successful stab at addressing these conceptual gaps. He notes that for decades he had "taken American furniture very seriously, but . . . stand[ing] aside from any over-reverence of the material" (p. 8). Working with a talented host of decorative arts scholars including, among others, Wendy Cooper, Nancy Evans, Dean Failey, Elisabeth Garrett, Brock Jobe, Karen Keane, Leslie Keno, Albert Sack, Gerry Ward, and Philip Zea, he has refined his sense of what makes furniture beautiful. "This book is about beauty," he writes. "It seeks to understand how beauty was created, and demonstrates the art of perceiving what was put there for the viewer. In addition there is encouragement to value the patina that time and use have added" (p. 10).[2]

Kirk elaborates on his admonition in his *Impecunious Collector's Guide to American Antiques* (1975), that a collector should "buy [a piece] ratty and leave it alone." His recommendation that painted surfaces, in particular, should be left alone to best reveal their beautiful patina came to be described in the antiques marketplace as a suggestion to prioritize the finding and preservation of objects with "Kirk surfaces." This concept was extended, often inappropriately, to evaluating the connoisseurship virtues of shimmering, high-gloss objects originally valued for the artisans' abilities to make their often-thinly veneered pieces reflect light. Applying the "Kirk surface" criterion to such high-style federal period and architectonic, neoclassical furnishings is antithetical to the value he had placed on celebrating the untouched patina of grungy painted surfaces that emerged from generations of plebeian domestic use. Here Kirk reminds his readers to look carefully at objects and to listen closely to what he has taught on discerning and understanding the intentions of the original artisans.[3]

American Furniture begins with an introduction to conceptual thinking about furniture connoisseurship and follows with six chronological sections comprised of admirably digestible vignettes detailing various aspects of how to examine and discriminate among comparable objects. The stylistic evolution of American design from the mid-seventeenth through the early nineteenth century is covered in great detail, including useful comparisons of authentic and fake objects. The text includes sections on classicism and the Shakers, and on mid-nineteenth-century revivals that hint at Kirk's studies of later designs, including his *The Shaker World: Art, Life, Belief.* He cuts off his chronological analysis at the point when machine production assumed a greater role than the hand in making the final statement. It is somewhat disappointing, given the emergence of collecting interest in much later material, that Kirk does not apply his aesthetic and design principles to work after 1850. Aesthetics and good design principles have continued to be applicable even in the machine age as American arts and crafts and mission styles emerged in the late nineteenth century, and as new technology influenced design throughout the twentieth century. For the past 150 years, architects, industrial designers, and artisans linked aesthetics, industrial innovation, and artisanry to push the limits of the existing design aesthetic. The reluctance of an aesthetician such as Kirk to address the twentieth-century's design aesthetics is particularly surprising in light of the other design influences. The task of producing such an opus remains for the generation of scholars Kirk has nurtured. Nonetheless, *American Furniture* puts a fitting asterisk on Kirk's ability to teach furniture aesthetics better than anyone else in the past quarter century. The work links aesthetics and construction details with a deep knowledge of contemporary cultural contexts and modern market forces that affect antiques collecting. Kirk demonstrates, again, that he is a brilliant and consummate educator who has influenced generations of dealers and collectors. He has significantly improved the level of scholarship into American decorative arts.[4]

Ted Landsmark
Boston Architectural Center

1. Barbara McLean Ward and Gerald W.R. Ward, "American Furniture to 1820," in Kenneth L. Ames and Gerald W.R. Ward, eds., *American Decorative Arts and Household Furnishings Used in America, 1650–1920: An Annotated Bibliography* (Winterthur, Del.: Henry Francis du Pont Winterthur Museum, 1989), p. 96. Ward and Ward, "American Furniture," p. 97.

2. Albert Sack, *The New Fine Points of Furniture—Early American* (New York: Crown, 1993).

3. John T. Kirk, *The Impecunious Collector's Guide to American Antiques* (New York: Alfred A. Knopf, 1982), p. 92.

4. John T. Kirk, *The Shaker World: Art, Life, Belief* (New York: Harry N. Abrams, Inc., 1997).

Compiled by Gerald W.R. Ward

Recent Writing on American Furniture: A Bibliography

▼ T H I S Y E A R' S L I S T includes works published in 2000 and roughly through July of 2001. As always, a few earlier publications that had escaped notice are also cited. The short title *American Furniture 2000* is used in citations for articles and reviews published in last year's issue of this journal, which is also cited in full under Luke Beckerdite's name. For the first time, this checklist includes a publication issued only in an electronic format—Jay Robert Stiefel's analysis of the account book of John Head of Philadelphia, issued by the American Philosophical Society Library.

For their assistance in a variety of ways I am grateful to Luke Beckerdite, Jonathan L. Fairbanks, Steven M. Lash, Milo Naeve, Rebecca Reynolds, Pat Warner, and Philip Zimmerman. Staff members of the library of the Museum of Fine Arts, Boston, the Portsmouth Athenaeum, and the Winterthur Museum Library, especially Neville Thompson, have also been helpful.

I would be delighted to receive suggestions for titles that should be included in these annual lists. Review copies of significant works would also be much appreciated.

Abbott, James. "In the Spotlight: American Empire Armchair." *BMA Today* (September/October 2000): 24–25. 1 bw illus. (Baltimore Museum of Art acquisition.)

Adamson, Glenn. "Recreations: The Furniture of Harold Ionson." *Woodwork*, no. 67 (February 2001): 24–31. 22 color and bw illus.

Albertson, Karla Klein. "Living with Antiques: San Francisco Shaker." *Antiques* 159, no. 5 (May 2001): 796–805. 18 color illus.

American Period Furniture 1, no. 1 (January 2001): 1–36. bw illus. (Seven articles are contained in this first issue of the newsletter of the Society of American Period Furniture Makers.)

[American Textile Museum, Lowell, Mass.]. "Antique New England Furniture Exhibition June 17 at American Textile Museum." *Antiques and the Arts Weekly* (June 1, 2001): 7.

Ames, Kenneth L. Review of Galen Cranz, *The Chair: Rethinking Culture, Body, and Design.* In *Studies in the Decorative Arts* 8, no. 2 (spring/summer 2001): 133–36.

Antonelli, Paola, ed. *Workspheres: Design and Contemporary Work Styles.* New York: Abrams, 2001. 176 pp.; numerous color illus.

Apicella, Mary Ann. "The Lum Chest: A Connecticut Yankee in Scotland?" *Regional Furniture* 14 (2000): 1–103. 6 bw illus.

[Art Complex Museum]. *Shaker Chairs: Their Story / Rotation: Seats, Etc. / Contemporary Studio Furniture (Shaker Inspired) / Unique Seats / More Unique Seats.* Duxbury, Mass.: Art Complex Museum, 2000. 18 pp.; illus.

Arthur, Catherine Rogers. "'The True Antiques of Tomorrow': Furniture by the Potthast Brothers of Baltimore, 1892–1975." *American Furniture 2000,* pp. 31–58. 49 color and bw illus.

Baarsen, Reinier. *17th-Century Cabinets.* Amsterdam: Waanders Publishers, Rijksmuseum, 2000. 64 pp.; 70 color and bw illus.

Bailey, Chris H. "Horological Gods and Heroes." *NAWCC Bulletin* 42, no. 5 (October 2000): 617–20. 8 bw illus.

Barron, Stephanie, et al. *Made in California: Art, Image, and Identity, 1900–2000.* Berkeley: Los Angeles County Museum of Art and University of California Press, 2000. 351 pp.; 402 color and 162 bw illus., checklist, bibliography, index.

Bartlett, Apple Parish, and Susan Bartlett Crater. *Sister: The Life of Legendary American Decorator, Mrs. Henry Parish II.* New York: St. Martin's, 2000. 357 pp.; illus.

Bartolucci, Marisa, and Cathy Ho. *American Contemporary Furniture.* Edited by Raul Cabra and Dung Ngo. New York: Universe, 2000. 208 pp.; illus., index.

Bates, Elizabeth Bidwell. "Study Project Reevaluates 19th-Century New York Chairmaking." *Maine Antique Digest* 29, no. 2 (February 2001): 11A. 1 bw illus.

Beach, Laura. "Bills of Sale Confirm Early Date of Beekman Family Furniture." *Antiques and the Arts Weekly* (January 12, 2001): 78–79. 3 bw illus.

Beach, Laura. "A Bombé Discovery." *Antiques and the Arts Weekly* (February 9, 2001): 65. 1 bw illus.

Beach, Laura. "An Engagement with Folk Art: Cyril I. Nelson's Gifts to the Museum." *Antiques and the Arts Weekly* (November 10, 2000): 1, 68–70. 13 bw illus.

Beach, Laura. "Highlights: With New Galleries, Milwaukee Becomes a Decorative Arts Hub." *The Catalogue of Antiques and Fine Art* 2, no. 4 (summer/fall 2001): 54–55. 2 color illus.

Beach, Laura. "Pendleton House in Providence: RISD's American Wing Reopens a Century After Its Founding." *Antiques and the Arts Weekly* (June 1, 2001): 1, 68–70A. 10 bw illus.

Beach, Laura. "A Tribute to Zeke [Liverant]." *Antiques and the Arts Weekly* (October 20, 2000): 1, 68–71. 13 bw illus.

Beckerdite, Luke, ed. *American Furniture 2000.* Milwaukee, Wis.: Chipstone Foundation, 2000. xii + 239 pp.; numerous color and bw illus., bibliography, index. Distributed by University Press of New England, Hanover, N.H., and London.

Beckerdite, Luke. "The Early Furniture of Christopher and Job Townsend." *American Furniture 2000,* pp. 1–30. 47 color and bw illus.

Beckerdite, Luke. "Introduction." *American Furniture 2000,* pp. xi–xii.

Binzen, Jonathan. "The First Years of Fine Woodworking." *Fine Woodworking*, no. 146 (winter 2000–2001): 46–51. Color and bw illus.

Binzen, Jonathan. "Spectacular! Stirring! Fun!" *Woodwork*, no. 71 (October 2001): 31. 1 color illus. (Re Garry Knox Bennett.)

Bjelajac, David. *American Art: A Cultural History.* New York: Harry N. Abrams, Inc., 2001. 416

pp.; numerous color and bw illus., bibliography, index.

Blackburn, Graham. "A Short History of Design." *Fine Woodworking*, no. 146 (winter 2000–2001): 56–63. Line drawings.

Boardman, Allan. "Sam Maloof." *Fine Woodworking*, no. 146 (winter 2000–2001): 52–54. 4 color illus.

Boggs, Brian. "Maloof's Challenging Chairs." *Fine Woodworking*, no. 146 (winter 2000–2001): 55. 1 color illus.

Bouler, Alissa L., comp. "Essays from *The Clarion* and *Folk Art*: Fall 1975 Through Summer 2001: A Subject Index." *Folk Art* 26, no. 2 (summer 2001): 59–72. Color illus.

Bourgeault, Ronald. *Northeast Auctions: Year 2000 in Review.* Portsmouth, N.H.: Northeast Auctions, n.d. [2001]. Color illus. (Includes some furniture.)

Boyce, Charles, ed. *Dictionary of Furniture.* 2d ed. New York: Facts on File, 2000. xxii + 378 pp.; illus., bibliography.

Bradford, Peter. *The Design Art of Nicos Zographos.* New York: Monacelli Press, 2000. Unpaged; numerous color illus.

Brawer, Nicholas A. *British Campaign Furniture: Elegance under Canvas, 1740–1914.* New York: Harry N. Abrams, Inc., 2001. 232 pp.; 140 color and 135 bw illus., directory, bibliography, index.

Brawer, Nicholas A. "Victorian Campaign Furniture." *Antiques* 158, no. 3 (September 2000): 346–53. 16 color and 3 bw illus.

[Brick Store Museum]. "Brick Store Museum Gets Major Gift." *Maine Antique Digest* 29, no. 5 (May 2001): 10A. 1 bw illus.

(Re gift of 1685 Essex County chest of drawers with history in Capen family. See also *The Boston Globe,* March 31, 2001, C1ff.)

Brown, Michael K. "Bombé Furniture at Bayou Bend, Museum of Fine Arts, Houston." *The Catalogue of Antiques and Fine Art* 2, no. 4 (summer/fall 2001): 182–85. 4 color illus.

Buchanon, Chris. "Appalachian Chairmakers: Tradition and Revival." *Woodwork,* no. 69 (June 2001): 48–53. Color and bw illus.

Burks, Jean M., and Rob Tarule. "Mystery Revealed: Unraveling the Story of a Hadley Chest." *The Catalogue of Antiques and Fine Art* 2, no. 1 (winter 2001): 195–97. 5 color illus.

"Cabinetmakers Database on Web." *Maine Antique Digest* 29, no. 7 (July 2001): 11A.

Carlisle, Nancy. "Inside SPNEA: Newbury Furniture." *Old-Time New England* 77, no. 267 (fall/winter 1999): 34–48. 19 bw illus.

Collins, Jeffrey. "*In Vino Veritas?* Death and the Cellarette in Empire New York." In *American Artifacts: Essays in Material Culture,* ed. Jules D. Prown and Kenneth Haltman, pp. 47–70. East Lansing: Michigan State University Press, 2000. 10 bw illus.

[Colonial Williamsburg]. *Colonial Williamsburg Celebrates 75 Years of Collecting.* Williamsburg, Va.: Colonial Williamsburg Foundation, 2001. 48 pp.; color illus. (Essay by Ronald L. Hurst.)

[Concord (Massachusetts) Museum]. "Keeping Time: Clockmaking in Concord, 1790–1835, at the Concord

Museum, Concord, MA." *NAWCC Bulletin* 42, no. 5 (October 2000): 621–22. 4 bw illus.

[Concord (Massachusetts) Museum]. "A Painted Rocking Chair." *Concord Museum Newsletter* (spring 2001): 3. 2 bw illus.

Congdon-Martin, Douglas. *Arts and Crafts Designs for the Home.* Atglen, Pa.: Schiffer Publishing, 2001. 254 pp.; color illus.

[Connecticut Historical Society]. "CHS Will Mount Chapin Exhibit." *Maine Antique Digest* 29, no. 3 (March 2001): 8A.

[Connecticut Historical Society]. "Connecticut Historical Society Plans Eliphalet Chapin Exhibit." *Antiques and the Arts Weekly* (March 2, 2001): 60. 1 bw illus.

[Connecticut Valley Historical Museum]. "Exhibitions . . . Through March 31, 2002." *Maine Antique Digest* 29, no. 8 (August 2001): 35E. 1 bw illus. (Re exhibition entitled "Valley Furniture, Valley Tools.)

Cooke, Edward S., Jr. "Women Furniture Makers: From Decorative Designers to Studio Makers." In *Women Designers in the USA, 1900–2000,* edited by Pat Kirkham, pp. 291–303. New Haven and London: Yale University Press for the Bard Center for Studies in the Decorative Arts, 2000. 15 color and bw illus.

Crowley, John E. *The Invention of Comfort: Sensibilities and Design in Early Modern Britain and Early America.* Baltimore: Johns Hopkins University Press, 2001. 384 pp.; illus., index.

[Currier Gallery of Art]. "Currier Gallery of Art Acquires 1780s Boston Chest-on-Chest." *Antiques and the Arts Weekly* (February 2, 2001): 64. 1 bw illus.

[Currier Gallery of Art]. "Currier Gallery of Art Announces Recent Furniture Acquisitions." *Antiques and the Arts Weekly* (February 23, 2001): 40. 1 bw illus. (Re contemporary studio furniture.)

[Currier Gallery of Art]. "Currier Gallery of Art Purchases Landmark Wendell Secretary." *Antiques and the Arts Weekly* (November 24, 2000): 40. 1 bw illus.

[Dallas Museum of Art]. "Dallas Museum of Art Reveals Silver and Gold Treasures." *Antiques and the Arts Weekly* (November 3, 2000): 99. 1 bw illus. (Re silver dressing table and stool of 1899, designed by William C. Codman for the Gorham Manufacturing Company. See also *Antiques and the Arts Weekly* [November 17, 2000]: 104.)

D'Ambrosio, Anna Tobin. Review of Donald C. Peirce, *Art & Enterprise: American Decorative Art, 1825–1917, The Virginia Carroll Crawford Collection.* In *American Furniture 2000,* pp. 206–11.

[DAR Museum]. "The Art of Upholstery on View at DAR Museum, Washington, D.C." *Antiques and the Arts Weekly* (December 8, 2000): 48.

Davidson, Paul. *The Antique Collector's Directory of Period Detail: How to Identify the Key Characteristics, Shapes, and Forms of Period Styles.* Hauppauge, N. Y.: Barron's, 2000. 224 pp.; 600+ color and bw illus., index.

Day, Ross. "A Krenov Student's Notebook." *Fine Woodworking,* no. 146 (winter 2000–2001): 98–103. Color illus.

[DeWitt Wallace Museum, Colonial Williamsburg]. "Curtains, Cases, and Covers: Textiles for the American Home, 1700–1845, at DeWitt Wallace Museum." *Antiques and the Arts Weekly* (November 17, 2000): 9. 3 bw illus.

Dias-Reid, Cynthia. "Willard House and Clock Museum: Benjamin Willard Tall Clock Donated to the Museum." *NAWCC Bulletin* 43, no. 3 (June 2001): 351. 2 bw illus.

"Discoveries." *The Catalogue of Antiques and Fine Art* 2, no. 1 (winter 2001): 167–69. 6 color and 2 bw illus.

"Discoveries." *The Catalogue of Antiques and Fine Art* 2, no. 2 (early spring 2001): 17–19. 5 color and 3 bw illus.

"Discoveries." *The Catalogue of Antiques and Fine Art* 2, no. 3 (summer 2001): 10–12. 6 color illus. (Re Capen Perkins chest of drawers, Ipswich or Newbury, Massachusetts, 1685.)

Donnelly, Max. "Cottier and Company, Art Furniture Makers." *Antiques* 159, no. 6 (June 2001): 916–25. 15 color and 3 bw illus.

Edwards, Clive. *Encyclopedia of Furniture Materials, Trades, and Techniques.* Brookfield, Vt.: Ashgate Publishing, 2001. 290 pp.; 24 color and 148 bw illus., bibliography.

Edwards, Robert. "Beyond Mission." *Antiques and the Arts Weekly* (November 3, 2000): 56–57. 6 bw illus.

Esperdy, Gabrielle. Review of J. Stewart Johnson, *American Modern, 1925–1940: Design for a New Age.* In *Studies in the Decorative Arts* 8, no. 2 (spring/summer 2001): 136–39.

Evans, Nancy Goyne. "The Windsor Side Chair in the Dining Room." *The Catalogue of Antiques and Fine Art* 2, no. 3 (summer 2001): 157–61. 7 color illus.

Feld, Stuart P. "Boston in the Age of Neo-classicism." In *Ellis Memorial Antiques Show 2000* (catalogue). Boston: Ellis Memorial Center, 2000, pp. 74–81. 12 color illus.

"The Fifth Annual Furniture Society Conference." *Woodwork,* no. 71 (October 2001): 68-76. 18 color illus.

Fisher, Marshall Jon. "The Ergonomic Rocking Chair." *The Atlantic* 287, no. 4 (April 2001): 93–95. 4 color illus.

Fleming, Elizabeth A. "Cultural Negotiations: A Study of the New Mexican Caja." *American Furniture 2000,* pp. 185–204. 22 color and bw illus.

Forman, Bruce Ross. *Clockmakers of Montgomery County, 1740–1850.* Norristown, Pa.: Historical Society of Montgomery County, 2000. 327 pp.; illus.

Forsyth, Amy. "Jere Osgood and Thomas Hucker." *Woodwork,* no. 69 (June 2001): 24–33. Color and bw illus.

Fuchs, Ron. "The Colonial Revival." *Winterthur Magazine* (summer 2001): 29–34. 6 color illus. (See also "The Oldest Piece of Colonial Revival Furniture," p. 35, and "Winterthur: The Quintessential Colonial Revival Artifact, "pp. 36–37, by the same author.)

Furniture History 35 (1999): 1–172. (Seven articles on English furniture.)

Furniture History 36 (2000): 1–251. (Eight articles on English furniture.)

"Gallery." *Fine Woodworking*, no. 146 (winter 2000–2001): 114–21. Color illus. (Re a variety of contemporary furniture.)

"Gallery." *Woodwork*, no. 70 (August 2001): 46–53. Color illus. (Re contemporary furniture from Northern Woods Exhibition, and by Guy Marsden, Meier Brothers, Robert Akroyd, and Doug Chamblin, and the Tercera Stool Show.)

"Gallery." *Woodwork*, no. 71 (October 2001): 46–53. 31 color illus. (Re contemporary furniture by Mark Levin, Jeff Hunt, John Grew Sheridan, William Locke, and others).

"Gallery: The Society of American Period Furnituremakers." *Woodwork*, no. 67 (February 2001): 33–37. 10 color illus.

"Gallery: Wornick Scholarship Winners." *Woodwork*, no. 67 (February 2001): 38–39. 8 color illus.

Garrett, Wendell. "All Things American." *Sotheby's Preview* (January 2001): 68–71. 3 color illus. (Re collection of Andrew D. Wolfe.)

Garrett, Wendell, and Allison Eckardt Ledes. "Harold Sack (1911–2000)." *Antiques* 158, no. 3 (September 2000): 316. 1 color illus.

Gaynor, James M. "Tools for Gentlemen." *Antiques* 159, no. 1 (January 2001): 234–41. 9 color and 5 bw illus.

Gill, Harold B., Jr. "Portrait of an Artisan." *Colonial Williamsburg* 23, no. 1 (spring 2001): 15–20. 7 color and 1 bw illus. (Re portrait of cabinetmaker Edmund B. Dickinson of Williamsburg.)

Gilpin, Hank. "Professor Frid." *Fine Woodworking*, no. 146 (winter 2000–2001): 80–85. Color illus.

Girouard, Mark. *Life in the French Country House*. New York: Alfred A. Knopf, 2000. 352 pp.; 239 color and bw illus., index.

Gordan, Liz, and Terri Hartman. *Decorative Hardware: Interior Designing with Knobs, Handles, Latches, Locks, Hinges, Lighting Fixtures, and Other Hardware*. New York: HarperCollins, 2000. 224 pp.; 300 color illus.

Graham, Judith S. *Puritan Family Life: The Diary of Samuel Sewall*. Boston: Northeastern University Press, 2000. xii + 283 pp.; 12 bw illus., bibliography, index. (Re a few remarks concerning children's furniture.)

Graves, Leroy, and Luke Beckerdite. "New Insights on John Cadwalader's Commode-Seat Side Chairs." *American Furniture 2000*, pp. 152–68. 33 color and bw illus.

Greenberg, Cara. "George Nakashima and the Modernist Movement: An Interview with Steven Beyer." *The Modernism Magazine* 4, no. 2 (summer 2001): 36–41. Color illus.

Greenhalgh, Paul. *The Essence of Art Nouveau*. New York: Harry N. Abrams, Inc., 2000. 96 pp.; illus., bibliography, index.

Greenhalgh, Paul, ed. *Art Nouveau, 1890–1914*. London: V & A Publications, 2000. 496 pp.; numerous color illus., bibliography, checklist, index.

Gustafson, Eleanor H. "Museum Accessions." *Antiques* 159, no. 1 (January 2001): 40–44. 7 color illus. (Includes illustrations of Hadley chest and seventeenth-century Virginia table on loan to Colonial Williamsburg.)

Gustafson, Eleanor H. "Museum Accessions." *Antiques* 159, no. 5 (May 2001): 686. 3 color illus. (Re acquisitions by Minneapolis Institute of Arts and Dallas Museum of Art.)

Gustafson, Eleanor H. "Museum Accessions." *Antiques* 160, no. 1 (July 2001): 34. 3 color illus. (Re acquisition of L.C. Tiffany & Associated Artists screen, 1881–1882, by Virginia Museum of Fine Arts).

Gustafson, Eleanor H. "Museum Accessions." *Antiques* 160, no. 2 (August 2001): 150. 4 color illus. (Re Shaker chest of drawers, New York State, ca. 1810–1830, acquired by the Seattle Art Museum in honor of John T. Kirk.)

Hanks, David A., and Anne Hoy. *Design for Living: Furniture and Lighting, 1950–2000, The Liliane and David M. Stewart Collection*. Edited by Martin Eidelberg. London: Thames and Hudson, 2000. 200 pp.; numerous color illus.

Hardiman, Thomas, Jr. "Veneered Furniture of Cumston and Buckminster, Saco, Maine." *Antiques* 159, no. 5 (May 2001): 754–61. 13 color and 1 bw illus.

Heath, Adrian, et al. *300 Years of Industrial Design*. New York: Watson-Guptill, 2000. 272 pp.; numerous bw illus., line drawings.

Heckscher, Morrison H., with Amelia Peck and Carrie Rebora Barratt. "Anatomy of an Acquisition: Treasures from the Ann and Philip Holzer Collection." *Antiques* 160, no. 2 (August 2001): 190–97. 10 color illus.

[Heritage Center Museum]. "Heritage Center Museum Acquires Rare Piece of Lancaster

Furniture." *Antiques and the Arts Weekly* (December 1, 2000): 49. (Re mahogany dressing table made by Jacob F. Markley [1800–1854] of Columbia, Pennsylvania.)

Hewett, David. "Stickley Sideboard Buried Inside Lake Camp Brings $107,250." *Maine Antique Digest* 29, no. 1 (January 2001): 7A. 2 bw illus.

Hewett, David. "The Twelve-Day Turnaround: $1650 Card Table in Florida Brings $1.32 Million in Massachusetts." *Maine Antique Digest* 29, no. 8 (August 2001): 21A. 1 bw illus.

Hindman, Leslie, with Dan Santow. *Adventures at the Auction: The Ultimate Guide to Buying and Selling at Auction, In Person and Online.* New York: Clarkson Potter, 2001. xiv + 242 pp.; color illus., appendixes, index.

[Historic Deerfield]. "Historic Deerfield Acquires Rare Seventeenth-Century Table." *Antiques and the Arts Weekly* (May 27, 2001): 27. 1 bw illus.

Hitchmough, Wendy. *The Arts and Crafts Lifestyle and Design.* New York: Watson-Guptill, 2000. 192 pp.; illus.

Hofer, Margaret K. "Furniture Makers and Allied Craftsmen in Plymouth and Bristol Counties, Massachusetts, 1760–1810." *Antiques* 159, no. 5 (May 2001): 806–13. 6 color and 4 bw illus.

Hood, Graham. "Attics Anonymous." *Colonial Williamsburg* 23, no. 1 (spring 2001): 56–60. 4 color and 1 bw illus.

Hunting, Mary Anne. "Living with Antiques: The Richard H. Mandel House in Bedford Hills, New York." *Antiques* 160, no. 1

(July 2001): 72–81. 17 color and 2 bw illus.

Hurst, Ronald L. "The Peyton Randolph House Restored." *Antiques* 159, no. 1 (January 2001): 178–85. 14 color and 2 bw illus.

Ilse-Neuman, Ursula, Arthur C. Danto, and Edward S. Cooke, Jr. *Made in Oakland: The Furniture of Garry Knox Bennett.* New York: American Craft Museum, 2000. 228 pp.; 300+ color illus., bibliography.

Indiana Cabinets with Prices. Gas City, Ind.: L-W Book Sales, 2001. 134 pp.; illus.

Israel, Barbara. "Know Your Antiques: British and American Cast-Iron Garden Seats." *The Catalogue of Antiques and Fine Art* 2, no. 4 (summer/fall 2001): 190–91. 2 color illus.

Jackman, Bob. "Restoring the Thomas Bailey Aldrich House." *Antiques and the Arts Weekly* (September 29, 2000): 1, 68–71. 7 bw illus.

Jackson, Lesley. *Robin and Lucienne Day: Pioneers of Modern Design.* New York: Princeton Architectural Press, 2001. 192 pp.; numerous color and bw illus., list of designs, bibliography, index. (Re twentieth-century English furniture.)

Jaffer, Amin. *Furniture from British India and Ceylon: A Catalogue of the Collections in the V & A and the Peabody Essex Museum.* London: V & A Publications, 2001. 384 pp.; 135 color and 250 bw illus.

Johnson, Don. "Odd Chest Sold in Indiana." *Maine Antique Digest* 29, no. 4 (April 2001): 10A. 1 bw illus.

Joyce, Henry. Review of Anna Tobin D'Ambrosio, ed., *Masterpieces of American Furniture from*

the Munson-Williams-Proctor Institute. In *Winterthur Portfolio* 35, no. 1 (spring 2000): 109–10.

Joyce, Henry, and Sloane Stephens. *American Folk Art at the Shelburne Museum.* Shelburne, Vt.: Shelburne Museum, 2001. 90 pp.; color illus. (Includes a few pieces of furniture.)

"Keeping Time in Concord." *Antiques and the Arts Weekly* (November 3, 2000): 1, 68–71. 14 bw illus.

Kelsey, John. "How To Be Garry Knox Bennett." *Woodwork,* no. 71 (October 2001): 32–35. 7 color illus.

Keno, Leigh, and Leslie Keno, with Joan Barzilay Freund. *Hidden Treasures: Searching for Masterpieces of American Furniture.* New York: Warner Books, 2000. 304 pp.; numerous color and bw illus., glossary, bibliography, index.

Ketchum, William C., Jr., revised by Elizabeth von Habsburg. *American Furniture.* Vol. 2, *Chests, Cupboards, Desks, and Other Pieces.* New York: Black Dog and Leventhal, 2000. 480 pp.; numerous color and bw illus., line drawings, glossary, price guide, bibliography, index.

Kirk, John T. *American Furniture: Understanding Styles, Construction, and Quality.* New York: Harry N. Abrams, Inc., 2000. 236 pp.; 57 color and 194 bw illus., 7 line drawings, bibliography, index.

Kirk, John T. "Our Evolving Understanding of Untouched Furniture Surfaces." *Antiques* 158, no. 4 (October 2000): 534–41. 12 color and 3 bw illus.

Kirkham, Pat, ed. *Women Designers*

in the USA, 1900–2000. New Haven and London: Yale University Press for the Bard Graduate Center for Studies in the Decorative Arts, 2000. 462 pp.; numerous color and bw illus., checklist of the exhibition, bibliography, index. (See especially the essay by Edward S. Cooke, Jr., cited above.)

Kirkham, Pat, and Ella Howard, guest editors. Special issue on Women Designers in the USA, 1900–2000. *Studies in the Decorative Arts* 8, no. 1 (fall/winter 2000–2001): 4–194. Numerous bw illus. (Seven articles, four interviews, and several book reviews.)

Kirtley, Alexandra Alevizatos. "A New Suspect: Baltimore Cabinetmaker Edward Priestley." *American Furniture 2000*, pp. 100–151. 31 color and bw illus., appendix.

Kramer, Fran. "And Now There Are Four." *Maine Antique Digest* 29, no. 1 (January 2001): 9A. 2 bw illus. (Re desk, 1904, designed by Harvey Ellis for Gustav Stickley.)

Kramer, Fran. "The Winning Card Table." *Maine Antique Digest* 29, no. 2 (February 2001): 10A. 1 bw illus.

Krenov, James. *With Weathered Hands: Furniture by James Krenov and Students*. Bethel, Conn.: Cambium Press; Fresno, Cal.: Linden Publishing, 2000. 136 pp.; 225 color illus., index.

Krill, Rosemary Troy, with Pauline K. Eversmann. *Early American Decorative Arts, 1620–1860: A Handbook for Interpreters*. American Association for State and Local History Book Series. Walnut Creek, Cal.: AltaMira Press, 2001. xii + 299 pp.;

numerous bw illus., index.

[Kuehne, Max]. "Max Kuehne: Artist and Craftsman Featured at Hollis Taggert Galleries." *Antiques and the Arts Weekly* (May 11, 2001): 36. 1 bw illus.

[Lakeview Museum, Peoria, Illinois]. "It's About Time: Clocks and Timekeeping." *NAWCC Bulletin* 42, no. 5 (October 2000): 604. 3 bw illus.

Landrey, Gregory J., ed. *The Winterthur Guide to Caring for Your Collection*. Winterthur, Del.: Winterthur Museum, 2001. 154 pp.; color and bw illus., bibliography. Distributed by University Press of New England, Hanover and London.

Lash, Steven M. "Benjamin Franklin's Armonica." *Franklin Gazette* 10, no. 2 (summer 2000): 7–8. 1 bw illus.

Lauria, Jo. "Riding the Wave: The California Design Exhibitions, 1955–1976." *The Modernism Magazine* 4, no. 2 (summer 2001): 18–35. Color illus.

Lavine, John. Review of Arthur Danto et al., *Made in Oakland: The Furniture of Garry Knox Bennett*. *Woodwork*, no. 71 (October 2001): 14. 1 color illus.

Ledes, Allison Eckardt. "Current and Coming: American Clocks." *Antiques* 158, no. 3 (September 2000): 252. 1 color illus.

Ledes, Allison Eckardt. "Current and Coming: Colonial Williamsburg at Home and on the Road." *Antiques* 159, no. 1 (January 2001): 28. 3 color illus.

Ledes, Allison Eckardt. "Current and Coming: Nineteenth-Century New York City." *Antiques* 158, no. 3 (September 2000): 248,

250. 2 color illus.

Lessard, Michel. *Meubles Anciens du Quebec: au carrefour de trois cultures*. Montreal: Editions de l'Homme, 1999. 543 pp.; color and bw illus., bibliography, index.

Linden, Diana L. "Lower East Side Tenement Museum, New York City." *Antiques* 160, no. 2 (August 2001): 198–205. 12 color and 1 bw illus.

Linley, David. *Design and Detail in the Home*. New York: Harry N. Abrams, Inc., 2000. 224 pp.; illus.

Little, Nina Fletcher. *Neat and Tidy: Boxes and Their Contents Used in Early American Households*. 1980. Reprint. Boston: Society for the Preservation of New England Antiquities, 2001. xxv + 204 pp.; 24 color and 190 bw illus., bibliography, index. Distributed by the University Press of New England, Hanover and London. (With a new foreword by Wendell Garrett.)

Locklair, Paula. "New in the MESDA Collection." *The Luminary, the Newsletter of the Museum of Early Southern Decorative Arts* 21, no. 2 (fall 2000): 6–7. (Includes several pieces of furniture.)

"Maine Contemporary Furniture." *Maine Antique Digest* 29, no. 5 (May 2001): 11A. (Re exhibition at Colby College Museum of Art, Waterville.)

Makinson, Randell, and Thomas Heinz. *Greene and Greene: The Blacker House*. Salt Lake City, Utah: Gibbs Smith, 2000. 132 pp.; illus.

Marshall, Jason. "SAPFM Report." *Woodwork*, no. 67 (February

2001): 32. 2 color illus.

Martin, Terry. "Questioning the Limits: Canadian Woodworker Michael Hosaluk." *Woodwork*, no. 70 (August 2001): 26–32. Color illus.

Mayer, Roberta A., and Carolyn K. Lane. "Disassociating the 'Associated Artists': The Early Business Ventures of Louis C. Tiffany, Candace T. Wheeler, and Lockwood de Forest." *Studies in the Decorative Arts* 8, no. 2 (spring/summer 2001): 2–36. 11 bw illus.

Mayor, Alfred. Review of *The Edinburgh Cabinet and Chair Makers' Books of Prices, 1805–1825*. In *Antiques* 159, no. 6 (June 2001): 874–76. 1 bw illus.

McLennan, Bill, and Karen Duffek. *The Transforming Image: Painted Arts of the Northwest Coast First Nations*. Vancouver and Toronto: UBC Press; Seattle: University of Washington Press, 2000. xii + 291 pp.; numerous color and bw illus., maps, appendix, bibliography.

Melchior-Bonnet, Sabine. *The Mirror: A History*. Trans. Katharine H. Jewett. New York: Routledge, 2001. xi + 308 pp.; bw illus., index.

[Metropolitan Museum of Art]. "Levy Donates Beekman Chair." *Maine Antique Digest* 29, no. 5 (May 2001): 8A. 1 bw illus. (Re gift to Metropolitan Museum of Art of New York armchair of 1819 by John Banks, possibly with upholstery by William Denny.)

[Michener Museum]. "George Nakashima Exhibition To Open at Michener Museum." *Antiques and the Arts Weekly* (June 1, 2001): 76. 1 bw illus.

Miller, Judith. *A Closer Look at Antiques: A Visual Guide to Identifying, Dating, and Authenticating*. Boston: Bulfinch Press, 2001. 224 pp.; 900+ color and bw illus.

[Minneapolis Institute of Arts]. "Dressing Table Built for Henry Clay Acquired by the Minneapolis Institute of Arts." *Antiques and the Arts Weekly* (December 1, 2000): 27. 1 bw illus.

"Moderne Gallery to Host 'George Nakashima Designing Nature' June 15 through Sept. 15." *Antiques and the Arts Weekly* (June 8, 2001): 39. 2 bw illus.

Monkman, Betty C. *The White House: Its Historic Furnishings and First Families*. Washington, D.C.: White House Historical Association; New York: Abbeville Press, 2000. 320 pp.; 260 color and 35 bw illus., catalogue, bibliography, index.

[Museum of American Folk Art]. "Museum of American Folk Art Receives Esmerian Collection." *Antiques and the Arts Weekly* (April 27, 2001): 100–101. 9 bw illus.

[Museum of Early Southern Decorative Arts]. "Index of Early Southern Artists and Artisans: Entries A–C." *Journal of Early Southern Decorative Arts* 24, no. 2 (winter 1998): 1–202. bw illus.

[Museum of Early Southern Decorative Arts]. "Index of Early Southern Artists and Artisans: Entries D–H." *Journal of Early Southern Decorative Arts* 25, no. 1 (summer 1999): 1–186. bw illus.

[Museum of Early Southern Decorative Arts]. "Index of Early Southern Artists and Artisans: Entries I–O." *Journal of Early Southern Decorative Arts* 25, no. 2 (winter 1999): 1–179. bw illus.

[Museum of Early Southern Decorative Arts]. "Index of Early Southern Artists and Artisans: Entries P–S." *Journal of Early Southern Decorative Arts* 26, no. 1 (summer 2000): 1–149. bw illus.

[Museum of Early Southern Decorative Arts]. "Index of Early Southern Artists and Artisans: Entries T–Z." *Journal of Early Southern Decorative Arts* 26, no. 2 (winter 2000): 1–138. bw illus., bibliography.

[Museum of Early Southern Decorative Arts]. "A Surprising New Addition to the MESDA." *The Luminary, the Newsletter of the Museum of Early Southern Decorative Arts* 22, no. 1 (spring 2001): 4–5. 2 bw illus. (Re mahogany stretcher-base table from South Carolina, made in the late seventeenth or early eighteenth century and owned by Thomas Broughton of Mulberry Plantation.)

[National Museum of American History, Smithsonian Institution]. "Within These Walls." *Antiques and the Arts Weekly* (July 27, 2001): 1, 68. 13 bw illus.

Nichols, Sarah. "Jewelry to Jets: Aluminum Design Since the 1850s." *Antiques* 158, no. 6 (December 2000): 864–73. 16 color illus.

Nichols, Sarah, ed., with the assistance of Elisabeth Agro and Elizabeth Teller. *Aluminum by Design*. Pittsburgh, Pa.: Carnegie Museum of Art, 2000. 296 pp.; 290 color and 95 bw illus., glossary, bibliography, checklist, index.

Norbury, Betty, ed. *Furniture for the 21st Century*. New York:

Viking Studio, 1999. 192 pp.; illus., index.

Northeast Auctions. *The Audrey and Tom Monahan Collection*. Auction catalogue. Portsmouth, N.H.: Northeast Auctions, August 4, 2001. 60 pp.; numerous color illus. (Re collection of "Pilgrim-Century American Furniture and Related Decorative Arts Featuring New England Eighteenth-Century Needlework" being offered at auction.)

Nye, John B.A. "East Coast Excellence." *Sotheby's Preview* (January 2001): 76–81. 7 color illus.

Nylander, Jane C. "William Sumner Appleton and Henry Davis Sleeper, Boston Collectors of Two Different Types." *Ellis Memorial Antiques Show 2000* (catalogue), pp. 62–68. Boston: Ellis Memorial Center, 2000. 6 color and 2 bw illus.

"189,000 Realized for Salem Joined Chest." *Antiques and the Arts Weekly* (June 15, 2000): 65. 1 bw illus. (Re Symonds shop example.)

"Period Card Table Sells for $181,500 at Hessney's Auction." *Antiques and the Arts Weekly* (January 19, 2001): 20. 1 bw illus. (Re Goddard-Townsend style Newport card table, 1760s–1780s.)

Perlman, Richard. "S. Willard's Patent Timepiece: A Clock (no. 27, 1809) Made by Ansel Turner (1787–1814)." *NAWCC Bulletin* 43, no. 3 (June 2001): 295–303. 16 bw illus.

Perry, Barbara Stone. *On the Surface: Late Nineteenth-Century Decorative Arts*. Charlotte, N.C.: Mint Museum of Art, 2001. 111 pp.; illus.

Piña, Leslie. *Graphic Herman Miller*. Atglen, Pa.: Schiffer Publishing, 2001. 160 pp.; 33+ illus.

Prebys, Henry J. "The Genuine Article? Analysis of a Bible Box." *The Catalogue of Antiques and Fine Art* 2, no. 3 (summer 2001): 192–93. 4 color illus.

Priddy, Sumpter, III, J. Michael Flanigan, and Gregory J. Weidman. "The Genesis of Neoclassical Style in Baltimore Furniture." *American Furniture 2000*, pp. 59–99. 57 color and bw illus.

Prown, Jules D., and Kenneth Haltman, eds. *American Artifacts: Essays in Material Culture*. East Lansing: Michigan State University Press, 2000. xiii + 255 pp.; bw illus.

Ramsey, Marianne, and Dianne Wach. *Fancy Forms and Flowers: A Significant Group of Kentucky Inlaid Furniture*. Lexington, Ken.: Headley-Whitley Museum, 2000. 39 pp.; illus.

Ramsey, Marianne, and Dianne Wach. *The Tuttle Muddle: An Investigation of a Kentucky Case-on-Frame Furniture Group*. Lexington, Ken.: Headley-Whitley Museum, 2000. 76 pp.; 30 illus.

Reade, Nathaniel. "Chairmen of the Board." *Attaché* (March 2001): 54–60. Color illus. (Woodworkers Hank Gilpin and Jack Kepler.)

"Record Hatrack." *Maine Antique Digest* 29, no. 6 (June 2001): 10A. 2 bw illus. (Re furniture by Mitchell & Rammelsberg.)

Regional Furniture 14 (2000): 1–103. Numerous bw illus.

Regional Furniture Society Newsletter, no. 32 (summer 2000): 1–17. bw illus.

Regional Furniture Society Newsletter, no. 33 (autumn 2000): 1–17. bw illus.

Regional Furniture Society Newsletter, no. 34 (spring 2001): 1–17. bw illus.

Remmey, Carolyn. "Leigh Keno and Leslie Keno and Their Hidden Treasures" (book review). *Antiques and the Arts Weekly* (November 24, 2000): 64N. 4 bw illus.

Richman, Irwin. *Pennsylvania German Arts: More Than Hearts, Parrots, and Tulips*. Atglen, Pa.: Schiffer Publishing, 2001. 144 pp.; 354 color and 7 bw illus., bibliography, index.

Rogers, Dominique A., and Graham Marley, eds. *Modern Materials, Modern Problems: Postprints of the Conference Organised by the UKIC Furniture Section Held at the Conservation Centre NMGM Liverpool, 17 April 1999*. London: The Furniture Section of The United Kingdom Institute for Conservation of Historic and Artistic Works, 1999. 45 pp.; bw illus., line drawings.

Rowland, Rodney. "The Genuine Article: Alterations, Repairs, or Colonial Revival?" *The Catalogue of Antiques and Fine Art* 2, no. 4 (summer/fall 2001): 200–201. 4 color illus.

Ruff, Joshua, and William Ayres. "H.F. du Pont's Chesterwood House, Southampton, New York." *Antiques* 160, no. 1 (July 2001): 98–107. 11 color and 6 bw illus.

"Sack Buys *Mona Lisa* of Card Tables for $1.32 Million." *Maine Antique Digest* 29, no. 7 (July 2001): 11A. 1 bw illus.

Sack, Albert. "The Role of the Dealer." *The Catalogue of Antiques and Fine Art* 2, no. 1 (winter 2001): 181–83. 2 color and 1 bw illus.

[St. Louis Art Museum]. "Alexandria Period Room at Saint Louis Art Museum." *Newsletter of the Decorative Arts Society* 9, no. 2 (summer 2001): 9. 1 bw illus.

Scherer, John L. "The Allison Brothers: New York City Cabinetmakers." *The Catalogue of Antiques and Fine Art* 2, no. 1 (winter 2001): 206–9. 6 color and 1 bw illus.

Schroy, Ellen T., ed. *Warman's American Furniture.* Iola, Wis.: Krause Publications, 2001. 352 pp.; numerous color and bw illus.

Schwartz, Marvin D., revised by Elizabeth von Habsburg. *American Furniture.* Vol. 1, *Tables, Chairs, Sofas, and Beds.* 2d ed. New York: Black Dog and Leventhal, 2000. 480 pp.; numerous color and bw illus., line drawings, glossary, price guide, bibliography, index.

Seibert, Peter S. "Decorated Chairs of the Lower Susquehanna River Valley." *Antiques* 159, no. 5 (May 2001): 780–87. 15 color illus.

"Shaker Inspiration." *American Craft* 61, no. 1 (February/March 2001): 92–95. 7 color illus.

"Shoptalk: Pritam & Eames Anniversary Show." *Woodwork,* no. 70 (August 2001): 22–23. 2 color illus.

Smith, Thomas Gordon. "Quervelle Furniture at Rosedown, In Louisiana." *Antiques* 159, no. 5 (May 2001): 770–79. 16 color and 2 bw illus.

Smithson, Peter, and Karl Unglaub. *Flying Furniture.* Köln: Verlag der Buchhandlung Walther König, 1999. 191 pp.; 126 color and 124 bw illus., line drawings, bibliography.

Snellenburg, Jonathan. "George Washington in Bronze: A Survey of the Memorial Clocks." *The Catalogue of Antiques and Fine Art* 2, no. 1 (winter 2001): 198–203. 6 color illus.

[Society for the Preservation of New England Antiquities]. "Boxes, Open and Shut." *Antiques and the Arts Weekly* (May 11, 2001): 83. 1 bw illus.

Solis-Cohen, Lita. "Account Book Becomes Rosetta Stone for Philadelphia Furniture." *Maine Antique Digest* 29, no. 4 (April 2001): 30E–31E. 1 bw illus.

Solis-Cohen, Lita. "Britton Gift of American Furniture on View at MFA, Houston." *Maine Antique Digest* 29, no. 2 (February 2001): 8A. 1 bw illus.

Solis-Cohen, Lita. "More on the Cogswell Chest-on-Chest." *Maine Antique Digest* 29, no. 3 (March 2001): 8A. 2 bw illus.

Solis-Cohen, Lita. "Rare Table Turns Up at Christie's East." *Maine Antique Digest* 29, no. 3 (March 2001): 8A. 1 bw illus.

Solis-Cohen, Lita. Review of Luke Beckerdite, ed., *American Furniture 2000.* In *Maine Antique Digest* 29, no. 4 (April 2001): 26C–27C. 1 bw illus.

Solis-Cohen, Lita. "Sack Sells Boston Chair That George Washington Sat In." *Maine Antique Digest* 29, no. 3 (March 2001): 1D–2D. 10 bw illus.

Solis-Cohen, Lita. "The Show Stopper that Stopped Short of the Show." *Maine Antique Digest* 29, no. 2 (February 2001): 8A. 1 bw illus. (Re Boston chest-on-chest attributed to John Cogswell and sold by Leigh Keno.)

[Sotheby's]. "American Decorative and Folk Art." In *Sotheby's Art at Auction 1999–2000,* pp. 154–55. London: Sotheby's, 2000. 3 bw illus.

Stephens, John R. "Benjamin Willard Grafton Wood Movement Tall Clock." *NAWCC Bulletin* 42, no. 4 (August 2000): 545–46. 6 bw illus.

Stiefel, Jay Robert. "The Head Account Book as Artifact: A Supplementary Essay." *Bulletin of the American Philosophical Society Library,* new series 1, no. 1 (winter 2001):1–7. Available online at http://www.amphilsoc.org/library/bulletin/20011.

Stiefel, Jay Robert. "Philadelphia Cabinetmaking and Commerce, 1718–1753: The Account Book of John Head, Joiner." *Bulletin of the American Philosophical Society Library,* new series 1, no. 1 (winter 2001): 1–58. Numerous illus. Available online at http://www.amphilsoc.org/library/bulletin/20011.

Stone, Michael A. "Garry Knox Bennett." *Woodwork,* no. 71 (October 2001): 24–30. 25 color illus.

Strasser, Susan. *Waste and Want: A Social History of Trash.* New York: Metropolitan Books, Henry Holt & Co., 2000. 355 pp.; bw illus., bibliography, index. (Some references to "recycled" furniture.)

Temin, Peter, ed. *Engines of Enterprise: An Economic History of New England.* Cambridge: Harvard University Press, 2000. vii + 328 pp.; bw illus., tables, figures, index. (Some scattered references to furniture making.)

Theobald, Mary Miley. "Colonial Williamsburg Partners with Historic Stickley Furniture." *Colonial*

Williamsburg 23, no.1 (spring 2001): 61–64. 5 color illus.

Thompson, Neville. Review of Henry Petroski, *The Book on the Bookshelf*. In *American Furniture 2000*, pp. 205–6.

Trench, Lucy, ed. *Materials and Techniques in the Decorative Arts: An Illustrated Dictionary*. Chicago: University of Chicago Press, 2000. ix + 572 pp.; 18 color and numerous bw illus., bibliography.

[Tubman African American Museum]. *Sankofa: A Century of African American Expression in the Decorative Arts*. Macon, Ga.: Tubman African American Museum, 2000. 16 pp.; illus.

Vaughn, Jeri. "Museum Focus: Long Beach Museum of Art." *The Catalogue of Antiques and Fine Art* 2, no. 4 (summer/fall 2001): 202–3. 4 color illus.

[Wadsworth Atheneum]. "Recent Shaker Gifts to be Exhibited at Wadsworth." *Antiques and the Arts Weekly* (December 8, 2000): 6.

Wahler, Joyce B. "The Evolution of the 1838–1848 Brewster Shelf Clocks as Reflected in Their Labels, Part I." *NAWCC Bulletin* 42, no. 3 (June 2000): 293–327. Numerous bw illus., tables.

Wahler, Joyce B. "The Evolution of the 1838–1848 Brewster Shelf Clocks as Reflected in Their Labels, Part II." *NAWCC Bulletin* 42, no. 4 (August 2000): 461–84. Numerous bw illus., tables.

Ward, Gerald W.R. Review of John Morley, *The History of Furniture: Twenty-five Centuries of Style and Design in the Western Tradition*. In *American Furniture 2000*, pp. 217–18.

Ward, Gerald W.R., et al. *American Folk: Folk Art from the Collection of the Museum of Fine Arts, Boston*. Boston: Museum of Fine Arts, Boston, 2001. 111 pp.; color illus., bibliography, index. (Includes some furniture.)

Ward, Gerald W.R., comp. "Recent Writing on American Furniture: A Bibliography." In *American Furniture 2000*, pp. 219–28.

Webster, Donald Blake. *Rococo to Rustique: Early French-Canadian Furniture in the Royal Ontario Museum*. Toronto: Royal Ontario Museum, 2000. ix + 238 pp.; numerous color and bw illus., bibliography.

"Wendell Family Secretary Brings $332,500 at Northeast." *Antiques and the Arts Weekly* (November 17, 2000): 109. 1 bw illus.

West, James B. "A Mission Clock Commentary." *NAWCC Bulletin* 42, no. 4 (August 2000): 439–49. 31 bw illus.

Wilner, Eli, ed. *The Gilded Edge: The Art of the Frame*. San Francisco: Chronicle Books, 2000. 203 pp.; illus., bibliography, index.

Willoughby, Martha H. "Patronage in Early Salem: The Symonds Shops and Their Customers." *American Furniture 2000*, pp. 169–84. 13 color and bw illus.

[Winterthur Museum]. "'That Classy Classical Style' On View at Winterthur." *Antiques and the Arts Weekly* (September 1, 2000): 74. 2 bw illus.

Wood, David F. "Concord, Massachusetts, Clockmakers." *Antiques* 159, no. 5 (May 2001): 762–69. 8 color and 1 bw illus.

Zea, Philip. " A Revolution in Taste: Furniture Design in the American Backcountry." *Antiques* 159, no. 1 (January 2001): 186–95. 16 color illus.

Zimmerman, Philip D. "Delaware Valley Chests of Drawers, 1725–1800." *Antiques* 159, no. 5 (May 2001): 788–95. 8 color and 1 bw illus.

Zimmerman, Philip D. Review of Jack Lindsey et al., *Worldly Goods: The Arts of Early Pennsylvania, 1680–1758*. In *American Furniture 2000*, pp. 212–16.

Index

Abbott, John L., 63(n61)

Adam, Robert, 248

Adams, Abigail, 243

Adams, Benjamin, 193

Adams, John Quincy, 245

Adams, Mehitable (Torry), 193

Adams, Nehemiah, 155, 161, 178, 192(n47), 193, 197

Aesthetics, furniture, 251–254

Affleck, Thomas, 77, 79

"AHP," 25

Albany Bicentennial display, 101(&fig. 17)

Alignment marks, 58(n16)

Allman, William G., 246

American Furniture of the 18th Century (Greene), 136(fig. 25)

American Furniture: Understanding Styles, Construction, and Quality (Kirk), 251–254

Ames, Burpee, 189

Anderrese, Nicholas, 128

Andover (Massachusetts), 1, 50

Antiques, 2, 121

Appleton, Elizabeth (Rogers), 16, 59–60(n27)

Appleton, Esther Knowlton (Annable), 60(n30)

Appleton, George, Jr., 60(n30)

Appleton, John, 16, 31, 59–60(n27)

Appleton, William, 155, 161, 163(&fig. 8), 179, 190(n8), 193, 194, 197

Appleton chest of drawers, 16, 17(fig. 21)

Appleton cupboard, 2, 17(fig. 21), 22

Appleton family (Ipswich, Massachusetts), 1, 54–55(&n55)

Applied ornament, 34, 35(figs.)

Appliqués, 26, 30, 41, 46

Apprentices, grievance procedures, 156

Arbitration, 78, 85(n1)

Arcades, 22, 38, 46, 59(n20); surface, 9(fig. 8), 10

Arch, 46

Arch appliqués, 14, 59(n20, 25)

Arched crests, 110

Arches, 46, 62(n50); surface, 11

Arch panels, 13–14(&fig. 17)

Architectural styles, furniture style and, 43–44, 54, 55, 63(n57)

Architettura (Serlio), 6

Architrave moldings, 235(figs. 17, 18)

Arentszen (Blom), Frederick, 89, 91(fig. 3)

Armchairs: Evans, 81(&fig. 15); New York, 93(fig. 6), 94(figs.), 103(fig. 21), 106(fig. 26), 110, 111(fig. 35); Salem (Massachusetts), 181–182(&fig. 38); Virginia, 93, 95(fig. 9)

Artisans: eighteenth-century estates of, 85(n2); intentions of, 253

Ash, 94(fig. 7), 105(fig. 25), 112(fig. 38) 113(fig. 39)

Ash splint loop, 60(n31)

Aspen, 144

Assembly marks. *See* Marking system

Astragal elements, 15–16, 39, 47(fig. 90)

Astragal molding, 13(&fig. 16), 26, 62(n50), 161

Austin, Isabel (Symonds), 194

Austin, Josiah, 154, 155, 189(n6), 193, 194, 197

Austin, Mary, 194

Austin, Richard, 155, 186, 189(n6), 194

Authenticating Antique Furniture, xii(n5)

Authenticity, 253

Back: of chest of drawers, 32; of cupboard, 27–28(&fig. 41)

Badger family (Newbury, Massachusetts), 54

Bailey, Constant, 128

Baker, Benjamin, 126, 128, 148(n7)

Balch, Benjamin, 191(n24)

Baldus, Edouard, 53(fig. 99)

Ball-shaped elements, in turned chairs, 103

Ball-turned posts, 106

Baluster elements, in turned chairs, 103

Balusters, 40, 44, 51, 105–106

Baluster-shaped pillars, 27(fig. 42), 28

Banister, John, 123

Banister backs, 110

Barnard, Elizabeth (Bond), 194

Barnard, Elizabeth (Cook), 194

Barnard, Samuel, 194, 196, 197

Baroque style, 55, 234, 238, 240, 247; chest of drawers, 52; high chest, 37; southern German, 231

Bartlett, Mrs. N. E., 49

Base: Appleton chest of drawers, 16, 17(fig. 21); cupboard, 14–15, 23(&fig. 34), 25, 44, 46, 47(fig. 90), 53(fig. 100)

Base molding, 22, 47(fig. 90), 136, 150(n12), 235(figs. 19, 20)

Basin stands. *See* Washstands

Bath (North Carolina), 226

Bayou Bend, 132, 151(n23)

Beauty, 253

Bed cornices, 185–186, 198

Bedsteads, Salem (Massachusetts), 157,

184–187(&figs.), 192(n52), 217

Beekman Patent, 241(n9)

Behrend, Mrs. B. A., 61(n35)

Benes, Peter, 249–251

Bentley, William, 155, 188–189

Bergen County (New Jersey), 97, 100, 117(n11)

Bergman, Andreas, 240

Bergman, Anna Elizabeth, 240

Bergman, Anna Sibylla, 240

Bergner, Jonas, 123(fig. 6)

Beverly (Massachusetts), seventeenth-century furniture in, 1, 8

Beyerle, J. A., 237(fig. 22)

Bidets, 156

Birch, 167, 172(fig. 22), 173(fig. 23), 184, 212, 217

"Bivinesque," xi

Bivins, John, xi–xiii, 93

Black-heath (England), 224, 225(fig. 5)

Black walnut, 82(fig. 16), 98

Blom, Arent, 116(n2)

Blom, Arent Frederickszen, 89, 118(n18)

Blom, Frederick, 89, 91(fig. 3)

Blom, Frederick Arentszen, 98, 99–100, 101, 116(n2)

Blom, Jacob, 89, 91, 116(n2)

Blue Room, 244, 245

Boardman, Langley, 191(n29)

Bogaert, William, 89, 116(n2)

Bolection, 39

Bookcase, Salem (Massachusetts), 164, 207. See also Desk-and-bookcases

Boskerk (Buskirk), Lourens Andrieszen van, 89, 91(&fig. 3), 92, 99, 100, 116(n2), 117(n6), 118(n18)

Bosses, 11, 17(fig. 21), 37(fig. 67), 38, 42, 62(n49), 62–63(n52), 63(n54)

Boston (Massachusetts): case pieces, 4, 5; chest, 11(&fig. 13); chest of drawers, 60(n28); competition from in Essex County, 39; desk-and-bookcase case construction, 150(n13); great chairs, 104; half-columns based on Tuscan order, 28; influence on Essex County furniture, 1, 30, 40; leaf table, 16, 18(fig. 23)

Bottle boxes, 156, 190(n12)

Bowen, Jabez, 123, 142

Boynton family (Newbury, Massachusetts), 54

Braces, 8

Bracket feet, 170, 172

Brackets: chest of drawers, 31, 32(fig. 55),

33(fig. 56); cupboard, 30(&fig. 48), 41, 42(fig. 78)

Bradstreet, Elizabeth, 61(n40)

Bradstreet, John, 61(n40)

Bradstreet, Priscilla, 61(n40)

Bradstreet, Simon, 1

Brands, on New York spindle-back chairs, 112(&figs.), 114. See also Marks

Brasier (Brasar), Henry, 116(n2)

Brass handles, 82

Bread board ends, 176

Breakfast table, 82, 174

Breed, Frederick, 186

Bresnan, Lauren, 100

Brick Store Museum (Kennebunk, Maine), 61(n40)

Briggs, Jeremiah, 187–188

Bright, Jonathan, 181, 192(n47)

Bringhurst, George, 79

British influence, on New York chair making, 104

British woodworkers, 56(n6)

Brocas, John, 38

Brown, John, 123, 128, 141

Brown, Joseph, 123, 128, 149(n9)

Brown, Moses, 123, 128, 142, 148(n4), 149(n9)

Brown, Nicholas, 121, 123, 128, 141

Brown, Sarah, 142

Brown chest, 61(n42)

Brown desk-and-bookcases, 128, 130(figs.), 139, 141–142, 146, 148(n11)

Bullock, John, 196

Burch, Hendrik van der, 95, 96(fig. 11), 100, 104

Burd, Edward, 81, 87(n24)

Bureaus, Salem (Massachusetts), 157, 171–172(&fig. 22), 210

Bureau tables, 139; Goddard, 149(n8)

Burnham family (Ipswich, Massachusetts), 54

Burpee Chair Manufactory, 154

Buskirk, Lourens Andrieszen, 89, 91(fig. 3)

Butt hinges, 83

Butt joints, 62(n51)

Byvanck, Evert, 91

Byvanck, Johannes, 89, 91, 116(n2)

Cabinet, price of Salem (Massachusetts), 205

Cabinet-Maker and Upholsterer's Drawing Book, The (Sheraton), 156, 159(&fig. 4), 178(fig. 32), 182, 192(n47)

Cabinet-Maker and Upholsterer's Guide, The (Hepplewhite), 156, 164(&fig. 9), 168(fig. 16), 170(&fig. 20), 174, 175(fig. 26), 177, 179, 181(fig. 37), 185(fig. 41), 190(n11)

Cabinet-Makers' London Book of Prices, and Designs of Cabinet Work, The 153–154, 156, 159, 160(fig. 5), 161, 163(fig. 8), 175

Cabinetmaking, prices for, 153–154. See also Price books; Salem (Massachusetts) Cabinet-Maker Society

Cabriole leg high chest, 66(fig. 1), 67

Cadwalader, Elizabeth, 87(n23)

Cadwalader, John, 87(n23)

Cahoone, John, 125, 126, 148–149(n7)

Camberwell (England), 224, 225(fig. 5)

Cambridge (Massachusetts): cupboards, 14–15(&fig. 18); joiners, 59(n25); influence on Essex County furniture, 40, 52

Candee, Richard, 57(n14)

Candelabra, 6

Canfield, Richard, 128

Canted corner bureau, 171

Canted imposts, 13, 46

Cantilevered rails, 63(n65)

Capen, Joseph, 31, 59(n27), 61(n43)

Capen, Priscilla (Appleton), 31, 59(n27), 61(n43)

Capen chest of drawers, 31–33(&figs.), 40, 44, 61(n42)

Capped urns, 40, 44

Card tables, 87(n24): Evans, 81–83(&figs.); Salem (Massachusetts), 173–174(&fig. 24), 194, 212; Sanderson, 197

Carpenter, Ralph, 151(n22)

Carpenters, 3–4

Carteret, Thomas, high chest, 66(fig. 1), 67–68(&figs.), 69(fig. 4), 70(figs.)

Cartouche, 68, 70(fig. 6)

Carved shells, desk-and-bookcase, 138, 139, 141(figs.), 143, 144(&figs.), 145

Carving: of bedposts, 184–185. See also McIntire, Samuel; as cost factor in Salem (Massachusetts), 157

Case construction: desk-and-bookcase, 150(n13); high chest, 68(figs.)

Cedar, 179, 187, 215. See also Red cedar

Cedrela, 4, 11(fig. 13), 18(fig. 23), 135(fig. 22)

Ceramics, 243, 248

C. G. Sloan and Company, 242(n18)

Chair making, 194; prices for, 154

Chairs: arms, 104; easy, 180–181(&figs.),

216; high, 107(figs.); klismos, 245; lolling chairs, 182–183(&fig. 39), 216; miniature, 95, 96(fig. 12), 100, 117(n10); rush-seated, 93; slat-back, 103–104(&figs.); Windsor, 189(n3); *See also* Armchairs; Side chairs; Turned chairs

Chalk inscriptions, 146

Chamber tables, 156

Chambers, William, 126

Chamfered decoration, 8, 52

Chamfered moldings, 62(n50)

Chandler, John, 176

Channel-molded muntins, 13

Channel moldings, 1, 38, 42, 52, 62(n50)

Chase-Follansbee family (Newbury, Massachusetts), 54

Chatter marks, 6

Checkered cock beading, 190(n15)

Cheever, Ames, 194

Cheever, Anna (Ropes), 195

Cheever, Hannah (Clark), 195

Cheever, Samuel, 155, 189, 194–195

Cheever, Sarah (Davis), 194

Cherry: armchairs, 112(fig. 38), 113(fig. 39), 114(fig. 41), 115(figs.), 94(fig. 7), 95(fig. 9), 111(fig. 35); desk, 167(&fig. 14); desk-and-bookcases, 130(fig. 13), 133(fig. 18), 134(fig. 20), 140; New England joined chair, 117–118(n12); side chairs, 88(fig. 1), 101(fig. 18), 102(fig. 19), 112(fig. 38), 113(fig. 39), 114(fig. 41), 115(figs.); use by New York Dutch artisans, 97; *wäscheschränk*, 236(fig. 21)

Chest: Boston, 11(&fig. 13); Brown, 61(n42); Columbia County (New York), 220(fig. 1); Schoharie County (New York), 221(fig. 2); seaman's, 187(&fig. 46), 218

Chests of drawers: Appleton, 16, 17(fig. 21); Capen, 31–33(&figs.), 40, 44, 61(n42); concept of, 4–5; Essex County, 3(&fig. 1), 4–8(&figs.), 13(&fig. 16), 34–35(&figs.), 51(fig. 98), 52; Perkins, 33–34(&figs.); Salem, 195; sides and back of, 7–8(&fig. 7)

Chestnut, 129(fig. 11), 130(fig. 13), 133(fig. 18), 134(fig. 20), 135(fig. 22), 141, 143, 144

Chest-on-chest, 139

Chippendale, Thomas, 68, 126, 180

Chisel marks, 33(&fig. 58), 34, 35(fig. 64)

Choate, Robert, 173, 196

Circular card table, 173

Circular doors, 161

Circular front bureau, 171, 172(&fig. 22)

Clarke, Daniel, 155, 156, 167, 177, 184, 189(n3), 190(n8, 14), 195; sideboard, 165(&fig. 10)

Clarke, Hannah, 195

Clarke, Peter, 195

Classical proportions, 6

Classicism, 248, 253

Claw-and-ball feet, 166, 190(n14)

Claypoole, George, 78, 86(n17)

Cliffton, Henry, 67, 70; high chest, 66(fig. 1), 67–68(&figs.), 69(fig. 4), 70(figs.)

Cliffton, Rachel, 70

Clock cases: Evans, 83(figs.), 84(&fig. 21), 85(fig. 22), 87(fig. 27); Salem (Massachusetts), 167(&fig. 15), 169, 191(n24), 209

Clocks, 243, 248

Clothes press, 139, 159, 160(fig. 5)

Clunie, Margaret, 154, 156

Coall (Cole), George, 57(n11), 59(n18)

Coffins, 84, 157; Salem (Massachusetts), 187, 192(n54)

Collared flanges, 41, 44, 49

Colonettes, 84

Colonial Furniture in America (Lockwood), 13, 121

Colonial Furniture of New England, The (Lyon), 2, 8

Commodes, Salem (Massachusetts), 156, 168–169(&figs.), 209

Connecticut, side chair, 105(fig. 25)

Conservative style, 81, 87(n23)

Construction: desk-and-bookcase, 136–139(&figs.), 150(n13); drawer, 7, 37–38(&fig. 68), 62(n47), 74, 239(&fig. 24); dressing table, 74(fig. 12); high chest, 68(figs.)

Cook, Clarence, 2, 23

Coolidge, Grace, 245

Cooper, Wendy, 121, 253

Cornè, Michele Felice, 187, 188(fig. 47)

Corner sideboards, 175, 191(n36)

Corner washstand, 191(n36)

Cornice moldings, 159

Cornices: bedstead, 185–186; *schränke*, 234, 235(figs. 17, 18); *wäscheschränk*, 239

Cost: labor as determinant of furniture, 157. *See also* Price books; Salem (Massachusetts) Cabinet-Maker Society

Cots, Salem (Massachusetts), 184, 186–187(&fig. 44)

Cotting family, 173

Cottonwood, 144

Court, Petronella de la, 95, 100

Cove elements, 15–16, 41

Cove molding, 28

Cowan, Robert, 187

Coxe, Rebecca, 75, 86(n12)

Coxe, Tench, 65, 85, 86(n12, 17); contract and dispute with David Evans, 75–80

Coxe, William, 75

Cradles: grisaille decoration of, 118–119(n23); price of, 157; Salem (Massachusetts), 179(&fig. 34), 215

Craftsmanship, eighteenth-century American, 65

Crossets, 33, 34(figs.)

Cummings, Abbott Lowell, 43

Cupboard base, Essex County, 23(&fig. 34), 25

Cupboards: "EP," 44–46(&figs.); Essex County, 12(&figs.), 13–16(&figs.), 19, 20(fig. 27), 21–23(&figs.), 24(fig. 36), 25–28(&figs.), 46–49(&figs.); by Harvard College joiners, 14–15(&fig. 18); Hitchcock, 28–31(&figs.); *kast*, 89, 229, 230(fig. 9), 231, 232(fig. 12), 235; Sawyer, 35–40(&figs.), 44, 46, 49, 62(n50); 62–63(n52); seventeenth-century English, 52, 53(fig. 100), 54; Weare, 40–44(&figs.), 49, 59(n23), 63(n56); Woodbury, 8–12(&figs.), 18, 28, 41

Currier, Edmund, 191(n24)

Curwen, George Rea, 181

Cushing, Joshua, 156

Cyma base moldings, 231

Cyma recta, 239

Dalrymple, James, 197

Dating, New York turned chairs, 114–115

Daybooks, David Evans, 71, 76(fig. 13), 86(n5)

Death of William, The (Cornè), 187, 188(fig. 47)

Decorative arts, White House collection of, 243–246

Demi-lune commode, 168(fig. 16), 169

Denison, Daniel, 1

Dennis, Thomas, 1, 2–3, 56(n9)

Dennis family (Ipswich, Massachusetts), 54

Derby, Elias Hasket, 169, 176, 192(n37)

Derby, John, 169, 175, 177

Desk-and-bookcases: bookcase partitions, 143, 144, 145(figs.); construction of, 136–139(&figs.); design of shell-carved, 132; details of, 144–145(&figs.); function of, 126; Goddard, 120(fig. 1), 121(&fig. 2), 122(figs.); Lisle, 120(fig. 1), 121(fig. 2), 122(figs.), 142–144, 145(fig. 44), 146–147, 148(n2), 149(n11); price of, 157, 148(n7); Rhode Island, 124(fig. 7), 125(fig. 8), 127(figs.), 129–137(figs.); Salem (Massachusetts), 197; straight-front, 147; upper case, 138–139(&fig. 31); writing compartment, 140–141. *See also* Secretary-and-bookcase

Desks: for export trade, 123; gentleman's secretary, 158–159(&figs.), 160(fig. 6), 161, 193, 196; lady's secretary, 157, 169–171(&figs.), 190(n14), 191(n27), 210; price of Rhode Island, 126; Salem (Massachusetts), 165–167(&figs.), 196, 208–209; slant-lid, 123; tambour, 193, 196, 197; traveling, 167; uses for, 148(n7)

Diamond doors, 161

Dinant, Peter, 238

Dinant, Susanna, 238

Dining tables: Evans, 80–81(&figs.); Goddard, 123; Salem (Massachusetts), 172–173, 211

Dispute resolution: price books and, 153, 156; Society of Friends and, 78, 85(n1)

Docents, guide for, 246–249

Doll house, miniature chairs, 95, 96(fig. 12), 100, 117(n10)

Doors: bookcase, 138–139, 140(fig. 32); circular, 161; cupboard, 39(fig. 70), 41(fig. 75), 44; diamond, 161; mullions, 170; *schränk*, 239; tambour, 171(&fig. 21)

Doty, Timothy, 250

Double-beaded turnings, 140

Dovetails: desk-and-bookcase, 136, 137(&fig. 28), 138; drawer, 1, 37(fig. 38), 38, 52, 62(n47), 143–144, 145(figs.); German, 242(n12); *schränk*, 234(&fig. 16), 239

Downs, Joseph, 151(n23)

Draaier, 116(n2)

Dragon beam, 43, 63(n56)

Draw-bar tables, 97

Drawer construction: cupboard, 37–38(&fig. 68); Evans' technique, 74; Essex County technique, 62(n47);

Staniford chest of drawers, 7; *wäscheschränk,* 239(&fig. 24)

Drawer fronts: cupboard, 23, 25, 39, 44; desk-and-bookcase, 137, 138, 139(fig. 30), 144

Drawer ornament, 4–5, 39

Drawer pull backplates, 39

Drawers: arrangement of, 52; bottom boards, 7(fig. 6), 9, 234(fig. 15); desk-and-bookcase interior, 138; dividers, 136–137; dovetail joints, 1, 52, 62(n47); thumbnail-molded, 71

Drawing tables, 156

Drayer, 89, 116(n2)

Dressing boxes, 156, 157, 190(n12)

Dressing glass, 195

Dressing tables: Evans, 71, 73–74(&figs.); New York, 109(fig. 31); Newport (Rhode Island), 150(n21); Salem (Massachusetts), 156, 176

Dressoir, 52, 53(fig. 99)

Drop-ground carving, 11

Drop-leaf table, 173

Drop-panel bureau, 172

Dublin Seminar for New England Folklife, 250

Dudley, Thomas, 1

Dummer, Richard, 1

Dunster, Henry, 1

du Pont, Henry Francis, 151(n23)

Dustboards, 67, 141

Dutch culture, persistence in New Amsterdam, 100

Dutch West India Company, 100

Dwarf clock, Salem (Massachusetts), 167(&fig. 15)

Earl of Sunderland, 226

Early American Decorative Arts, 1620–1860: A Handbook for Interpreters (Krill and Eversmann), 246–249

Early American Furniture: How to Recognize, Evaluate, Buy and Care for the Most Beautiful Pieces–High Style, Country, Primitive, and Rustic (Kirk), 252

Early baroque style, 247

Early classical revival style, 247

East Camp (New York), 228(fig. 8), 229, 241(n9)

Easton's Point (Rhode Island), 123, 128

Easy chairs, Salem (Massachusetts), 180–181(&fig. 36), 216

Ebony, 97, 98, 99(&fig. 16), 190(n8)

Ehinger, Mike, xi

Eight-day movements, 167

Ekelen, Albert Van, 89, 116(n2, 3)

Eliot, John, 16

Eliot bureau, 16, 60(n28)

Elliptical turnings, 92, 95, 97(fig. 14), 105, 106

Elting, Jan, 242(n13)

Elting-Beekman shops, 238, 242(n13); *kast,* 232(fig. 12), 235

Emery shop tradition (Newbury, Massachusetts), 4, 54

England, lumbering practices, 58(n15)

English arts and crafts movement, 2

English Board of Trade Lists, 242(n16)

English cupboard, seventeenth-century, 52, 53(fig. 100), 54

English rococo style, influence on Rhode Island cabinetmakers, 126

"EP" cupboard, 44–46(&figs.), 49

Escutcheons, 33(fig. 57)

Esens (Holland), 89

Essex (Massachusetts), 61(n42)

Essex County (Massachusetts), mannerist furniture in, 1–64(&figs.): Appleton chest of drawers, 16, 17(fig. 21); Capen chest of drawers, 31–33(&figs.), 40, 44, 61(n42); chest of drawers, 3(fig. 1), 4–8(&figs.), 13(fig. 16), 34–35(&figs.), 51(fig. 98), 52; context and catalysts, 52–53; cupboards, 20(fig. 27), 21–23(&figs.), 24(fig. 36), 25–26, 46–49(&figs.); "EP" cupboard, 44–46(&figs.), 49; experimentation with style and structure, 19–35; Foster cupboard, 26–28(&figs.), 46; historiography of, 2–4; Hitchcock cupboard, 28–31(&figs.); leaf table, 16–19(&figs.); Perkins chest of drawers, 33–34(&figs.); Sawyer cupboard, 35–40(&figs.), 44, 46, 49, 62(n50), 62–63(n52); square joined table, 49–51(&fig. 97); Staniford chest of drawers, 3–8(&figs.), 18, 25, 41, 56(n8), 59(n23); Waters cupboard, 13–16(&figs.); Weare cupboard, 40–44(&figs.), 49, 59(n23), 63(n56); Woodbury cupboard, 8–12(&figs.), 18, 28, 41

Ethnicity, occupation in New Amsterdam and, 91

European walnut, 97

Evans, David, 65–87: apprenticeship, 67–68, 70, 86(n4); armchair, 81(&fig. 15); biography, 65, 67–75; card table, 81–83(&figs.); career during

Revolutionary War, 74–75; clock cases, 83(figs.), 84(&fig. 21), 85(fig. 22), 87(fig. 27); coffin and Venetian blind production, 84; contract and dispute with Tench Coxe, 75–80; dining tables, 80–81(&figs.); dressing tables, 71, 73–74(&figs.); economic setbacks, 79–80

Evans, Edward, 65

Evans, Elizabeth, 65

Evans, Evan, 67

Evans, Nancy, 253

Evans, Rebecca, 67

Evans, Sarah, 85(n2)

Evans, Sidney, 67

Eversmann, Pauline K., 246–249

Ewing, John, 84

Export trade, in Rhode Island desks, 123. *See also* Venture cargo trade

Failey, Dean, 253

Fakes, 253

Fallboard, 137, 138, 140(fig. 32), 141, 144–145(&figs.), 150(n15), 165–166

Family ties, occupation in New Amsterdam and, 91

Fanny, 193, 197

Faries, William, 79

Fascia, 22, 239

Faux marble tops, 17(fig. 22), 176

Faux surfaces, 157

Federal furniture, 248

Federal style, 247

Feet: base moldings, 38(fig. 69); bracket, 136, 172; chest of drawers, 34(&fig. 61); claw-and-ball, 71; cupboard, 26(fig. 40), 30, 42, 43(fig. 81); desk, 166, 190(n14); desk-and-bookcase, 136, 137(fig. 26), 143(&fig. 40), 145, 146, 150(n22), 151(n25); French, 170; ogee, 171; turned, 18, 92, 105

Felt, George Washington, 152(fig. 1)

Fenced rabbet plane, 22, 39, 62(n50)

Field beds, 184

Filister plane, 22

Fillet, 22

Fine Americana and Silver (Sotheby's), 25(fig. 36)

Finials: desk-and-bookcase, 139, 142(&fig. 37); turned-chair, 101–102, 104–106, 118(n23), 150(n19); urn-shaped, 95, 97(&fig. 14), 103, 108, 117(n11)

Firebacks, 11

Fireplaces, jambless, 100

Firescreen, Salem (Massachusetts), 177(&fig. 31), 214

First ladies, White House collection of decorative arts and, 243

Fiske, Samuel, card table, 173, 174(fig. 24)

Fiske, William, card table, 173, 174(fig. 24)

Five Books of Architecture (Serlio), 7(fig. 5)

Flame finials, 68, 70(fig. 6)

Flanged collars, 41, 44, 49

Flap leaf, 177

Floor coverings, 248

Floral rosettes, 68, 70(fig. 6)

Fly leg, 18, 19(fig. 26), 40

Flyrail, 82(figs.)

Folding board, 176

Folding tables, 174

Folklife, 250

Follansbee, Peter, 250

Foot blocks, 84(&fig. 21)

Foot molding, 235(figs. 19, 20)

Ford, Mary, 198

Forman, Benno M., 3–4, 57(n14), 63(n62)

Fort Orange (Albany, New York), 101

Foster, Ephraim, 26, 61(n37)

Foster, Hannah (Eames), 26, 61(n37)

Foster, Lucy Hill, 193

Foster cupboard, 26–28(&figs.), 46

Frame sawing, 58(n15)

Frame saw marks, 25(fig. 38)

Framing: chest of drawers, 52; Weare cupboard, 43–44(&figs.); Woodbury cupboard, 11, 12(fig. 14)

Framing members, 8

Francis, Tench, 75

Frantzner, J. L., 237(fig. 22)

French court styles, 6

French feet, 170

French furniture, 6, 243

French joinery, 1

French turning, 119(n25)

Friendship, 194, 196, 197

Frieze, 22

Frieze/column/surbase composition, 5

Frieze rail, 63(n54)

Front rail, 28

Front skirts, 71

Frothingham, Samuel, 155, 197

Furness, James C., 60(n30)

Furness, Lillie M., 60(n30)

Furness, Lily May (Appleton), 60(n30)

Furniture aesthetics, 251–254

Furniture of Charleston, 1680–1820, The (Bivins), xii, xiii

Furniture of Coastal North Carolina 1700–1820 (Bivins), xi, xii(n4), xiii

Furniture of the North Carolina Roanoke River Basin in the Collection of Historic Hope Foundation (Bivins), xiii

Furniture Treasury (Nutting), 2, 14(fig. 17), 35, 44, 60(n31), 112, 118(n13)

Furniture workers, 251

Game of Cards, The (van der Burch), 95, 96(fig. 11), 100, 104

Gardiner, Richard, 67

Gardner, Elizabeth, 165, 183

Gardner, Elisabeth West, 180

Gardner, John, 165, 180, 183

Gardner-Pingree House, 183, 186

Garrett, Elizabeth, 253

Garrett, Wendell, 246

Garrigues, William, 78, 86(n9, 18)

Garvan, Francis P., 112, 128

Gasburn, Benjamin, 72(fig. 8)

Gateleg tables, 97

Gavet, John, 177

Gavet, Jonathan, 177, 179, 184, 190(n14)

Gaynor, Jay, 57(n11)

Genealogical research, to assess histories of ownership, 2

Gentleman and Cabinet-Maker's Director, The (Chippendale), 68, 126, 180

Gentleman's secretary, Salem (Massachusetts), 158–159(&figs.), 160(fig. 6), 161, 167, 193, 196

Geometric-panels, in seventeenth-century Essex County furniture, 3

Gerritsen, Class, 116(n2)

Gilding, 157

Gilles (Gülch), Melchior, 237–238

Gillingham, James, 67, 68, 70, 86(n5); side chair, 71(fig. 7)

Glass, 243, 248

Gleason, Tara, 121

Glyphs, 26(fig. 40)

Goddard, Daniel, 122, 126, 128, 150(n19, 20)

Goddard, Hannah (Townsend), 122

Goddard, James, 122

Goddard, John, 121–126, 142, 147, 148(n4), 150(n21); desk-and-bookcase, 120(fig. 1), 121(&fig. 2), 122(figs.); house and shop, 123(fig. 6)

Goddard, Stephen, 124, 125

Goddard, Susannah (Townsend), 122

Goddard, Thomas, 121–122, 124–126, 147, 148(n3), 150(n19)

"Golden Book," 241(n4)

Good Intent, 194
Goodfriend, Joyce, 91
Goodnow, Ezekiel, 189, 195
Goodnow, Sophia (Farrington), 195
Goodwill, Harold, 241(n10)
Goodwill, Muriel, 241(n10)
Gookin, Daniel, 59(n27)
Gostelowe, Jonathan, 84
Gothic cupboard door, 41(fig. 75)
Gouge-carved moldings, 31
Graffenreid, Christoph Baron von, 226
Gray, William, 173, 176
Greene, Jeffrey P., 136(fig. 25)
Grendy, Giles, 84
Grisaille decoration, 118–119(n23)
Guilford-Saybrook area (Connecticut), 105(fig. 25), 106, 118(n23)
Gülch, Heinrich, 238
Gülch, Magdelena, 238
Gülch, Melchior, 237–238
Gum wood, 238

Hale family (Newbury, Massachusetts), 54
Half-columns: Appleton chest of drawers, 17(fig. 21); chest of drawers, 13(&fig. 16), 32(fig. 54); cupboard, 21(&figs.), 23, 24(fig. 36), 25(fig. 38), 26(&fig. 40), 27(fig. 44), 28(&figs. 45, 46), 29(fig. 47), 30–31(&figs.), 37(fig. 67), 38(fig. 69), 39, 40(&figs.), 42, 43(figs.), 44, 47(figs.), 49(&fig. 94), 50(figs.), 63(n52); leaf table, 18; Staniford chest of drawers, 5(&fig. 2), 6–7; Woodbury cupboard, 9, 11(figs.)
Half-lap, 12
Hamilton (Massachusetts), 63(n57)
Handbook for Winterthur Interpreters: A Multidisciplinary Analysis of the Winterthur Collection, 246–247
Handles, baroque brass, 236(fig. 21)
Hardware, restoration of desk-and-bookcase, 146
Harris family (Ipswich, Massachusetts), 56(n9)
Harrison, Ada, 241(n10)
Harrison, Caroline, 245
Hartford (Connecticut) price book, 153, 154
Hartman, Christian, 240
Hatfield (Massachusetts) price books, 153, 154
"HEA," 30
Head-moldings, 170

Heard family (Ipswich, Massachusetts), 4
Helme, James, 128
Helme desk-and-bookcase, 127(fig. 9), 128, 144–147, 149(n11)
Hendrickson, Daniel, Sr., 101
Hendrickson family (Flatbush, New York), 94(fig. 7)
Henri II style, 6
Henri IV style, 6
Hepplewhite, George, 156, 164(&fig. 9), 168(fig. 16), 169, 170(&fig. 20), 174, 175(fig. 26), 177–179, 181(&fig. 37), 183, 185(fig. 41), 190(n11), 248
Hermann, Johann, 240
Hewitt, Benjamin, 173
"HH" brand, 112(figs.)
Hickory, 97, 98(fig. 15)
Higgins, Solomon, 50
Higgins table, 49–51(&fig. 97)
High chairs, New York, 107(figs.)
High chest, Clifton and Carteret, 66(fig. 1), 67–68(&figs.), 69(fig. 4), 70(figs.)
High-style furniture, 248
Hilg (Gülch), Melchior, 237–238
Hill, Lucy, 192(n47)
Hinges, 16
Hitchcock cupboard, 28–31(&figs.)
Hoban, James, 244
Hodges, George, 195
Hodgkins, Thomas, 173, 174, 187
Hodgson, Thomas, 177
Hoffman, Charles, 187
Hogg, Ima, 132, 151(n23)
Hollow plane, 39, 62(n50)
Holsapple, Catharina, 241(n10)
Holstein (Denmark), 89
Holyoke, Edward A., 176
Hood, desk-and-bookcase, 138
Hook, Abigail (Greenleaf), 195
Hook, William, 155(&fig. 2), 178, 195–196
Hoover, Lou, 245
Hopkins, Stephen, 123
House Beautiful, The (Cook), 2, 23
Howard, Joshua, 186
"HT 1685," 61(n42)
Hudson River Valley: Palatine immigration to, 221, 226–229; *schränke*, 220–242(&figs.)
Huguenot craftsmen diaspora, 52, 63(n64)
Hunter, Robert, 226(&fig. 6), 227, 228, 229
Hunter Subsistence Lists, 240

Huntington, David, 128
Husk inlay, 190(n21)
Husks, 165
Hutchins, Levi, 169
Hutchinson, Israel, 155

"IAE," 16
"IK," 35
Imbrication, 13
Impecunious Collector's Guide to American Antiques (Kirk), 253
Imported furniture: in eighteenth-century New York, 110; after Revolutionary War, 80
Inlay, 173, 177, 190(n21)
Inserts, 26, 38, 52, 62(n49)
Interior struts, 63(n55)
Interpretation, handbook of, 246–249
Inventories: eighteenth-century New York, 117(n9); of John Goddard, 148(n5); of New Amsterdam chairs and, 93; Newport (Rhode Island), 126, 149(n7)
"IPC," 31
Ipswich (Massachusetts), 1, 4, 9, 16, 26, 54–55, 57(n14), 60(n27), 61(n42), 64(n67)
Iron and copper, 248
Ironing board, 175, 176
Isham, Norman, 121
Italo-Netherlandish case pieces, 4

Jackson, Andrew, 245
Jacobean style, 247
Jamb plinths, 14, 46
Janzen, Jan, 99
Jaques, Henry, 54
Jaques, Stephen, 50, 54
Jaques shop tradition, 54, 64(n67)
Jenks, John, 156, 190(n11)
Jetty(ies), 12(&fig. 15), 16, 23, 24(fig. 36), 25, 26(fig. 39), 42, 43–44, 54, 63(n55, 57)
Jig, 138
Jobe, Brock, 253
John, 173, 180, 182
John Nicholas Brown Center for the Study of American Civilization, 149(n9)
Johns, Philip, 98
Johnson, Betsy (Smith), 196
Johnson, Edmund, 155, 156, 160(fig. 6), 189(&n3), 190(n8), 194–197; desk, 167(&fig. 14); sideboard, 165(fig. 11)

Johnson, Edward, 154, 196
Johnson, Micaiah, 154
Joined case forms, 24(fig. 36), 37(&fig. 66)
Joined leaf tables, 16–19(&figs.)
Joiners: additional jobs for, 64(n66); Boston, 11; Cambridge (Massachusetts), 59(n25); Essex County (Massachusetts), 3–4; Palatine, 220–242(&figs.)
Joinery, French, 1
Joint production of furniture: in Newport (Rhode Island), 128; in Salem (Massachusetts), 155
Jones, Henry Z., Jr., 224
Jones, Thomas, 87(n26)
Josefs Guild, 242(n19)
Journal of Early Southern Decorative Arts, xi
Journal of Historic Arms Making Technology, xi
Journeymen: network of in Rhode Island, 124–125; price books and, 156

Karolik, Maxim, 128
Kasten, 89, 97, 100, 118(n23), 229, 230(fig. 9), 231, 232(fig. 12), 235, 242(n13)
Keane, Karen, 253
Kennedy, Jacqueline, 245–246
Kennedy, John F., 246
Kenny, Peter, 97
Keno, Leslie, 253
Keyhole escutcheon, 62(n50)
Keystone, 13
Kimball, Lydia, 178
King, William, 177
Kirk, John R., 251–254
Kirtley, Alexandra, 149(n7), 151(n23)
Kitchen table, Salem (Massachusetts), 176, 213
Kleiderschränk (clothing cupboard), 229, 231
Klismos chairs, 245
Kneller, Godfrey, 226(fig. 6)
Knife boxes, 156, 190(n12), 196
Kniskern, Johannes, 241(n1)
Knobs, 26(fig. 40)
Knuckle joint, 82(fig. 17)
Kocherthal, Joshua, 221
Krill, Rosemary Troy, 246–249

Labor, as proportion of furniture cost, 157
Lady's secretary, Salem (Massachusetts),

157, 169–171(&figs.), 210, 190(n14), 191(n27)
Lake, John, 4
Lake, Margaret Reade, 4
Latrobe, Benjamin Henry, 245
Laurence, William, 100, 118(n18)
Lawton, Elizabeth, 11
Lawton, Isaac, 11
Leaf table, 174; Boston, 16, 18(fig. 23); Essex County (Massachusetts), 16–19(&figs.), 50(fig. 97), 51; fly leg, 18, 19(fig. 26), 40; function of, 16, 18
Leath, Robert, 93
Lee, George, 62(n46)
Lee, Hannah Farnham Sawyer, 37
Legs: fly, 18, 19(fig. 26), 49; Marlboro, 174; reeded, 191(n21); swing, 82(fig. 18)
Lemon, William, 180, 182
Library Company of Philadelphia, 68
Lincoln, Mary Todd, 245
Lincoln Bedroom, The, 243
Link, Susanna, 241(n10)
Lisle, Arthur, 121, 149(n9)
Lisle desk-and-bookcase, 120(fig. 1), 121(&fig. 2), 122(figs.), 142–144, 145(fig. 44), 149(n11); maker's identity, 147; provenance, 148(n2); restoration of, 146
Little, James Lovell, 23
Livingston, John, 230(fig. 9)
Livingston, Robert, 227(&fig. 7), 228–229, 230(fig. 9)
Livingston Manor (New York), 228(fig. 8)
Locks: chest of drawers, 33(fig. 57); *schränk,* 233(fig. 13), 234
Lockwood, Luke Vincent, 13, 59(n22), 121, 128
Lolling chairs, Salem (Massachusetts), 182–183(&fig. 39), 216
London Chair-Makers' and Carvers' Book of Prices, The, 182
London furniture styles: eighteenth-century, 68; influence on seventeenth-century American furniture, 1
London price books, 153–154
Longrifles of North Carolina, The (Bivins), xi, xii
Looking glasses, 157
Lopez, Aaron, 123
Louis XIII style, 6
Low, Anthony, 123
Lower rail, Essex County cupboard, 15–16(&fig. 19), 49

Loxley, Benjamin, 71
Lunette and trefoil motif, 39
Lunt family (Newbury, Massachusetts), 54
Luscomb, William, 174
Luscomb family (Salem, Massachusetts), 187
Lutheranism, 117(n6)
Luxe et Indigence, 186(fig. 45), 187
Lyon, Irving P., 2–3, 16, 25, 37, 49, 60(n29)
Lyon, Irving W., 2, 8

MacWhinnie, Morgan, 242(n18)
Madison, James, 245
Maes, Nicolaes, 95(&fig. 10), 100, 104
Mahoganized rails, 17(fig. 22)
Mahogany: armchair, 81(fig. 15), 182 (fig. 38); bedstead, 186(fig. 43), 217; bureau, 172(fig. 22); card table, 82(figs.), 174(fig. 24); clock case. 167(fig. 15), 209; coffin, 187, 192(n54); commodes, 168(fig. 17), 169(fig. 18); cradle, 179(fig. 34), 215; desk-and-bookcases, 120(fig. 1), 124(fig. 7), 126, 128(fig. 9), 129(fig. 11), 130(fig. 13), 131(fig. 15), 133(fig. 18), 134(fig. 20), 135(fig. 22), 140, 150(n17); dining table, 80(fig. 14); dressing tables, 73(fig. 9), 109(fig. 31); easy chair, 181(&fig. 36); firescreen, 177(fig. 31); gentleman's secretary, 159(fig. 3), 160(fig. 6); high chest, 66(fig. 1), 69(fig. 4); joint purchase of, 155; lady's writing table, 171(fig. 21); lolling chair, 183(fig. 39); night table, 174(fig. 25); pembroke table,175(fig. 27); quarter table, 175(fig. 28); secretary-and-bookcases, 162(fig. 7), 163(fig. 8); side chair, 71(fig. 7); sideboards, 165(figs.), 166(figs.); sofa, 180(&fig. 35), 215; stand, 176, 177(fig. 30), 213; washstand, 178(fig. 33); window stool, 184(&fig. 40)
Maine Antique Digest, 242(n18)
Mandarino, Monte, xi
Mannerist style, 52–53, 247; vs. baroque style, 55. *See also* Essex County (Massachusetts), mannerist furniture in
Map of the Province of New York, Part of New England, with Part of New France, A, 228(fig. 8)
Maple: armchairs, 93(fig. 6), 94(fig. 7), 103(fig. 21), 106(fig. 26); beds,

186(figs.); chests of drawers, 3(fig. 1), 5, 13(fig. 16), 17(fig. 21), 32(fig. 53), 33(fig. 57), 51(fig. 98); cupboard, 9(fig. 8), 14(fig. 17), 15(fig. 18), 20(fig. 27), 23(fig. 34), 24(fig. 36), 26(fig. 40), 29(fig. 47), 37(fig. 66), 41(fig. 75), 43(fig. 81), 45(fig. 85), 47(fig. 90), 48(fig. 91); desk-and-book-cases, 120(fig. 1), 124(fig. 7), 126, 131(fig. 15), 134(fig. 20), 135(fig. 22), 143; high chair, 107(fig. 28); kitchen tables, 176; leaf table, 17(fig. 22), 18(&fig. 23); *schränke*, 222(fig. 3), 223(fig. 4), 240; side chairs, 104(fig. 23), 105(figs.), 106(fig. 27), 110(figs.), 111(fig. 34); tables, 63(n61); in turned chairs, 97

Marbleized top, 17(fig. 22), 176

March family (Newbury, Massachusetts), 54

Marking system, 8, 52, 54, 58(n16)

Marks, New York furniture, 112(&figs.), 114, 119(n26)

Marlboro legs, 174

Marston, Elisha, 196

Marston, Jonathan, 189, 194, 196, 197

Marston, Sarah (Holt), 196

Martin, George, 189

Martin, George W., 155, 194, 196

Martin, George Whitefield, 173, 196–197

Martin, Sally (Bullock), 197

Maryland, quarter table, 175(fig. 28)

Mason and Messinger families, 4

Mass-produced furniture, 250

McCall, Catherine, 75

McCall, Samuel, 75

McGuffin, Robert, 190(n12)

McIntire, Samuel, 154, 157, 169(&fig. 18), 180(&figs. 35), 183, 184(fig. 40), 185(&fig. 42), 190(n14)

Mead, Elizabeth Pink, 241(n10)

Meetinghouses, Essex County (Massachusetts), 54–55

Metropolitan Museum of Art, 128

Milne, Edmond, 75–77

Miniature chairs, 95, 96(fig.12), 100, 117(n10)

Miter joints, 235(&figs. 17, 18)

Mitered cleats, 51

Mixing tables, 156

Molded decoration, 8

Molding planes, 57(n11), 59(n18)

Moldings: architrave, 235(figs. 17, 18); astragal, 13(&fig. 16), 26, 62(n50), 161; base molding, 22, 47(fig. 90), 136,

150(n12), 235(figs. 19, 20); base, 22, 47(fig. 90), 136, 150(n12), 235(figs. 19, 20); chamfered, 62(n50); channel, 1, 38, 42, 52, 62(n50); chest of drawer, 33, 34, 35(figs.); cornice, 159; cove, 28; cupboard, 22, 25, 47, 62(n51); cyma base, 231; desk-and-bookcase, 136, 137; dressing table, 74; foot, 235(figs. 19, 20); gouge-carved, 31; head, 170; quirk, 231, 234; *schränk* door, 239; scratch-stock, 11, 62(n50); spandrel, 47; Staniford chest of drawers, 5–6(&fig. 4); sweep-generated, 11; waist, 137, 150(n13); Woodbury cupboard, 11

Monkman, Betty C., 243–246

Monmouth County Historical Society, 119(n25)

Monroe, James, 244

Montgomery, Charles, 151(n23), 153, 157, 174–175

Moravian Decorative Arts in North Carolina: A Guide to the Old Salem Collection (Bivins), xii

Moravian Potters in North Carolina, The, (Bivins), xi, xii, xii(n2)

Morris, Lydia Thompson, 73(fig. 9)

Morris, Samuel, 86(n4, 18)

Morris, Thomas, 78

Morse, Frances Clary, 2

Mortise-and-tenon joints, 74

Moxon, Joseph, 57(n11), 58–59(n18)

Mulberry, 97, 112, 113(fig. 40)

Mulliken, John, 191(n24)

Mulliken, Mary, 197

Mulliken, Samuel, 191(n24), 197

Mulliken, Samuel, II, 167(&fig. 15)

Muntins, 23; channel-molded, 13

Museum of Fine Arts (Boston), 128, 132, 149(n9), 150(n22)

Museum of Fine Arts, Houston, 132

Muzzleblasts, xi

Narrden, Teuis Tomassen van, 99

Nasenschränk (nose cupboard), 231(&fig. 10)

Nash, Gary, 85(n2)

Nathan Read house (Salem, Massachusetts), 154

National Muzzleloading Rifle Association Gunsmithing Seminars, xi

Neat and plain style, 81–82, 87(n24)

Needham, Thomas, 172, 173, 189, 192(n52)

Needlework, 248

Neoclassical style, 154–155; in Salem (Massachusetts), 156–157, 172

Neoclassicism, 248

Netherlands, side chair, 92(fig. 4), 93(fig. 5), 97(fig. 13)

Neutrality, 190(n12)

New Amsterdam, redraft of the Castello plan of, 90(fig. 2), 91(fig. 3)

New England: joined chair, 117(n12); turned chairs, 105

New England Begins: The Seventeenth Century (Trent), 4

New England Historic and Genealogical Register, 2

New Fine Points of Furniture–Early American (Sack), 252

New Haven (Connecticut), chest of drawers, 60(n28)

New Netherlands. *See* New York

New York: armchairs, 93(fig. 6), 94(figs.), 103(fig. 21), 106(fig. 26), 110, 111(fig. 35); chests, 220(fig. 1), 221(fig. 2); culture, context, and dating of turned chairs, 100–111; dressing table, 109(fig. 31); high chairs, 107(figs.); *kast* (Ulster County), 232(fig. 12); price books, 153; redraft of the Castello plan of, 90(fig. 2), 91(fig. 3); Remensnyder *schränk,* 222(fig. 3), 229, 231(&fig. 11), 234, 235(figs. 17, 19), 238; *schränke* (Dutchess or Ulster County), 222–223(figs.); side chairs, 88(fig. 1), 98(fig. 15), 99(fig. 16), 101(fig. 18), 102(fig. 19), 104(fig. 23), 105(fig. 24), 106(&fig. 27), 108(&fig. 30), 110(figs.), 111(fig. 34), 112(fig. 38), 113–115(figs.); *wäscheschränke,* 236(fig. 21), 238–239(&figs.), 240

Newburgh (New York), 127, 221

Newbury (Massachusetts), 1, 4, 9, 40, 50, 54, 55, 57(n14), 63(n57)

Newport (Rhode Island), cabinetmaking in, 120–151(&figs.); career of John Goddard, 121–125; career of Thomas Goddard, 125–126; craftsmen, 150(n18); desk-and-bookcases, 120(fig. 1), 121(&fig. 2), 122(figs.), 126–147(&figs.), 150(n13); dressing tables, 150(n21); effect of Revolutionary War on furniture making in, 123; inventories, 126, 149(n7); joint production of furniture in, 128; network of journeymen in, 124–125

Nichols, Walter, 128
Night tables: Hepplewhite design, 175(fig. 26); Salem (Massachusetts), 174(&fig. 25), 175, 197, 212
North Andover (Massachusetts), 1, 26
North Carolina: armchairs, 93; furniture of, xi–xiii; rail-and-spindle back chairs, 117(n7)
Norton family (Ipswich, Massachusetts), 54
Norwich (England) price book, 153
Notch, 12
Numbering system, 34, 35(fig. 62)
Nutten (Governor's Island, New York), 227
Nutting, Wallace, 2, 14(fig. 17), 16, 18, 35, 44, 46, 60(n31), 112, 116(n1), 118(n13)

Oak: chest, 11(fig. 13); chests of drawers, 3(fig. 1), 4, 13(fig. 16), 32(&fig. 53), 33(&fig. 57), 35(fig. 62), 51(fig. 98), 57(n15); cupboards, 14(fig. 17), 15(fig. 18), 17(fig. 21), 20(fig. 27), 23(fig. 34), 24(fig. 36), 26(fig. 40), 29(fig. 47), 37(fig. 66), 41(fig. 75), 45(fig. 85), 47(fig. 90), 48(fig. 91), 53(fig. 100); dining table, 80(fig. 14); English shortage of, 58(n15); kast, 230(fig. 9); leaf table, 18(fig. 23); table, 50(fig. 97); water-sawn, 18, 20(fig. 27), 34, 35(fig. 63), 57(n14), 62(n48). See also Red oak; White oak
Oeuvre de Jacques Androuet dit Du Cerceau (Baldus), 53(fig. 99)
Ogee, 14, 22
Ogee bracket feet, 190(n14)
Ogee feet, 166, 171
Old-Time New England, 2
Olive Branch, 155, 193, 194, 197
Open bonnets, 139
Orientation marks. See Marking system
Ornament, hierarchy, 9–10
Orne, Joseph, 164
Oval Room (Blue Room), 244, 245
Oval-top candlestand, Salem (Massachusetts), 176–177(&fig. 30)
Ovolo corners, 161, 173
Ovolo element, 23
Oxbow, 165

Page, Samuel, 186
Paine, Charles, 37
Paine, John, 37
Painted decoration: on bedsteads, 186; on

chests, 5, 25, 61(n34), 220–221(&figs.); on cradles, 179(fig. 34); on cupboards, 20(fig. 27), 23, 37(fig. 66), 41, 42; faux marble, 176; on high chair, 107(fig. 29); on leaf table, 17(fig. 22); price of in Salem (Massachusetts), 157; on Salem tables, 173–174
Paintings, 248
Palatinate, 241(n1)
Palatines: exodus from Germany, 224–226; immigration to America, 221, 224–229; joiners, 239–240. See also Turned chairs
Parisian furniture styles, 63(n64)
Park, Helen, 3
Parker family (Newbury, Massachusetts), 54
Partridge, Nehemiah, 227(fig. 7)
Paschall, Beaulah, 71, 73(fig. 9)
Paschall, Elizabeth Coates, 73(fig.9)
Paschall, Joseph, 71, 73(fig. 9)
Patera, 173
Patroonships, 100, 118(n17)
Patterned inlay, 173
Paulus, Thomas, 89, 116(n2)
Peabody, Benjamin, 128
Peabody Essex Museum, 153, 167, 191(n36), 192(n52), 195, 197, 198
Peckham, Robert, 250
Pediments, 84, 142(fig. 37), 146, 149(n11), 161, 163
Pediment façade, desk-and-bookcase, 138
Peirce, Jerathamiel, 185
Peirce-Nichols family (Salem, Massachusetts), 176
Peirce-Nichols House, 183
Pembroke table, Salem (Massachusetts), 157, 174–175(&fig. 27), 197
Pendants, 11, 13, 17(figs. 21, 22), 25, 26(figs. 39, 40), 31, 38, 61(n41), 63(n57)
Pendleton, Charles, 128
Pendleton desk-and-bookcase, 131(fig. 15), 132(figs.), 143, 146, 150(n20)
Perkins, Abraham, 25, 55
Perkins, Edna (Hazen), 33
Perkins, Hannah (Beamsley), 25
Perkins, Timothy, 33, 61(n43)
Perkins, William, 33
Perkins cabinet, 250
Perkins chest of drawers, 33–34(&figs.)
Perkins cupboard, 24(fig. 36), 25–26, 31, 41, 63(n52)
Perkins families, 1
Perry, Marsden J., 128, 141

Peterson, Ernst, 151(n23)
Pewter, 243, 248
Peyster, Johanne De, 101
Pfhister, Frances, 228(fig. 8)
Pfuhl, Anna Catharina, 238
Pfuhl, Anna Sophia, 238
Pfuhl, Peter, 238
Philadelphia: career of cabinetmaker David Evans, 65–87(&figs.); Cliffton and Carteret high chest, 66–70(figs.); Evans armchair, 81(&fig. 15); Evans card table, 81–83(&figs.); Evans dining table, 80–81(&figs.); Gillingham side chair, 71(fig. 7); map of eighteenth-century, 72(fig. 8); price books, 153; tall clock cases, 83(fig. 19), 84(&fig. 21), 85(fig. 22)
Phillips, Samuel, 1
Piecework, journeymen rates and, 153
Pier table, 156, 176
Pieters, Grietie, 89
Pigeonholes, 150(n21)
Pigmented varnishes, 234
Pilgrim Century Furniture (Nutting), 2
Pillars: on cupboards, 9–10(&figs.), 16(&fig. 20), 21, 22(fig. 32), 23(figs. 34, 35), 25(&fig. 38), 27(figs. 42, 43), 30(&fig. 50), 39–40(&figs.), 40(&fig. 72), 41–42(&figs.)44, 46(&figs.), 49(figs.), 63(n56); on leaf table, 18, 19(fig. 25); for stands, 177
Pine: bedstead, 186(fig. 43); bureau, 172(fig. 22); card table, 174(fig. 24), 212; chest of drawers, 13(fig. 16), 51(fig. 98); chests, 220(fig. 1), 221(fig. 2); commodes, 168(fig. 17), 169(fig. 18); cot, 186(fig. 44); cradles, 179(fig. 34), 215; cupboards, 14(fig. 17), 15(fig. 18), 20(fig. 27), 37(fig. 66), 41(fig. 75), 48(fig. 91); desks, 166(fig. 13), 167(fig. 14); dwarf clock, 167(fig. 15); gentleman's secretary, 159(fig. 3), 160(fig. 6); in desk-and-bookcases, 141; night table, 174(fig. 25); pembroke table, 175(fig. 27); quarter table, 175(fig. 28); sea chest, 187(&fig. 46); secretary-and-bookcases, 162(fig. 7), 163(fig. 8); sideboards, 165(fig. 11), 166(fig. 12); table, 176(&fig. 29); tambour writing table, 171(fig. 21); washstand, 178(fig. 33); water-sawn, 38, 57(n14). See also White pine; Yellow pine
Pintles, 16

Pit sawing, 58(n15)

Pitman, Mark, 164, 167, 192(n54)

Plane marks, 25(fig. 38)

Planes: fenced rabbet, 22, 39, 62(n50); filister, 22; hollow, 39, 62(n50); molding, 57(n11), 59(n18); revolving, 59(n18)

Plaques, 5, 33, 34

Plummer Hall (Salem, Massachusetts), 2

Plymouth Colony, 52, 62(n51)

Pommels, 104

Poplar, 120(fig. 1), 135(fig. 22). *See also* Tulip poplar; Yellow poplar

Poppen, Jan, 89, 116(n2), 117(n3), 118(n20)

Portsmouth, bureau style, 172

Posts: with ball and/or baluster elements, 92; ball-turned, 106

Potter, Elisha Reynolds, 128, 149(n9)

Potter, Thomas Mawney, 121, 128, 149(n9)

Potter family (Kingston, Rhode Island), 121

Powell, Thomas, 79

Price books, 153–154, 159, 248. *See also* Salem (Massachusetts) Cabinet-Maker Society

Prince, Henry, 167

Prince, Jonathan, 173

Prints, 248

Probate inventories, joiner/carpenter distinction and, 3–4

Prouty, Dwight M., 59(n22)

Provenance: of Appleton table, 60(n30); of Essex County furniture, 2–3; of Lisle desk-and-bookcase, 148(n2); of shell-carved desk-and-bookcases, 128; of Staniford chest, 56(n8)

Providence (Rhode Island), 150(n18); desk-and-bookcases, 121, 141–142, 148(n2), 149(n9); price book, 153, 154

Pruyn family (Albany, New York), 119(n25)

Public records, using to identify craftsmen, 2–3

Pulcifer, Francis, 197

Pulcifer, Hannah (Haskell), 197

Pulcifer, Hannah (Trask), 197

Pulcifer, Lydia (Lakeman), 197

Pulcifer, Martha (Hodgkins), 197

Quakers. *See* Society of Friends

Quality: assessing, 252–253; as determinant of price, 157

Quarter-columns: on clock case, 84; on desk-and-bookcases, 140(fig. 33),

142(&fig. 38), 143, 144(fig. 43), 150(n20); on dressing table, 71

Quarter tables: Maryland, 175(fig. 28); Salem (Massachusetts), 175, 213

Queens' Bedroom, The, 243

Queens' Sitting Room, The, 243

Quirk moldings, 231, 234

Rabbet, 28

Radson, B., 156

Rails: cantilevered, 63(n65); cupboard, 15–16(&fig. 19), 23, 28, 49, 59(n21), 63(n54); frieze, 63(n54); mahoganized, 17(fig. 22); rear, 46, 62(n51); table, 51

Rauschner, John Christian, 155(fig. 2)

Reade, Elizabeth, 4

Reade, Martha, 4

Rear post, 95, 97(fig. 14)

Rear rail, 46, 62(n51)

Red cedar, 120(fig. 1), 124(fig. 7), 131(fig. 15), 133(fig. 18), 135(fig. 22), 140, 143, 150(n17)

Red gum, 232(fig. 12), 236(fig. 21)

Red mulberry, 112, 113(fig. 40)

Red oak, 9(fig. 8), 99(fig. 16)

Reeded legs, 191(n21)

Regional Arts of the Early South: A Sampling from the Collection of the Museum of Early Southern Decorative Arts, The (Bivins), xiii

Religion, as vehicle for transmission of design and patronage, 91–92

Remensnyder, John Paul, 229

Remensnyder *schränk,* 222(fig. 3), 229, 231(&fig. 11), 234, 235(figs. 17, 19), 238

Rensselaer, Alida Schuyler Van, 230(fig. 9)

Restoration: of Appleton chest of drawers, 16; of desk-and-bookcases, 146(&fig. 48), 151(n23); of Eliot bureau, 60(n28); of Essex County chest of drawers, 13(fig. 16); of Essex County cupboard, 14(fig. 17), 60(n29); of Hitchcock cupboard, 29(fig. 47); of Perkins cupboard, 61(n35); of Staniford chest of drawers, 5; of Weare cupboard, 41(fig. 75)

Retail prices, furniture price books and, 153, 156, 157

Revolutionary War: effect on furniture making in Philadelphia, 74–75, 79; effect on furniture making in Newport (Rhode Island), 123

Revolving planes, 59(n18)

Rhinebeck (New York), 228(fig. 8), 229

Rhode Island. *See* Newport (Rhode Island); Providence (Rhode Island)

Rhode Island Historical Society, 149(n9)

Rhode Island School of Design, 121, 128, 149(n9), 151(n25)

Rifle Magazine, xi

Rindge, Daniel, Jr., 54, 55

Rindge family (Ipswich, Massachusetts), 54

Ring elements, in turned chairs, 103

Rittenhouse, Benjamin, 85(fig. 22)

Rittenhouse, David, 83(fig. 19), 84

Riven oak, 2, 7, 20(fig. 27), 21, 26(fig. 40), 32, 46, 51, 57(n14), 62(n51), 63(n61)

Robert Hunter, 226(fig. 6)

Robert Livingston, 227(fig. 7)

Robinson, Thomas, 123

Rococo ornament, 66(fig. 1), 67

Rococo style, 68, 87(n23), 126, 172

Rogers, John, 16

Rogers, Nathaniel, 1

Rope beckets, 187

Roper family (Ipswich, Massachusetts), 54

Ropes, Abigail, 192(n54)

Ropes, Elizabeth, 167

Ropes, Nathaniel, 165, 195

Rosettes, on desk-and-bookcase, 139

Rosewood, 93(fig. 5), 98

Rosewood graining, 234

Ross Tavern (Ipswich, Massachusetts), 43, 63(n57)

Rotary button bits, 61(n39)

Rotary cutter, 30

Rowley (Massachusetts), 3, 33

Roxbury (Massachusetts), 16

Roxbury clock case, 167

Ruhl, Philip, 6(fig. 3)

Rural New England Furniture: People, Place, and Production (Benes), 249–251

Rural, meaning of, 250

Rush-seated chairs, 93

Rust, Henry, 195

Rynders, William, 241(n10)

Sack, Albert, 252, 253

Safford, Nathaniel, 183, 184; sideboard, 165, 166(fig. 12); sofa, 180(fig. 35)

Salem (Massachusetts), furnituremaking industry, 152–219(&figs.); armchair, 181–182(&fig. 38); bedsteads, 184–187(&figs.); bookcase, 164; bureaus, 171–172(&fig. 22); card tables, 173–174(&fig. 24); chest of drawers,

195; clock cases, 167(&fig. 15), 169, 191(n24), 209; coffins, 187, 192(n54); commodes, 168–169(&figs.); competition in, 39; cot, 186–187(&fig. 44); cradles, 179(&fig. 34); decline of furniture industry in, 188–189; desks, 165–167(&figs.); dining tables, 172–173(&fig. 23); dressing tables, 156, 176; dwarf clock, 167(&fig. 15); easy chairs, 180–181(&fig. 36); firescreen, 177(&fig. 31); gentleman's secretary, 159(&fig. 3), 160(fig. 6), 161; kitchen table, 176; lady's secretary, 157,169–171(&figs.), 190(n14), 191(n27), 210; lolling chairs, 182–183(&fig. 39); night table, 174(&fig. 25); oval-top candlestand, 176–177(&fig. 30); pembroke tables, 174–175(&fig. 27); prosperity of, 154–155; quarter table, 175; seaman's chest, 187(&fig. 46); secretary-and-bookcase, 161–163(&figs.); seventeenth-century furniture in, 3; sideboard, 164–165(&figs.); slab table, 175–176; sofas, 157, 180(&fig. 35); stand, 176; table, 176(fig. 29); tambour table, 171(&fig. 21); view of Court House Square, 152(fig. 1); washstands, 178–179(&fig. 33); window stool frame, 183–184(&fig. 40). *See also* Essex County (Massachusetts)

Salem (Massachusetts) Cabinet-Maker Society, 152–219; founding, 155–156; member biographies, 193–198; price list facsimile, 199–219

Salem Charitable Mechanic Association, 189

Sallows, Thomas, 62(n48)

Sanders, Barent, 106

Sanders, Maria, 106

Sanders, Maria (Wendell), 106

Sanders, Robert, 106

Sanderson, Elijah, 154, 155, 156, 161, 167, 173, 174, 180, 187, 190(n12), 191(n27), 197–198; desk, 166(&fig. 13); night table, 174(&fig. 25); tambour table, 171(&fig. 21)

Sanderson, Jacob, 154, 155, 167, 169, 171, 173, 174, 175, 177, 180, 186, 188, 192(n52), 197, 198

Sanderson, Katherine (Harrington), 198

Sanderson, Mary, 195

Sanderson, Mary (Mulliken), 167, 197

Sanderson, Sally, 191(n27)

Sandersons, 157, 172, 174, 177, 179, 181, 184, 187, 188, 189(n6), 190(n8, 14), 193, 194, 195

Sargent, Mrs. Charles Sprague, 63(n59)

Sash-cornered card table, 173

Sash corners, 165, 173

Satinwood, 160(fig. 6)

Saugus Ironworks, 11

Savery, William, 87(n23)

Saw kerfs, 45(fig. 85), 58(n15), 83

Sawn oak, 59(n23)

Sawyer, Hannah, 62(n46)

Sawyer, Micajah, 37, 62(n46)

Sawyer, Sibyll (Farnham), 37, 62(n46)

Sawyer cupboard, 35–40(&figs.), 44, 46, 49, 62(n50), 62–63(n52)

Scalloped front bureau, 171, 172

Scalloped lower rail, 15–16(&fig. 19)

Scalloped ornament, 13(&fig. 16)

Schoharie (New York), 229

Schränke: cornices, 234, 235(figs. 17, 18); dovetails, 234(&fig. 16); drawer bottom, 234(fig. 15); drawings of, 237(fig. 22); Dutchess or Ulster County (New York), 222–223(figs.); identifying artisans, 235, 237–238; isometric drawing, 233(fig. 14); locking system, 233(fig. 13), 234; Remensnyder *schränk,* 222(fig. 3), 229, 231(&fig. 11), 234, 235(figs. 17, 19), 238

Schuyler, Margareta, 117(n9)

Scratch bead, 23

Scratch-stock, 5–6(&fig. 3), 57(n11), 59(n18), 138

Scratch-stock cutter, 10, 14, 22, 39, 47, 239

Scratch-stock iron, 39, 62(n50)

Scratch-stock moldings, 11, 62(n50)

Scribe marks, 74(fig. 11)

Scrole head, 161

Scrole volute, 161, 163(fig. 8)

Scrolled motif, 41

Scrolled sofa arms, 180

Seaman's chest, Salem (Massachusetts), 187(&fig. 46), 218

Second base torus, 21

Second School of Fontainebleau, 1, 6, 52

Secretary-and-bookcases, Salem (Massachusetts), 161–163(&figs.), 193, 206. *See also* Desk-and-bookcases

Secretary drawer, 165, 166

Sergeant, Elizabeth (Rittenhouse), 85(fig. 22)

Sergeant, Jonathan Dickinson, 84, 85(fig. 22)

Serlio, Sebastiano, 6, 7(fig. 5)

Serpentine fronts: bureau, 251; sideboards, 165; sofa backs, 180; table top, 174

Sewing desk, 251

Shaker furniture, 251

Shaker World: Art, Life, Belief, The (Kirk), 253

Shaw, Francis, 61(n35)

Shearer, Thomas, 160(fig. 5)

Shelf, of leaf table, 18

Sheraton, Thomas, 156, 159(&fig. 4), 173, 174, 178(&fig. 32), 182, 192(n47), 248

Sideboards: corner, 191(n36); Salem (Massachusetts), 156, 164–165(&figs.), 190–191(n21), 195, 196, 207

Side chairs: Connecticut, 105(fig. 25); Gillingham, 71(fig. 7); Netherlands, 92(fig. 4), 93(fig. 5), 97(fig. 13); New York, 88(fig. 1), 98(fig. 15), 99(fig. 16), 101(fig. 18), 102(fig. 19), 104(fig. 23), 105(fig. 24), 106(&fig. 27), 108(&fig. 30), 110(figs.), 111(fig. 34), 112(fig. 38), 113–115(figs.)

Side panels: cupboard, 16; desk-and-bookcase, 143(&fig. 39)

Side rails, 28, 59(n21), 63(n54)

Side skirts, 71

Side table, 123

Side-hung drawers, 7

Silver, 243, 248

Silver, Mark, xi

Simmendinger, Ulrich, 224, 225, 227–228

Simmendinger Register, 240

Singleton, Esther, 2

"SK" cupboard, 46

Slab table, Salem (Massachusetts), 175–176, 213

Slant top desk, 196, 197

Slat-back chairs, 103–104(&figs.)

Slaves, as journeymen, 124

Sleepy Hollow Dutch Reformed Church, 101, 102(fig. 20)

Slingelandt, Pieter Cornelis van, 104(fig. 22)

Smit, Jacob, 89, 116(n2)

Society of Friends, 67; role in arbitration, 78, 85(n11)

Society of Upholsterers, 160(fig. 5), 163(fig. 8)

Sofas, Salem (Massachusetts), 157, 180(&fig. 35), 192(n47), 215

Soffit boards, 12, 43, 63(n55, 56)

South Africa, *tolletjie* chair, 117(n7)

South Carolina, joined chair, 118(n12)

Spandrel appliqués, 13

Spandrel moldings, 47

Spandrels, 22, 140

Spaulding, Philip L., 60(n29), 60(n31)

Spindle-back chairs. *See* Turned chairs

Spindles, 95, 97(fig. 14)

Splines, 235

Split spindles, 7

Square-backed sofas, 192(47)

Square head, 161

Square-shouldered pillars, 27(fig. 42), 28

Square tables, 50(fig. 97), 63(n61), 174

Stair and Company, 151(n23)

Stand, Salem (Massachusetts), 176, 213

Stand pillars, 177

Staniford, Hannah (Rindge), 55

Staniford, Margaret, 56(n9)

Staniford, Margaret (Harris), 3, 4

Staniford, Thomas, 3, 4, 55, 56(n9)

Staniford chest of drawers, 3–8(&figs.), 18, 25, 41, 56(n8), 59(n23)

Staniford family (Ipswich, Massachusetts), 56(n9)

State of the Palatines For Fifty Years past to this present Time, The, 225(fig. 5)

Steenwyck, Cornelius, 93

Steenwyck inventory, 117(n9)

Stepped dentil, 26

Stevens, Samuel Dale, 33

Stiles, 11, 12, 14, 16, 18, 25, 26(fig. 40), 34, 39, 42, 49, 59(n21), 62(n51), 63(n54)

Stoel, 116(n2)

Stoelendraaiers, 89, 100.

Stone, Isaac, 154

Stone, Robert, 37

Stopped moldings, 6(fig. 4)

Storage compartments, cupboard, 20(fig. 27), 21, 27–28, 46

Straight bracket feet, 166

Straight front bureau, 171

Straight-sided vase turning, 13(&fig. 16), 14(fig 17), 17(fig. 22)

Strawbery Banke, 191(n30)

Stretcher turnings, 92

String inlay, 175, 190(n21)

Stringing motifs, 165

Strong family (Ipswich, Massachusetts), 54

Style names, 247

Stylistic comprehension, 247

Subcontracting, in Salem (Massachusetts), 177, 179, 184–185, 197

Sudbury communion table, 57(n15)

Sumner, William H., 2, 16

Superposition of orders, 9–10

Surface arcades, 9(fig. 8), 10, 44

Surface arches, 11

Swags, 185

Swarte Sluis (Holland), 89

Sweep, 10, 11, 58–59(n18)

Sweep-generated moldings, 11

"Swelled" desks, 165

Swelled facade, 191(n22)

Swett, John, 195

Swing leg, 82(fig. 18)

Sycamore, 2, 3(fig. 1), 7(fig. 6), 9(&fig. 8), 33(fig. 57), 35(fig. 62); water-sawn, 7(&fig. 7), 9, 17(fig. 21), 57(n14)

Symonds, Samuel, 4, 33, 61–62(n43)

Symonds shops (Essex County, Massachusetts), 3

Tables: breakfast, 82, 174; bureau, 139, 149(n8); card, 81–83(&figs.), 87(n24), 173–174(&fig. 24), 194, 197, 212; chamber, 156; dining, 80–81(&figs.), 123, 172–173, 211; draw-bar, 97; drawing, 156; dressing, 71, 73, 74(&fig. 31), 109(fig. 31), 150(n21), 156, 176; drop-leaf, 173; folding, 174; gateleg, 97; joined leaf, 16–19(&figs.); kitchen, 176, 213; leaf, 40, 50(fig. 97), 51, 60(n30), 174; mixing, 156; night, 174–175(&figs.), 197, 212; pembroke, 157, 174–175(&fig. 27), 197; pier, 156, 176; Salem (Massachusetts), 157, 176(fig. 29), 191(n30); side, 123; slab, 175–176, 213; square, 63(n61); square joined, 49–51(&fig. 97); tambour, 171(&fig. 21); tea, 123, 174; tilt-top, 123; tops of, 51, 63(n61); types of, 156; work, 156, 157, 190(n12); writing, 171(&fig. 21)

Tall clock cases, 167, 169

Tambour desk, 193, 196, 197

Tambour doors, 171(&fig. 21)

Tambour table, 171(&fig. 21)

Tassels, 185

Taylor, Nicholas, 121

Tea caddys, 156, 190(n12)

Tea tables, 123, 174

Ten Eyck family (Albany, New York), 106, 119(n23)

Tenons, 8(fig. 7), 19(fig. 25)

"TEP," 33–34

Textiles, 243, 248

Theoda, 196

Thompson, Charles, 82

Tiebout, Johannes, 89, 116(n2)

Tilton, Abraham, Jr., 55

Tilton, Abraham, Sr., 54, 55

Tilton family (Ipswich, Massachusetts), 54

Tilt-top table, 123

Timbering practices, seventeenth-century New England, 7–8

Titcomb family (Newbury, Massachusetts), 54

Tolletjie chairs, 117(n7)

Tongue-and-groove joints, 62(n51)

Tools, seventeenth-century innovations in, 39

Topham, Susan (Goddard), 122

Topham, Theophilus, 121–122

Topsfield (Massachusetts), 1, 3, 31, 33, 61(n40), 63(n57); meeting house, 61–62(n43)

Torus, 28

Townsend, Christopher, 128, 147, 148(n1), 150(n21), 151(n25)

Townsend, Edmund, 128, 147

Townsend, Job, 122, 126, 147, 151(n25)

Townsend, Job, Jr., 126, 128, 147, 148(n7)

Townsend, John, 123, 124, 128, 147

Townsend, Thomas, 128, 147

Trapezoidal storage compartment, 12(&fig. 14), 13, 14(&fig. 17), 44, 49, 50(figs.)

Traveling desks, 167

Traver, Rosina Mead, 241(n10)

Traver, Samantha, 241(n10)

Traver, Stephen L., 241(n10)

Traver *schränk,* 223(fig. 4), 229, 231, 235(figs. 18, 20), 238, 241(n10), 242(n11)

Trays, 156

Trefoil carving, 41

Trent, Robert F., 4, 63(n62), 250, 251

Trompe d'oeil, 157

True poplar, 144

Trumble, Francis, 77, 79

Trunnels, 242(n13)

Tucker, Andrew, 186

Tulip poplar, 3(fig. 1), 5, 9(fig. 8), 20(fig. 27), 66(fig. 1), 69(fig. 4), 73(figs.), 80(fig. 14), 109(fig. 31), 175(fig. 28)

Türck, Isaac, 238

Turned chairs, eighteenth-century New

York, 89–119(&figs.); culture, context, and dating of, 100–111; marking, sets, and makers, 112–115; Netherlandish sources, 92–100; prices of, 99–100; uses of, 93, 95. *See also* Armchairs; Side chairs

Turned ornament, 15, 26

Turners, 28, 116(n2)

Turnings, cupboard, 30, 41, 44. *See also* Half-columns; Pillars

Turning sequences, 1

Tuscan half-columns, 28, 30–31(&figs.), 42, 44

Tuttle, James C., 154

Tyler, Charles Hitchcock, 28

Tympana, 146

Tympanum appliqué, 68, 70(fig. 5)

Ulster County (New York): Elting-Beekman makers, 242(n13); *kasten,* 235

Unicorn, 193, 197

United States Magazine, 244

Updike, Lodowick, II, 128

Upholstery nails, 62(n50)

Urn ornament, 161

Urn stands, 156

Urn-shaped finials, 92, 95, 97(&fig. 14), 103, 108, 117(n11)

Uses: for desks, 148(n7); for turned chairs, 93, 95

Valance drawers, 138, 139(fig. 29), 140–141, 150(n17)

Van Buren, Martin, 245

Varlet, Sieur Nicolaes, 98, 118(n13)

Varnish: analysis of *schränk,* 242(n11); pigmented, 234

Vases, classical, 6, 7(fig. 5)

Veneer, 173, 177

Venetian blinds, 84

Venture cargo trade, 154, 155, 161, 167, 171, 176, 179, 180, 182, 187–188, 190(n12), 191(n24), 193–197, 248

View of Court House Square (Felt), 152(fig. 1)

Virginia: armchairs, 93, 95(fig. 9); rail-and-spindle back chairs, 117(n7)

V-joints, 62(n51)

Waist molding, 137, 150(n13)

Waite, Aaron, 172(&fig. 22), 173, 176, 181, 192(n52)

Waite, Lydia, 179

Waite family (Ipswich, Massachusetts), 54

Waitt, Elizabeth (Wildes), 61(n40)

Waitt, William, 61(n40)

Waldron, Rutgert, 89, 91, 116(n2)

Wallis, Mary Polly (Aveson), 198

Wallis, Robert, 198

Walnut, 4, 11(fig. 13), 18(fig. 23), 73(fig. 10), 92(fig. 4), 93(fig. 5), 97(&fig. 13), 98(&fig. 15), 106, 108(fig. 30), 126, 230(fig. 9)

Walton, John, 151(n23)

Wanton, Gideon, 123

Ward, Gerald W. R., 249, 253

Ward, Joshua, 176

Wardell family (Ipswich, Massachusetts), 54

Wardrobe, 161, 206

War of 1812, effect on Salem (Massachusetts) furniture industry, 188

Wäscheschränke (linen cupboard), 231, 236(fig. 21), 238–239(&figs.), 240

Washington, George, 176, 245

Washstands, Salem (Massachusetts), 156, 175, 178–179(&fig. 33), 191(n36), 214

Waterhouse, Timothy, 128

Water-powered saw marks, 25(fig. 38)

Waters, Henry Fitz Gilbert, 2, 13–14(&fig. 17)

Waters cupboard, 13–16(&figs.)

Water-sawn woods, 18(fig. 24), 57(n14), 57–58(n15); oak, 18, 20(fig. 27), 34, 35(fig. 63), 57(n14), 62(n48); pine, 38, 57(n14); sycamore, 7(&fig. 7), 9, 17(fig. 21), 57(n14); white pine, 62(n51)

Watson, Elizabeth, 185

Watson, Elizabeth Leach, 179

Watson, George, 179, 185

Way, George, 79

Weare, Huldah (Hussey), 40

Weare, Mary (Wait), 40

Weare, Meshech, 40

Weare, Nathaniel, 40

Weare cupboard, 40–44(&figs.), 49, 59(n23), 63(n56)

Weathervane, 101, 102(fig. 20)

Webb family (Salem, Massachusetts), 187

Well, desk-and-bookcase, 137–138

Wellington, Arthur W., 44

Wessels, David, 89, 91(&fig. 3), 92, 99, 116(n2), 117(n6)

West, Elizabeth Derby, 171, 180, 190(n15)

West Camp (New York), 241(n9)

Weston (Massachusetts), 44

White, Bruce, 244, 246

White, Joseph, 178

White cedar, 66(fig. 1), 69(fig. 4)

White House Historical Association, The, 246

White House: Its Historic Furnishings and First Families, The (Monkman), 243–246

White oak, 17(fig. 21), 101(fig. 18), 115(figs. 43, 45)

White pine: armchair, 81(fig. 15); chest, 11(fig. 13); desk-and-bookcases, 120(fig. 1), 124(fig. 7), 129(fig. 11), 130(fig. 13), 131(fig. 15), 133(fig. 18), 134(fig. 20), 135(fig. 22), 140; dining table, 80(fig. 14); dressing tables, 73(figs.); *kast,* 232(fig. 12); leaf table, 18(fig. 23); New England use of, 7; *schränke,* 222(fig. 3), 223(fig. 4); water-sawn, 62(n51)

Wildes, Mary (Bradstreet), 61(n40)

Wildes, Sylvanus, 61(n40)

Willard, Simon, 167

Willard family (Grafton, Massachusetts), 167

William and Mary style, 247

William Hook (Rauschner), 155(fig. 2)

Williams, Jesse, 78, 86(n17)

Williams, Thomas Russell, 193

Wilmington Furniture, 1720–1860 (Bivins), xii

Wilson, John, 60(n28)

Wind braces, 8

Window stool frame, Salem (Massachusetts), 156, 183–184(&fig. 40), 216

Windsor chair makers, 189(n3)

Windsor furniture, 248

"Wing" clothes press, 159, 160(fig. 5)

Winterthur Museum, 151(n23), 181, 197, 246

Winthrop, John, 1

Winthrop, John, Jr., 4

Witwerkers, 240

Woburn (Massachusetts), 52

Woman Making Lace with Two Children (Slingelandt), 104(fig. 22)

Wood, Charles B., III, 189(n1)

Wood, David F., 250

Woodbridge, John, 1

Woodbury, Peter, 8, 58(n17)

Woodbury cupboard, 8–12(&figs.), 18, 28, 41

Woods, types of: ash, 94(fig. 7), 105(fig.

25), 113(fig. 39); aspen, 144; birch, 167, 172(fig. 22), 173(fig. 23), 184, 212, 217; black ash, 112(fig. 38); black walnut, 82(fig. 16), 98; cedar, 179, 187, 215; cedrela, 4, 11(fig. 13), 18(fig. 23), 135(fig. 22); chestnut, 129(fig. 11), 130(fig. 13), 133(fig. 18), 134(fig. 20), 135(fig. 22), 141, 143, 144; cottonwood, 144; ebony, 97, 98, 99(&fig. 16), 190(n8); gum, 238; hickory, 97, 98(fig. 15); mulberry, 97, 112, 113(fig. 40); poplar, 120(fig. 1), 135(fig. 22); red cedar, 120(fig. 1), 124(fig. 7), 131(fig. 15), 133(fig. 18), 135(fig. 22), 140, 143, 150(n17); red gum, 232(fig. 12), 236(fig. 21); red oak, 9(fig. 8), 99(fig. 16); riven oak, 2, 7, 20(fig. 27), 21, 26(fig.40), 32, 46, 51, 57(n14), 62(n51), 63(n61); rosewood, 93(fig. 5), 98; satinwood, 160(fig. 6); sycamore, 2, 3(fig. 1), 7(fig. 6), 9(&fig. 8), 17(fig. 21), 33(fig. 57), 35(fig. 62), 57(n14); tulip poplar, 3(fig. 1), 5, 9(fig. 8), 20(fig. 27), 66(fig. 1), 69(fig. 4), 73(figs.), 80(fig. 14), 109(fig. 31), 175(fig. 28); used in construction of New Netherland turned chairs, 97–99; walnut, 4, 11(fig. 13), 18(fig. 23), 73(fig. 10), 92(fig. 4), 93(fig. 5), 97(&fig. 13), 98(&fig. 15), 106, 108(fig. 30), 126, 230(fig. 9); white cedar, 66(fig. 1), 69(fig. 4); white oak, 17(fig. 22), 101(fig. 18), 115(figs. 43, 45); yellow pine, 66(fig. 1), 69(fig. 4), 71(fig. 7), 120(fig. 1), 133(fig. 18), 222(fig. 3), 223(fig. 4); yellow poplar, 124(fig. 7), 129(fig. 11), 131(fig. 15), 133(fig. 18), 134(fig. 20), 135(fig. 22), 141, 143, 236(fig. 21). *See also* Cherry; Mahogany; Maple; Oak; Pine; Water-sawn woods; White pine

Woodward family (Ipswich, Massachusetts), 54

Woodworkers, British, 56(n6)

Woodworking practices, New England, 7–8, 13

Work tables, 156, 157, 190(n12)

Writing compartment, 145

Writing slides, 141

Writing table, 171(&fig. 21)

Yale University, 128

Yellow pine, 66(fig. 1), 69(fig. 4),

71(fig. 7), 120(fig. 1), 133(fig. 18), 222(fig. 3), 223(fig. 4)

Yellow poplar, 124(fig. 7), 129(fig. 11), 131(fig. 15), 133(fig. 18), 134(fig. 20), 135(fig. 22), 141, 143, 236(fig. 21)

Young Woman Sewing, A (Maes), 95(&fig. 10), 100, 104

Zea, Philip, 253